Praise for *Mastering Data Modeling: A User-Driven Approach*

This is without doubt the most complete and worthy "common sense" approach to data modeling that I have read. It spans the 'stupidity wars' of differences of notation and nomenclature with a clear and easy elegance that espouses common sense over dogma. . . . An excellent work which deserves to be a foundation of every programmer and software designer's bookshelf. Without understanding of data, there can be no intelligent software design.

Paul Irvine
Senior Manager
Emerald Solutions

I will also be able to use this book to make myself not only a better data modeler and database designer, but a better overall systems analyst, project planner, and business communicator. A second (and perhaps third) reading is definitely in order!

Matthew Keranen
Consulting Database Administrator

An invaluable resource for anyone who wants to learn about data modeling, this book is exceptionally powerful because its developed from real world experiences— its a pragmatic guide for data modeling practitioners.

Peter O'Kelley
Senior Consultant/Analyst
The Patricia Seybolt Group

This book presents a detailed, structured approach to the process of data modeling with emphasis on interacting with users, a unique feature which impressed me.

David McGoveran
Alternative Technologies, Inc.

I hope the book is well received. It deserves to be, as it provides extremely clear, practical thinking on an important but often misunderstood subject.

Mitch Kapor
Founder of the Lotus Development Corporation

Mastering Data Modeling

A User-Driven Approach

John Carlis

Joseph Maguire

Addison-Wesley

Boston • San Francisco • New York • Toronto • Montreal
London • Munich • Paris • Madrid • Capetown
Sydney • Tokyo • Singapore • Mexico City

The publisher offers discounts on this book when ordered in quantity for special sales. For more information, please contact:

Pearson Education Corporate Sales Division
One Lake Street
Upper Saddle River, NJ 07458
(800) 382-3419
corpsales@pearsontechgroup.com

Visit AW on the Web: www.awl.com/cseng/

Library of Congress Cataloging-in-Publication Data
Carlis, John Vincent.
   Mastering data modeling : a user driven approach / John V. Carlis and Joseph D. Maguire.
      p. cm.
   ISBN 0-301-70045-X (alk. paper)
    1. Database design. 2. Data structures (Computer science) I. Maguire, Joseph D. II. Title.
   QA76.9.D26 C37 2000
   005.7'3—dc21   00-061845

ISBN 0-201-70045-X
Text printed on recycled paper
1 2 3 4 5 6 7 8 9 10-CRS-04 03 02 01 00
First printing, November 2000

Contents

Foreword

The world of Web-based retail, financial, medical, educational, and business-to-business applications is rapidly expanding as the infrastructure for moving vast amounts of information around the world is being put into place. But, as is often the case, hardware advances are ahead of the necessary corresponding software advances. This has led to an explosion of reuse and integration problems, as designers seek to use existing information systems in new ways.

But many, many existing legacy systems embed in highly ad-hoc fashions the "meaning" of data in the code that manipulates it, thus forever entangling the nature of the application and data. Clearly, the evolution, reuse, and integration of information systems require that this separation be made as cleanly and expressively as possible.

Notice the focus on *information*. The successful development of Internet applications very frequently rides on the ability to easily capture the properties and "meaning" of stored information. This means that the nature of information should be specified before "source" information systems are deployed, since the likelihood of these systems being evolved and reused is very high. But since proper modeling techniques are often not applied when source systems are created, modeling procedures must often be applied after the fact.

Given the extreme size, complexity, and number of new information applications, the need for effective information modeling facilities is bigger than ever. The notation presented in this book, called LDS, emphasizes the careful separation of application code and data. The book contains detailed, real world examples, and advice, based on the authors' many years of practical experience with large systems. This book presents a time-tested, intelligently-crafted, and carefully-explained graphical notation for extracting the representation of a given information set—in the terminology and structures familiar to the users of this information.

This notation serves to guide developers in the implementation of information systems; it also provides for the documenting of information systems in a way that is easy to understand. It should be of great value to developers of built-from-scratch information systems, as well as to those who seek to build new systems out of old ones.

Preface

This book teaches you the first step of creating software systems: learning about the information needs of a community of strangers. This book is necessary because that step—known as data modeling—is prone to failure.

This book presumes nothing; it starts from first principles and gradually introduces, justifies, and teaches a rigorous process and notation for collecting and expressing the information needs of a business or organization.

This book is for anyone involved in the creation of information-management software. It is particularly useful to the designers of databases and applications driven by database management systems.

In many regards, this book is different from other books about data modeling. First, because it starts from first principles, it encourages you to question what you might already know about data modeling and data-modeling notations. To best serve users, how should the process of data modeling work? To create good, economical software systems, what kind of information should be on a data model? To become an effective data modeler, what skills should you master before talking with users?

Second, this book teaches you the process of data modeling. It doesn't just tell you what you should know; it tells you what to do. You learn fundamental skills, you integrate them into a process, you practice the process, and you become an expert at it. This means that you can become a "content-neutral modeler," moving gracefully among seemingly unrelated projects for seemingly unrelated clients. Because the process of modeling applies equally to all projects, your expertise becomes universally applicable. Being a master data modeler is like being a master statistician who can contribute to a wide array of unrelated endeavors: population studies, political polling, epidemiology, or baseball.

Third, this book does not focus on technology. Instead, it maintains its focus on the process of discovering and articulating the users' information needs, without concern for how those needs can or should be satisfied by any of the myriad technological options available. We do not completely ignore technology; we frequently mention it to remind you that during data modeling, you should ignore it. Users don't care about technology; they care about their information. The notation we use, Logical Data Structures (LDS), encourages you to focus on users' needs.

We think a data modeler should conceal technological details from users. But historically, many data modelers are database designers whose everyday working vocabulary is steeped in technology. When technologists talk with users, things can get awkward. In the worst case, users quit the conversation, or they get swept up in the technological details and neglect to paint a complete picture of their technology-independent information needs. Data modeling is not equivalent to database design.

Another undesirable trend: historically, many organizations wrongly think that data modeling can be done only by long-time, richly experienced members of the organization who have reached the status of "unofficial archivist." This is not true. Modeling is a set of skills like computer programming. It can be done by anyone equipped with the skills. In fact, a skilled modeler who is initially unfamiliar with the organization but has access to users will produce a better model than a highly knowledgeable archivist who is unskilled at modeling.

This book has great ambitions for you. To realize them, you cannot read it casually. Remember, we're trying to foster skills in you rather than merely deliver knowledge to you. If you master these skills, you can eventually apply them instinctively. Study this book the way you would a calculus book or a cookbook. Practice the skills on real-life problems. Work in teams with your classmates or colleagues. Write notes to yourself in the margins.

An ambitious book like this, well, we didn't just make it up. For starters, we are indebted to Michael Senko, a pioneer in database systems on whose work ours is based. Beyond him, many people deserve thanks. Most important are the many users we have worked with over the years, studying data: Gordon Decker; George Bluhm and others at the U.S. Soil Conservation Service; Peter O'Kelly and others at Lotus Development Corporation; John Hanna, Tim Dawson, and other employees and consultants at US WEST, Inc.; Jim Brown, Frank Carr, and others at Pacific Northwest National Laboratory; and Jane Goodall, Anne Pusey, Jen Williams, and the entire staff at the University of Minnesota's Center for Primate Studies. Not far behind are our students and colleagues. Among them are several deserving special thanks: Jim Albers, Dave Balaban, Leone Barnett, Doug Barry, Bruce Berra, Diane Beyer, Kelsey Bruso, Jake Chen, Paul Chapman, Jan Drake, Bob Elde, Apostolos Georgopolous, Carol Hartley, Jim Held, Chris Honda, David Jefferson, Verlyn Johnson, Roger King, Joe Konstan, Darryn Kozak, Scott Krieger, Heidi Kvinge, James A. Larson, Sal March, Brad Miller, Jerry Morton, Jose Pardo, Paul Pazandak, Doug Perrin, John Riedl, Maureen Riedl, George Romano, Sue Romano, Karen Ryan, Alex Safonov, Wallie Schmidt, Stephanie Sevcik, Libby Shoop, Tyler Sperry, Pat Starr, Fritz Van

Evert, Paul Wagner, Bill Wasserman, George Wilcox, Frank Williams, Mike Young, and several thousand students who used early versions of our work. Thanks also go to Lilly Bridwell-Bowles of the Center for Interdisciplinary Studies of Writing at the University of Minnesota. Several people formally reviewed late drafts of this book and made helpful suggestions: Declan Brady, Paul Irvine Matthew C. Keranen, David Livingstone, and David McGoveran. And finally, thanks to the helpful and patient people at Addison-Wesley. Paul Becker, Mariann Kourafas, Mary T. O'Brien, Ross Venables, Stacie Parillo, Jacquelyn Doucette, the copyeditor, Penny Hull, and the indexer, Ted Laux.

How to Use This Book

To study this book rather than merely read it, you need to understand a bit about what kind of information it contains. The information falls into eight categories.

- **Introduction and justification.** Chapters 1 and 2 define the data-modeling problem, introduce the LDS technique and notation, and describe good habits that any data modeler should exhibit. Chapters 22 and 24 justify in more technical detail some of the decisions we made when designing the LDS technique and notation.
- **Definitions.** Chapter 4 defines the vocabulary you need to read everything that follows. Chapter 13 defines things more formally—articulating exactly what constitutes a syntactically correct LDS. Chapter 23 presents a formal definition of our Logical Data Structures in a format we especially like—as an LDS.
- **Reading an LDS.** Chapter 3 describes how to translate an LDS into declarative sentences. The sentences are typically spoken to users to help them understand an in-progress LDS. Chapter 5 describes how to visualize and annotate sample data for an LDS.
- **Writing an LDS.** Chapter 13 describes the syntax rules for writing an LDS. Chapter 14 describes the guidelines for naming the parts of an LDS. Chapter 15 describes some seldom-used names that are part of any LDS. Chapter 16 describes how to label parts of an LDS. (Labels and names differ.) Chapter 17 describes how to document an LDS.
- **LDS shapes and recipes.** Chapter 7 introduces the concept of shapes and tells how your expertise with them can make you a master data modeler. Chapters 8 through 12 give an encyclopedic, exhaustive analysis of the shapes you will encounter as a data modeler. Chapter 26 describes some recipes—specific applications of the shapes to common problems encountered by software developers and database designers.
- **Process of LDS development.** Chapters 6 and 21 give elaborate examples of the process of LDS development. Chapter 18 describes a step-by-step script, called The Flow, that you follow in your conversations with users. Chapters 19 and 20 describe steps you can take to improve an in-progress LDS at any time— steps that do not fit into the script in any particular place because they fit in *every* place. Considered as a whole, Chapters 18 through 20 describe the process of **controlled evolution,** the process by which you guide the users through a

conversation that gradually improves the in-progress LDS. "Controlled" implies that the conversation is organized and methodical. "Evolution" implies that the conversation yields a continuously, gradually improving data model.

- **Implementation and technology issues.** Chapter 22 describes in detail the forces that compel us to exclude constraints from the LDS notation. Many of these forces stem from implementation issues. Chapter 25 describes a technique for creating a relational schema from an LDS.

- **Critical assessment of the LDS technique and notation.** Chapter 24 describes the decisions we made in designing the LDS technique and notation and describes how our decisions differ from those made by the designers of other notations. Chapter 22 is devoted to one such especially noteworthy decision. And throughout the book appear sets of "Story Interludes," which relate anecdotes about our successes and failures learning and using the LDS notation and technique. Taken as a whole, these stories constitute a critical assessment of the technique.

Reading Paths Through This Book

To become a master data modeler, you must appreciate the interplay among four areas of expertise: LDS reading, LDS writing, LDS shapes, and controlled evolution. These four areas are equally important and interrelated.

This book presents these four topics in a sensible order, but you cannot master any one of these areas without mastering the other three. Even if you study this book sequentially, when you get to controlled evolution (Chapters 18 through 20), you will find yourself referring to earlier chapters. Controlled evolution integrates virtually everything preceding Chapter 18. As you study that chapter, your incipient mastery of LDS reading, LDS writing, and shapes will be put to the test.

Chapters 3 and 4 are prerequisites to everything that follows. Chapter 13 is a prerequisite to Chapters 14 through 20.

As you work your way toward mastery, you should do the specific exercises at the end of chapters and the whole-skill mastery exercises in the Appendix. You might want to take a peek at Chapter 6 now to get a feel for how a master data modeler works with users.

John Carlis
Joseph Maguire
September 2000

1
Chapter

Introduction

This book can help you become a master at creating data models—diagrammatic and textual expressions of the kinds of data that an organization, a business, or a culture considers worth remembering. Data modeling is an important part of software development, so it is worth reviewing some essential characteristics of software systems.

A software system should help people do work. That sounds simple enough, but right away there are questions. Which work? We're not talking about physical work here, like serving in-flight snacks to passengers or transporting luggage through airports. We're talking about work with data:

- Remembering things—like seat assignments, flight schedules, and airplane maintenance histories
- Calculating things—like pilot performance statistics and passenger frequent-flyer mileage
- Displaying things—like flight schedules and routes

We're not saying that software cannot contribute to physical work. Indeed, software-controlled conveyors can transport luggage through airports. We are merely saying that in this book, we focus on how software can improve the storage, manipulation, and display of data. With that focus, this book is of particular interest to users of database management systems (DBMS).

Questions remain. Who gets helped? Does the system help all its users equally, or are there some users who endure costs (say, their workload increases because they must collect more data) so that some other users can realize benefits (say, their decision making improves because they have more data to justify their decisions)?

When do people get helped? Does the system pay dividends immediately, or must users work with it for a while before it becomes beneficial? We're not merely referring to the learning curve—the lag time between when a system is deployed and when users become proficient at using it. We're talking about systems that by design require an initial user investment. For example, a system that analyzes the annual buying patterns of customers pays dividends only after users have recorded several years worth of data—a significant investment. Even if the data entry clerks learn the system perfectly and instantaneously, they still have plenty of work to do before the system contains enough data to be useful.

Exactly what constitutes "help"? Should the system make work easier? Faster? More reliable? More secure? Should it enlarge the set of work actually performed?

To help answer these questions, you can apply a simple economic principle: *Do what's worth doing.* If a system's costs outweigh its benefits, don't bother building that system. If an individual feature's costs outweigh its benefits, don't include that feature in the system. Of course, this principle is a preposterous platitude; no one would disagree with it. But in practice, applying this simple economic principle to the design of software systems is terribly difficult for several reasons.

One reason is that work is complex. In a large organization, it is hard to understand what work is getting done, much less to quantify the cost of the work or the value of improvements to the work.

Another reason is that software is complex. The complexity of an implemented software system stems from both the complexity of the work and from the inherent complexity of software technology. Programming languages are tricky. Mastering data structures and algorithms requires devoted study. Configuring hardware systems requires knowledge and skill. Technology adds complexity; the complexity of a software system exceeds the complexity of the work it performs. All this complexity makes it difficult merely to build a software system and makes it almost impossible to know in advance how much it will cost to build it and use it.

Because the complexity of work and of software is a fact of life, a detailed, quantitative assessment of the costs and benefits of a software system seems impossibly out of reach. But remember, complex software does get built. Even if an economic assessment is impossible, a useful approximation is attainable, because sooner or later, the system designers understand the work and its technological automation quite well. The trouble is, such understanding often comes too late—at least, too late to affect the overall design of the software system.

It doesn't have to be that way. With a sensible, disciplined approach to system development, a team of people can learn much about a to-be-implemented system—enough to make sound economic decisions about what is worth doing. What's more, the same disciplined approach can help the team reduce system development costs, enlarging the set of things that are worth doing.

In this book, we focus on two parts of the team: you (the data modeler) and them (the users).

It's all about decision making; the team decides what is worth doing. Deciding what is worth doing really comes down to this: deciding where to shift the burden of work.

Remember that a typical software system has a number of components. The details depend on the technological environment and the goals of the system, but in the broadest sense, the following components are in any system:

- Data storage—e.g., a DBMS or a file-based system
- Data processing—e.g., implemented algorithms that create and manipulate the data
- Data input and display—e.g., human/computer interfaces for entering and reading data
- System documentation—instruction guides for using and understanding the automated system
- Business documentation—e.g., policy and procedure manuals for the organization
- Users—human beings who interact with the system through the human/computer interface

The burden of remembering a particular piece of information can be imposed on any of these components. For example, in certain environments, it might be reasonable to allow the users to shoulder the burden of remembering that a *status* value of 1 indicates a good customer and a value of 0 indicates a bad customer. It might not be so reasonable to expect the users to remember that *zoning ordinance number* 867 means "no liquor advertising within 200 yards of a school or day-care center." If there are hundreds of different zoning ordinances, this is an unreasonable burden to place on users.

When you consider where to situate the burden for retaining certain kinds of data, many factors come into play. If the data changes frequently (say, hourly), it is foolish to retain it in hard-copy manuals that need to be printed or in software programs that need to be compiled. In such situations, storing the data electronically seems best. If there is little data and it is used by a single individual—say, a saleswoman wants to remember the names and birthdays of her clients' children—storing the data in a database seems wasteful.

Throughout history, the trend has been to shift more and more of the burden toward the top of the list—away from the humans and toward the data storage. Millennia ago, humans began to write things down, effectively shifting the burden off themselves onto documentation. More recently, computer pioneers recognized a distinction between data and the procedures that manipulate data. The distinction has proved useful, and increasingly, software designers have described more and more of their technical solutions in the stored data.

For example, in some situations the data storage component shoulders some of the burden for remembering the processing steps. In such environments, the programmatic algorithms are reduced to the simplest, most abstract, content-neutral instructions: *Read the next instruction from the database and do what it says.*

Similarly, the details of the user interface can be stored as data. Programs needing to display data can simply contain instructions like *Display the customer input screen, which is described in the database.*

Rendering all this information as data to be interpreted while a program is running means that user interfaces and algorithms can be replaced with improved versions quickly, merely by updating data in the database. That is, programs do not need to be recompiled and redeployed after each modification.

It is worth stating again: The trend toward shifting ever-increasing portions of the memory burden away from users and onto software systems makes economic sense. It is a second-order principle that derives directly from our "preposterous platitude" of doing what is worth doing. Indeed, the trend to shift more and more burden ever further—from the user interface and data processing components toward the data storage component—is also motivated by economics.

Our brief historical study of the fundamentals of software is over. The chapter, however, continues:

- First, it describes Logical Data Structures (LDSs) and shows how any logical data model can be represented (stored) in several different ways. That is, it shows how decisions about WHAT is worth storing are separate from decisions about HOW to store it.
- Second, it presents some thoroughly analyzed sample data and the attendant LDS for that data and shows a simple modification to the LDS to accommodate more data.

Logical Data Structures and Physical Data Storage

A logical data structure, or LDS, is a graphical data model—that is, a diagram depicting what kinds of data some person or group wants to remember. As such, an LDS can depict the types of data contained in a database. An LDS reflects decisions made by the database users about what the database management system (DBMS) should remember.

An LDS helps people learn and communicate about an enterprise, specifically by focusing their attention on the enterprise's data. An LDS helps many different people. Technical analysts (e.g., software application developers and database designers) can use the LDS to communicate with each other or with users. Building the LDS formalizes the vocabulary with which they communicate. Software application developers are helped too. They can use the LDS to understand what information is in a database. That is, they use the LDS to plan the interaction between their programs and the DBMS. Developers and analysts can use an LDS both for understanding existing systems and for designing new ones.

What's more, an LDS can help even if you are not working on any software system, old or new. The process of constructing a good LDS fosters learning and communication among members of any enterprise, even if the enterprise has no software, no databases, and no computers.

Each LDS has two desirable properties making all this communication possible. First, it is precise, which ensures that LDS-induced communication will not be vague or sloppy. Second, its notation is simple. The simple, spare notation makes an LDS easy to read, which encourages all members of an enterprise to participate in discussions. A needlessly complex notation can shroud the important details from the users. If the users cannot read the data model, they cannot assess its accuracy or participate in its evolution. Without the users, the discussion is futile because the users are the only people who can judge what is worth remembering. The spare notation also ensures that the difficult task of creating an LDS is no more difficult than it needs to be. (Comprehending the data needs of a complex, alien enterprise is hard enough without having to grapple with a tedious or quirky notation.) Thus the notation does not interfere with the design task. Through the simplicity of its notation, the LDS supports the design task.

This book encourages you to master the skills, rather than merely learn the material.

Much of what has been written about data modeling emphasizes syntax and vocabulary. However, merely learning what constitutes a well-formed data model and what to call its parts will not give you useful data-modeling skills. This book will. Don't expect to acquire the skills by reading the book passively. Read LDSs aloud, build LDSs, write down sample data and check that the in-progress LDS accommodates it, and reflect on your in-progress LDSs. If you don't work at the skills, you won't master them. In particular, we want you to acquire these skills:

- Know what an LDS is and isn't.
- Be able to read any LDS precisely.
- Be able to build good LDSs.
- Be able to visualize data that an in-progress LDS can accommodate.

In this book we do not attempt to present a comprehensive study of all aspects of DBMSs. There are several books available that do a good job of introducing a reader to the DBMS realm (for recommendations, see Chapter 24).

"Logical Data Structures" is an apt name for this data modeling technique. The following sections elaborate.

Logical : Thinking About WHAT Without HOW

Each LDS is a Logical Data Structure because it excludes any description of how data is physically expressed or recorded. An LDS depicts WHAT data there is without regard for HOW the data gets stored. The distinction between WHAT and HOW is fundamental to the LDS technique. By expressing WHAT without HOW, an LDS lets users disregard unimportant or tangential details about the physical expression of data. Remember that this is one of the fundamental benefits of database management; DBMSs shoulder the burden of organizing and maintaining data so that users can concentrate on what the data means.

An analogy will help. Using a DBMS is like using a library with closed stacks. In such a library, you do not need to know where the books are physically arranged on the shelves—and you do not have direct access to the books. To retrieve a book, you tell the library staff which book you want, and the staff retrieves it for you. The library staff shoulders the burden of knowing where the books are. If you are a do-it-yourself kind of person, this might seem exasperating; you probably think you could fetch the book faster yourself. And if you were King of the World, you would rearrange the library to have all your favorite books easily accessible. But the library is a public facility, and you share the books with many other people. It is your civic duty to relinquish the privilege of strolling through the stacks so that the professional staff of librarians can protect, maintain, and organize the books in a way that will serve all the citizens equally well.

The benefits and sacrifices of using a DBMS are similar. The DBMS shoulders the burden of organizing and retrieving the data for you, and it mediates the sharing of data among a wide range of users. But you cannot directly design an algorithm to retrieve the data because you do not know HOW the data is stored. That is, you do not know the physical organization of the data; you know only the logical meaning of the data.

Unfortunately, the word "logical" is an overloaded word.[1] Many database analysts and database publications characterize a "schema"—a model of the structure of a database—as a logical model. However, the structure of a database, even a well-designed database, does not necessarily reflect the users' perceptions of the data. In particular, a schema describes the kinds of data as realized in a specific implementation model, such as the relational model or the object-oriented model. However, few users conceptualize their data as purely relational or object-oriented data, and no data-modeling technique purporting to be "logical" should force users to think of their data that way.

By stressing <u>logical</u> data structures, we are not saying that physical database design is unimportant or trivial. Choosing an efficient way to store the data is very important and notoriously challenging. The choice depends on a host of factors, including the volume of data, how it is used, how often it is updated or deleted or enlarged, and what kind of physical storage devices contain it. But during logical data modeling—when the goal is to learn and communicate about WHAT kind of information is worth remembering—concerns about efficiency can serve only to mystify the users and distract the data modelers. It is not merely a happy coincidence that logical data modeling disregards efficiency; it is an intentional aspect of the LDS technique. Efficiency, a legitimate concern of database designers, is irrelevant when developing an LDS or assessing its quality.

Data analysts and database designers are not the only people who tend to mix HOW with WHAT. Many users fail to distinguish the media containing data from the data itself. For example, users often describe their data as consisting of forms, reports, or screens of data. In most cases, what's important is what data these media contain. Nevertheless, you can use such forms and reports to investigate what information is important to an enterprise—if data appears on a report, it is probably important to someone.

---

[1] In data modeling, "semantic" and "conceptual" are approximately equivalent to "logical."

Data : Thinking About Data Without Processing

Each LDS is a Logical <u>Data</u> Structure because it excludes any indication of processing: when data is created, where it comes from and goes to, who interprets it, and how all this creation, transmission, and interpretation of data occurs.

By focusing purely on data, the data modeler in effect seeks to learn the names for the kinds of data important to the organization. Any information that does not change the names of the things on the LDS is tangential to the data modeling effort.[2] This includes all information about process and—perhaps surprisingly—it includes information about restrictions (constraints or business rules) on legal data values. The next chapter includes a justification for excluding process information from any LDS. See Chapter 22 for a justification for excluding data constraints from any LDS.

Structure : Articulating Types Without Instances

Each LDS is a Logical Data <u>Structure</u> because it depicts the form of the data rather than the data values. This distinction between data form and data values is profoundly important but simple to articulate: A database contains descriptions of things. An LDS names the types of things described.

A "type of thing" is simply a named category. Categorization is a natural human activity; we categorize to organize and conceptualize our experience. When the members of a culture recognize a category, they recognize that a certain class of noteworthy things share characteristics. Likewise, when a culture distinguishes between two categories, it recognizes that the same characteristics (or "descriptors") do not apply equally well to things in those categories. We have separate categories for "fish" and "dogs" because some characteristics that apply to fish do not apply to dogs. "Gill size" is not a characteristic of dogs.

Three fundamental characteristics of categorization affect the construction of data models. First, no set of categories is "correct." Rather, a set of categories recognized by an enterprise reflects decisions made by members of that enterprise about what distinctions are worth making and what categories are worth recognizing. A system of categories is neither true nor false. It merely is more or less useful to some set of people. For example, a laboratory of marine biologists might consider "gill size" to be a noteworthy characteristic of fish, whereas a restaurant chain might consider "gill size" to be insignificant but "fat calories per serving" to be noteworthy. For this reason, the data modeler must not impose his or her opinion about what is worth remembering. The members of the enterprise choose what to remember; the data modeler is there only to assist.

---

[2]Some experienced modelers object to this sentence because their experience is limited to modeling notations that use fewer names than the LDS notation uses. As you will see in Chapters 14 and 15, virtually everything on an LDS has a name. In modeling, you succeed if you get all these names right.

Second, all cultures and enterprises seem to go about categorization the same way. Although different cultures care about different categories, the act of categorization is consistent across cultures. And even wildly disparate cultures use systems of categories that *look* similar, even if the names of the categories differ. This lets a data modeler recognize structural similarities between seemingly unrelated sets of categories—and these structural similarities encourage analogical thinking.

Third, categorization is an attempt to organize individual things. That is, categories have instances (e.g., the thing LASSIE is an instance of the category DOG). As you struggle[3] to name a culture's categories, you should frequently study particular instances. Convince yourself that an in-progress LDS can actually accommodate the sample instances provided by users. Think hard about what kinds of instances are not accommodated by the LDS and make sure that the users accept these exclusions. As you try to acknowledge a category by naming it, you and the users will think hard about the question *What do we mean by one of these?* For example, when you think hard about the category DOG, you will ask yourself What is one of THESE? What is a DOG? Such thinking will help the users tell you exactly what the category is. For example, it will help them tell you that *LASSIE* is a DOG and that *COLLIE* is not a DOG.

Example

This section presents a lengthy example of a small amount of data. The example has several noteworthy features:

- **The data is relatively simple, but the example is exhaustive.** Thus the example shows you how to analyze a simple set of data thoroughly. Such thorough analysis is an important part of learning the LDS technique and an important part of creating LDSs.
- **The example shows several ways to express the same data.** Thus it illustrates several different formats for visualizing data. You can use any or all of these formats when helping users understand an in-progress LDS. The example also points out how some formats make it easy to answer certain questions by merely glancing quickly at the data but make answering other questions quite tedious. This is reminiscent of the affinity that some on-disk data structures have with certain patterns of data access.
- **The example gives a single LDS that accommodates the data.** Thus it illustrates that a single WHAT (the LDS) can be realized by many different HOWs (the data formats). This is important for you to appreciate early on in your learn-

---

[3] We are not being pessimistic here, but realistic. Naming a culture's categories is a struggle for you and for the members of that culture. In data modeling, you ask the users to think about their data and its categories harder and more explicitly than they have ever thought about them before. Although your role as modeler differs from their role as users, you will struggle along with them. Your job—helping them express their categories rigorously—is no easier than their job.

ing. Many beginning data modelers *insist* on thinking about HOW because they erroneously believe that thinking about HOW cannot be postponed. This example plants within you the seed of faith—faith that for any LDS, many different data structures are possible. As you become a master data modeler, this faith will become confidence earned through experience. But as you begin learning this material, you must resist the temptation to design physical data structures or to worry about implementation details or data-access efficiency. Believe it: There will be time to address these important issues after the logical data structure has become stable. But if you do not focus steadfastly on WHAT the users need to remember, you will not become a master data modeler.

What's more, by showing a single LDS alongside five ways to visualize the data, this example delivers an implicit warning: Do not be deceived by surface differences in the way data is presented. Users will often present sample data to you, and in most cases, the data will be similar to data you have seen before. But the particular way the data is presented might be quite idiosyncratic. An important data-modeling skill is recognizing these underlying similarities—despite surface differences—so that you can leverage your experience as often as possible.

- **The example describes sample data that the LDS cannot accommodate.** This is important. To understand an in-progress LDS, you must understand what data it can and cannot accommodate.
- **The example shows how a small increase in the kinds of data worth remembering yields an equally small modification to the LDS.** That is, the example illustrates an important characteristic of the LDS technique. As the users gradually refine and enlarge their data requirements, the LDS changes and grows accordingly. Because the LDS changes gradually, the users can follow the LDS's evolution. This keeps the users engaged in the process, and we cannot overstate how important it is for the users to remain engaged.

Figure 1-1 shows the data; you can think of it as a tiny database. The database has a set of creatures, a set of skills, and the skills that the creatures have achieved. The data provides answers to questions like the following:

1. Are there any floaters?[4]
2. Who floats?
3. What are the unachieved skills?
4. Are there any unachieving creatures?
5. Who has the most skills?
6. Who has the fewest skills?

---

[4] Strictly speaking, these questions could all be rephrased in a way that acknowledges the boundary between what is in the database and what is outside the database. For example, question 5 could be rephrased *Who—among the creatures that we remember—has the most skills?* Admittedly, it is important to acknowledge the distinction between data and the "real world" described by the data. Nevertheless, rephrasing all these questions amounts to awkward pedantry.

Creature			Skill (code and description)				
			A	E	O	U	Z
ID	Name	Type	float	swim	sink	walk on water	gargle
1	Bannon	person	1	3			3
2	Myers	person	3				
3	Neff	person	2				1
4	Neff	person	2	2			
5	Mieska	person					3
6	Carlis	person					
7	Kermit	frog		1			
8	Godzilla	monster			1		

Figure 1-1 A Tiny Database in Matrix Form

7. Are there any universally achieved skills?
8. Are there any all-achieving creatures?

Notice that we can rearrange the rows or columns of the table in Figure 1-1 without losing any information. The data happens to be arranged by ascending creature ID and by alphabetical skill code, but that is merely a convenience—it helps us find particular IDs or codes more quickly.

Other aspects of Figure 1-1 are less convenient. For a large set of hard-to-achieve skills, viewing the data in this format might prove less than ideal. The chart would have vast amounts of white space, and only occasionally would a cell contain a 1, 2, or 3. The same problem occurs if the data describes a large set of low-achieving creatures. Happily, there are other formats for viewing the same data.

Figures 1-2, 1-3, and 1-4 show exactly the same data in some of these other formats. Obviously, there are many different ways to render the same information. Figures 1-1 through 1-4 illustrate the same WHAT with different HOWs.

Creature		
ID	Name	Type
1	Bannon	person
2	Myers	person
3	Neff	person
4	Neff	person
5	Mieska	person
6	Carlis	person
7	Kermit	frog
8	Godzilla	monster

Achievement		
ID	Code	Proficiency
1	A	1
1	E	3
1	Z	3
2	A	3
3	A	2
3	Z	1
4	A	2
4	E	2
5	Z	3
7	E	1
8	O	1

Skill	
Code	Description
A	float
E	swim
O	sink
U	walk on water
Z	gargle

Figure 1-2 The same tiny database in a simple tabular form

We can visually compare these various HOWs for arranging the data. Figure 1-1 seems best, except for large, sparse data sets. For especially dense data sets, an on-disk structure analogous to Figure 1-1 will consume less disk space than an on-disk structure based on Figure 1-2. Each table of Figure 1-2 is simple, but answering questions often requires that we look at several different tables. When comparing formats, it is useful to consider particular questions, such as questions 1 through 8 listed on pages 9 and 10.

A little reflection about these questions reveals some interesting differences between the formats, but it also shows the essential similarity of the formats. Notice

Skills of creatures					Skill	
ID	Name	Type	Codes, proficiencies		Code	Description
1	Bannon	person	(A,1), (E,3), (Z,3)		A	float
2	Myers	person	(A,3)		E	swim
3	Neff	person	(A,2), (Z,1)		O	sink
4	Neff	person	(A,2), (E,2)		U	walk on water
5	Mieska	person	(Z,3)		Z	gargle
6	Carlis	person				
7	Kermit	frog	(E,1)			
8	Godzilla	monster	(O,1)			

Figure 1-3   The same tiny database in a nonsimple tabular form

that every format can answer questions 1 through 8. That is because each format contains exactly the same data so the sets of answerable questions must be the same. There are many HOWs evident, but only one WHAT—one corresponding LDS. Fragment 1-1 shows that LDS.[5]

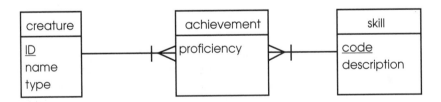

Fragment 1-1

---

[5] Throughout this book we use the word "fragment" to mean the portion of an LDS of interest at the moment. The fragment might encompass the entire LDS or be just a small portion of a large model.

Creatures of skill				Creature		
Code	Description	IDs, proficiencies		ID	Name	Type
A	float	(1,1), (2,3), (3,2), (4,2)		1	Bannon	person
E	swim	(1,3), (4,2), (7,1)		2	Myers	person
O	sink	(8,1)		3	Neff	person
U	walk on water			4	Neff	person
Z	gargle	(1,3), (3,1), (5,3)		5	Mieska	person
				6	Carlis	person
				7	Kermit	frog
				8	Godzilla	monster

Figure 1-4   The same tiny database in another nonsimple form

Notice that Fragment 1-1 shows no data instances—we cannot determine anyone's name, and so on. Although the LDS notation has not yet been explained, the meaning of this little LDS should be clear to you from the following italicized paragraph. It has declarative sentences that constitute a "reading" of the LDS. You will soon learn how to translate an LDS into such sentences.

There are creatures, skills, and achievements. About each creature we can remember its ID, name, type, and achievements. About each skill we can remember its code, description, and achievements. About each achievement we can remember its creature, its skill, and its proficiency. About each creature we must remember its ID, and no two creatures can have the same ID. We must remember each skill's code, and no two skills can have the same code. About each achievement we must remember its creature and its skill, and no achievement can have the same combination of creature and skill.

Like every LDS, Fragment 1-1 depicts the limited scope of its corresponding data. Obviously, there is an endless list of kinds of data not accommodated by the LDS. Here are a few questions that, therefore, cannot be answered with the data:

- To which skills does each creature aspire?
- Was there ever a time when Bannon floated with some proficiency other than 1? We cannot retain a dated progression of proficiencies for each creature-skill pair.
- What are the two-creature skills, and what creatures have acquired them? That is, we cannot remember anything about two-creature skills, such as "waltzing together."
- What are the two-skill achievements? A typical two-skill achievement is "simultaneous walking and gum chewing."

In effect, when this LDS was created, the users effectively made **boundary decisions;** they decided that creature aspirations, two-skill achievements, and so on were not worth remembering, so they were left outside the boundary of the database.

You should not necessarily perceive these limitations on the scope of the data as shortcomings of the LDS. The LDS reflects users' decisions about what's worth remembering. So far, we have seen no sample data that this LDS cannot accommodate, so we have no evidence indicating that the LDS is inaccurate—that the boundary is too restrictive. Data modelers should, however, be able to articulate what kinds of data fall within and outside the scope of the LDS—and should be able to make up allowed and disallowed instances accordingly.

As you build LDSs, you will constantly check your work with sample data to make sure that the LDS accommodates the data needed by the users. You can visualize sample data in any format that helps you and the users understand things. But remember that each format carries some extra connotation about how easy or difficult it is to answer specific questions. Don't allow yourself or the users to be swayed by these HOW connotations.

Ideally, we could devise a HOW-neutral format for visualizing data values. Figure 1-5 shows one such attempt. It is intended to indicate no commitment to any data structure; it's just data floating on a surface (although you might look at it and visualize an on-disk pointer structure). Each dot represents an instance; ovals encircle instances of the same type.

Study Figures 1-1 through 1-5 to internalize the distinction between WHAT and HOW; your success as a data modeler depends on it for several reasons. First, as we've said before (but it's worth repeating), separating WHAT from HOW lets users and data modelers disregard tangential details about physical data storage.

Second, as you design and study sample instances, you ought to feel free to express these instances in whatever form is convenient or illustrative. If you fail to appreciate the relative insignificance of HOW you express the data, you will inappropriately restrict yourself to a particular way of writing down instances. Such a restriction needlessly impedes your comprehension of and communication about the data.

Third, as you study multiple sets of user-provided sample instances, you need to recognize analogous shapes despite grossly differing ways of expressing the data. As a data modeler, you must recognize that Figures 1-1 and 1-2 reflect identical shapes; they look different only because of insignificant HOW decisions.

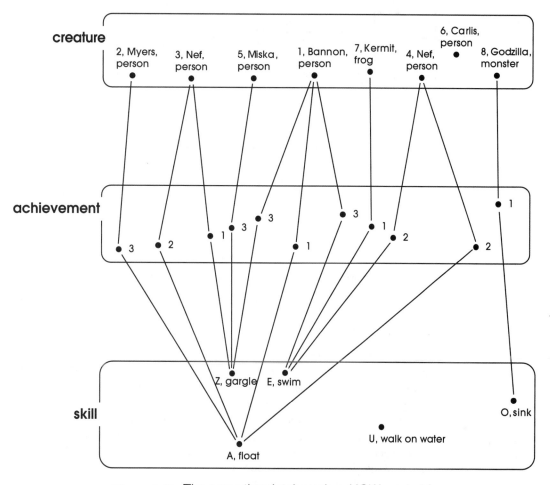

Figure 1-5 The same tiny database in a HOW-neutral form

Extending the Example LDS: Shifting the Burden

Remember, we typically want a DBMS to do as much work as possible. For example, we want to relieve users from having to remember the following data:

Proficiency 1 means "good."

Proficiency 2 means "fair."

Proficiency 3 means "poor."

Then we modify the LDS as in Fragment 1-2. With this change to the LDS, we shift the burden of work onto the DBMS by enlarging the database boundary to include more kinds of data. We now impose on the DBMS the burden of remembering

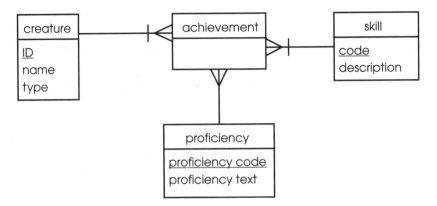

Fragment 1-2

the valid set of proficiency codes and for each such code the corresponding proficiency text.

Summary

Creating software is about deciding where to situate the burden of work with data. That means understanding the work and, first and foremost, that means understanding the data. You need to secure such an understanding from the users, which means talking to them about WHAT the data is but not HOW it is stored. There is a certain knack to this because the very act of writing down some data means arranging it on the page and that can reveal a subconscious bias toward how that data ought to be stored. There are many different ways to store the same data, but in trying to understand data, the different storage options are immaterial.

It is also important to focus initially on the data regardless of the processes used to collect, manipulate, and analyze it. The reasons for this are described in the next chapter.

Economically, it often makes sense to shift more and more of the work burden onto the DBMS. Enlarging the work burden shouldered by the DBMS means expanding the database boundary. With assistance from a data modeler, the users decide what the boundary of the DBMS should be.

To help users choose and record boundary decisions, data modelers can create Logical Data Structures (LDSs). The rest of this book is about creating Logical Data Structures—starting in the next chapter with a few good habits employed by any good data modeler.

Exercises

1. Think about "burden" applied to systems you use or have developed.
   - Where or on whom are various burdens imposed?
   - Is each burden appropriate? What other choices are available?
   - From version to version of the system how have burdens shifted?
2. Think about "logical."
   - What are the benefits and costs of a closed-stack library?
   - What are the benefits and costs of an open-stack library?
   - Suppose you wanted to rearrange the books in a library by author (instead of by the usual call-number order). What happens to library users with open versus closed stacks?
3. Think about "data."
   - To what extent can you think about data without thinking about processing?
   - To what extent can you think about processing without thinking about data?
   - What are the benefits and costs of thinking about one before the other?
   - What are the benefits and costs of mingling together your thinking about data and processing?
4. Think about "structure."
   - What is wrong with saying "COLLIE is a DOG"?
   - What is wrong with thinking about instances entirely without types?
   - What is wrong with thinking about types entirely without instances?
5. Think about "example data."
   - Look at some data, for example, from your personal accounting software or from work, and come up with several different HOWs for it.
   - Look at some data, for example, from your personal accounting software or from work, and find burden-shifting decisions.
   - In Fragment 1-2, should "skill code" replace "code"?
   - Redraw Figure 1-5, replacing the ID numbers with a chain of pointers from which you can deduce the correct ID for each creature. For example, Godzilla is last on the chain.

2
Chapter

Good Habits

To become a master data modeler, you must commit yourself to good data-modeling work habits. Here are several:

1. Employ the users' language and vocabulary.
2. Be rigorous
3. Don't rely on the opinion of a single expert; ask several.
4. Ask first about data, not processing.
5. Master the shapes of data.
6. Choose a notation that helps you realize habits 1–5.

These habits are worth mastering because you can apply them to virtually any system development effort.

Employ the Users' Language and Vocabulary

Together, you and the users must articulate the system requirements. If you talk to users in your idiosyncratic, high-tech language, you will achieve little. You must converse with them in their language.

During your conversations with users, the important distinction is between WHAT and HOW. The users care only about WHAT their data is and WHAT manipulations they perform on it. The users' language is for discussing the WHAT questions—WHAT is a customer? WHAT is the procedure for testing a circuit? Your high-tech language is for discussing HOW questions—HOW will the system electronically store and manage a description of each customer? HOW will the system automate the circuit-testing procedure? The users do not care HOW the storage and manipulation of the data is implemented in a deployed software system. To users, HOW language is nerdy; it bores some and intimidates others. Bored, intimidated users become disengaged, and disengaged users describe their needs vaguely. A system with vague goals fails.

Employing the users' language is not merely polite; it is absolutely necessary. To describe their information, users must employ the vocabulary of their culture because information is a cultural phenomenon. This means that different cultures will disagree about which things are worth remembering. For example, a university and a hospital are two different cultures. When you enroll in the university, you must supply information about yourself: your name, address, and planned course of study. But when you enter the hospital, you supply different information: your name, address, and blood type. The university does not ask for your blood type because within the university culture, blood type is not worth remembering.

Cultures can also disagree about what distinctions are worth making. For example, a bookstore need not distinguish among its three in-stock copies of *Hamlet;* it merely needs to know that it has three copies in stock. A library, on the other hand, must distinguish among its three copies, because the library must keep track of which copy is loaned out to which borrower.

Cultures can also disagree about vocabulary. These disagreements might be a simple matter of synonymy. For example, the bookstore considers *Hamlet* to be a "title" but the library considers it to be a "volume." On the other hand, these disagreements could be more serious. For example, two cultures could use the same word to mean two different things. It is very likely, for example, that a commercial courier service and a mail-order retailer use the word "shipment" to mean different things.

It is hard to understand another culture's information. After all, information truly is a cultural phenomenon, so if a certain culture is alien to you, so are that culture's vocabulary and value judgments about what distinctions are worth making. This should not surprise you; there is no reason to expect that you can participate fully in a conversation among, say, cardiac surgeons. You are (probably) not a member of the culture of cardiac surgery.

What's more—and maybe this will surprise you—a culture's information is never understood with absolute precision, not even by members of that culture. This is not so bad, because in many situations, absolute precision is neither needed nor desirable.

- It is not needed because in typical discourse, humans can make do with an inexact system of categories. On occasions when a more refined understanding is required, humans are flexible enough to make the refinements as needed. For example, you can say "I like music," even though there is no universal (or even culturewide) agreement about what exactly constitutes music.
- It is not desirable because for ordinary discourse, increased precision means decreased flexibility. The world is full of exceptional situations—things that do not fit squarely into our categorical systems. When we encounter such things, we need the flexibility to respond accordingly.

It happens more often than you might guess. Even a culture's most basic categories are imprecise and subject to such ad hoc fine-tuning. For example, a basic, seemingly well understood category used by the hospital culture is "patient." As it turns out, the concept of patient is not absolutely precise. The imprecision reveals itself in exceptional situations. For example, when cardiac surgeons repair a heart defect in a fetus while it is still in the mother's uterus, who is the patient? Are there two patients or just one? Suppose the fetus has a twin who will remain undisturbed during the surgery. During the surgery, the operating room personnel monitor the fetal heart rate and other vital signs of the other fetus. Is this second fetus a patient or not?

The point is not for you to debate these questions or even for you to debate whether medical experts and administrators would have difficulty answering these questions. The point is that the culture's concept of patient cannot accommodate all situations. In exceptional situations, the members of the culture must decide how (and whether) to adjust the culture's system of categories to accommodate the exception.

Humans are smart enough to recognize these exceptional situations and flexible enough to adjust to them. But a software system is dumb and inflexible. When a culture enlarges or revises its system of categories, the culture's attendant software systems can become obsolete. Users endure the obsolete software until it is improved or replaced. Typically, the replacement effort begins in earnest when the user's threshold of intolerance or irritation with the existing system is exceeded. That's just a fancy way of saying that the users get so fed up with a system that they stop using it.

Of course, a great way to prolong a system's life is to make sure that its initial design is as faithful as possible to the users' needs. So you need to give the users every chance to describe their needs completely and accurately. That means letting them use their own vocabulary.

Be Rigorous

Just because the users get to speak their own language does not mean it will be easy for them to describe their information to you. For several reasons, users' language will be vague, and you need to demand precision. The trick is to allow the users to use their own vocabulary but to disallow the customary vagueness common to all spoken language.

One reason users have difficulty describing their information needs to software designers is this: Software designers need to establish a purely symbolic representation of information. In ordinary discourse, humans need not go to such lengths, because humans can supplement their symbolic expressions of data with nonsymbolic expression. For example, during a field trip, a high school science teacher can distinguish between two elm trees merely by pointing. To her students, the teacher can say, "Look, this tree shows symptoms of Dutch elm disease, but that tree does not." In contrast, consider a botanist of the United States Forestry Service studying the spread of Dutch elm disease. She must write down the facts observed by the high school teacher. And writing it down means symbolically distinguishing between the two trees. The botanist need not name the two trees because there are other ways to distinguish the trees (e.g., by location). But one way or another, the scientist must devise some symbolic way to distinguish the trees. As it turns out, devising symbolic ways to express things we would ordinarily express in other ways (e.g., by pointing) is quite difficult. As a thought experiment, consider how you would symbolically instruct a dancer to perform a specific dance. The dancer cannot see you, so you are not allowed to demonstrate any of the motions. You can use words only, no pictures.

The trick is to let users employ their customary vocabulary but not their customary vagueness or nonverbal shortcuts or, equivalently, to force users to use the rigor required by software systems without also forcing them to endure the cryptic vocabulary of software technology. Most of this book is about performing this trick.

The data-modeling technique we describe in this book is rigorous. There is a syntax, and good data modelers *always* keep their in-progress models well formed. You should learn the modeling technique's syntax the way you learn a programming language's syntax—thoroughly. You should consider a data model with a syntax error to be as useless as a program with a syntax error. Honoring the data-modeling syntax presented in this book requires even more discipline than honoring programming language syntax, because when data modeling in a conference room with a group of users, there is no data-modeling equivalent of a syntax-checking language compiler. As data modeler, you must do your own syntax checking.

Don't Rely on the Opinion of a Single Expert; Ask Several

Another reason users will have difficulty describing their information to you is that different users will disagree about what their information needs are and about how best to describe them. Such disagreements come from what we call a "provincial view of data."

Work is so complex that no one person understands the information needs of the organization. For example, an employee in the marketing department is likely to understand the information used by the manufacturing personnel only vaguely. Conversely, the assembly line worker has only a sketchy understanding of the marketing information. What's worse, these misunderstandings might go beyond mere sketchiness or vagueness—they might be contradictory.

These differences between how two different "provinces" of an organization can view the same data can take on many forms. In fact, provincial disagreements about data can be just like the cultural differences we've already mentioned. You can think of two provinces (say, two departments) as subcultures within the larger culture. Just like any cultures, these two subcultures can disagree about what things are worth remembering, about what distinctions are worth making, and about vocabulary. And to a certain extent, the members of two subcultures will be alien to each other and, therefore, will have difficulty understanding each other.

If it's so difficult, why bother? In a large enterprise that has many subcultures, who cares if everyone speaks the same language? Provincialism in vocabulary and diction is a natural, even useful phenomenon. It is unreasonable to expect the personnel in a hospital's laundry to use the same vocabulary as the personnel in the on-site pharmacy. Within each subculture, the language evolves as needed; presumably each localized, departmental language is sufficient (maybe even ideal) for that department's needs.

But remember, there is a global, integrated perspective. As different as the pharmacy and the laundry might seem, the overarching culture—the hospital as a whole—can derive some benefit if the two departments can share data. For example, both the pharmacy and the laundry care about the allergic reactions patients can have to certain chemical agents found in both detergents and some ointments. The hospital can save money by collecting and storing this data only once about each patient and allowing any department concerned with patient allergies—laundry, pharmacy, kitchen services, or internal medicine—to use the data.

The pharmacy/laundry example only seems farfetched. It emphasizes that you can find opportunities for data sharing in surprising places, even among the most separate, seemingly disjoint departments. And data becomes more valuable when it is shared.

Ask First About Data, Not About Processing

There's another reason why people fail to realize how much data they share—they tend to think of data according to how it is used and manipulated. Two departments might use the same data, but if they use it in profoundly different ways, they might never realize that they have similar data needs. This is wasteful because they overlook an economic benefit—the chance to share the costs of collecting, verifying, and maintaining the data. To help users recognize this economic opportunity, you must concentrate on what their data is, regardless of what processing they perform on it.

Don't misunderstand us. Process models are very important, and process models should be closely related to data models. In particular, good process models should make it very clear how the processing affects the data. (For example, *Step 1 creates data describing a customer. Step 2 reads data about a customer's credit limit and outstanding balances, reads the price of the to-be-purchased item, and updates the customer's outstanding balance to reflect the new purchase. Step 3 reads data about the customer's address and creates data describing a shipping request.*) But the data model itself should merely express what kinds of data need to be there. The process models describe how the data is used.

Ours is not a data-without-processing perspective; it is a data-before-processing perspective. We are merely suggesting that there are good reasons to think about data models first and to keep process models integrated with, but separable from, data models.

Not surprisingly, these good reasons are based on economics. Modeling a system takes time and money. It represents a substantial investment. If the model becomes obsolete too soon, the investment is lost. But if the model's validity endures, the investment continues to yield returns. When modeling a culture (with an eye toward automating some of the culture's information processing), it is best to create a model that will endure so that the model can contribute to many different automated systems or to many different versions of a software system. And data models endure longer than processing models.

In fact, process models can change frequently because people are constantly trying to do things faster or more efficiently. Often, a change in a process model has no corresponding effect on the attendant data model. In designing the assembly line, Henry Ford might have changed the way cars are built, but he did not change what we consider worth remembering about cars (number of gears, number of cylinders, and so on). He changed the processing but not the kinds of data.

A more elaborate example will help. Consider a hospital with well-defined policies and procedures for admitting patients. In the emergency ward, each walk-in patient is interviewed by a nurse who assesses the urgency of the medical need based on the interview. The most urgent patients are admitted first. After admission, the blood pressure, pulse, and temperature of each patient are recorded.

To improve triage, the hospital changes its processing. Now patients have their blood pressure, pulse, and temperature taken before admittance to help the nurses choose the most urgent cases. Note that this new way of work does not affect the kinds of data the hospital requires. It merely changes the timing of the data's collection.

As it turns out, many changes in processing have exactly this characteristic — they do not affect the kinds of data. Since so many changes affect process models only, it is wise to create a model that expresses the data only, a model that will remain unaffected by process-only changes. A data model can remain valid for a long time, effectively preserving the team's initial investment in creating the model. And the urge to protect that investment does not excessively impede the organization's natural tendency to fine-tune its processing.

As you postpone any discussion of what users <u>do</u> with data in favor of discussing what the data <u>is</u>, users might struggle. Remember, users tend to think of their data according to how they interact with it — how they collect it, how they manipulate it, what questions they ask of it. Some users initially find it unnatural to discuss the data without discussing processing.

You can let users frame their initial descriptions of data according to how they manipulate it. But as you press the users for details, you will probe about the data, and you will (temporarily) ignore the fine details about the processing. Some users might never notice your unwavering focus on the data. It doesn't really matter because this book teaches you some specific techniques for getting the users to discuss what the data *is*. Even if the users are unaware of your focus, you inexorably drive them to provide more and more detail about the data.

Working this way makes sense because, sadly, most data is grossly underanalyzed. That is, what the users do with their data represents a small fraction of what they could do with it. If you allow the users' descriptions of their data to be colored by their current manipulations of that data, you will get an incomplete understanding of the data.

What's worse, you will implement a software system that resists enhancement. The deployed database will support the initial processing well. But as the users demand enhancements to the deployed system, they will effectively demand new processing. Your database, designed from an incomplete, processing-colored appreciation of the organization, will accommodate these changes awkwardly, if at all. To prolong the life of the implemented system and to reduce the cost of modifying the system to accommodate new user demands, it is important that the data storage portion of the system make few presumptions about data processing.

There's another benefit to working this way. Many users will pick up your habit of focusing on data. You and those users will shortly notice that you work especially well together. And later, you will notice something more remarkable. Those users will forge a new relationship with their data; they will truly understand their data independent of any particular processing that occurs against it. And when the time comes to think about processing, these users will not be constrained by the current processing environment or by their immediate processing needs. They will conceive of new ways of processing the data. In effect, they will be able to look into the future and anticipate new processing that other, less perceptive users might have requested only after the system was deployed. These clever users are helping you anticipate the evolutionary path of the system through several software-deployment cycles.

Master the Shapes of Data

There's no mystery to becoming a master data modeler. Each time you work with users to create a good data model, you gain experience that you can leverage during your next data-modeling effort. As you work to leverage experience into subsequent data-modeling projects, the specific content of your previous data-modeling efforts is immaterial. This is true because there are limits to the seemingly endless differences between cultures.

As noted in the previous chapter, all cultures and enterprises seem to go about categorization the same way. Yes, different cultures make different decisions about what categories exist. But categorization is common to all cultures. To become a master data modeler, you must appreciate the content-neutral characteristics of categorization—the essential nature of information. For example, most cultures arrange some of their information in taxonomies. As it turns out, there are a limited number of shapes that a taxonomy can exhibit. If you master these shapes, you will be prepared to understand any taxonomy. You will understand more than just a specific taxonomy like "country-state-county-city" or "kingdom-phylum-class-order-family-genus-species"—you will understand the general concept of taxonomy. You must study how taxonomies evolve over time, how people tend to talk about taxonomies, how people tend to cope with exceptions to their taxonomic structures, and what choices you have for visualizing taxonomic data for users. You study these aspects of taxonomy by studying the various shapes a taxonomy can take.

With such a content-neutral toolkit, a master data modeler can help museum curators as easily as chemists. A master data modeler can help them because a data modeler can ignore the surface differences (the culture-specific differences in vocabulary) to recognize the underlying similarities (the content-neutral similarities) between curators' data and chemists' data. And once the modeler recognizes the underlying similarities, she can leverage experience with the curators' data into the chemists' domain. (With the users' help, she will also quickly learn a lot about chemistry.)

When two seemingly different data models share an underlying, content-neutral similarity, they are said to have the same **shape.** A major portion of this book is devoted to teaching you the shapes of data.

Use a Notation That Helps You Realize These Good Habits

These good habits are so important, we have designed a data-modeling notation, Logical Data Structures (LDS), that encourages you to adhere to them. We use this notation throughout this book. The LDS notation itself has these important characteristics:

- **It is spare.** LDS notation has very few diagrammatic constructs. Thus it is not distracting and lets users concentrate on what is important (the names of the kinds of data) without worrying about comparatively trivial things (anything that does not help get the names right).
- **It encourages rigor.** LDS notation has an accompanying set of syntax rules, and it is easy to distinguish well-formed diagrams from ill-formed diagrams.
- **It is nontechnological.** LDS notation yields data models that are technology-neutral. Models created in this notation do not burden users with the idiosyncratic language of DBMSs or programming languages.
- **It fosters communication and consensus.** The spare, easy-to-read, nontechnological LDS notation welcomes all users into the discussion of their data needs. Because it is rigorous, it helps disparate users reach consensus by helping them detect, appreciate, and reconcile their different opinions about what data they need, even when those differences are subtle and might remain undiscovered in another, less rigorous notation.
- **It is processing-neutral.** LDS notation shows kinds of data only, not kinds of processing.

Summary

Data modeling—the careful articulation of the kinds of data important to a group of people—is an important initial step toward the creation of enduring, useful databases and software systems. You can become a master data modeler if you learn to exhibit these good habits, all of which stem from universal truths about culture, language, technology, and information. To end this chapter we provide an additional thought about each habit.

1. Employ the users' language and vocabulary.	It's about them, not you.
2. Be rigorous.	It's about being precise and overcoming natural vagueness.

3. Don't rely on the opinion of a single expert; ask several.	It's about users' sharing sets of data and coming to a consensus about data vocabulary.
4. Ask first about data, not about processing.	It's about relatively stable kinds of data, not about relatively short-lived processing.
5. Master the shapes of data.	It's about vision—seeing shapes and applying lessons learned.
6. Choose a notation that helps you realize these good habits.	It's about notation fostering and not impeding precise communication.

Exercises

1. For each good habit answer these questions:
   - What are its benefits?
   - What are its costs?
2. For each of the first four good habits, recall from your own system development experiences what happened when the habits were not practiced. Collect such stories from others, both systems people and users.
3. Think about another realm where you have expertise and try to articulate the "shapes" you use. To prepare for this exercise, you might find it helpful to read Robert Floyd's Turing Lecture article, "The Paradigms of Programming," in *Communications of the ACM* 22, 8 (August 1979). (He said, "Identify the paradigms you use, as fully as you can, then teach them explicitly.")
4. Think about some notation you use well. (It can be about anything: software development, chemical formulae, dance (Labanotation), genealogy, and so on). Answer these questions:
   - What are its strengths and weaknesses?
   - Does it have the characteristics that we claim are important in data-modeling notation?
   - How did you acquire skill in using it?

3
Chapter

Reading an LDS with Sentences

This chapter shows you how to say an LDS aloud—or equivalently, how to write sentences meaning precisely what the LDS means. This fundamental LDS-reading skill is quite mechanical and therefore quite easy to learn.

After you learn the material in this chapter, you will be able to generate accurate declarative sentences about an LDS, and you will be able to recognize inaccurate sentences and know why they are inaccurate. These seemingly modest goals deserve an entire chapter because these skills are fundamental. If you do not master the skills in this chapter, you will never learn the skills in the rest of the book.

We intentionally exclude from this chapter material that is not immediately useful to you. Notably, we don't distract you with LDS vocabulary, which we present in the next chapter. You don't need any vocabulary or special preparation to begin this chapter. We've seen hundreds of people master this material without any new vocabulary whatsoever. You're ready now.

Sentences About What Users Can Remember

On any LDS diagram, you'll notice some boxes, each of which indicates what users want to remember about a particular type of memorable thing. About each box there are several sentences you can say; we'll cover them in turn.

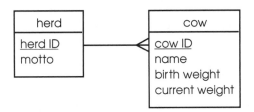

Fragment 3-1

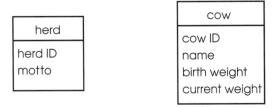

Fragment 3-2

Sentences About Words Inside Boxes

For each box, there is a sentence about the words inside the bottom part of the box. For example, consider Fragment 3-1. Focus only on the boxes and the words inside the boxes (Fragment 3-2). You can say the following sentences:

- *About each cow we[1] can remember its cow ID, its name, its birth weight, and its current weight.*
- *About each herd we can remember its herd ID and its motto.*

Although it is almost too simple for elaboration, we'll be explicit. To construct a sentence, simply say, "About each *<box name>* we can remember its *<list of text lines from inside the same box>*." The two box names in this diagram are *cow* and *herd*. The *<list of text lines from inside the same box>* includes those lines of text in the bottom portion of the box. Note that each line of text is considered as a unit. For example, users don't remember a cow's *birth* and a cow's *weight;* they remember a cow's *birth weight*. Notice that each line of inside-the-box text is a singular noun or noun phrase.

If you prefer, you can say a single sentence for each line of text within each box. For example, you can say four distinct sentences about the four lines of text in the cow box:

- *About each cow we can remember its cow ID.*
- *About each cow we can remember its name.*
- *About each cow we can remember its birth weight.*
- *About each cow we can remember its current weight.*

These declarative sentences—small, particular, tiresome in speech—correspond to individual assertions contained in the LDS. That is, each small portion of the LDS asserts that something is memorable; each such assertion has a corresponding sentence. Each minor extension to the LDS extends the number of assertions the LDS makes.

Despite the mechanical, repetitive simplicity of these rules for constructing sentences, many people make mistakes. We mention a few—when you are a master modeler you'll avoid them.

- Don't use the plural form of *<box name>*. For example, don't say, "About cows, we can remember cow IDs." This sentence is vague because it does not express that users can remember one cow ID for each cow.
- Don't use an article ("a" or "the") in place of "each." For example, don't say, "About a cow, we can remember its cow ID, its cow name, and its weight." This

---

[1] The "we" in these LDS-reading sentences means you and the users, not "we," the authors.

sentence can be misleading because the LDS asserts more than what users can remember about a mere cow; it asserts what they can remember about each remembered cow.

- Don't take shortcuts that make your sentences unclear. For example, don't say, "About each cow, we can remember its weight." The LDS is more specific; users can remember each cow's <u>current</u> weight. Actually, they remember the cow's last measured weight, which the users (the dairy farmers) refer to as the *current weight.*

- As you describe one box, don't mention lines of text inside other boxes. For example, don't say, "About each cow, we can remember its motto."

If you stick to the rules, you'll avoid these mistakes and accurately construct the sentences about the text lines inside the boxes.

Sentences About (Unlabeled) Box-to-Box Lines

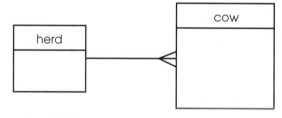

Fragment 3-3

✹ **WARNING**
This illustration shows a syntactically incomplete portion of an LDS.

Train yourself to read *two* sentences for each line.

There are more sentences about Fragment 3-1—sentences about the lines connecting the boxes. For each such box-to-box line, there are two sentences.

Concentrating only on the boxes and the lines connecting the boxes (Fragment 3-3), you can say the following sentences:

- *About each cow we can remember its herd.*
- *About each herd we can remember its cows.*

Notice that a single line induces <u>two</u> sentences. That's because each line indicates that there are two questions the data can answer. In the example, the two questions are *About each cow, what is its herd?* and *About each herd, who are its cows?*

Chicken Feet

When you say either sentence about a box-to-box line, you need to think about whether to use a singular or plural noun. For example, compare these two sentences:

1. *About each herd we can remember its cow.*
2. *About each herd we can remember its cows.*

Only one of these sentences is right. You pick a noun by looking for a chicken foot. A **chicken foot**[2] is a symbol on the LDS that looks like this:

A chicken foot indicates plural. In our example, we see a chicken foot near the *cow* box, so we say, *About each herd we can remember its cows.*

---

[2] Some modelers call it a crow's foot. Either term will do.

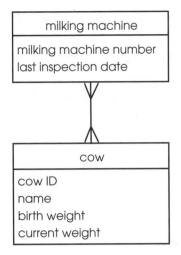

Fragment 3-4

✳ **WARNING**
This illustration shows a syntactically incomplete portion of an LDS.

Notice that the word "its" appears repeatedly; it is not "factored."

Because you must say two sentences for each box-to-box line, you must make a singular or plural decision twice. For example, after you choose between sentences about the herd, you must choose between sentences about the cow:

A. *About each cow we can remember its herd.*
B. *About each cow we can remember its herds.*

Once again, you choose by looking for a chicken foot. There is no chicken foot near the *herd* box, so you say, *About each cow we can remember its herd.*

Most box-to-box lines have exactly one chicken foot. Occasionally, however, a box-to-box line can have two. No matter how many chicken feet a box-to-box line has, each chicken foot affects exactly one sentence. In Fragment 3-4, the top chicken foot affects a sentence you say about cows: *About each cow we can remember its milking machines.* But it does not affect any sentence you say about milking machines. Similarly, the bottom chicken foot affects only a sentence you say about milking machines: *About each milking machine we can remember its cows.*

Similarities Between Sentences

You should recognize the essential similarity between what you say about a box-to-box line and what you say about inside-the-box text. Admittedly, you look at different portions of the LDS to construct these sentences, but don't let that obscure the basic similarity. Each kind of sentence indicates that users can remember a particular thing about one of the boxes. Combining and reformatting the various sentences reveals the similarity.

For example, these reformatted sentences express Fragment 3-5:

About each milking machine, we can remember
- *its milking machine number.*
- *its last inspection date.*
- *its cows.*

About each cow, we can remember
- *its cow ID.*
- *its name.*
- *its birth weight.*
- *its current weight.*
- *its milking machines.*
- *its herd.*

About each herd, we can remember
- *its herd ID.*
- *its motto.*
- *its cows.*

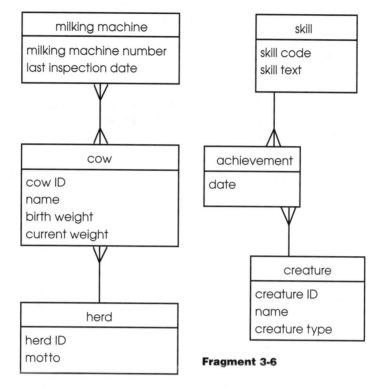

Fragment 3-5

Fragment 3-6

About each herd, there are three things to be remembered. Two of them correspond to inside-the-box text. The other (*its cows*) corresponds to the way you read a box-to-box line in one direction. (Counting helps. Look at a box and count how many named things will be in the sentence.)

Here is another example using Fragment 3-6. Following are the formatted sentences you can say about the inside-the-box text and the unlabeled box-to-box lines:

About each creature we can remember
- *its creature ID.*
- *its name.*
- *its creature type.*
- *its achievements.*

About each achievement we can remember
- *its creature.*
- *its skill.*
- *its date.*

About each skill we can remember
- *its skill code.*
- *its skill text.*
- *its achievements.*

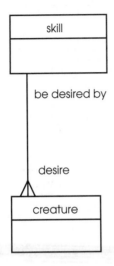

Fragment 3-7

Sentences About Labeled Box-to-Box Lines

Occasionally, a box-to-box line has labels you use to construct your sentences.

For example, in Fragment 3-7, consider the line connecting *creature* to *skill*. Like every box-to-box line, this line indicates two things. The best way to understand what the line asserts is to use the labels verbatim in two sentences:

- *Each creature <u>can desire</u> a skill.*
- *Each skill <u>can be desired</u> by creatures.*

You use the labels to construct predicates for the sentences. A predicate[3] is the portion of a sentence that indicates the action performed.

Notice that when you read a sentence about a box, you use the label near that box. Thus the predicate of the sentence about each creature is *can desire*. The other predicate is *can be desired*. Notice also that most rules for reading unlabeled box-to-box lines apply. That is, you still handle chicken feet the same way, and you still speak about *each creature* or *each skill* rather than *a creature* or *a skill*.

When you construct sentences using labels as predicates, there is a drawback: the sentences do not sound like all the other sentences you say. To sound the same, the sentences should read, *About each . . . we can remember its. . . .* The next section describes how to overcome this apparent dissimilarity.

Labels and Similarities Between Sentences

There are two ways to construct sentences about box-to-box lines. In the previous section, we describe what might be called the **label-as-predicate** method, so named because you use the label as the predicate of the sentence you construct. The label-as-predicate method is valuable because it makes the relationship very easy to understand.

In this section we describe the second method, the **noun-phrase** method, so named because for each "direction" of the labeled box-to-box line, you construct a

---

[3] Here we are using the word "predicate" as a teacher of English grammar would, not as a logician would.

noun phrase describing the memorable tidbit of information. The noun-phrase method is valuable because it highlights the similarities between inside-the-box text and box-to-box lines.

For example, here are the sentences about the desire for skills by creatures using the noun-phrase method (with the noun phrases underlined):

- *About each creature we can remember <u>a skill it desires</u>.*
- *About each skill we can remember <u>the creatures desiring it</u>.*

There is no template for constructing the noun phrases from the label-as-predicate sentences. You should use the label-as-predicate sentences to understand what the relationship means, then carefully construct the noun-phrase sentences so that they conform to the structure *About each . . . we can remember. . . .*

Especially careful sentence construction is required whenever you encounter a box-to-box line whose labels are both *be*. You can still use the label-as-predicate method. For example, to read the relationship in Fragment 3-8, you can say these two sentences:

- *Each patient can be a blood donor.*
- *Each blood donor can be a patient.*

The hard thinking comes when you try to use the noun-phrase method. As always, you use the label-as-predicate sentences to understand what the relationship means.

A relationship whose labels are both *be* has a meaning that is fundamentally different from other relationships. Other relationships indicate an association between two different things. (A creature is one thing and a skill is another associated thing. A cow is one thing and a herd is another associated thing.) But a relationship whose labels are *be* indicates an equivalence: there's only one thing, but there are two different ways to interpret the thing. The relationship indicates the association between one interpretation of the thing and another interpretation of the same thing. The relationship in Fragment 3-8 indicates that some things are both patients and blood donors.

So when it comes time to paraphrase the sentences to make them sound like other sentences, you need to ensure that the new sentences connote this equivalence—the sameness of the two associated things. In our experience, using the word "interpretation" works best when paraphrasing (once again, the noun phrases are underlined):

- *About each patient we can remember <u>its interpretation as a blood donor</u>.*
- *About each blood donor we can remember <u>its interpretation as a patient</u>.*

Whether the labels are *be* or some other words, you should be prepared to read a labeled box-to-box line using the label-as-predicate technique and the noun-phrase technique because each technique is useful in its own way. The label-as-predicate technique is a more direct and forceful way to read the box-to-box line; users will easily grasp its meaning. The noun-phrase technique highlights the basic similarity between labeled box-to-box lines and all the other memorable things on an LDS.

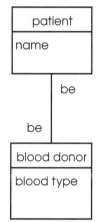

Fragment 3-8

✹ **W A R N I N G**
This illustration shows a syntactically incomplete portion of an LDS.

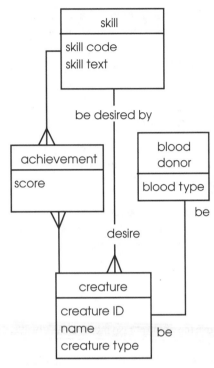

Fragment 3-9

Similarities Between Sentences Revisited

Fragment 3-9 includes box-to-box lines—some labeled and some unlabeled. Read it as follows:

About each creature we can remember
- *its creature ID.*
- *its name.*
- *its creature type.*
- *its achievements.*
- *its desired skill.*
- *its interpretation as a blood donor.*

About each skill we can remember
- *its skill code.*
- *its skill text.*
- *its achievements.*
- *the creatures desiring it.*

About each achievement we can remember
- *its score.*
- *its skill.*
- *its creature.*

About each blood donor we can remember
- *its blood type.*
- *its interpretation as a creature.*

Because this example includes a relationship whose labels are *be,* it gives you a chance to practice reading such relationships using the noun-phrase method. Even though such relationships are fundamentally different from all other relationships, the example bears out our previous assertion: With a little rhetorical effort, you can make the sentences sound somewhat like all the others.

But what's the point? The two kinds of relationships are fundamentally different, and it's no shame if the differences become manifest when you read relationships aloud. The goal remains—helping the users understand the LDS. Most users will grasp the meaning of a *be*-labeled relationship from the labels-as-predicate sentences. You should say the noun-phrase sentences for *be*-labeled relationships only if the users remain confused.

Before moving on, you should practice counting. Notice that about *creature,* users can remember six named things: three are due to inside-the-box names, while three are due to box-to-box lines. Two of the names come from lines with labels; one does not. One labeled line is *be;* the other is not. Two have have singular names; one has plural. Notice that about *achievement,* users can remember three named things: one is due to an inside-the-box name, while two are due to box-to-box lines. Both names from lines are singular, unlabeled, and not *be.* What should you notice about *skill* and *blood donor?*

Realize that novice modelers need to count to avoid errors; master modelers count as a natural part of their expertise.

Sentences About Differentiating Things from Each Other

The LDS diagram does more than enumerate the kinds of memorable information. For each box the LDS diagram indicates how to distinguish each memorable thing from every other memorable thing of that type. For example, the diagram indicates how we distinguish each cow from every other cow or each milking machine from every other milking machine.

One-Bar Boxes

Consider again Fragment 3-1 for cows and herds. Concentrate on the inside-the-box text that has bars, as shown in Fragment 3-10. (The bars look like underlines, but you should think of the symbol as a bar, not an underline.) Focusing on only this portion of the LDS, you can construct some sentences.

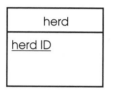

First of all, you can construct some sentences merely because the boxes contain some text. You already know how to construct these sentences. They are *About each herd we can remember a herd ID* and *About each cow we can remember a cow ID*. It is important to remember that these sentences are not changed by the addition of the bar.

But you can say some further sentences because the boxes have bars. About the *herd* box, you can say the following:

1. *About each herd we must remember its herd ID.*
2. *No two herds can have the same herd ID.*

Together, these two sentences mean that users employ the values of *herd ID* to distinguish herds from each other.

In the *cow* box, *cow ID* has a bar, so you say:

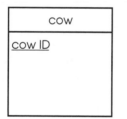

Fragment 3-10

1. *About each cow we must remember its cow ID.*
2. *No two cows can have the same cow ID.*

These sentences mean that users employ the values of *cow ID* to distinguish cows from each other.

Multiple-Bar Boxes

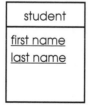

Fragment 3-11

A box can have more than one bar, in which case the sentences are slightly different.

A box can contain two bars, as in Fragment 3-11.

First of all, you can construct a sentence merely because the box contains some text: *About each student we can remember a first name and a last name.*

You construct additional sentences because the box contains bars:

1. *About each student we must remember its first name and its last name.*[4]
2. *No two students can have the same first name and same last name.*
3. *Two students could have the same first name or the same last name.*

Notice the third sentence. It indicates that taken individually, neither first name nor last name is guaranteed to distinguish each instance of student from every other instance. That is, it indicates that each bar is necessary; fewer bars will not suffice. You could paraphrase the third sentence as *Two students could share any one of first name and last name.*

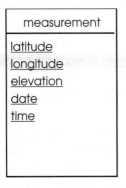

Fragment 3-12

This paraphrased form of the third sentence—admittedly awkward when used for a two-bar box—becomes especially useful if a box contains many bars, as in Fragment 3-12.

Because the box contains bars, you can say the following:

1. *About each location we must remember its latitude, its longitude, and its elevation.*
2. *No two locations can have the same latitude, same longitude, and same elevation.*
3. *Two locations could share any two of latitude, longitude, and elevation.*

You could replace sentence 3 with this cumbersome equivalent: *Two locations could share latitude and longitude or latitude and elevation or longitude and elevation.*

There is no limit to the number of bars for a box, as in Fragment 3-13.

Fragment 3-13

As in the previous examples, you first construct the sentence corresponding to the box's text, regardless of the bars. It is *About each measurement we can remember a latitude, a longitude, an elevation, a date, and a time.*

Then you construct sentences such as the following because the box contains bars:

1. *About each measurement we must remember its latitude, its longitude, its elevation, its date, and its time.*
2. *No two measurements can have the same latitude, longitude, elevation, date, and time.*
3. *Two measurements could share any four of latitude, longitude, elevation, date, and time.*

---

[4] The order in which you say the individual nouns is immaterial. You can say *its first name and its last name,* or you can say *its last name and its first name.*

Outside-the-Box Bars

A bar can appear just outside the box on a box-to-box line. Such a bar applies only to the nearby box. For example, in Fragment 3-14, one of the three bars present is on the box-to-box line.

Start by articulating the sentences you need regardless of each box's bars. They are *About each state we can remember its state name, its state flower, its state motto, and its cities* and *About each city we can remember its city name, its population, and its state.*

Now focus on the portions of Fragment 3-14 that contain bars. Articulate the sentences induced by the bars. In the following, the *city* box has two bars inside or near it, so you say:

1. *About each city we must remember its city name and its state.*
2. *No two cities can have the same city name and same state name.*
3. *Two cities could share a city name or a state name.*

The *state* box has only one bar inside or near it, so you say the following:

1. *About each state we must remember its state name.*
2. *No two states can have the same state name.*

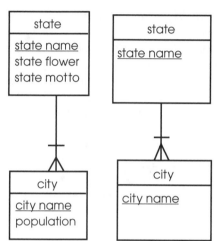

Fragment 3-14   Fragment 3-15

Inside some boxes, no bar appears; all bars are on box-to-box lines. In Fragment 3-16, *achievement* is one such box.

To construct the sentences indicated by Fragment 3-16, start with the sentences about the boxes and box-to-box lines, disregarding the bars. The three sentences are *About each skill we can remember its achievements, About each creature we can remember its achievements,* and *About each achievement we can remember its creature and its skill.*

The *achievement* box has bars near it, so you say the following:

1. *About each achievement we must remember its skill and its creature.*
2. *No two achievements can have the same skill and the same creature.*
3. *Two achievements could share skill or creature.*

A Shorthand

Because each box's bars can induce two or three sentences, it is useful to introduce a one-sentence equivalent—a shorthand. (Remember, the bar of a single-bar box induces two sentences; the bars of a multiple-bar box induce three.) The shorthand constructs sentences of this form: "Each <*box name*> is identified by <*list of barred data that we remember about that box*>."

For single-bar boxes, the shorthand yields sentences like these:

• *Each herd is identified by its herd ID.*
• *Each cow is identified by its cow ID.*

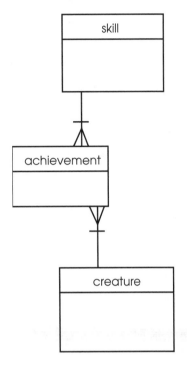

Fragment 3-16

- *Each state is identified by its state name.*
- *Each skill is identified by its skill code.*
- *Each creature is identified by its creature ID.*

For multiple-bar boxes, the shorthand yields sentences like these:

- *Each student is identified by the combination of its first name and its last name.*
- *Each location is identified by the combination of its latitude, its longitude, and its elevation.*
- *Each measurement is identified by the combination of its latitude, its longitude, its elevation, its date, and its time.*
- *Each city is identified by the combination of its city name and its state.*
- *Each achievement is identified by the combination of its creature and its skill.*

A Common Error You Should Avoid

Some students misinterpret the presence of multiple bars for a box. Look again at the *state-city* LDS in Fragment 3-15 and try to answer these four questions:

1. How many bars does the *state* box have?
2. How many ways are there to distinguish instances of *state* from each other?
3. How many bars does the *city* box have?
4. How many ways are there to distinguish instances of *city* from each other?

The answers to these questions are one, one, two, and one. Note that even though the *city* box has two bars, there is still only one way to distinguish instances of city from each other. In the *one* method of distinguishing cities from each other, users must be prepared to inspect *two* data values for each instance.

Here is a trick to help you interpret bars correctly. Look again at Fragment 3-15 and write down the following:

- *About each state we can remember its state name and its cities.*
- *About each city we can remember its city name and its state.*

Then, for each place on the diagram with a bar, put a bar under the corresponding name:

- *About each state we can remember its <u>state name</u> and its cities.*
- *About each city we can remember its <u>city name</u> and its <u>state</u>.*

Finally, form the identifier sentence using exactly those names:

- *State is identified by its state name.*
- *City is identified by the combination of its city name and its state.*

Sentences You Should Not Say

When you read an LDS, say as much as the diagram says, but no more.

The important phrase worth repeating is "When you read an LDS." Although you will sometimes know more than what is expressed on the diagram, remember that you are not saying everything you know; you are simply reading the diagram. Such extra knowledge is not worthless, but it is important to distinguish between the assertions on the diagram and assertions known from other sources. This distinction is important for many reasons, most of which we'll postpone discussing until Chapters 17 and 22. But one benefit worth immediate mention is this: If you read only and exactly what the diagram says, your audience will easily and quickly learn how to read the diagram merely by watching and listening to you.

Don't say too little. That is, don't omit any assertion evident in the diagram. You can avoid the common types of understatement by following these rules:

- **Don't overlook a chicken foot.** If the diagram says that users can remember the *cows* of each herd, don't understate it by saying that they can remember the *cow* of each herd.
- **Don't use an article instead of "each."** *About a cow we can remember its herd* says less than the diagram indicates. The stronger, correct assertion is *About each cow we can remember its herd.*

Don't say too much. That is, don't include any assertion not evident on the diagram. You can avoid the common types of overstatement by following these rules:

- **Don't use *must* without a reason.** If you know that each cow belongs to some herd, you will be tempted to say *About each cow, we must remember its herd.* Resist the temptation while you're reading the LDS. Remember, the goal is not to say what you know; the goal is to say what the LDS—the graphical description of the data model—says.
- **Don't imagine a chicken foot where there is none.** If you say *About each cow we can remember its herds,* you're overstating things. The LDS diagram has no such chicken foot.
- **Don't say *or* when you mean *and.*** For example, don't say *About each cow we can remember cow ID, name, birth weight, or current weight.* This is an overstatement because the LDS makes no assertions about what combinations of values are possible. The LDS indicates that about each cow we can remember cow ID, name, birth weight, and current weight.

For example, when *first name* and *last name* are barred, do not say *Each student is identified by its first name or its last name.* This is an understatement because the LDS asserts that first name and last name together form the identifier.

Some Complete Examples

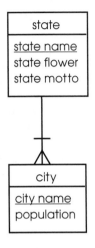

- *About each state we can remember its state name, its state flower, its state motto, and its cities.*
- *Each state is identified by its state name.*

- *About each city we can remember its city name, its population, and its state.*
- *Each city is identified by the combination of its city name and its state.*

Fragment 3-17

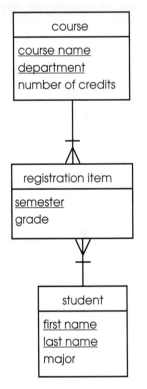

- *About each course we can remember its course name, its department, its number of credits, and its registration items.*
- *Each course is identified by the combination of its course name and its department.*

- *About each registration item we can remember its course, its student, its semester, and its grade.*
- *Each registration item is identified by the combination of its course, its student, and its semester.*

- *About each student we can remember its first name, its last name, its major, and its registration items.*
- *Each student is identified by the combination of its first name and its last name.*

Fragment 3-18

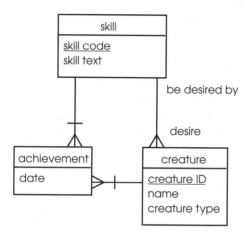

Fragment 3-19

- *About each skill we can remember its skill code, its skill text, its achievements, and the creatures desiring it.*
- *Each skill is identified by its skill code.*

- *About each achievement we can remember its skill, its creature, and its date.*
- *Each achievement is identified by the combination of its skill and its creature.*

- *About each creature we can remember its creature ID, its name, its creature type, its achievements, and its desired skill.*
- *Each creature is identified by its creature ID.*

Summary

When you say a sentence like *About each creature we can remember its . . .* , you complete the sentence by looking for four kinds of things:

1. A piece of inside-the-box text
2. A box connected to *creature* via an unlabeled line
3. A box connected to *creature* via a line whose labels are not *be*
4. A box connected to *creature* via a line whose labels are *be*

The first kind of thing makes the simplest sentence: you complete the sentence simply by appending the inside-the-box text: *About each creature we can remember its creature ID.* The second kind of thing can make a slightly more complex sentence: you complete the sentence by appending the name of the connected box. But note that you might use the plural form of the connected box, as in *About each creature we can remember its achievements.* The third kind of thing can make an even more complex sentence: you use the (singular or plural) name of the connected box, but you modify it accordingly to preserve the meaning of the box-to-box line, as in *About each creature we can remember its desired skill.* The fourth kind of thing yields a sentence that is quite different from the simple sentences you say about inside-the-box text, as in *About each creature we can remember its interpretation as a blood donor.*

After saying what can be remembered about a box, you should also say how instances are distinguished; look for the bars. You can say explicit sentences, such as

About each herd we must remember its herd ID and *No two herds can have the same herd ID.* If a box has several bars, there is a third sentence, such as *Two students could have the same first name or the same last name.* You can summarize these explicit sentences in a single sentence, such as *Each herd is identified by its herd ID* or *Each student is identified by the combination of its first name and its last name.*

To help users understand a box-to-box line, you can read both directions of the line consecutively. For example, you can say *About each herd we can remember its cows* and *About each cow we can remember its herd.* To choose singular or plural nouns at the end of the sentences, look for the presence or absence of a chicken foot at the end of the appropriate line.

Exercises

1. This exercise stresses the underlying similarity between box-to-box lines and inside-the-box text. Complete the following table using Fragment 3-14.

What is the question that we can answer?	How does the LDS indicate that we can answer this question?	What is the name of the data that answers this question?
What is the state name of a particular state?	Inside-the-box text	"State name"
What are the cities of a particular state?	A box-to-box line, read in a particular direction	"Cities of state"
What is the state flower of a particular state?		
What is the state motto of a particular state?		
What is the city name of a particular city?		
What is the population of a particular city?		
What is the state of a particular city?		

2. Make a similar table about Fragment 3-18.
3. Fragment 3-20 is missing bars. Based on the following sentences, draw in the bars where they belong.
   - *About each course we must remember its course number.*
   - *No two courses can have the same course number.*

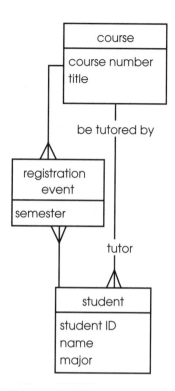

Fragment 3-20

✹ **WARNING**
This illustration shows a syntactically incomplete portion of an LDS.

- *About each registration event we must remember its course and its student.*
- *No two registration events can have the same course and the same student.*
- *Each student is identified by student ID.*

4. For Fragments 3-17, 3-18, and 3-19, answer the following questions.
   - How many bars does each box have?
   - How many ways are there to distinguish the instances of each from one another?

4
Chapter

Vocabulary
of LDS

The parts of an LDS need names because we need to talk about the parts. Indeed, we have already used some conversational, unofficial names in the previous chapter: box, box-to-box line, inside-the-box text, and so on. There are several reasons why we now present more official names that we will use throughout the remainder of this book. First, the unofficial names are cumbersome. Second, the data-modeling community already has a vocabulary for these concepts. Third, different members of the data-modeling community can use subtly different variations in their vocabulary. The subtlety of these distinctions is sometimes overlooked, leading to confusion when two data modelers confer. We need to be explicit about our vocabulary.

The vocabulary we present in this chapter can intimidate users. However, a data modeler does not need to use this vocabulary with users; in fact, a good data modeler scrupulously hides it from them. When a data modeler and users meet to record the decisions about what kinds of things are worth remembering, the discussion should take place in the users' vocabulary. The vocabulary we present here will become part of *your* vocabulary. You can use these words when you discuss an LDS with other data modelers.

Restraining yourself from using this vocabulary with users requires self-discipline. Data modelers who allow this vocabulary to creep into their discussions with users are ineffective. Recall that in Chapter 3 we managed to interpret and discuss many different LDS fragments. In every case, we took the vocabulary directly from the words in the LDS fragment itself. For example, we talked about *herds, cows, farms, creatures,* and *achievements.* You'll notice that your ability to interpret the LDS fragments in that chapter was not impeded by our decision as authors to withhold the data-modeling vocabulary until now. That chapter should help to convince you that you really can talk effectively about an LDS without using data-modeling vocabulary.

There's another reason why we withheld the data-modeling vocabulary until now. Now that you have read Chapter 3, you implicitly understand the definitions we're going to give in this chapter. That is, you already understand (to a certain extent) what a box represents, what a box-to-box line represents, and what inside-the-box text represents. You just need the formal names for concepts you've already been using.

Vocabulary Overview

The vocabulary we present falls into two categories: words about types and words about instances. The distinction between type and instance is important; the next paragraph reviews the distinction.

Remember, a database contains descriptions of things. Any database has an explicit structure that defines (and limits) the kinds of things that can be described. This explicit structure is simply an articulation of the **types** of things the database can remember. So when a database contains a description of a thing, we can equivalently say that the database contains a description of some **thing of a particular type.** (For example, if a database contains a description of Bessie, we say that it contains a description of some cow, where *cow* is a type of thing.) We call a description of a thing of a particular type an **instance** of that type of thing. And in general, we can say that a database contains instances of types of things. An LDS diagram shows the types of things that users consider worth remembering. The descriptions of the actual memorable things, which are not shown on an LDS diagram, are instances of those types.

The words about types that we define are entity, attribute, relationship, link, descriptor, maximum degree, and identifier.[1] The words about instances that we define are entity instance, attribute value, relationship instance, link value, descriptor value, and identifier value.

We also define other useful words: identifying descriptor, one-many relationship, many-many relationship, one-one relationship, to-be relationship, not-to-be relationship, describing entity, described entity, and tiebreaker.

---

[1] You will notice that the words "identifier" and its cousin "identify" have special status. Although these words are part of your vocabulary as a data modeler, you are allowed to use them in your conversations with users. Recall that the preceding chapter taught you how to say shorthand sentences using the expression "is identified by." Users are comfortable with these sentences because users are comfortable with the concept of using symbolic identifiers to distinguish things from each other.

cow
cow ID
name
birth weight
current weight

Fragment 4-1

Entity and Entity Instance

An **entity** is a kind of memorable thing. Each entity is represented on an LDS by a box. An entity has descriptors, each of which is either an attribute or a link.

An **entity instance** is a description of a memorable thing that conforms to some entity. An entity instance has a value for each of its descriptors. For example, Fragment 4-1 shows the entity whose name is *cow*, which has four attributes. Following are two instances of the cow entity.

Cow ID	Name	Birth weight	Current weight
57	Elsa	30	389
Q2	Beth	28	

Attribute and Attribute Value

An **attribute** is a kind of memorable thing whose instances are scalar values. Each attribute is represented on an LDS by a line of inside-the-box text. An **attribute value** is a memorable thing that conforms to some attribute. Because each attribute value is a scalar quantity, each attribute value is atomic—it cannot be decomposed. It does not contain a complex value that has individual components. Nor does it contain a list of values.

Every attribute has a name, which appears as inside-the-box text. For example, Fragment 4-1 and its accompanying sample data include the birth weight attribute and two values of that attribute, 30 and 28.

By including an attribute in an entity, we let users ask simple questions about the instances of that entity, such as *What is Beth's birth weight?* But this does not mean that the answer to every such question is always available. For example, the answer to *What is Beth's current weight?* is not available because the data does not include it. We say that the attribute's value is **null.**

Alternatively, we can say that *Beth does not have a current weight.* However, some people are misled by this diction into a too-strong conclusion: that Beth <u>cannot</u> have a current weight. It remains possible for us to store Beth's current weight; you can see in the sample data exactly where we would write it. By contrast, we cannot remember Beth's *horn size;* there is no such attribute for Beth or for any cow because *horn size* describes bulls, not cows. The distinction here is between attributes that have unknown values and attributes that are not applicable to a particular entity. For more information about this distinction, read about too-inclusive and too-exclusive descriptor misplacement in Chapter 19.

How could an attribute value not conform to its attribute? Here is an example: Put "target weight 1492" as Beth's birth weight. That value is not a birth weight.

```
┌─────────────────────┐
│       person        │
├─────────────────────┤
│    person name      │
│    home phone       │
│                     │
│                     │
└─────────────────────┘
```

Fragment 4-2

```
┌─────────────────────┐
│       person        │
├─────────────────────┤
│ person name         │
│ home area code      │
│ home phone number   │
│                     │
└─────────────────────┘
```

Fragment 4-3

Like everything else on an LDS, each attribute represents one or more user decisions. Of course, each attribute indicates that the users consider something worth remembering. But each attribute also indicates that the users consider a particular memorable thing to be atomic. Consider Fragments 4-2 and 4-3. By choosing Fragment 4-2, the users are deciding that phone numbers are atomic. By choosing Fragment 4-3, the users are deciding that phone numbers are not atomic but consist of two components: area code and number.

When the users decide that certain values are atomic, there are ramifications. First, users avoid having to think up names for the individual components (like *home area code* and *home phone number*) of the values. Second, users are effectively accepting that the database management system on which the LDS is eventually implemented is free to consider the values to be atomic.[2]

We do not mention an attribute's datatype because datatype is not important during logical data modeling. What is important is a related concept called **scale.** Datatype is not important during logical data modeling because users do not care whether the DBMS stores something in a byte or a word or a longword or a string. Datatype is a technological solution to the problem of expressing scale in an implemented system. We devote Chapter 9 to scale.

Relationship and Relationship Instance

A **relationship** is a kind of memorable thing whose instances associate two entity instances. Each relationship is represented on an LDS by a box-to-box line. A **relationship instance** is a description of a memorable thing that conforms to some relationship.

Fragment 4-4 and its sample data show a relationship and five relationship instances that conform to it. In the sample data, each entity instance is represented by a dot, and each relationship instance is represented by a line connecting two dots. The leftmost line indicates that *Bessie is a member of Herd 043.* That line conforms to the relationship because it associates a cow with a herd.

---

[2]It is a bit beyond the scope of this book, but we'll elaborate. By choosing Fragment 4-2 rather than Fragment 4-3, the users are effectively relinquishing the potential to ask the DBMS to retrieve persons "WHERE HOME_AREA_CODE = 617." Instead, the users are accepting that extracting such information from the database will require a more elaborate expression performing string manipulations to extract the first three characters of the HOME_PHONE column and then comparing the extracted three-character substring with the value "617."

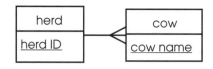

Fragment 4-4

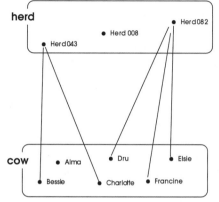

Every relationship has a name. In this example, the relationship's name is *membership of cow in herd*. You might find this name awkward, but this awkwardness is not a serious problem because in most situations, you can talk clearly about relationships without using relationship names. (The preceding chapter accomplished exactly this.) You can ignore relationship names for a while; we say more about them in Chapter 15.

A relationship instance must conform to a relationship. But how exactly could a relationship instance fail to conform to a relationship? Suppose we drew a line from Bessie to Alma and then tried to interpret that line as an instance of the relationship of Fragment 4-4. We might try to say that *Alma contains Bessie*. However, the purported relationship instance does not conform because it does not associate a cow with a herd.

Link and Link Value

A **link** is a kind of memorable thing corresponding to a relationship as interpreted in one direction only. Because you can interpret any relationship in two directions, each relationship has two links. For example, Fragment 4-4 shows two links: *cows of herd* and *herd of cow*. A **link value** is a memorable thing that conforms to a link. In the sample data for Fragment 4-4, there are three values of the *cows of herd* link (because there are three herds), and there are six values of the *herd of cow* link (because there are six cows). The following tables show the values of the links.

Herd	Value of the cows of herd link
Herd 043	{Bessie, Charlotte}
Herd 008	{}
Herd 082	{Dru, Francine, Elsie}

Cow	Value of the herd of cow link
Bessie	{Herd 043}
Alma	{}
Charlotte	{Herd 043}
Dru	{Herd 082}
Francine	{Herd 082}
Elsie	{Herd 082}

Note that a link value can be a set containing more than one element. For example, for Herd 082 the *cows of herd* descriptor value is a set with three elements. It is wrong to say that the descriptor has three values; the descriptor has one value, which is a set.

Note also that a link value can be the null set. For example, *herd of cow* for Alma is the null set. Note that strictly speaking, it is wrong to say that Alma does not have a value of the *herd of cow* descriptor; it is right to say that the value exists, but it is the null set value. Similarly, Herd 008 has a value of the *cows of herd* descriptor; the value is the null set.

Alternatively, we can say that *Alma does not have a herd.* However, some people are misled by this diction into the too-strong conclusion that Alma *cannot* have a herd. It remains possible for us to store Alma's herd; you can see in the sample data where we would draw the line connecting Alma to a herd.

(We are scratching the surface of a problem somewhat beyond the scope of this book: the many interpretations of "null" in storage systems. DBMS systems use null values to represent any number of things. A few uses for null are (1) to represent an unknown value such as Beth's current weight in Fragment 4-1; (2) to represent a nonexistent value, such as the value of *last immunization date* for a cow that has never been immunized; (3) to represent the null set, such as the value of *cows of herd* for Herd 008; (4) to represent an inconceivable value, such as the horn size of a cow or the udder size of a bull. You can study the portions of this topic that are germane to data modeling in the discussion of too-inclusive and too-exclusive descriptor misplacement in Chapter 19.)

Every link has a name. The names of the two links in this example are *cows of herd* and *herd of cow.* These names are relatively clear, but some links have peculiar names that sound awkward. For more information, see Chapter 14.

Maximum Degree

The **maximum degree** of a link is an indication of whether the descriptor's values (which are sets) can contain more than one element. In Fragment 4-4, for example, the maximum degree of the *cows of herd* is "many" because a herd can contain more than one cow. The maximum degree of the *herd of cow* link is "one" because each cow can be contained in at most one herd. On an LDS diagram you indicate maximum degree with the presence or absence of a chicken foot.

Each link can also have a **minimum degree,** which is an indication of the minimum number of elements that can be in the descriptor's value. During logical data modeling, minimum degree is of little or no importance for a number of reasons. The most important reason is that minimum degree does not affect the entity names or descriptor names, and the most important part of data modeling is getting the names right. To learn the other reasons why minimum degree is not important during logical data modeling, see Chapter 22.

Because maximum degree is so much more important than minimum degree, we sometimes call it simply **degree.**

Descriptor and Descriptor Value

A **descriptor** is a link or an attribute. A **descriptor value** is a link value or an attribute value. We use the word "descriptor" because a descriptor value serves to describe its entity instance.

It is useful for us to have a single word that refers to both links and attributes, because there are some things that are true for both kinds of descriptors. For example, we can assert that a descriptor can contribute to an identifier. The next section elaborates on this assertion.

Identifier and Identifier Value

An **identifier** is a minimal set of an entity's descriptors whose values distinguish entity instances from each other. LDS diagrams typically use bars to show identifiers. That is, you mark each descriptor contributing to the identifier with a bar. An **identifier value** is a set of descriptor values for the descriptors that contribute to an identifier of an entity instance.

A set (call it set S) of descriptors of an entity can serve as an identifier only if all three of the following statements are true:

1. Every current instance of the entity and every possible future instance of the entity has a nonnull value for every descriptor in S.
2. At no moment in time can two instances of the entity simultaneously exist while having identical values for every descriptor in S.
3. If S contains more than one descriptor, then for each strict subset T of S, it is possible for two instances of the entity to have identical values for every descriptor in T. (This requirement is why the first sentence of this section includes the word "minimal.")

(This is a good time for you to return to the previous chapter. Look again at the examples in the section "Sentences About Differentiating Things from Each Other," and study the sentences that you say when you are interpreting the bars for a box. Do you see how the sentences you say are consistent with the official definition of identifier given here?)

A picture can help you understand why each entity must have an identifier. Consider Figure 4-1, where a wall separates the users from their data stored in the database. Users cannot see through the wall; they cannot tell HOW the data is arranged. Thus, when they request information from the database, they cannot request it by pointing at it. That is, they cannot request a piece of data about a cow by saying, *Get me that cow there*. Instead, they must indicate which data they want symbolically, as in *Get me the data about the cow named Alma*. Because the users will sometimes need to request information about a specific cow as distinguished from all other cows, they need to use identifiers to make that distinction.

Think again about the analogy presented in Chapter 1. The wall in Figure 4-1 is like the wall of a closed-stack library, separating the borrowers from the books. Borrowers request books not by pointing at them (*Give me a copy of that book there*) but by identifier (*Give me the book*

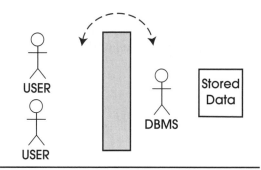

Figure 4.1 Simplified DBMS realm

whose Library of Congress catalog number is QA141.H86). The Library of Congress number serves as an identifier so that users can demand of the library staff exactly the book they want as distinguished from all other books.

An entity can have more than one identifier. That is, a user can assert that (a) each of two[3] sets of descriptors forms an identifier, and (b) the DBMS should enforce both identifiers.

It is very rare for an entity to have two identifiers, although some users and novice modelers believe otherwise. When a novice modeler erroneously asserts that a particular entity has two identifiers, he or she is probably overlooking one of the three requirements of identification.

Specifically, novice modelers tend to ignore requirements 2 and 3, concentrating exclusively on the first requirement in this list (no identifying descriptor can be null for any entity instance). Because users are likely to describe many sets of descriptors that satisfy requirement 1, novice modelers who overlook requirements 2 and 3 will erroneously create entities with multiple identifiers.

In the rare case that users legitimately decide to have more than one identifier for an entity, you can use two different symbols to mark the descriptors of the two identifiers. For example, use bars to mark the descriptors of one identifier, and use dotted or dashed lines to mark the descriptors of the other.

Can an identifier value change? From an LDS point of view the answer is yes. However, users generally pick an identifier whose values are relatively stable. For example, an employee's weight would make a worse identifier than his or her name because weight changes frequently. For some applications, identifiers are not allowed to change.

Identifying Descriptor

A descriptor that contributes to an identifier is called an **identifying descriptor.**

Degree-One Descriptor

A link whose maximum degree is one is called a **degree-one descriptor.**

Degree-Many Descriptor

A link whose maximum degree is many is called a **degree-many descriptor.**

One-Many Relationship

A relationship with one degree-one descriptor and one degree-many descriptor is called a **one-many relationship.**

---

[3] Actually, an entity can have any number of identifiers, but we have never seen more than two enforced.

Many-Many Relationship

A relationship with two degree-many descriptors is called a **many-many relationship.**

One-One Relationship

A relationship with two degree-one descriptor is called a **one-one relationship.**

To-be Relationship

A one-one relationship whose labels are both *be* is called a *to-be* **relationship.**

Not-to-be Relationship

A relationship whose labels are not both *be* is called a *not-to-be* **relationship.** Note that every relationship with a degree-many descriptor is a not-to-be relationship, and some but not all one-one relationships are not-to-be relationships.

Described Entity and Describing Entity

Remember, we use the word "descriptor" because each descriptor value <u>describes</u> an entity instance. When discussing a link, it is useful to distinguish between the described entity and the describing entity. The **described entity** of a link is the entity to which that descriptor belongs. The **describing entity** of a link is the entity whose instances can be included in the value of the descriptor.

Consider the link *cows of herd* and the entities *herd* and *cow*. *Herd* is the described entity and *cow* is the describing entity because you can (partially) describe a herd by indicating what cows are in it. Conversely, consider the link *herd of cow*. For that descriptor, *cow* is the described entity and *herd* is the describing entity because you can (partially) describe a cow by indicating what herd it belongs to.

Note that when discussing an attribute, the only entity involved is the described entity. Thus we sometimes refer to an attribute's entity simply as "the entity" rather than "the described entity." When the context demands it, we use the more explicit diction.

Tiebreaker

Tiebreaker is a somewhat informal term that can be applied to any identifying descriptor that contributes to a multiple-descriptor identifier.

A Bit More About Entities, Attributes, and Relationships

You will notice the similarity among the definitions of entity, attribute, and relationship. They are all "kinds of things." It is worth revisiting and stressing the differences.

Entities versus Attributes

How do you decide that a kind of thing is an entity rather than, say, an attribute? The users will tell you. For example, suppose the users provide some sample data.

Customers

Soon Lee	32 Excelante Dr.	St. Paul	MN
Joe Smith	101 Murms Av.	Albany	NY
Greg Wong	11 Frank Lane	Hellertown	PA

From the second column of this data, it becomes clear to you that one kind of thing is a street address. But you need to determine if street address is an attribute, a relationship, or an entity. It is easy enough to see that it is not a relationship—it obviously does not associate pairs of other things. But it could be an attribute or an entity, depending on the users' perspective.

- If the users sell magazine subscriptions, they might consider a street address to be merely a scalar part of the description of a customer. Each customer has one and only one street address, and there is no reason to remember a street address except as part of the description of a memorable customer.
- If the users sell home real estate, they might consider a street address to be memorable in its own right. That is, a street address might be worth remembering even if no one lives in that house. (If the users build the homes they sell, they might consider a street address worth remembering, even if the address is an empty lot.)

Having instances that are memorable in their own right is a good reason to use an entity rather than an attribute, but it is not the only reason. See "Promoting Attributes" in Chapter 19.

An aside about other modeling techniques: Some data modeling experts define an entity as a "kind of thing whose instances can exist independently." The crux of this definition is a contrast between attributes and <u>some</u> entities—that attribute instances cannot exist independently because attribute instances are remembered only as part of the description of some entity instance. This definition of entity does not work for us because it wrongly suggests that what makes an entity different from an attribute is that every entity can have an independent existence. This is not true. That is, some things deserve to be entities even though their instances cannot exist independently. For example, any entity categorized as a dependent entity or an intersection entity cannot exist independently. For more information about categorizing entities in this way, see Chapter 8. For more information about other modeling techniques, see Chapter 24.

Entities versus Relationships

What makes a kind of thing an entity rather than, say, a relationship? Once again, the users decide. Specifically, if the users indicate that a kind of thing has descriptors, it must be an entity. For example, if the users indicate that each farm can have many herds and each herd can have many farms, the resulting LDS could look like Fragment 4-5.

However, the users might want to remember additional information about each farm's association with each herd. For example, the users might want to remember a percent of ownership, as in the following sample data. In such a situation, a relationship does not suffice to store all the needed data; an entity is needed.

Fragment 4-5

Herd ID ·	Motto	Farm ID	Farm Name	Farmer	Percent
777	Happy Cow	0011	Jones	Jones	51
777	Happy Cow	0022	Big Acre	Smith	49
888		0011	Jones	Jones	100
999	Moo Moo	0022	Big Acre	Smith	50
999	Moo Moo	0033	Blue Sky	Newman	25
999	Moo Moo	0044	Good Earth	Pembleton	25

The LDS that accommodates this data replaces the relationship of Fragment 4-5 with a longer path between *farm* and *herd* (Fragment 4-6). The longer path includes an entity with an attribute for the percent of ownership.

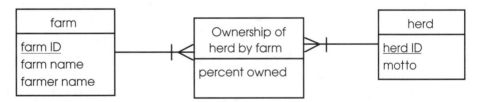

Fragment 4-6

LDS Reading Rules Revisited

The previous chapter describes how to translate an LDS diagram into declarative sentences. To convince you that LDSs are easily read by people who have not formally studied the method, the previous chapter carefully avoids using any of the vocabulary introduced in this chapter. But now that you *do* know the official LDS vocabulary, you should understand the rules for reading sentences, as rephrased in the table that follows.

If you see a (n)	. . . then you say:	. . . and you can also say:
Attribute	About each *<entity name>*, we can remember its *<attribute name>*.	
Unlabeled degree-one link	About each *<described entity name>*, we can remember its *<describing entity name>*.	
Unlabeled degree-many link	About each *<described entity name>*, we can remember its *<plural of the describing entity name>*.	
Degree-one link that is labeled with a word other than "be"	About each *<described entity name>*, we can remember *<meaningful noun phrase using the describing entity name>*.	Each *<described entity name>* can *<link label near the described entity>* a *<describing entity name>*.
Degree-one link that is labeled with the word "be"	Each *<described entity name>* can be a *<describing entity name>*.	About each *<described entity name>* we can remember its interpretation as a *<describing entity name>*.
A labeled degree-many link	About each *<described entity name>*, we can remember its *<meaningful noun phrase using the plural of the describing entity name>*.	Each *<described entity name>* can *<link label near the described entity>* some *<plural of describing entity name>*.
A single-descriptor identifier	Each *<entity name>* is identified by *<descriptor name>*.	About each *<entity name>*, we must remember its *<identifying descriptor name>*; no two *<plural of entity name>* can have the same *<identifying descriptor name>*.
A multiple-descriptor identifier with *n* descriptors	Each *<entity name>* is identified by the combination of its *<list of identifying descriptor names>*.	About each *<entity name>*, we must remember *<list of identifying descriptor names>*; no two *<plural of entity name>* can have the same values for *<list of identifying descriptor names>*; any two *<plural of entity name>* can have the same values for any *<(n−1)>* of *<list of identifying descriptor names>*.

The last row of the preceding table is expecially important.
Learn it now!

Responsibility for Speaking Well

It is not just a good idea to use vocabulary appropriately; it really is a matter of responsibility. Here are three examples of how participants in discourse can encounter this responsibility.

- You are a professional data modeler, hired by a particular business to help its employees articulate their data needs; you will eventually assist the database designers in creating the database. When you meet with users, you are responsible for using only the vocabulary of that business. That is, you should not allow your technical vocabulary (about data modeling or database technology, for example) to intrude into the discourse. Even though you were hired in part because of your considerable expertise in data modeling and database technology, the users do not want to hear you think aloud about such technological issues. Users want to hear you think aloud about their data. From the users' perspective, the best way for you to impose your technological expertise onto their business is quietly.
- You are one of several users describing your shared enterprise to a professional data modeler. When you meet with the modeler, whose goal is to learn your vocabulary, you must speak precisely and consistently. (Remember, the data modeler wants to learn the names for the types of things you consider worth remembering. These names will appear on the LDS diagram as entity names and descriptor names. And these names are nothing more or less than your business vocabulary.) Suppose you realize that you and a colleague use the word "shipment" slightly differently. Your colleague believes that a shipment is a single carton containing goods, whereas you believe a shipment can span several cartons, provided those cartons are sent to the same address on the same day. You and your colleague share a responsibility to agree on definitions and use them consistently. The data modeler will help you and your colleagues discover such inconsistent nomenclature.
- We are the authors of this book. We are responsible for saying precisely what we mean. And that means defining our vocabulary and using it consistently. By using our vocabulary consistently, we encourage you to speak clearly and precisely with your classmates and colleagues. This will help you learn from each other. But remember, when you later use the LDS technique to learn about some enterprise, you must not allow the language of data modeling to intrude.

Summary (and a Chance to Check Your Progress)

Now you know the names of the building blocks of an LDS: entity, attribute, relationship, descriptor, link, maximum degree, identifier. Hereafter, we will use this vocabulary in the book—no more talking about boxes and lines.

You can start getting accustomed to it immediately. Using the official vocabulary, we now present a list of common errors that novice data modelers make when reading an LDS. The material is not new to you; it derives directly from Chapter 3. It is a good chance to use the new vocabulary in material you already know. It is also a good chance for us to remind you about these errors so that you can watch out for them as you proceed. We illustrate these errors with Fragment 4-7.

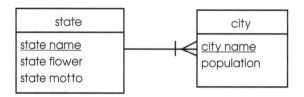

Fragment 4-7

Using a Plural Noun for the Described Entity

Don't do that. When you read the sentences, the described entity should <u>always</u> be a singular noun (see Fragment 4-7). Don't say *States have cities* or *States have state flowers.*

Overlooking Links

Don't do that. An entity has a set of descriptors; some are attributes, and some are links. When reading the sentences about an entity, don't forget to say the sentences about the links. For example, don't leave out the sentences like *About each city, we can remember its state.* (The link in this case is *state of city.*)

To overcome this problem, you can count the number of syntactic elements on a few small LDSs. Count the number of descriptors, the number of attributes, and the number of links.

Overlooking the Conventional Role of Identifying Descriptors

Within an entity, every descriptor describes, but only some descriptors identify. Identifying descriptors is special, so say extra sentences about them. But don't forget, identifying descriptors has all the other trappings of more conventional, nonidentifying descriptors. Just because a descriptor contributes to an identifier does not mean that the descriptor does not also describe the entity. So you say, *About each city, we can remember its city name, population, and state,* no matter what the identifier of the *city* entity is.

Confusing Identifiers with Identifying Descriptors

Some novice modelers would say that *city* has two identifiers. That is wrong. It has one identifier that consists of two descriptors. Because the two descriptors contribute to the identifier, they are called identifying descriptors.

Counting helps here, too. Count the number of identifiers and the number of identifying descriptors.

Overlooking the Similarity Between an Identifying Attribute and an Identifying Link

A descriptor can contribute to an identifier. On the LDS diagram, such a contribution is indicated with a bar. A bar under an attribute and a bar on a link mean the same thing: "This descriptor contributes to the entity's identifier." Some beginning modelers think that the bars mean different things, but they don't. A bar is a bar no matter where it appears. For example, the bar on *city name* means that it contributes to the identifier of *city* and the bar on *state of city* means that it too contributes to the identifier.

Neglecting to Read Both Links of a Relationship

Some beginning modelers look at a relationship and read only one link. For example, some might say, *About each state, we can remember its cities* but never say, *About each city, we can remember its state.* That's wrong; if you are reading the entire LDS, you must eventually say both these sentences. You'll probably say them at different times because one sentence is about *city* and the other is about *state.* If you are reading the relationship itself—to call the users' attention specifically to the relationship—you say one sentence right after the other.

Novice modelers with implementation experience might try to justify this error. They might say: "In the implemented database, we will store the state name with each city, but we won't store the list of cities with each state. That's why it is OK to read the relationship in one direction only." This is not a justification, because an LDS is a <u>logical</u> data structure, and the database implementation should have no effect whatever on how the users perceive the LDS.

Novice modelers who are process oriented also might try to justify this error. They might say: "As users process this data, they would never change context from *city* to *state.* Once the information about a city is found, all processing focuses on that city; we would never subsequently seek that city's state for additional processing. On the other hand, users do traverse the relationship from *state* to *city* because a primary way to retrieve the information about a city is according to what state it is in." This is no justification either. An LDS is a logical <u>data</u> structure, and the anticipated processing should have no effect on how the users perceive the LDS.

Exercises

1. In Fragments 3-17, 3-18, and 3-19, count how many of the following are evident.
   - Entities
   - Identified entities
   - Nonidentified entities

- Relationships
- Labeled relationships
- To-be relationships
- Not-to-be relationships
- One-many relationships
- Labeled one-many relationships
- Unlabeled one-many relationships
- Many-many relationships
- Labeled many-many relationships
- Unlabeled many-many relationships
- One-one relationships
- Labeled one-one relationships
- Unlabeled one-one relationships
- One-one, not-to-be relationships

2. For each entity in Fragments 3-17, 3-18, and 3-19, count how many of the following are evident.
   - Descriptors
   - Attributes
   - Singular attributes
   - Plural attributes
   - Links
   - Unlabeled links
   - Unlabeled degree-many links
   - Unlabeled degree-one links
   - Labeled links
   - Degree-one links
   - Degree-one labeled not-to-be links
   - To-be links
   - Degree-many labeled to-be links
   - Identifiers

3. For each identifier of each entity in Fragments 3-17, 3-18, and 3-19, indicate what symbol is used to annotate the identifier. Then count how many of the following contribute to the identifier.
   - Descriptors
   - Attributes
   - Links
   - Degree-many links
   - Unlabeled degree-many links
   - Labeled degree-many links
   - Degree-one links
   - Not-to-be degree-one links
   - To-be links

4. For each error in the Summary, make up an example, and show its negative consequences.

5. Suppose you are helping dairy farmers model and have this fragment:

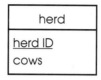

a. What is wrong with the fragment?
b. What is wrong with replacing *cows* with *cow?*
c. What should you do?
Note: We do not expect you to be able to answer part c fully. To do so, you need to have the "Promoting Attributes" skill in Chapter 20. However, you should try answering it now anyway; then after you have read Chapter 20, review your answer to see how good it was.

6. For each of the following, make up an example or say why it is impossible to do so.
   - Entity with one identifier and one identifying descriptor
   - Entity with one identifier and two identifying descriptors
   - Entity with two identifiers and one identifying descriptor
   - Entity with n identifiers and p identifying descriptors, where $n > p$

7. Look again at the definition of the word *tiebreaker*. Why do you think we chose that word to refer to that concept? Feel free to use sample data to illustrate your thinking.

5
Chapter

Visualizing Allowed and Disallowed Instances

There is more to reading an LDS than merely articulating the correct sentences. The sentences deserve scrutiny because they are pithy; that is by design. An LDS should be brief but richly substantive. Understanding the sentences means understanding their substance and all its ramifications.

When you read the LDS, either to yourself or aloud to someone else, you must be able to call attention to the ramifications of each sentence. Like the original sentences themselves, these ramifications are about what data the users want to remember. We describe in this chapter how to show typical and atypical data that an LDS accommodates—and how to show noteworthy data that an LDS cannot accommodate.

These data visualization techniques are useful at many times during the process of creating an LDS. For example you can use these techniques for the following:

- You can visualize instances to ensure that an entity is correctly named. (If an entity's name is inaccurate, the LDS will confuse users and mislead everyone.)
- You can visualize instances to ensure that the LDS is sufficiently accommodating—that it lets users remember all the data they require.

- You can visualize instances to ensure that the LDS is sufficiently restrictive—that it prevents users from remembering data they do not require.
- You can visualize instances any time you need to read and understand the LDS—for example, at any natural stopping point during a data-modeling session with users.

Master data modelers do not hesitate to write down sample data. They follow the mantra "Anchor your understanding with instances."

Show the Data and Say Something About It

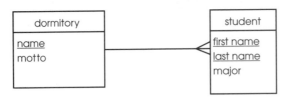

Fragment 5-1

To illustrate what data users can remember, show some data (see Fragment 5-1.) There is no better way to understand what an LDS says than to write out and study the data the LDS accommodates.

Dormitory name	Motto	Student first name	Student last name	Student major
Wilson	Study hard	Eddie	Mulderry	Math
Wilson	Study hard	Alice	Georgeopolos	History
Byner	Carpe diem	Andrew	Castro	Math
Byner	Carpe diem	Elphaba	Gale	Education
Byner	Carpe diem	Isaac	Wilson	History

You should note in words what the data illustrates. For example, you can call attention to particular aspects of the sample data with the following words:

- Note that each student has a first name.
- Note that there are some dormitories with several students. (Wilson and Byner have two and three students, respectively.)
- Note that no student has two dormitories.

The notes call attention to specific ramifications of the LDS's assertions, as manifested by the sample data. That is, the notes do not call attention to coincidental aspects of the sample data. Notice, for example, that you did not explicitly note that each student's first name begins with a vowel. That's a mere curiosity about the sample data, not an illustration of the LDS's assertions.

In many ways, the notes are more important than the sample data itself. Specifically,

- You assess the quality of the sample data by assessing the notes.
- You choose to add more sample data, not because "more is better" but because you need to illustrate a particular ramification, and there is no sample data whose note would provide such an illustration.
- You design sample data by first deciding what notes you want to write, then creating the sample data accordingly.

This chapter shows you what notes are possible.

Plan Your Notes by Considering Elemental Parts of the LDS

A note within the sample data illustrates or elaborates on an assertion of the LDS. Because you can read these assertions directly from the diagram, you can plan what notes to include simply by inspecting the diagram itself.

Some Notes Apply Simply Because the Diagram Includes an Attribute

Recall that each attribute can induce a particular sentence. For example, the motto attribute induces the sentence *About each dormitory we can remember a motto.* There are several aspects of this sentence to which you might like to call attention:

- When users remember a motto, they remember it about a particular dormitory.
- For each dormitory, users *can* remember a motto. "Can" does not mean "must," so perhaps there are some dormitories about which they remember no motto.
- For each dormitory, users can remember a (single) motto, so they cannot remember two mottos for any dormitory.
- Users can remember the same motto for two different dormitories. That is, there is nothing in the diagram indicating that a dormitory's motto is used by that dormitory exclusively.

So there are several notes that immediately leap to mind. Keeping these notes in mind, it is easy to sketch out sample data; in the following table, the notes follow the data.

Dormitory name	Dormitory motto	Student first name	Student last name	Student major
Wilson	Study hard	Eddie	Mulderry	Math
Wilson	Study hard	Alice	Georgeopolos	History
Byner	Carpe diem	Andrew	Castro	Math
Byner	Carpe diem	Elphaba	Gale	Education

(continued)

Byner	Carpe diem	Isaac	Wilson	History
Tesla		James	Johnson	Education
Tesla		Leo	Mandell	Football
Frankel	Study hard	Keith	Conway	Physics
Frankel	Study hard	Alexander	Kowalski	Physics

Notice that each dormitory can have a motto. (That is, it's a dormitory that can have a motto, not a student.)

Notice that one dormitory (Tesla) has no motto.

Notice that no dormitory has two mottos.

Notice that two dormitories (Wilson and Frankel) use the same motto.

Some Notes Apply Because the Diagram Includes a Degree-One Link

Recall that each link can induce a sentence, and one of the sentence's nouns will be either singular or plural, depending on the degree of the link. For example, the link *dormitory of student* induces the sentence *About each student, we can remember a dormitory.* There are several aspects of this sentence to which we'd like to call attention:

- For each student, users *can* remember a dormitory. "Can" does not mean "must." So perhaps there are some students about whom users remember no dormitory. (Maybe some students live off campus.)
- For each student, users can remember a (single) dormitory. So users cannot remember two dormitories for any student.

So there are several notes that immediately leap to mind. It is easy to sketch out the sample data with accompanying notes.

Dormitory name	Dormitory motto	Student first name	Student last name	Student major
Wilson	Study hard	Eddie	Mulderry	Math
Wilson	Study hard	Alice	Georgeopolos	History
Byner	Carpe diem	Andrew	Castro	Math
Byner	Carpe diem	Elphaba	Gale	Education
Byner	Carpe diem	Isaac	Wilson	History
Tesla		James	Johnson	Education

Tesla		Leo	Mandell	Football
		Louise	Pagnini	Politics
Frankel	Study hard	Keith	Conway	Physics
Frankel	Study hard	Alexander	Kowalski	Physics

Notice that one student (Louise Pagnini) has no dormitory.

Notice that no student has two or more dormitories.

Some Notes Apply Because the Diagram Includes a Degree-Many Link

Remember, the sentence induced by a link might include a plural noun. For example, the link *students of dormitory* induces the sentence *About each dormitory, we can remember its students*. There are several aspects of this sentence to which you can call attention:

- For each dormitory, users *can* remember some students. "Can" does not mean "must." So perhaps there are some dormitories about which users remember no student. (Maybe some dormitories are unoccupied.)
- For each dormitory, users can remember some students. Perhaps a dormitory has two students, perhaps three, perhaps only one.

So there are several notes that immediately leap to mind. Keeping these notes in mind, it is easy to sketch out sample data, followed by the desired notes.

Dormitory name	Dormitory motto	Student first name	Student last name	Student major
Wilson	Study hard	Eddie	Mulderry	Math
Wilson	Study hard	Alice	Georgeopolos	History
Byner	Carpe diem	Andrew	Castro	Math
Byner	Carpe diem	Elphaba	Gale	Education
Byner	Carpe diem	Isaac	Wilson	History
Marquez	Excelsior			
Tesla		James	Johnson	Education
Tesla		Leo	Mandell	Football
Gushikin	G.W. slept here.	Maureen	Oesterhout	
		Louise	Pagnini	Politics

(continued)

Frankel	Study hard	Keith	Conway	Physics
Frankel	Study hard	Alexander	Kowalski	Physics

Notice that one dormitory (Marquez) has no students.

Notice that one dormitory (Gushikin) has exactly one student.

Notice that some dormitories (Wilson and Byner) have several students.

Some Notes Apply Because the Diagram Includes a Single-Descriptor Identifier

Remember that each identifier induces a single sentence, such as *Each dormitory is identified by its name.* Also remember, however, that this single sentence is a shorthand for some other sentences. For a single-descriptor identifier, there are two other sentences, such as *About each dormitory, we must remember a name* and *No two dormitories have the same name.* These two sentences deserve illustration in the sample data.

So there are two notes that immediately leap to mind. The sample data is shown below, followed by the desired notes.

Dormitory name	Dormitory motto
Wilson	Study hard
Byner	Carpe diem
Marquez	Excelsior
Tesla	
Gushikin	G.W. slept here
Frankel	Study hard

Notice that every dormitory has a name.

Notice that every dormitory has a unique name.

Some Notes Apply Because the Diagram Includes a Multiple-Descriptor Identifier

For a multiple-descriptor identifier, the single sentence (e.g., *Each student is identified by its first name plus its last name*) is a shorthand for three other sentences, such as

- *About each student, we must remember a first name and a last name.*

- *No two students have the same first name and the same last name.*
- *Two students could have the same first name or the same last name.*

These three sentences deserve illustration in the sample data.

So there are several notes the immediately leap to mind. *Every student has a first name. Every student has a last name. No two students have the same (first + last) name. These two (particular) students have the same first name. These two (particular) students have the same last name.* Keeping these notes in mind, it is easy to sketch out the sample data.

Student first name	Student last name	Student major
Betsy	Pedersen	History
Drucinda	Pedersen	Math
Betsy	Schultz	Physics

Notice that two students have the same first name (Betsy Pedersen and Betsy Schultz).

Notice that two students have the same last name (Drucinda Pedersen and Betsy Pedersen).

Notice that no two students have the same first name and last name.

Notice that every student has a first and a last name. (If the single-named rock star Sting enrolls in the school, the database will not be able to accommodate the data about him.)

If an Identifier Has Three or More Descriptors, the Notes Can Be More Elaborate Than the Notes for a Two-Descriptor Identifier

Remember that you can paraphrase the sentence *Two students could have the same first name or the same last name* with the following seemingly more awkward equivalent: *Two students could share any one of first name and last name.* As we mentioned in Chapter 3, this diction is useful for multiple-descriptor identifiers using more than two descriptors. The diction is useful in such cases because it is spare.

Consider these two equivalent sentences about the LDS in Fragment 5-2:

location
latitude
longitude
elevation

Fragment 5-2

- Two locations could share any two of latitude, longitude, and elevation.
- Two locations could share latitude and longitude or latitude and elevation or longitude and elevation.

The first sentence is admirably brief, but the second sentence has its merits, too. It helps you see what notes you might want to include alongside the sample data: *These two (particular) locations have the same latitude and the same longitude. These two (particular) locations have the same latitude and the same elevation.*

These two (particular) locations have the same longitude and the same elevation. Keeping these notes in mind, it is easy to sketch out the sample data.

Latitude	Longitude	Elevation
42 north	90 west	100 feet
42 north	90 west	200 feet
78 north	90 west	200 feet
78 north	62 west	200 feet

Notice that two locations have the same latitude and longitude (42 north, 90 west).

Notice that two locations have the same longitude and elevation (90 west, 200 feet).

Notice that two locations have the same latitude and elevation (78 north, 200 feet).

As You Visualize Data, Don't Lose Sight of the Goal

You are trying to comprehend the LDS. Visualizing data is a means, not an end unto itself. Take care to avoid these pitfalls.

More Data Is Not Necessarily Better

Do not waste time making too much sample data that illustrates and reillustrates the same point over and over.

Less Data Is Not Necessarily Better

Do not struggle to squeeze as many notes as possible into as little sample data as possible. The best sample data clearly elucidates the ramification of the LDS. Sample data is not good merely because it uses minimal ink.

Don't Limit Yourself to a Single Way of Visualizing the Data

In this chapter, we present all sample data in a consistent format. But as you know, there are several ways to visualize data (see Figures 1-1 through 1-5). You can use any of them.

Exercises

1. Create examples to illustrate the three pitfalls in visualizing data.
2. Look in books and manuals for ways in which people visualize their data. Compile a list of techniques that you find effective and ineffective. Explain your findings. (Attach your list here so you can refer to it.)
3. LDS Fragment 5-3 is about entertainment in an arena.

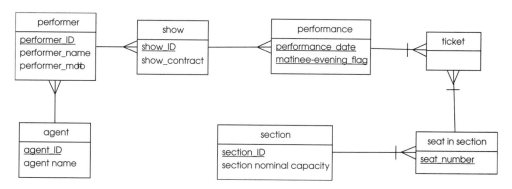

Fragment 5-3

Your tasks:
   a. Make up sample data and notes that illustrate what can and cannot be accommodated.
   b. Create sample data for this LDS that illustrates each visualizing data pitfall.
   c. Suppose your user wants to remember *price*.
      (a) Make *price* an attribute of each entity in turn, and explain what it means for *price* to be an attribute of that entity.
      (b) Decide (as a user) which, if any, of the *price* attributes should be kept and if its name could be improved.
      (c) Decide (as a user) which, if any, other price attributes should be kept. (You may need to expand the LDS.)

After you have read more of this book (or now, if you want to try them), do these tasks.
   a. Modify the LDS to accommodate warm-up acts or, perhaps, an entire bill.
   b. Modify the LDS to accommodate different seating configurations. Include a planned configuration, deciding if it should be describe a show or a performance.

6

Chapter

A Conversation with Users About Creatures and Skills

During data modeling, you converse with users about their data, gradually improving the LDS as the conversation proceeds. This chapter presents a somewhat idealized conversation and shows the gradual improvement to the LDS.[1] We show very few instances and give you the opportunity to practice the instance visualization techniques you just learned. For each fragment, think about the pros and cons of the various visualization techniques, choose one, and make up some instances.

Suppose an in-progress LDS includes the entities *creature* and *skill*. While conversing with users, you, the modeler, learn that there is a relationship between these two entities. Users say *Creatures have skills.* You draw a line between these two entities, yielding Fragment 6-1. Notice that the line you draw has two question marks to remind you that you do not yet know the degrees of its two links.

You ask the users a question: *Can some creature have several skills?* The users say yes, yielding Fragment 6-2.

---

[1] This conversation is an example of controlled evolution, which you will learn about in Chapters 18 through 20. For now, just follow along. After you have read those chapters, reread this conversation, and see how the modeler has led the users through a decision-making process.

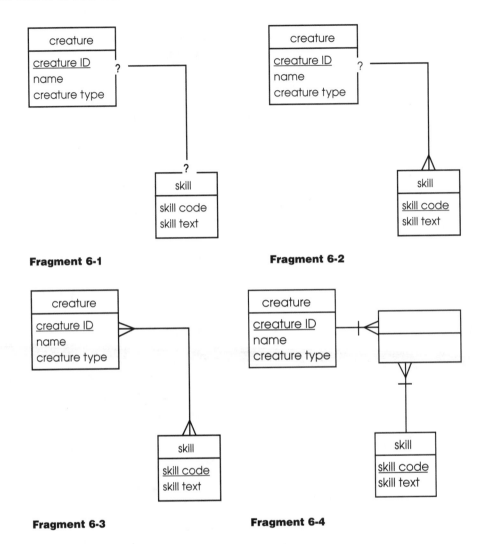

Fragment 6-1

Fragment 6-2

Fragment 6-3

Fragment 6-4

You ask the users a question: *Can some skill have several creatures?* The users say yes, yielding Fragment 6-3.

Without asking another question, you immediately replace Fragment 6-3 with Fragment 6-4. (Chapter 18 explains why this replacement happens.)

Notice that the new entity has no name. You must secure a name from the users. To help the users name the entity, you help them understand what each instance of the entity is. You draw the diagram on page 77 for the users.

You say that each dot in the upper set represents a creature, so the data shows four instances of the *creature* entity. Likewise, you point out that the data shows five instances of the *skill* entity. Then you say that each line represents an instance of the unnamed entity and that the sample data shows four instances of that entity. You ask the users: *What is each one of these lines?*

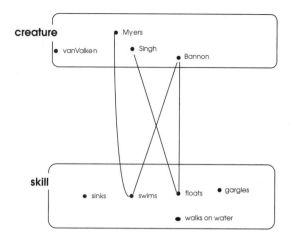

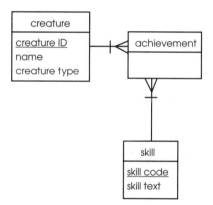

Fragment 6-5

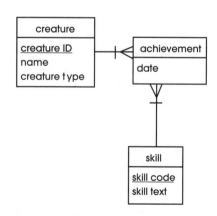

Fragment 6-6

The users have trouble answering, so you ask a more specific (and presumably easier) question. Pointing to the leftmost line, you ask, *What is this?* One articulate user says it is *the achievement of swimming by Myers.* Pointing to the rightmost line, you ask the same user, *What is this?* She says it is *the achievement of floating by Bannon.*

You say *So each of these lines is an achievement? And there are four achievements shown here?* The users say yes, so you draw Fragment 6-5.

You ask the users a question: *Is there anything else you want to remember about each achievement?* The users say *Yes, we want to remember the date on which the achievement occurs,* yielding Fragment 6-6.

You ask the users a question: *Can a creature achieve the same skill more than once?* The users say yes, so you ask a follow-up question: *How do you distinguish the two achievements of the same skill by the same creature?* The users say *If a creature achieves the same skill more than once, the achievements must happen on separate dates.* As a result of this discussion, you draw Fragment 6-7.

You ask the users a question: *Can a creature have two achievements on the same date?* The users say no, yielding Fragment 6-8.

You ask, *Can there be two achievements on the same date?* The users say yes, so you leave Fragment 6-8 unchanged.

You ask, *Is there ever an achievement whose date you do not know? And can you know about an achievement but not know what creature made it?* Answering the first question, users say *Yes, we sometimes know of some really old achievements —achievements that occurred before we bothered to record*

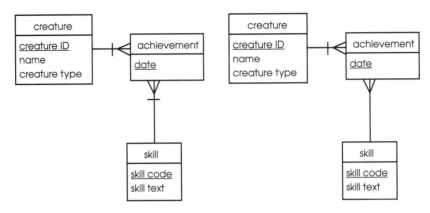

Fragment 6-7   **Fragment 6-8**

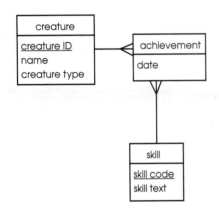

Fragment 6-9

Revisiting and revising earlier decisions are common. As the LDS evolves, users make finer and finer distinctions in how they describe their data.

achievement dates. To answer the second question, users have a longer discussion among themselves. Some users insist that in peculiar cases, there are achievements that they know about even though they do not know what creature made them. Eventually, these users convince the others.

Now you know that *date* can be null and that *creature of achievement* can be null, so you need to find an identifier for the *achievement* entity.

To the users, you explain that because not every instance (of achievement) has a creature and not every instance has a date, they cannot be assured that every instance will be distinguishable from every other instance. You remove the identifier from the entity (Fragment 6-9), and you say *Suppose you have two achievements that do not have a creature. How do you distinguish those achievements from each other?*

Users grapple with the question, offering different opinions, debating the various possibilities. You listen for a while, hoping that you might hear the users mention a new descriptor that could contribute to the identifier of *achievement*. When you are convinced that the discussion will yield no new identifier, you interrupt.

You recap the situation, including the facts that are evident on the LDS and the important facts that you just overheard. You say: *The diagram needs to say how to distinguish achievements from each other. A moment ago (Fragment 6-8) it said that we can use the combination of the creature and the date, but we know that this is unreliable because some achievements have no creature and some achievements have no date. It appears that we will need to use an arbitrary identifier—a meaningless number or piece of text—to identify each achievement. If we carefully assign an identifier value to each achievement, we can use that value forevermore to refer to that achievement.*

With the users' approval, you modify the LDS to include an arbitrary identifier for *achievement,* as shown in Fragment 6-10. Then you reread the *achievement* entity aloud to ensure that the users still agree with the assertions on the LDS.

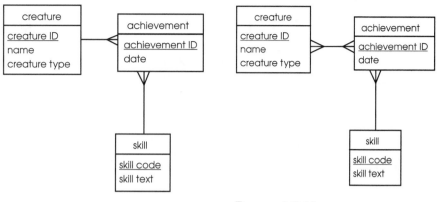

Fragment 6-10   **Fragment 6-11**

You ask the users a question: *Can an achievement require several skills?* The users say no, leaving Fragment 6-10 unchanged.

Then you ask a similar question: *Can an achievement require several creatures?* The users say yes. When you ask users for examples, they offer two:

- Waltzing is a skill that can be achieved by pairs of creatures—waltzing alone is no accomplishment.
- Bobsledding is a skill that can be achieved only by groups of four creatures.

From this discussion, Fragment 6-11 results.

> Notice that you *suggest* names for the new entity, but you allow the users to name the entity.

Without asking another question, you immediately replace Fragment 6-11 with Fragment 6-12. Notice that Fragment 6-12 is syntactically incomplete; the new entity has no name. You help the users understand what the unnamed entity means. You say *Each instance of this* (you point to the unnamed entity) *describes an individual creature's participation in a particular achievement.* You draw sample data of creatures, achievements, and instances of the unnamed entity. You ask users to name the unnamed entity, reminding them that the name should apply to each instance of the entity. Because the users have difficulty naming the entity, you make these suggestions:

- Participation—each instance describes a creature's participation in an achievement.
- Contribution—each instance describes a creature's contribution in an achievement.
- Work—each instance describes the work an individual creature performed for a particular achievement.

Fragment 6-12

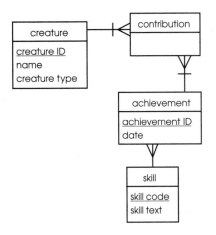

Fragment 6-13

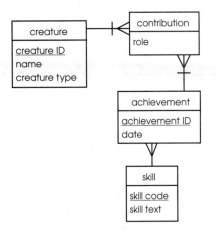

Fragment 6-14

The users become confused. You cannot follow their discussion, but it appears that they are talking at cross purposes. You let them go for a while (a brief while!) until one astute user points out that *work* is a terrible suggestion because that word has a very particular meaning to them. Once you remove that word from your list of suggested entity names, the conversation settles down. (You make a note to yourself to ask the users about *work* at a later time.)

You refocus the users, pointing to the unnamed entity and saying, *We are talking about this. I want the word for what each one of these is.* Users reject *participation* and accept *contribution* since they can think of no better name. As a result, you draw Fragment 6-13.

Aloud to the users, you reread the short path between *creature* and *achievement*. What you say includes the sentence *About each contribution, we can remember its creature and its achievement.* You then ask the users a question: *Is there anything <u>else</u> worth remembering about a contribution?*

Users say yes, because they need to remember for each contribution the role the creature played in the achievement. To clarify, you ask the users for some examples. They explain to you that some skills that can be achieved only by groups require the members of the achieving groups to assume particular roles. For example, to achieve the skill of waltzing, one person must be the leader, and the other must be the follower. To achieve the skill of bobsledding, one person must be the driver, one person must be the brake operator, and two people must be pushers. As a result of this discussion, you draw Fragment 6-14.

You ask the users if a creature can contribute to the same achievement in several different ways. Users say no, so you leave Fragment 6-14 unchanged.

You ask users if they want to remember what roles are possible. The question confuses them, so you help them understand a ramification of Fragment 6-14. You say *According to this diagram (Fragment 6-14), we can remember a role only when some creature assumes the role in some contribution. If by some coincidence the database contains no instance of this* (you point to the contribution entity), *we are not remembering any of the possible roles that <u>could</u> be assumed by creatures. Do you want to remember the roles themselves, independent of the decision to remember any particular contributions?*

Users say yes. You then draw Fragment 6-15. Note that you know that the link *role of contribution* was degree one because the attribute *role* was, by definition, a singleton. However, you do not yet know the degree of the other link of the new relationship, so you use a question mark as a reminder.

You ask users how they distinguish roles from each other. They indicate that each role has a unique name. You draw Fragment 6-16.

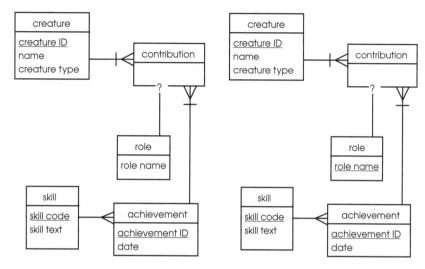

Fragment 6-15   **Fragment 6-16**

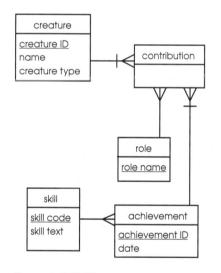

Fragment 6-17

Thinking about roles and contributions, you remember what the users said about bobsledding—that in bobsledding, two different participants fill the role of pusher. Thus you can replace the question mark with a chicken foot. You draw Fragment 6-17, explaining to the users that the chicken foot accommodates the bobsledding example.

You ask the users if there is anything else they want to remember about roles. They say no, so you leave Fragment 6-17 unchanged.

You seek other relationships between pairs of entities. During the search, you ask: *Can a creature be associated with an achievement in some way other than by contributing to that achievement?* The users say *Yes, creatures witness achievements.* You draw Fragment 6-18.

You ask: *Can a creature witness several achievements?* Users say yes, so you draw Fragment 6-19.

You ask: *Can an achievement be witnessed by several creatures?* Users say yes, so you draw Fragment 6-20.

Without asking another question, you immediately replace Fragment 6-20 with Fragment 6-21. Notice that the new entity has no name.

You ask the users to name the unnamed entity. To help them understand it, you say *Each instance of this* (you point to the unnamed entity) *indicates that a particular creature witnesses a particular achievement.* Based on this understanding, you suggest a name for the entity: *witness episode.* The users reject this suggestion because they already use a different word: *observation.* You draw Fragment 6-22.

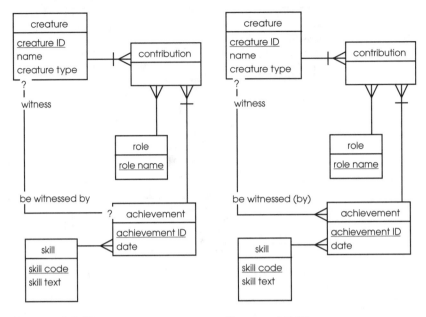

Fragment 6-18

Fragment 6-19

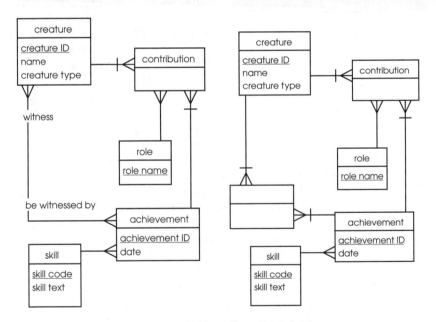

Fragment 6-20

Fragment 6-21

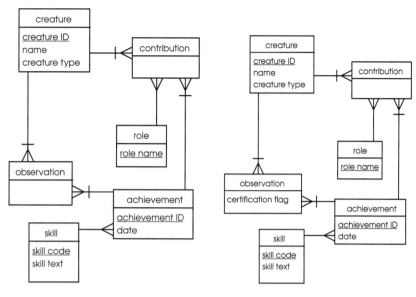

Fragment 6-22   **Fragment 6-23**

You say *About each observation, we can remember its achievement and its creature. Is there anything else you want to remember about each observation?* The users say *Yes, whether the observation is official or not. Some observations are official; the observer actually certifies that the achievement occurred. Other observations are not official, but we want to remember them along with the official ones.* You draw Fragment 6-23.

You ask *Can a creature observe the same achievement more than once?* Users say no, so you leave Fragment 6-23 unchanged.

You continue to seek other relationships between pairs of entities. You ask:

- *Can a creature be associated with an achievement in some way other than contributing to it or observing it?* Users say no.
- *Can a creature be associated with an observation in some way other than as the creature actually making the observation?* Users say no.
- *Can a creature be associated with a contribution in some way other than as the creature actually making the contribution?* Users say no.
- *Can an achievement be associated with an observation in some way other than as the achievement actually observed?* Users say no.
- *Can a creature be associated with a contribution in some way other than as the achievement actually contributed to?* Users say no.

Because users say no to all these questions, you leave Fragment 6-23 unchanged.

You continue to seek other relationships between pairs of entities. You ask: *Can a creature be associated with a skill in some way other than contributing to an*

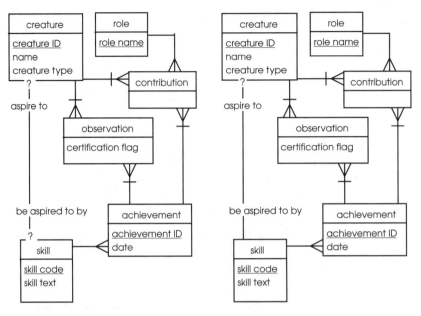

Fragment 6-24   **Fragment 6-25**

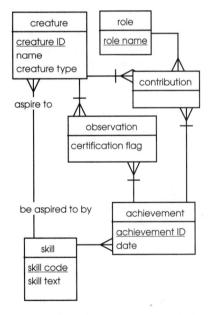

Fragment 6-26

achievement of that skill or observing an achievement of that skill? Users say *Yes, creatures aspire to skills.* You draw Fragment 6-24.

You ask: *Can a creature aspire to several skills?* Users say no, so you draw Fragment 6-25.

You ask: *Can a skill have several creatures aspiring to it?* Users say yes, so you draw Fragment 6-26.

At this point, your meeting with users is drawing to a close. Aloud to the users, you reread the LDS once more. You ask the users for a printout of sample data showing real creatures, skills, achievements, observations, contributions, and roles. The users agree to deliver such data to you. Leaving yourself enough time to study these printouts thoroughly, you arrange for another meeting with the users to enlarge the LDS further.

Summary

What is happening? How does this conversation transpire so smoothly? The data modeler (whom we optimistically refer to as "you") has prepared for the conversation by mastering four areas.

- **Reading an LDS.** Say sentences, visualize allowed instances, and visualize disallowed instances. The information you need to master LDS reading is in Chapters 3 through 5.

- **LDS shapes.** A shape is a canonical form that can appear on an LDS. LDS shapes are analogous to programming shapes (like loops). The material you need to master LDS shapes is in Chapters 7 through 12.
- **Writing an LDS.** Keep the LDS syntactically valid, and secure good names (for entities and attributes) and labels (for links). The information you need to master LDS writing is in Chapters 13 through 17.
- **Controlled evolution.** Controlled evolution is a partially scripted process by which you and the users gradually modify an LDS to make it more and more faithful to their information needs. The material you need to master controlled evolution is in Chapters 18 through 20.

Exercises

1. If you failed to make up instances for each fragment as you read the conversation, then do so now.
2. Pretend that you are a user. Dispute everything. That is, for each user response in the conversation, say, *No, I disagree, because . . . ,* and then explain your disagreement. (Show counterexample instances so that you can make a strong argument.)
3. Make up another conversation using Fragment 6-27 as the starting point.
4. Make up another conversation using Fragment 6-28 as the starting point.

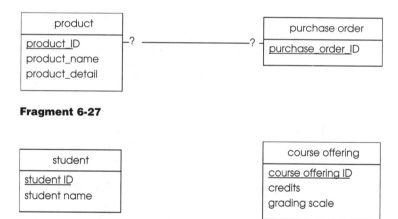

Fragment 6-27

Fragment 6-28

Story Interlude

As data modelers and as teachers of data modelers, we have real, in-context stories to tell about mistakes, successes, interesting things that happened, what novice modelers did, and so on. We tell stories to enrich what we say in university classes, in industrial training, while consulting, and while talking with fellow teachers. Inspired by Gary Klein, we decided to write down some stories for you to read and ponder as you acquire the skills and culture of data modeling.[1] As you gain experience, you should craft and tell your own stories.

The stories appear in "interludes," here and after Chapters 12, 17, 21, and 26. Each interlude contains seven or eight stories. The stories are loosely grouped but really are in no particular order—after all, they are just stories.

These several dozen stories are about people: modelers and users, teachers and students. The stories follow a template: a pithy title, a body as brief as we can make it, and a moral. The stories are told from a first person singular perspective because we think they read better that way; it doesn't matter if a story is by Carlis or Maguire or both.

We use dummy names for organizations, arbitrarily pick names and genders for people, and slightly distort some situations. We do so to improve the stories and

---

[1] G. Klein, *Sources of Power: How People Make Decisions,* MIT Press, Cambridge, MA, 1999.

to shield individuals from negative comments. While some stories are critical of behaviors, we do not intend to ridicule anyone; indeed, we readily acknowledge our debt to users, students, and fellow modelers, without whom there would be no stories.

Short, Frequent, Few

This story has three parts.

Long meetings do not work well. Data modeling is hard intellectual work and people get tired. At company X, a four-day modeling blitz was not very productive. After a few hours people faded out. After a few days people got punchy.

Long intervals between meetings do not work well. At company Y, users who came back after several weeks either had forgotten a lot or had done a lot of hard thinking that put them out of sync with other users.

Large meetings do not work well. At company Z, a big meeting with two dozen users caused problems. A few users did most of the talking. A number of users listened at the beginning, but, because they were not participants, their attention faded. The users who did most of the talking were frustrated because, even though they dominated the meeting, they still had lots more to contribute.

Moral: *Have short, frequent meetings with a few users.*

Slower and Louder

At agency X, partway through a three-day modeling meeting, I was locked in a room with about a score of scientists plus a few others. (Yes, I know, too many users and too long a meeting, but I was a novice then and did not frame the meeting well.) We had about 70 entities on an in-progress LDS. Things were going very well when I made a mistake. After listening to the scientists for a bit, I wrote down an entity and asked them to name it. However, they said nothing. Wanting to make progress and knowing what they meant, I said, *let's use this name for now and we'll change it later if need be.* I was in charge so I wrote down my perfect name and moved on.

Thirty minutes later, the positive feeling in the room was gone. People had become tense and were fidgeting and speaking slower and louder (a sure sign that the speaker thinks the listener is dense). Disaster was imminent when I got lucky and realized that they did not understand my perfect entity name and, therefore, might accordingly misunderstand anything closely connected to it. I pointed to this entity and again sought a user name for it. We examined and discarded several possibilities until a previously silent user contributed a name. That word was really perfect because the users understood it. It pricked the bubble of tension and rescued the meeting and me, a misbehaving modeler.

Moral: *Use user words, or else!*

Aha!

At agency X, after that slower and louder modeling meeting, three economists who worked with the scientists came up to me and said, "We learned more in three days than we have in three years on the job." They found an LDS a great vehicle for communication. During the meeting they had several "aha" reactions, as in "Aha! now I know what that means."

Moral: *Users learn a lot during data modeling.*

Read to New Users

At company X, I was observing at an LDS review meeting. Users and modelers were sitting around a conference table. A 600-entity model was up on the wall. One brand-new user, Ruth, was obviously shying away from the rather imposing LDS. Her coworker, Janet, who had participated in the modeling, saw Ruth's fear and said, *Come on, I'll show you.* They went up to the LDS, and Janet properly read the LDS aloud, with editorial comments, convincing Ruth that she knew this data. Janet pointed out one portion of the model and said, *Look, we collect this data and pass it on to department AAA where they add this other data.* Within a few minutes Ruth was jabbing at the LDS and asking questions with no fear.

Moral: *New users can learn a lot by having the model read to them.*

Thin LDS, Lost Users

At company X, I was observing a meeting run by a novice modeler, Mario. Although Mario did nothing overtly wrong, within 30 minutes the users were lost. During a break, Mario and I determined that the model was too thin. That is, many entities had just identifying descriptors. While this is syntactically okay, when he revisited those entities asking, *What else is memorable here?* the users had lots to say. When there was flesh on the bones, the uncertainty abated and the session took a positive course.

Moral: *Adding descriptors deepens users' understanding of an entity.*

Data Modelers Must Understand Identifiers Deeply

This story surprises many people. Pay attention to it.

In a university class I gave an in-class exercise to build an LDS for the local movie guide. A few teams put their models on the board. I said, *Fred, your identifier for the entity named* show *means that a movie could be shown at only one time of day and that cannot be right.* Fred's reply was, *So what?* It was not a surly answer. Despite knowing the definition of "identifier," Fred did not see the consequences of his decision.

Here is another story with the same moral.

At company X, I was observing Liz, a novice modeler but an experienced programmer, model with users. At one point when she wrote down an entity plus its identifier, a user said, *Whoa, that identifier prevents us from remembering. . . .* Liz looked puzzled. She did not see the user's point.

Moral: *Novice modelers have trouble with the notion of identifier, but users do not.* [2]

Sandbox

A team of students in a university class came to me asking for help with their homework assignment, which was to reverse engineer the university's class schedule booklet into an LDS. They said, *We keep going round and round and cannot agree. This LDS stuff is useless.* I asked to see their in-progress LDS, looked at it for a bit, and said, *Sandbox!*

"Sandbox" is shorthand for *You have an ill-formed model with syntax errors in it, so of course you cannot agree!* I establish this shorthand on the first day of the course. I write

I the sandbox

on the board, ask students to talk with neighboring students and decide what it means, and then ask for their interpretations. Of course, the point is that they will produce lots of differing answers. A syntactically incorrect sentence or LDS is imprecise and therefore is subject to interpretation (it's poetry); it's certainly not a vehicle for rigorous communication.

"Sandbox" woke up those students. They focused on identifiers and finished the project expeditiously.

Here is a second sandbox story.

At company X, I gave an in-class exercise in which teams were to draw an LDS by reverse engineering a company X form. For a while all the teams worked hard, hunching over their shared paperwork. Then I noticed that the members of one team were slouching in their chairs, leaning back—away from their work. I went over to observe and found that, with the worthy goal of jump starting the model, they had taken each keyword on the form and put it in a box (no attributes). Then they had drawn some lines (no chicken feet, labels, or bars) connecting boxes where those words might be associated somehow. (They had about 12 boxes and 30 lines.) After

---

[2] Since this story is such a surprise, we will editorialize a bit. We seldom see users misunderstand identifiers, but we have seen hundreds of computer science students and professional programmers stumble over them. We think two factors cause them to err. First, computer scientists develop the habit of capitalizing on the position of their data (via pointer structures and subscripts). Through this habit, they can distinguish individual instances without inspecting the values of the instances. Second, they manipulate data but generally do not generate it or really use the results they produce. Beware: Until you understand identifiers, you cannot be a master modeler.

doing so, they stopped making progress and withdrew emotionally and physically from the task.

They had a drawing, not an LDS; it was beyond poetry—it was art. I reminded them about sandbox and had them start over and keep their LDS well formed as they proceeded. They did so and succeeded.

In retrospect, I realized that I had failed to say, *Don't just write down keywords and then try to fix it;* now I do so explicitly.

These and similar experiences have raised *Be rigorous* to the level of a good habit.

Moral: *An ill-formed LDS fails to communicate.*

Drifting

At company X, back when I was a novice modeler, the users and I reverse engineered an existing application. We finished quickly because they answered no to many of my shape-based questions. The model seemed a bit small to me, but it did reflect their decisions and was backed up by their manuals, so I said *fine, we are done.* However, I had made two mistakes.

I failed to frame the meeting properly and emphasize that we were not looking just for typical instances but were looking also for odd ones that our LDS also had to accommodate.

I also failed to look at real instances. They later became available, and they provided handy examples that led the users to change their early noes into yeses.

Moral: *Anchor your understanding with instances, or else!*

7
Chapter

Introduction to Mastering Shapes

Unrelated LDSs can look similar. You can use their similarities to make analogies between the shapes. By making analogies, you can leverage your experience with a familiar LDS into expertise about an unfamiliar one.

Definition of Shape

Compare LDS Fragments 7-1 and 7-2 describing data from unrelated endeavors.

When LDS fragments resemble each other like this, we say they have the same shape. As it turns out, there is a small set of fundamental shapes that recur throughout all LDSs. If you understand these shapes well, you can quickly come to understand any well-formed LDS.

We use the word "shape" because the resemblance between LDS fragments is often pictorial. You recognize most shapes by recognizing certain patterns of boxes, lines, chicken feet, and bars—that is, you temporarily ignore the words on the LDS. However, there are limits to this pictorial similarity. In fact, two LDS fragments that conform to the same shape can look strikingly different because the entities can be oriented differently on the page. For example, Fragment 7-3 looks different from Fragment 7-1, but they are identical; both fragments contain the same assertions about what kinds of things are worth remembering.

Nevertheless, pictorial similarity remains useful as a way to recognize that two fragments conform to the same shape.

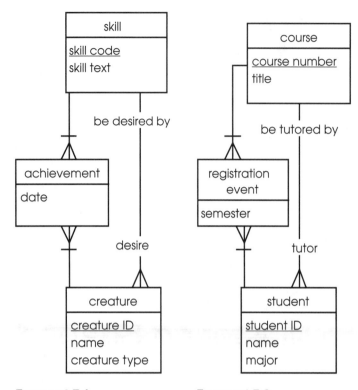

Fragment 7-1

Fragment 7-2

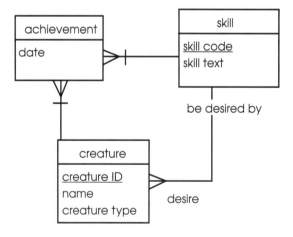

Fragment 7-3

Recognizing a shape is merely a beginning. A shape is important because of the things you can do after you detect it within a fragment. First, you can interpret the LDS, even if it contains words you do not know. For example, when you encounter a shape like the one in Fragment 7-4, you can immediately interpret the LDS with sentences like these:

- *About each* P, *we can remember the As it includes.*
- *About each* A, *we can remember a* P *that includes it.*

P and *A* might be words familiar to you—say, "play" and "actor." But they might be words entirely unfamiliar to you—say, "plasticity mechanism" and "axon." Nevertheless, because you recognize a shape, you can say meaningful sentences using the alien vocabulary: *About each plasticity mechanism, we can remember the axons it includes.*

Second, recognizing a shape helps you gradually improve the LDS. For example, when you encounter the shape in Fragment 7-4, you can immediately wonder whether it should evolve to the shape in Fragment 7-5. To find out, you can ask users this question: *Can an* A *be included in more than one* P? If the users respond affirmatively, the LDS evolves. If the users respond negatively, the LDS does not evolve. Once again, you can frame these questions even if *P* and *A* are words that are unfamiliar to you.

What you learn about a shape can be applied to any LDS fragment conforming to the shape. Each time you recognize that a fragment conforms to a shape, you gain experience working with the shape that you can later apply to other, seemingly unrelated LDS fragments.

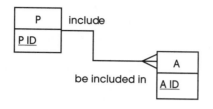

Fragment 7-4

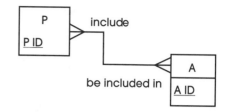

Fragment 7-5

This all leads to a semiformal definition of shape. A **shape** is a category of LDS structure that presents two opportunities:

- A shape presents an opportunity to make rigorous analogies between a familiar LDS and an unfamiliar LDS, thereby helping you understand the unfamiliar LDS.
- A shape presents an opportunity to anticipate incremental improvements to any LDS.

Shapes are small; a typical shape has one to three entities. This has several benefits:

- You can recognize shapes easily, even within a larger LDS.
- You can work on a complex LDS, even if it is unfamiliar to you. Faced with a large, daunting LDS, you do not need to take it in all at once. Instead, you can focus your attention on a small part of the LDS that conforms to a shape you recognize. Thus you decompose seemingly unwieldy problems into manageable portions.
- You can analyze shapes thoroughly. Because a shape is small, there is not that much to study about it. You can comprehensively examine the various options for reading the shape, for visualizing its sample data, and for anticipating how it might evolve.

There's more good news. You can analyze all the shapes you need to because there are not that many shapes to begin with. And remember, shapes are **content neutral**—they recur throughout all LDSs regardless of the specific content. This is the best news of all—it means that you can thoroughly analyze shapes on your own time before you ever meet with users. Later, when you meet with users and detect a shape within an in-progress LDS, you will know exactly what to do.

Mastering Shapes

Mastering shapes is a major part of mastering the LDS technique as a whole. Mastering shapes means mastering the following skills:

Shape-reading skills
- Reading shape aloud in several ways
- For any shape, creating and visualizing sample data in several ways
- For any shape, discussing and illustrating noteworthy disallowed data

Shape-recognition skills
- Finding and focusing on shapes within a large LDS
- Recognizing the differences between shapes that are similar but not identical
- Recognizing the similarity between seemingly dissimilar shapes
- Distinguishing between legitimate shapes and syntactically invalid LDS fragments

Shape-evolution skills
- Knowing how shapes are likely to evolve
- Asking questions that help users choose between two similar shapes
- Knowing when to ask questions of users
- Knowing when and how to modify the LDS to make a shape evolve
- Understanding the relative frequency of the various shapes

Shape-studying skills
- Referring to each fundamental shape by its name

The remainder of this chapter elaborates on these aspects of shape mastery.

Reading a Shape Aloud in Several Ways

There will be times when you or the users become confused by an in-progress data model. You should not be discouraged when confusion arises. In fact, you should expect it, so you can prepare for it and conquer it. One excellent way to combat confusion is to be able to read an LDS fragment in several ways.

Facing confusion, you'll naturally want to help the user by paraphrasing the LDS in more conversational diction. If you're not careful, however, you'll resort to vague statements and imprecise hand waving. Remember, there is no room for imprecision. For each shape, you need to be able to say in several ways exactly what the shape means.

For example, consider LDS Fragment 7-6. You can read this shape according to the guidelines for reading LDSs presented in Chapter 3.

- *About each course, we can remember its name and its enrollment events. Each course is identified by its name.*
- *About each enrollment event, we can remember its course and its student. Each enrollment event is identified by its course and its student.*
- *About each student, we can remember its student ID. Each student is identified by its student ID.*

Fragment 7-6

Because these sentences conform to the guidelines for reading LDSs, we know they are accurate. However, they effectively read the shape piecemeal—in installments.

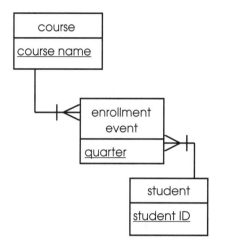

Fragment 7-7

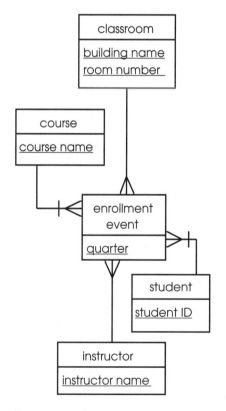

Fragment 7-8

They fail to give an overall picture of the shape. You can say other accurate sentences about this shape, such as the following:

- *Each course can have many enrolled students* and *Each student can have many enrolled-in courses.* These sentences together stress that the enrollment event entity effectively constitutes a many-many relationship between student and course.
- *Each enrollment event indicates that a particular student enrolls in a particular course.* This sentence stresses the meaning of the word enrollment. It also stresses that each enrollment event is about a (*course, student*) pair.

Note that these conversational sentences supplement the original sentences but do not substitute for them. For example, these conversational sentences say nothing about how to distinguish instances from one another.

Looking back at the conversation about creatures and skills in the previous chapter, we can see several times when this conversational diction might come in handy. For example, if you read Fragment 6-5 with this diction, you can help users understand the similarity between Fragments 6-5 and 6-3.

What's more, as shapes grow more complex, these conversational sentences grow more enlightening to confused persons. For example, consider the two successively more complex shapes in Fragments 7-7 and 7-8 and the corresponding sentences:

- *Each enrollment event indicates that a particular student enrolls in a particular course during a particular quarter.*
- *Each enrollment event indicates that during a particular quarter, a particular student enrolls in a particular course from a particular instructor in a particular classroom.* When you say this sentence for users, you can further help them understand the diagram by pointing to portions of the diagram as you say the corresponding portions of the sentence.

Visualizing Sample Data in Several Formats

Just as some users find some diction more helpful than other diction, some users prefer to view sample data in particular formats, that is, with different HOWs. Thus you need to be able to visualize data in several different formats. Throughout this book, you'll notice that we use different formats depending on what we're trying to illustrate. And sometimes

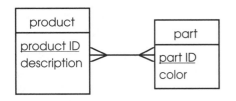

Fragment 7-9

we use a less typical format to remind you that such a format exists or to remind you that you have choices about how you visualize the data.

Although there are many formats for illustrating any ramification of a shape, each format offers particular shortcuts for illustrating particular ramifications. For example, suppose you want to illustrate the left chicken foot from the shape in Fragment 7-9. That is, you want to illustrate that each *part* can have more than one *product*.

If you use the format in the accompanying table, you illustrate the effect of the chicken foot by saying, *Notice that within any particular column, there can be several X's* (you can point to the column for Part 8777 when you say this). *That's because a part can have many products* (point to the left chicken foot).

In a diagram format, you illustrate the same ramification by saying, *Notice that from a particular part, there can be several emerging lines* (point to part 8777). *That's because a part can have many products* (point to the left chicken foot).

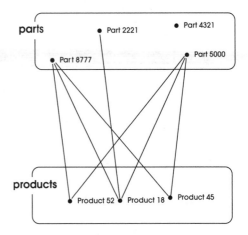

	Part 2221	Part 8777	Part 4321	Part 5000
Product 45		X		X
Product 52	X	X		X
Product 18		X		X

In the conversation about creatures and skills, notice that the data modeler used one of these visualization techniques to discuss Fragment 6-4.

Discussing and Illustrating Noteworthy Disallowed Data

Remember that as the LDS gradually evolves, the database boundary gradually moves. Each incremental change to the LDS connotes a correspondingly small expansion or contraction of the boundary. Until the LDS matures, most of these modifications are expansions of the boundary, as the users describe more and more of their data to you.

You can cue the users by anticipating how the boundary will expand and explicitly asking them about what you anticipate. That is, you can talk about interesting data that is just outside the boundary of an in-progress LDS.

For example, consider Fragment 6-14. You anticipated that the LDS could evolve into Fragment 6-15 because you realized that Fragment 6-14 could not accommodate some potentially noteworthy data. Specifically, you realized that a role could be worth remembering even if no creature has ever fulfilled that role in any achievement.

In that conversation, you merely talked about the disallowed data. But sometimes it is helpful to illustrate such data. This can get tricky because you need to make it clear to the users that you are illustrating the impossible. One good way to do this is to choose a format that illustrates the allowed data, jot down some sample data, then try to add the disallowed data. If you choose your format carefully, it will be clear that there is "no room" for the data.

Finding and Focusing on Shapes Within a Large LDS

After finding a shape, you can focus on it, temporarily ignoring the rest of the LDS. For example, in Fragments 6-18 through 6-23, you and the users focused on a small portion of the LDS, ignoring the entities named *contribution, role,* and *skill.* Such focus is possible because in Fragment 6-18, you recognized a shape, anticipated how it would evolve, and began to lead the users through a discussion that revealed the evolution.

Shapes overlap. That is, when you focus your attention on a small LDS fragment, it can participate in several shapes. That's okay. In fact, you should expect that several shapes will apply to any particular LDS fragment. Because a fragment participates in several shapes, you can apply your knowledge about all the applicable shapes to it. You do not have to choose which shape is "most important" or which one is the "best match" for the fragment.

Look at Fragment 7-10 and consider two shapes:

- **Chicken feet in.** Shape in which an entity has several one-many relationships with the chicken feet near the entity. *Achievement* participates in the chicken-feet-in shape.
- **Chicken feet out.** Shape in which an entity has several one-many relationships with the chicken feet away from the entity. *Date* participates in the chicken-feet-out shape.

Notice that both shapes apply to the *aspiration* entity. You can see this easily from the diagram: *creature-aspiration-skill* looks like *creature-achievement-skill* (feet in), and *practice session-aspiration-exam* looks like *practice session-date-exam* (feet out).

Fragment 7-10 makes it easy to see that *aspiration* is like both *achievement* and *date,* even though *achievement* and *date* are not alike at all. Speaking realistically, things won't always be this easy. Keep the following in mind.

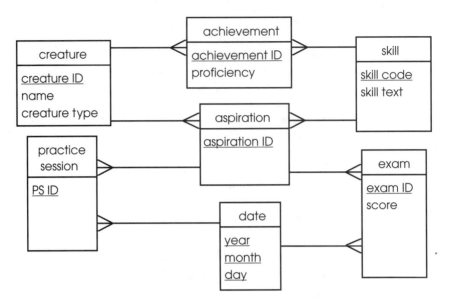

Fragment 7-10

- **Shapes are independent of layout.** You detect shapes by detecting patterns of entities, descriptors, and identifiers. Variations in layout might obscure these patterns. For example, *creature-aspiration-skill* is parallel to *date-exam-aspiration;* both exhibit the chicken-feet-in shape.
- **Fragments need not share any entities to share a shape.** For example, *practice session-date-exam* and *aspiration-skill-achievement* both exhibit the chicken-feet-out shape.
- **Fragments can be compared to canonical shapes.** Comparing fragments to one another is useful, and you will do this a lot while you are a novice modeler. You will make analogies between a new fragment and another fragment you have already scrutinized. But as you become a master, you will develop an abstract, content-neutral appreciation of the shapes. You won't always compare a new fragment to an old one; you will perceive a new fragment according to your masterful expectation of how fragments and shapes behave. This is what happened during the conversation about creatures and skills in Fragments 6-3 through 6-5. There was no other many-many relationship available for comparison, but the modeler knew in general how to work with many-many relationships.
- **Recognizing shapes is not a raw talent or gift; it requires knowledge.** You need to learn what the shapes are and how to recognize them. In particular, this means learning what to observe and what to ignore (temporarily) on an in-progress LDS. In Fragment 7-10, for example, you can perceive that *aspiration* participates in the chicken-feet-in shape by temporarily ignoring the lower relationships to *practice session* and *exam.* Likewise, in Fragment 7-11, you can appreciate that *aspiration* participates in the chicken-feet-in shape despite the

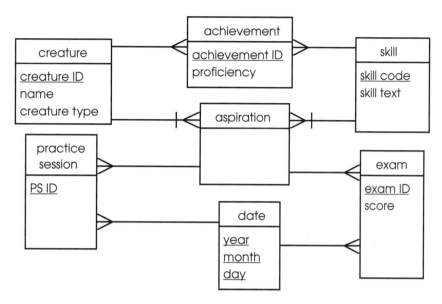

Fragment 7-11

change in the identifier. Part of the knowledge you need about the chicken-feet-in shape is that identifiers have no bearing on the shape. This is exactly the kind of information in Chapters 8 through 12.

You will find that every entity participates in many shapes. Consider the *contribution* entity of Fragment 6-22. It conforms to at least two shapes, *intersection entity* (see Chapter 8) and chicken feet in. Thus, when you discuss this fragment with users, you can leverage your skill with both of these shapes. Any data-visualization technique that applies to chicken feet in can apply to this fragment. Any conversational diction that can apply to intersection entities can apply to this fragment.

Recognizing the Differences Between Shapes That Are Similar but Not Identical

For any pair of similar but not identical shapes, you need to be able to articulate immediately the differences between them. One good way to articulate these differences is with sample data. That is, you design some sample data that is accommodated by one of the shapes but not by the other.

For example, consider the two similar shapes of Fragments 7-12 and 7-13. The top shape shows a two-part identifier for the *enrollment event* entity, whereas the bottom shape shows a three-part identifier. To appreciate the differences between these two shapes, you can design some sample data that highlights them.

For example, the data in the accompanying table shows that a student (ID number 123456) can take the same course (history of Peru) in several different quarters.

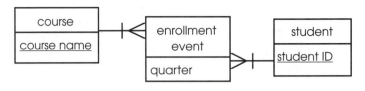

Fragment 7-12

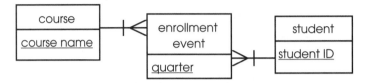

Fragment 7-13

Course	Student ID	Quarter
History of Peru	123456	Fall
History of Peru	123456	Spring
Calculus	777777	Winter
History of Peru	777777	Spring

The top shape cannot accommodate this data because the two-part identifier of *enrollment event* cannot distinguish between these two instances.

In the conversation about creatures and skills, shapes like these came up in Fragments 6-6 and 6-7. In that case, you helped the users choose Fragment 6-7 merely by asking a question; you did not need to draw sample data. But if the users had become confused or had misunderstood your question, you could have used sample data to help them.

More generally, *any* pair of consecutive fragments in Chapter 6 illustrates the differences between similar but not identical shapes. That's the whole point of controlled evolution. The LDS evolves because you continuously modify it. But the evolution is controlled because each revision is a small step that users can understand.

When you are designing sample data that helps you compare two shapes, do not assume that one shape is absolutely superior to the other. That is, do not assume that because one shape surpasses the other in some respect, it surpasses the other in all respects. For example, the preceding sample data shows that the shape of Fragment 7-13 is (in some respect) more accommodating than the shape of Fragment 7-12. However, the shape of Fragment 7-13 is also less accommodating than the shape of Fragment 7-12 in some respects. Specifically, Fragment 7-13 cannot accommodate any instance of *enrollment event* that leaves the *quarter* attribute null.

Remember, shapes are not superior or inferior to each other. Rather, they are more or less faithful to the kinds of data the users want to remember and more or less effective at fostering communication among system designers and users. You cannot find a perfect, all-encompassing shape that accommodates any data anyone might want to remember. You seek shapes that accurately reflect what the users want to remember. Together, you and the users decide which shapes best suit their data needs.

Recognizing the Similarity Between Seemingly Dissimilar Shapes

In some cases, shapes that look dissimilar can be quite similar in that they accommodate nearly the same data. You must be able to look beyond the surface differences to perceive the similarities in such pairs of seemingly dissimilar shapes.

For example, although the two shapes of Fragments 7-14 and 7-15 look grossly different, they are quite similar. In fact, they can both accommodate the data shown in the subsequent table.

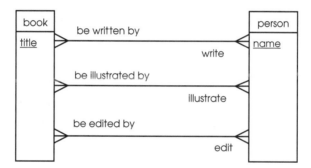

Fragment 7-14

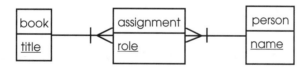

Fragment 7-15

In the sample data, notice the following:

- A book can have several authors (*Logical Data Structures* does).
- A book can have several editors (*Innocence and Experience* does).
- A person can write several books (Jane Langton does).
- A person can fill multiple roles on the same book (Gregory Maguire does for *Innocence and Experience;* Barbara Harrison does for *Innocence and Experience;* Jane Langton does for *Murder at the Gardner*).

Books	John Carlis	Joseph Maguire	Gregory Maguire	Barbara Harrison	Jane Langton	Alex Humez	Nick Humez	Erik Blegvad
Innocence and Experience			writer, editor	writer, editor	writer			
Logical Data Stuctures	writer	writer						
Wicked			writer					
Zero to Lazy Eight		writer				writer	writer	
Latina pro Populo						writer	writer	
The Diamond in the Window					writer			illustrator
Murder at the Gardner					writer, illustrator			

A quick exercise: Fragment 7-14 has six chicken feet, but the sample data in the table illustrates only some of them. Which chicken feet are not illustrated by the sample data? With a pencil, add sample data to ensure that all of the chicken feet are illustrated.

Another quick exercise: Nick Humez sometimes reviews books. Assume that he has reviewed *Wicked*. With a pencil, modify the table to so indicate. How would you change each of the attendant LDS fragments to accommodate this data?

Distinguishing Between Legitimate Shapes and Syntactically Invalid LDS Fragments

An LDS with bad syntax is like a program with bad syntax—meaningless. Programmers have it relatively easy because they can use compilers to perform automatic syntax checking. But a data modeler must rely on his or her wits to detect and correct syntax errors.

You might think that a good piece of data-modeling software could shoulder the burden of syntax checking for you. But this is not true for two reasons. The first reason is practical: You need to detect syntax errors as soon as they creep onto an in-progress LDS. If a syntax error remains uncorrected on an LDS, any conversation about that portion of the LDS is useless. During a data-modeling meeting with users, you typically are not using software; you are more likely standing at the front of a conference room with a marker in one hand and an eraser in the other, asking questions, listening to users, drawing sample data, and gradually modifying the LDS. Detecting a syntax error after the meeting is over—say, when you enter the model into your data-modeling software—is too late. You and the users will have to revisit all the decisions made about that portion of the LDS since the error appeared. Needless to say, users do not like this kind of hazing.

The second reason is theoretical. Being able to understand syntax errors is inseparable from being able to read and write LDSs. For the most part, LDS syntax rules are manifest—inescapable consequences of the definitions of entity, attribute, relationship, and identifier. No one can claim fluency with LDS without knowing the syntax rules backward and forward.

During the conversation about creatures and skills, you encountered Fragment 6-4, which contained a syntax error (an entity with no name; see Chapter 13). You did not let the syntax error remain on the LDS for long, for the very next fragment is syntactically valid. Similarly, Fragment 6-9 is invalid (an entity has no identifier). You fixed that right away, too.

Knowing How Shapes Are Likely to Evolve

Refresh your memory: The point of shape mastery is to ensure that your conversations with users transpire as smoothly as possible. Inevitably, there will be times when the conversations are not so smooth because the users will struggle as you ask them to think harder about their data than they ever have before. (Recall how users struggled with a question you asked about Fragment 6-9.) But your shape mastery can ensure that *you* are not the impediment.

That's why you cannot waste a lot of time trying to remember how shapes are likely to evolve. During the time you waste, users will lose interest in the LDS or lose faith in your ability or start listening to messages on their cell phones.

In the conversation about creatures and skill, almost every question you ask is motivated by your anticipation of how the LDS can evolve. Sometimes the users' answer indicates that the LDS should not evolve, and sometimes it indicates that it should. But in almost every case, you ask the question in anticipation of evolution.

Asking Questions That Help Users Choose Between Two Similar Shapes

When you anticipate evolution of the LDS, you are effectively comparing a shape on the in-progress LDS with a shape that *could be* on the LDS. You must help the users choose between these shapes. The best way is to ask a yes-or-no question.

For example, suppose the shape of Fragment 7-16 is on an in-progress LDS, but you anticipate that it might evolve into the shape of Fragment 7-17. You ask the following question:

Can a part be contained in several products?

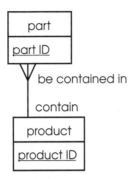

Fragment 7-16

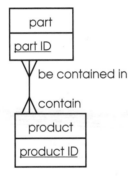

Fragment 7-17

Shape mastery means being able to formulate these questions quickly for any shape. When you ask these questions, you must choose your language carefully. Just as in reading an LDS, vagueness is anathema. A good question has these characteristics:

- It employs the users' words. For example, notice that the entity names *part* and *product* appear in the preceding question.
- It is a yes-or-no question.
- Each possible answer has an immediate, minor (or null) effect on the LDS. For example, a yes answer to the preceding question changes Fragment 7-14 to Fragment 7-15. A no answer leaves it unchanged.

Knowing When to Ask Questions of Users

At any given moment, there are dozens or hundreds of questions you could ask users. You have some leeway about which question you ask, but there are some guidelines:

- Some questions seek to remedy syntax errors on the LDS. These questions receive high priority. Among them, the questions that seek to remedy bad identifiers, missing identifiers, and bad or missing entity names are especially urgent.
- Some questions focus on the same portion of the LDS that users are already concentrating on. Ask these questions before moving on to another portion of the LDS.

Beyond these admittedly minimal guidelines, in Chapter 18 we offer much more explicit advice about knowing when to ask questions.

Knowing When and How to Modify the LDS to Make a Shape Evolve

Ordinarily, it goes like this: You ask a question, modify the LDS accordingly, and move to the next question. Obviously, this repetitive cycle fails if you do not know how to modify the LDS. We devote Chapters 13 through 16 to the fundamentals of writing syntactically valid, high-fidelity LDSs. And Chapter 18 shows how to modify the LDS for particular questions.

Sometimes you modify the LDS without even asking a question. This happens when you encounter a many-many relationship: You automatically replace the relationship with an entity and two one-many relationships. For an example of this, see Fragments 6-3 and 6-4.

And on rare occasions you ask a question even though you do not intend to modify the LDS immediately. That is, you ask a yes-or-no question even though neither answer will induce you to change the LDS. There are two reasons why you might do this:

- The users' answer will help you eliminate certain possible evolutionary paths for the LDS.
- The users' answer will help you recognize worthy constraints that apply to the LDS.

We call such questions "delayed-effect" questions, and they apply only to a few particular shapes. We will tell you about them when we describe each of these shapes.

Understanding the Relative Frequency of the Various Shapes

Some shapes are so rare that when you see them during controlled evolution of an LDS, your first reflex should be to scrutinize the fragment for immediate improvement. When an in-progress LDS contains too many rare shapes, you are probably misrepresenting the users' assertions, you are expressing physical database design decisions on the LDS, or you are making unwise stylistic choices that make the LDS hard to understand. When you understand the relative frequency of the various shapes, you'll be able to look at an in-progress LDS and quickly diagnose whether it is peculiar or conventional. If it is peculiar, you are probably not serving your users well.

In the next few chapters about specific shapes, we will tell you which shapes occur infrequently on mature LDSs.

When you are a novice modeler, you should explicitly check your in-progress LDS every so often for rare shapes. But as you become a master, you will find yourself making this check instinctively because you will have developed a feel for LDS quality.

Referring to Each Fundamental Shape by Its Name

Shape mastery means being able to talk about shapes with your data modeling colleagues. Thus you need names for certain fundamental shapes that will arise in conversation often. We give each shape a name.

Exercises

1. Notice that Fragment 7-12 is like Fragment 1-1.
   a. Modify Fragment 1-1 so that it is like Fragment 7-13.
   b. Mimic the discussion about Fragments 7-12 and 7-13, creating sample data that illustrates the differences between Fragment 1-1 and its modified version.

2. Make a shape-by-skill spreadsheet with a column for each mastering-shape skill and a row for each shape in Chapters 8 through 12. For each cell in the spreadsheet you can
   a. mark that you have the skill for the shape.
   b. write specific examples from your own modeling experiences.
   c. note questions that you have.
3. Find fragments in this book that contain a shape like Fragment 1-1. Mark them somehow, and then, after you have read Chapter 11, look at the marked shapes again and see if you were correct.
4. Compare Fragment 7-1 with Fragment 21-6. Describe in words how they differ.

8
Chapter

One-Entity, No-Relationship Shapes

You categorize an entity by looking at what kinds of descriptors contribute to its identifier. Following are the kinds of entity.

Independent. There are three variations of the independent entity shape:

- Common independent entity. The identifier includes no links. The entity includes at least one attribute that contributes to the identifier and at least one attribute that does not.
- Lonely-attribute independent entity. The identifier includes no links. The entity includes only one attribute, and that attribute constitutes the entity's identifier.
- Aggregate independent entity (sometimes simply called aggregate entity). The identifier includes no link. The entity includes two or more attributes, and every attribute contributes to the identifier.

Lonely-attribute independent entities and aggregate independent entities are rare. Thus we sometimes refer to common independent entities simply as independent entities. When the context demands it, we'll be more specific.

Dependent. The identifier includes exactly one link and one or more attributes. The link that contributes to the identifier is the degree-one link of a one-many relationship.

Intersection. The identifier includes more than one link and zero or more attributes. The links are degree-one links of one-many relationships.

Subordinate. The identifier includes exactly one link and zero attributes. The link is part of a one-one relationship.

Collection. The identifier includes exactly one descriptor, a degree-many link. There are two variations of the collection entity shape.

- One-many collection entity. The degree-many link contributing to the identifier is part of a one-many relationship.
- Many-many collection entity. The degree-many link contributing to the identifier is part of a many-many relationship.

Notice that you recognize an entity's kind by characterizing that entity's identifier. Thus, because an entity can have several identifiers, one entity can fall into several of these categories.

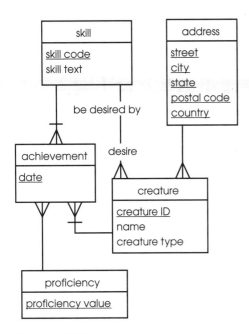

Fragment 8-1

Shape: Common Independent Entity

A common independent entity has an identifier that includes no links, includes at least one attribute, and excludes at least one attribute.

In LDS Fragment 8-1, some of the entities are common independent entities, and some are not.

- *Proficiency* is not a common independent entity because no attribute is excluded from its identifier.
- *Skill* is a common independent entity because its identifier includes no link, includes an attribute (skill code), and excludes an attribute (skill text).
- *Creature* is a common independent entity because its identifier includes some but not all of the attributes and none of the links.
- *Achievement* is not a common independent entity because its identifier includes some links.
- *Address* is not a common independent entity because there is no attribute excluded from the entity's identifier.

Entities that users think of as fundamental or pivotal to their endeavors tend to be common independent entities.

A common independent entity rarely evolves into another kind of entity. However, when the scope of the endeavor expands, some common independent entities can become dependent entities. For example, Fragment 8-2 shows a common independent entity that accommodates data about a particular campus's students.

Fragment 8-2

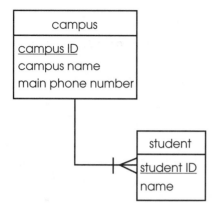

Fragment 8-3

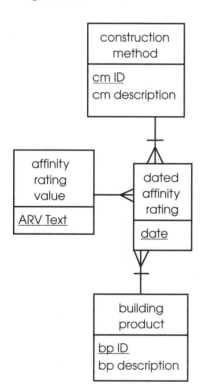

Fragment 8-4

Lonely-attribute
independent entities
are rare.

Fragment 8-3 shows the corresponding LDS fragment for accommodating students from any campus within the university system. Because each campus has complete control over what ID numbers it assigns to students, it is possible that two students from different campuses can share a student ID number. Therefore the identifier of student must include the link *campus of student.* Because the scope of the endeavor expanded from a single campus to several campuses, a common independent entity evolved to a dependent entity.

Shape: Lonely-Attribute Independent Entity

A lonely-attribute independent entity has only one attribute. The entity's identifier includes that attribute but no links.

In Fragment 8-4, one of the entities is a lonely-attribute independent entity.

- *Affinity rating value* is a lonely-attribute independent entity because it has only one attribute and that attribute is the only descriptor contributing to the identifier.
- *Dated affinity rating* is not a lonely-attribute independent entity. Although it has only one attribute and that attribute contributes to the identifier, it is not a lonely-attribute independent entity because the identifier also includes some links.
- *Building product* is not a lonely-attribute independent entity because it has more than one attribute.
- *Construction method* is not a lonely-attribute independent entity because it has more than one attribute.

We have seen only one use for lonely-attribute independent entities—they are sometimes used to model the existence of lookup tables. Lookup tables let you make user interfaces table-driven. That is, they let you store in the database a list of values from which users can choose. For example, in an application using the data of Fragment 8-4, users can assert that a particular building product works well (or poorly) for a particular construction method. After the user indicates which construction method and which building product she wishes to rate, the user interface can provide her a list of possible affinity ratings (such as "Recommended," "Approved," and "Not Recommended"). The user interface can look up these values from the database.

A lonely-attribute independent entity can become an independent entity when you add an attribute—typically, you add such an attribute to provide explanatory

Recommended	Recommended by the manufacturer.
Approved	Workable, but the product was not specifically designed for this purpose.
Not Recommended	Using this product with this construction method will be unsafe or too costly.

affinity rating
value

ARV text
ARV description

Fragment 8-5

text. For example, suppose that the users want to remember brief explanations of the possible affinity rating values, as in the accompanying sample data. Fragment 8-5 shows the evolved *affinity rating value* entity. It is now a common independent entity.

Look again at Fragment 8-4. Suppose you removed the *affinity rating value* entity and added an attribute called *affinity rating* to the *dated affinity rating* entity. The resulting shape differs only slightly from Fragment 8-4 in the data that it accommodates. (We leave the articulation of exactly how it differs as an exercise for you.)

Shape: Aggregate Independent Entity

An aggregate independent entity has more than one attribute, each of which contributes to the identifier. The identifier includes no link.

In Fragment 8-6, one of the entities is an aggregate independent entity; the others are not.

- *Address* is an aggregate independent entity because its identifier includes more than one attribute, excludes no attribute, and includes no link.
- *Customer* is not an aggregate independent entity because there is an attribute that is excluded from the identifier.
- *Trucking route* is not an aggregate independent entity. Although its identifier includes several attributes and excludes none, it cannot be an aggregate entity because its identifier includes one or more links.

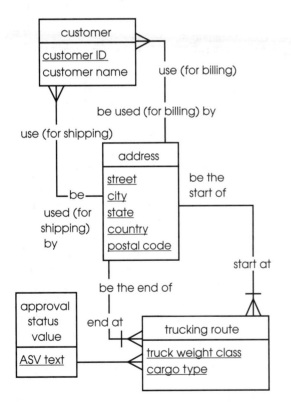

Fragment 8-6

date
year
month
day

Fragment 8-7

Aggregate independent entities are rare.

- *Approval status value* is not an aggregate independent entity. Although its identifier excludes no attribute and includes no link, it cannot be an aggregate because it contains only one attribute.

We commonly see only two uses for aggregate independent entities: addresses (as in Fragment 8-6) and dates (Fragment 8-7). Note that if an aggregate entity participates in a chicken-feet-out shape, the multiple descriptor identifiers can become inconvenient for some implementation models, particularly the relational model.

Aggregate independent entities tend to evolve in two different ways:

- If an aggregate independent entity's multiple descriptor identifier becomes inconvenient, then it can evolve into a common independent entity with an arbitrary identifier.
- If you promote one of the attributes into a more complex structure (see "Promoting Attributes" in Chapter 19), the aggregate entity becomes a dependent entity. If you make two such promotions on two different attributes, the aggregate entity becomes an intersection entity. For example, Fragments 8-8 and 8-9 show the subsequent evolutionary phases for the aggregate entity in Fragment 8-7. Fragment 8-8 shows that date has evolved into a dependent entity. Fragment 8-9 shows that date has evolved into an intersection entity.

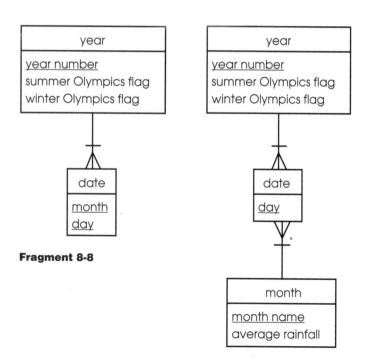

Fragment 8-8

Fragment 8-9

Shape: Dependent Entity

A dependent entity has an identifier including exactly one degree-one link of a one-many relationship, plus one or more attributes.

In Fragment 8-10, some of the entities are dependent entities, and others are not.

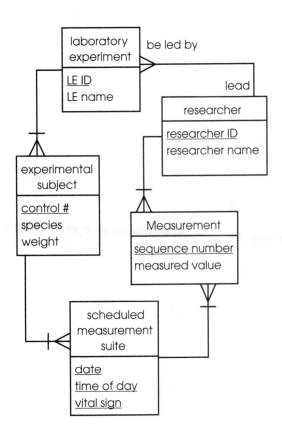

Fragment 8-10

- *Laboratory experiment* is not a dependent entity because its identifier includes no link.
- *Researcher* is not a dependent entity because its identifier includes no link.
- *Experimental subject* is a dependent entity because its identifier includes exactly one degree-one link of a one-many relationship plus one or more attributes.
- *Scheduled measurement suite* is a dependent entity because its identifier includes exactly one degree-one link of a one-many relationship plus one or more attributes. (In fact, the identifier includes all of the entity's attributes.)
- *Measurement* is not a dependent entity because its identifier includes more than one link.

During controlled evolution, dependent entities can sometimes evolve into independent entities.

Shape: Intersection Entity

An intersection entity has an identifier with all of the following characteristics:

- The identifier includes two or more degree-one links of one-many relationships.
- The identifier includes no other links (that is, it includes no degree-many links or links from one-one relationships).
- The identifier includes zero or more attributes.

In Fragment 8-11, some of the entities are intersection entities, and some are not.

- *Skill* is not an intersection entity because its identifier includes no links.
- *Achievement* is an intersection entity because its identifier includes two degree-one links from one-many relationships plus no other links plus zero attributes.
- *Exam* is an intersection entity because its identifier includes three degree-one links from one-many relationships plus no other links plus zero attributes.
- *Date* is not an intersection entity because its identifier includes no links.
- *Creature* is not an intersection entity because its identifier includes no links.

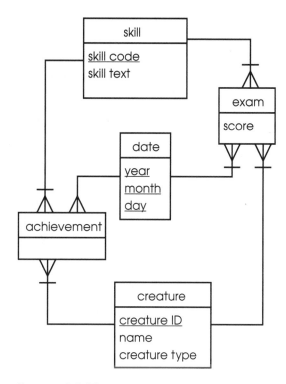

Fragment 8-11

For another example of an intersection entity, see the *measurement* entity in Fragment 8-10.

An intersection entity is a special case of the chicken-feet-in shape; you should apply all your mastery of that shape to intersection entities. See Chapter 11 for more information.

Intersection entities can evolve to dependent entities. See Chapter 18 for more information.

If the identifier of an intersection entity has no tiebreaker, you can visualize its instances as cells of an *n*-dimensional matrix, where *n* is the number of links contributing to the identifier.

Shape: Subordinate Entity

A subordinate independent entity has an identifier that includes exactly one descriptor—a link from a one-one relationship.

In Fragment 8-12, one of the entities is a subordinate entity, and the other is not.

Subordinate entities are rare.

- *Employee* is not a subordinate entity because its identifier includes an attribute.
- *Part-time employee* is a subordinate entity because its identifier consists of one link from a one-one relationship.

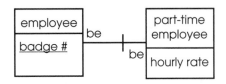

Fragment 8-12

If an in-progress LDS you are working on has many subordinate entities, scrutinize it. Subordinate entities should be rare on an LDS. Students with significant backgrounds in object-oriented programming techniques are especially prone to overuse subordinate entities. For more information, read the "Subordinates Out" and "Subordinates Across" sections in Chapter 11.

Shape: One-Many Collection Entity

A one-many collection entity has an identifier containing exactly one descriptor—the degree-many link of a one-many relationship.

In Fragment 8-13, one of the entities is a one-many collection entity, and the other is not.

- *Herd* is a one-many collection entity because its identifier consists of a degree-many link of a one-many relationship.
- *Cow* is not a one-many collection entity because its identifier consists of one attribute.

This is a *very* rare shape.

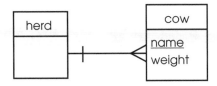

Fragment 8-13

In the accompanying sample data, notice the following:

- The *herd* entity is a collection entity, so herds do not have single-valued identifiers. Rather than refer to "Herd 082" (as in Fragment 8-2), we refer to "the herd containing Dru, Elsie, and Francine."
- Each herd must contain at least one cow. That is, we cannot remember the "null" herd.

You should also realize these ramifications of the identifier of the *herd* entity:

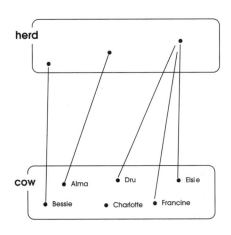

- If a cow quits a herd, the herd becomes obsolete. For example, if Francine leaves her herd, we can no longer refer to the herd containing Dru, Elsie, and Francine. Rather, we must refer to a new, different herd, the herd containing Dru and Elsie.
- Similarly, if a new cow is born into a herd or if a cow joins a herd for any reason, the result is a new herd. For example, if Charlotte joins the herd containing Alma, the result is a new herd, and the previous herd containing only Alma ceases to exist.

The one-many collection entity shape is very rare; it endures only on very abstract data models.

A one-many collection entity can evolve in either of two ways:

- If a one-many collection entity's multivalued identifier becomes inconvenient or confusing to the users, it can evolve into an entity with an arbitrary identifier.
- If the one-many relationship evolves to a many-many relationship, the entity consequently becomes a many-many collection entity.

This is a delayed-effect question.

When you encounter a one-many collection entity, you should consider whether every instance of the entity has the same number of instances of the related entity. That is, you should ask a question like *Can different instances of <collection entity name> have different numbers of related <related entity name>?*

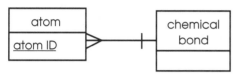

Fragment 8-14

For Fragment 8-13, the question is *Can different herds have different numbers of cows?* In this case, the users (dairy farmers) indicate that the answer is yes; herds have different sizes. However, for Fragment 8-14, the related question is *Can different chemical bonds have different numbers of atoms?* In this case, the users indicate that the answer is no; every chemical bond has exactly two atoms.

Shape: Many-Many Collection Entity

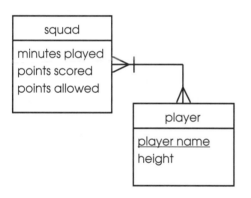

Fragment 8-15

A many-many collection entity has an identifier containing exactly one descriptor—a link of a many-many relationship.

There are some concrete, albeit slightly contrived examples that illustrate this shape. For example, a very thorough, quantitative basketball coach maintains statistics about her team's performance. In particular, she is interested in particular combinations of five players, which she calls squads. Fragment 8-15 describes part of the coach's data.

About each squad, we can remember its minutes played, points scored, points allowed, and its players. Each squad is identified by its players.

In the fragment, one of the entities is a many-many collection entity, and the other is not.

- *Squad* is a many-many collection entity because its identifier consists of a link of a many-many relationship.
- *Player* is not a many-many collection entity because its identifier consists of an attribute.

This shape is very rare.

Noncontrived examples of the many-many collection entity shape endure only on very abstract data models. For typical commercial applications, you might never see it during an entire career of data modeling.

If the many-many relationship evolves into an intersection entity, the identifier of the collection entity must change because when you replace the many-many relationship with an intersection entity, you eliminate the very link that has been contributing to the identifier of the collection entity.

This is a delayed-effect question.

When you encounter a many-many collection entity, you should consider whether every instance of the entity has the same number of instances of the related entity. That is, you should ask a question like *Can different instances of <collection entity name> have different numbers of related <related entity name>?*

For Fragment 8-15, the question is *Can different squads have different numbers of players?* In this case, the users (basketball coaches) indicate that the answer is no; every squad has exactly five players. However, for Fragment 8-16, the related question is *Can different nonnull sets have different numbers of elements?* In this case, the users (mathematicians) indicate that the answer is yes because sets can have different sizes.

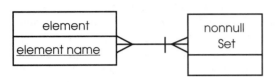

Fragment 8-16

Unnamed Possibilities

There are several syntactically valid possibilities for identifiers that have never occurred—or have occurred only momentarily on a rapidly evolving LDS—in all of our combined years of data modeling. These possibilities are so rare that they do not require names. Remember, people use names so that they can refer to things within spoken and written language. If a certain thing never (or rarely) arises in discourse, people will never (or rarely) need a name for the thing. We tell you about these identifiers in Chapter 13, and we tell you about them for two reasons:

- Conceivably, someone might encounter one of these peculiar identifiers during controlled evolution of a very abstract LDS.
- A thorough understanding (rather than just rote memorization) of the syntax rules for identifiers will make it clear why these peculiar shapes are theoretically valid. And conversely, if you understand why these peculiar shapes are valid, it will help you understand the syntax rules.

Exercises

1. Make a chart with a column for each kind of entity and with these row headings:
   - kind of entity
   - number of identifying attributes
   - number of identifying degree-one links
   - number of identifying degree-many links
   - number of nonidentifying attributes
   - number of nonidentifying links
   - likelihood of evolving (low, medium, high)
   - example
   - evolved-to example
2. Go through this book, and for each entity you see, write down what kind of entity it is. Do so until you find that assessing an entity's kind becomes automatic.
3. Compare your answers to question 2 to your classmates' or colleagues' answers.

9 Chapter

One-Attribute Shapes

When you encounter an attribute, you should be able to say what kind of attribute it is. That is, you should know the attribute's **scale.** An attribute's scale constitutes a shape. Thus recognizing scale yields some of the same benefits as recognizing any other shape.

The rest of this chapter elaborates on the preceding paragraph and describes some common scales.

Scale

An attribute's scale is a general classification of the kind of values it contains. For example, in LDS Fragment 9-1, the attributes *team name* and *city* are both nominal-scale attributes; each attribute has values that are names. The attribute *place* is an ordinal-scale attribute; its values are ordinal numbers (first, second, third, and so on). The attribute *finish time in seconds* is an arithmetic-scale attribute; its values are numbers that can be used as any operand in an arithmetic expression.

A data modeler's interest in scale mirrors a statistician's interest in scale. Statisticians care about the scale of variables because certain statistical analyses and arithmetic operations are valid only for certain scale. (For example, it is nonsensical to compute the mean for a nominal-scale variable—there is no "average team name.") Similarly, data modelers care about the scale of attributes because an attribute's scale

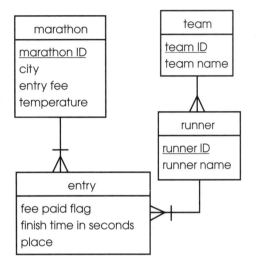

Fragment 9-1

restricts how you can use the attribute and how the LDS fragment containing the attribute can evolve.

You can make very fine distinctions between scales, but while developing an LDS, you rarely need to. You can understand most of the information you need about scale merely by making some very coarse distinctions. For example, although you can distinguish between arithmetic-scale and logarithmic-scale attributes, the distinction makes little difference to the LDS. Ordinarily, it suffices merely to recognize that the scale of both attributes is numeric.

And in general, the distinctions that are worth making are coarse. Specifically, it is worthwhile to differentiate among nominal-scale, numeric-scale, ordinal-scale, and Boolean-scale attributes. These four scales are described in the next sections.

Shape: Nominal-Scale Attributes

The values of a nominal-scale attribute are not numbers but names. There is no implied ordering of attribute values or magnitude associated with the values. The attribute's values cannot serve as operands in any arithmetic operation. Note, however, that you can use the attribute's values in equality tests (e.g., if *RunnerName* = "Frank Shorter," then . . .) and inequality tests (if *RunnerName* <> "Bill Rogers," then . . .).

In Fragment 9-1, these attributes have nominal scale: *marathon ID, city, runner ID, name, team ID,* and *team name.*

Two issues are important here. One is "not numbers but names." We discuss it soon in the "Scale and Datatype" section. The other is the atomicity of nominal-scale attributes. Is "Frank Shorter" atomic—that is, is it one thing or two (first and last name)? The answer is "one" because an attribute is *always* atomic. Users can make burden-shifting decisions that hide internal structure of attributes. For example, an attribute could be unstructured text remarks, semistructured text remarks (perhaps encoded in XML), a picture, a recording, and so on.

Shape: Numeric-Scale Attributes

The values of a numeric-scale attribute are real numbers that can be used as operands in arithmetic expressions. Individual numeric-scale attributes might have other restrictions, like allowing only a certain subset of the real numbers (such as an integer-only restriction or a positive-only restriction).

In Fragment 9-1, the following attributes have numeric scale: *entry fee, temperature,* and *finish time in seconds.*

It is very rare for a numeric-scale attribute to contribute to an identifier. When you encounter an entity whose identifier includes a numeric-scale attribute, study the shape especially hard to improve the identifier.

Shape: Ordinal-Scale Attributes

The values of an ordinal-scale attribute are sequence numbers (first, second, third, and so on) that impose an order on an entity's instances.

In Fragment 9-1, there is one ordinal-scale attribute, *place*.

An ordinal-scale attribute can contribute to an identifier.

Note that an ordinal-scale attribute does not necessarily impose an order over all the instances of an entity. An ordinal-scale attribute can order instances within groups. For example, in Fragment 9-2, the attribute *class* indicates which class (freshman, sophomore, junior, or senior) each student is in. The attribute *rank in class* indicates each student's ranking within his or her class. There is no absolute ranking of all the instances of the entity. Instead there are four separate rankings—one for each class.

When you encounter an ordinal-scale attribute, you should remember that there might be other shapes that are more faithful to the users' needs. These shapes include reflexive relationships. See the section "Sequence Data and Cyclic Sequence Data" in Chapter 12.

student
student ID
name
class
rank in class

Fragment 9-2

Shape: Boolean-Scale Attributes

The values of a Boolean-scale attribute are TRUE or FALSE. In Fragment 9-1, there is one Boolean-scale attribute, *fee paid flag*. Ordinarily, a Boolean-scale attribute does not contribute to an identifier.

Scale and Datatype

Although they refer to related concepts, "scale" and "datatype" are not synonyms. In an implemented system, two attributes that have the same scale might yield two variables or database columns with different datatypes. For example, the numeric-scale attribute *entry fee* might be implemented as an integer (or in a system that includes a primitive datatype for money, as "currency"), whereas the numeric-scale attribute *finish time in seconds* might be implemented as a real number because it is important to record each finish time very accurately—to fractions of seconds.

Conversely, an implemented system might accommodate different scales with the same datatype. For example, a system might use the integer datatype to store both the nominal-scale attribute *marathon ID* and the numeric-scale attribute *temperature*.

Now is a good time to think about WHAT vs. HOW. "Scale" matters when you think about WHAT is worth remembering. "Datatype" matters when you think about HOW to remember it in some implementation.

Mismatches between datatype and scale can induce sloppy, meaningless calculation. If a nominal-scale attribute is implemented with a numeric datatype, the DBMS or compiler will allow you to calculate meaningless values such as the product of two *marathon ID*s or the sum of two *team ID*s. Nevertheless, the convenience of using a numeric variable to accommodate a nominal-scale attribute often outweighs the potential confusion resulting from the scale/datatype mismatch. This point is important enough for you to hear it another way: A nominal attribute encoded with integers is still nominal scale. When faced with a scale/datatype mismatch, you can reduce the likelihood of performing meaningless calculations by choosing attribute names (and variable names in the attendant implemented system) that accurately reflect the scale.

Scale and Attribute Names

Try to give each attribute a name that makes the attribute's scale obvious. When an attribute's name reveals its scale, users are less likely to request (and programmers are less likely to perform) the meaningless calculations described in the previous section. For example, when naming an attribute that will serve as an arbitrary identifier for an entity, do not use a suffix of *_number*. Instead, use a suffix of *_ID*. Similarly, when naming an ordinal-scale attribute, use a suffix of *_sequence* or *_rank*.

It won't always be possible to make the name reveal the scale, because the user vocabulary will require that you use a name that does not meet this standard. For example, users will rightly insist on the attribute name *phone number*, even though phone numbers are nominal-scale data. The principle of respecting the user's vocabulary outweighs the principle of making an attribute's name reveal its scale.

Fine Distinctions of Scale

Although the finer distinctions of scale are a bit beyond the scope of this book, you should know the general principles for making these fine distinctions. The basic principle is this: A variable's scale allows some operations on its values and disallows others. Using this principle, you can classify numeric-scale attributes into two finer categories: arithmetic-scale attributes and interval-scale attributes. You make this fine distinction by thinking carefully about the division operation.

The values of arithmetic-scale attributes are numbers that can function as any operand of any arithmetic expression. Most notably, the value can be the denominator of a fraction. In Fragment 9-1, *finish time in seconds* is an arithmetic-scale attribute because it is meaningful to divide one entry's finish time by another entry's finish time. If you divide Isabella's finish time by Ferdinand's finish time to get a quotient of 2, you can say that Ferdinand went twice as fast as Isabella.

On the other hand, if such division yields a meaningless value, the attribute is not arithmetic scale; it is interval scale. In Fragment 9-1, *temperature* is an interval-scale attribute because it is meaningless to divide one marathon's temperature by another marathon's temperature. If one marathon's temperature is 32 degrees Fahrenheit and another's is 64 degrees Fahrenheit, it is wrong to say that the second marathon is "twice as hot" as the first.

Scale and Abstract Datatypes

As you make finer and finer distinctions of scale you will encounter some of the same issues encountered by programmers creating abstract datatypes. Although creation of abstract datatypes is beyond the scope of this book, we give here a brief example of an attribute whose scale might induce you to implement an abstract datatype.

Consider an attribute called *day of week,* whose seven legal values are Sunday, Monday, Tuesday, . . . , Saturday. Because each value is the name of a day of the week, you might reasonably conclude that the attribute's scale is nominal. But note that the values exist in a specific order; each value has exactly one predecessor and one successor. Perhaps the attribute's scale is ordinal.

While it may be convenient or useful to think of *day of week* as a nominal-scale attribute, that gives a somewhat incomplete view of things. It's best to think of it as a cyclic-scale attribute, a special case of an ordinal-scale attribute. A cyclic-scale attribute is an attribute whose legal values are finite and exist in a particular order that has no "lowest" element or "highest" element. By "no lowest element," we mean that there is no element without predecessor. Sunday might be the first day of the week, but it does have a predecessor: Saturday. Similarly, by "no highest element," we mean that there is no element without a successor. December might be the last month of the year, but it does have a successor: January.

Suppose that the order of the days of the week is important to your application.[1] Suppose further that the implementation system does not provide primitive operations for manipulating days of the week. For example, your system cannot answer questions like *What day is two days after Thursday?* In this situation, you might decide to implement an abstract datatype exposing both the nominal-scale characteristics of the data (i.e., the name of each day) and the cyclic-scale characteristics of the data (i.e., the predecessor and successor operators).

Summary of How Scale Restricts an Attribute

Remember, an attribute's scale restricts the following:

- **Mathematical operations.** For example, you can divide by an arithmetic-scale attribute, but you cannot divide by an interval-scale attribute.
- **LDS evolution.** For example, an entity including an ordinal-scale attribute can evolve to a shape including a reflexive one-one relationship.
- **Identification.** For example, it is very rare for a numeric-scale attribute to contribute to an identifier, but it is quite common for a nominal-scale attribute to contribute to an identifier.

---

[1] Suppose, for example, that your users are social scientists studying the effects of vacation time and scheduled nonwork days on daily workforce productivity. Among other things, the users hope to determine the effect of weekends on employee productivity and absenteeism patterns throughout the work week. To these users, "Tuesday" is more than merely the name of a day; it is a day that is two days after the weekend. It is significant that Friday is the day before the weekend. In short, these users care about the cycle of days of the week.

Exercises

1. Here are some possible suffixes for attribute names: *name, flag, title, payment, weight, gender, color, amount, place, rank, code, text, remark, description, ID, number, elevation, status, position, suffix.* You might, for example, have *creature_name* and *department_name.* For each suffix,
   a. State what scale an attribute with that suffix should have.
   b. Find (in this book or in real databases) or create several attributes with that suffix.
   c. Find or create with that suffix several attributes that are mistakes, and explain what the mistakes are.
2. Your friend Esther calls and says, *Look, we need help here at our university. We are building an LDS for courses and are trying to decide what to do about prerequisites of various kinds. In our legacy system we have prerequisites stored in a free-form VarChar field, and it's very difficult to search. What do you think we should do?*
   a. Determine what else, if anything, you need to know from Esther before you form an answer.
   b. Form a scale-based answer to Esther's question, making up as many attributes as you think she might need.
3. A user says, *No two chimps were born at the same time, and every chimp was born. So let's use birth_time as the identifier.*
   a. Determine what else, if anything, you need to know from the user before you reply.
   b. Form a response to the user, discussing the pros and cons of using this identifier.
4. Where you work (or in textbooks), find out what naming conventions exist for data, programs, forms, and so on.
   a. Critique the conventions for sensibility and completeness.
   b. Determine to what extent the conventions are followed.

10
Chapter

Two-Entity Shapes

Some shapes involve exactly two entities and some relationships. This chapter describes them.

Two Entities, One Relationship

Some shapes have one relationship between two entities.

One-many shapes
- Plain one-many relationship
- One-many relationship making a dependent or intersection entity
- One-many relationship making a collection entity

One-one shapes
- Plain one-one relationship
- One-one relationship making a subordinate entity
- *To-be* one-one relationship
- *Not-to-be* one-one relationship
- *To-be* one-one relationship making a subordinate entity
- Plain *to-be* one-one relationship
- Plain *not-to-be* one-one relationship
- *Not-to-be* one-one relationship making a subordinate entity

Many-many shapes
- Plain many-many relationship
- Many-many relationship making a collection entity

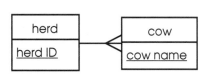

Fragment 10-1

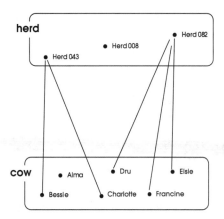

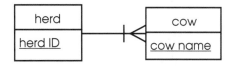

Fragment 10-2

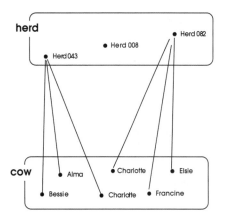

One-Many Shapes

Some shapes have a one-many relationship between two entities.

Shape: Plain One-Many Relationship

LDS Fragment 10-1 illustrates the plain (plain means "without bars") one-many shape, accompanied by sample data. The shape indicates the following:

- *About each cow, we can remember its name and herd.*
- *About each herd, we can remember its herd ID and cows.*
- *Each cow is identified by its name.*
- *Each herd is identified by its herd ID.*

The sample data illustrates some ramifications of the shape. Notice that each cow has a unique, nonnull name, that there is a cow (Alma) that belongs to no herd, and that there is a herd (Herd 008) containing no cows.

Shape: One-Many Relationship Making a Dependent or Intersection Entity

A one-many relationship can have a bar near the chicken foot. Fragment 10-2 shows an LDS similar to the previous one, with revised sample data. Notice that the sample data differs from the data for the plain one-many relationship: Every cow belongs to a herd, and two cows (e.g., the cows named Charlotte) can share a name (because those cows are in different herds). Notice also that Herd 008 contains no cows.

Fragment 10-3 is another example illustrating the same shape, along with some typical data. The shape indicates that each line item is identified by its order and its line number. Suppose we wanted to alter the LDS so that each line item is identified by its order and its product name. This identifier would prevent us from remembering any order that includes both black umbrellas and brown umbrellas. (Notice that the sample data shows both black and brown umbrellas.)

Notice that Order 1072 includes no line item. This is analogous to the sample for Fragment 10-1, in which Herd 008 contains no cow.

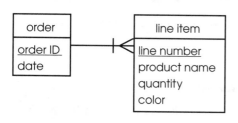

Fragment 10-3

Line no.	Product	Qty	Color
Order 1071, October 10, 1996			
1	gloves	1	black
2	umbrella	1	brown
3	hatbox	2	
Order 1072, October 10, 1996			
Order 1073, October 10, 1996			
1	galoshes	1	black
2	umbrella	1	black

For an example illustrating a one-many relationship with an intersection entity, see the relationship between *Skill* and *Achievement* in the section "Shape: Intersection Entity" in Chapter 8.

Shape: One-Many Relationship Making a Collection Entity

When a one-many relationship has a bar away from the chicken foot, it makes a **collection entity.** LDS fragments conforming to this shape are extremely rare. For a description of this shape, see the section "Shape: One-Many Collection Entity" in Chapter 8.

One-One Shapes

Some shapes have a one-one relationship between two entities. There are two ways to classify a one-one relationship:

1. Is the relationship *to-be* or *not-to-be?* An instance of a *to-be* relationship indicates an association between two different interpretations of the same thing. An instance of a *not-to-be* relationship indicates an association between two different things.
2. Is the relationship *plain,* or does it *make a subordinate entity?* A *plain* one-one relationship is a one-one relationship with no bars. A one-one relationship making a subordinate entity is a one-one relationship with a bar.

Next we present eight one-one relationship shapes, and then we address several issues that arise in thinking about one-one relationships.

Shape: Plain One-One Relationship

If a one-one relationship has no bar, it conforms to the shape called plain one-one relationship.

Shape: One-One Relationship Making a Subordinate Entity

If a one-one relationship has a bar on it, it conforms to the shape called one-one relationship making a subordinate entity.

Shape: *To-be* One-One Relationship

If a one-one relationship has both links labeled with *be,* it conforms to the shape called to-be one-one relationship.

Shape: *Not-to-be* One-One Relationship

If a one-one relationship has both links labeled with other than *be,* it conforms to the shape called not-to-be one-one relationship.

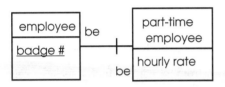

Fragment 10-4

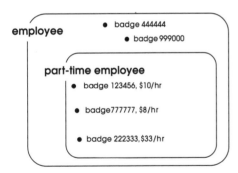

Shape: *To-be* One-One Relationship Making a Subordinate Entity

If a *to-be* one-one relationship has a bar, it makes a subordinate entity. For example, Fragment 10-4 indicates that each part-time employee is identified by its interpretation as an employee.

The accompanying sample data shows five instances of *employee.* Three of them are also *part-time employees.* It illustrates that each employee has a badge number, but only part-time employees have an hourly rate.

The layout of this sample data illustrates the subordinate aspect of this shape. One cannot be a *part-time employee* without also being an *employee.* In other words, the set of *employee* instances contains the set of *part-time employee* instances.

To master this shape, be sure to study the subordinates-out and subordinates-across shapes described in Chapter 11.

Shape: Plain *To-be* One-One Relationship

Fragment 10-5, with sample data, illustrates a plain to-be one-one relationship.

The sample data illustrates that some employees are also persons, that some persons are also employees, and that not every employee is a person. In other words, the set of *employee* instances overlaps the set of *person* instances.

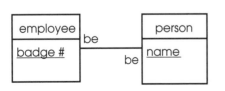

Fragment 10-5

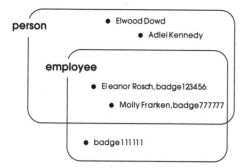

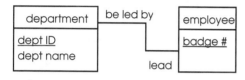

Fragment 10-6

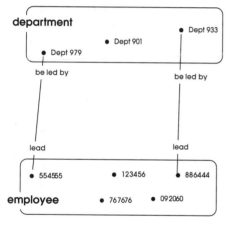

The reason why some employees are not persons is because the users are managers of a circus that employs some animals.

Shape: Plain *Not-to-be* One-One Relationship

Fragment 10-6 illustrates a plain not-to-be one-one relationship:

- Each employee can lead one department.
- Each department can be led by one employee.

The accompanying sample data illustrates that either link can be null. That is, a department can be without a leader (such as Department 901), and not every employee must lead a department.

When you encounter this shape on an in-progress LDS, scrutinize it. It is likely to evolve into a one-many relationship. For example, the LDS as shown indicates that no employee can lead two different departments. While this might seem reasonable, exceptional situations to the contrary can arise. For example, during job vacancies, a single employee could be called on to manage two departments.

Shape: *Not-to-be* One-One Relationship Making a Subordinate Entity

A not-to-be one-one relationship making a subordinate entity is syntactically correct and has occasionally appeared on an in-progress LDS. However, it has never survived scrutiny.

Fragment 10-7 illustrates this shape. Note that we use largely meaningless names because we have no real names to use. This shape can evolve into one like Fragment 10-8 or one like Fragment 10-9.

Thinking About One-One Relationship Shapes

We need to address three more issues in thinking about one-one relationships.

First, it might seem that relationships labeled with *be* are unnecessary, but it is not so. Consider again Fragment 10-4. The sample data shows that every part-time employee is an employee. Why not use a simpler fragment such as Fragment 10-10, thereby eliminating the one-one relationship altogether?

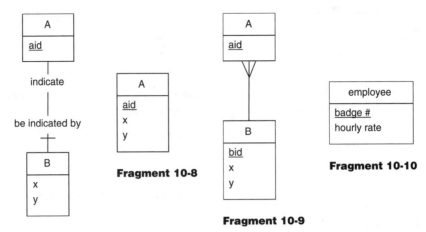

Fragment 10-8

Fragment 10-10

Fragment 10-9

Fragment 10-7

Although there are some justifications for using this simpler shape, the simpler LDS conceals some detail from the users who read the LDS. (Specifically, it conceals the fact that hourly rate applies only to persons who are part-time employees.) By neglecting to reveal this detail, the data modeler who created the simpler LDS has shifted the burden from the LDS to the users, who must now use some means other than the LDS to remember to whom hourly rate applies. There may be some situations in which the simpler, less accurate LDS is worth the irritation. But there are surely other situations in which the accuracy must prevail, so the option of a one-one relationship with the *be* link labels is necessary. Similarly, replacing Fragment 10-5 with a single entity called *person* would present to the users an oversimplified view of their data.

Second, the sample data for Fragment 10-5 shows that either link can be null. What if neither can be null? In that case, the two entities are describing exactly the same sets, and the two entity names are synonyms. The shape should evolve into a single entity. The entity's descriptors should include any descriptor that was in either of the two previous entities.

For example, Fragment 10-11 indicates that each job can be a task and each task can be a job. Suppose the users convince you that every task is a job and that every job is a task. In effect, the users are telling you that you that the words "task" and "job" are synonyms. You can replace Fragment 10-11 with either entity in Fragment 10-12. You should let the users decide between the two. By choosing one, they effectively choose which word they will continue to use.

Third, whenever you encounter any one-one relationship on an in-progress LDS, your first instinct should be to determine whether it is a *to-be* or a *not-to-be* relationship. If you learn that

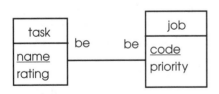

Fragment 10-11

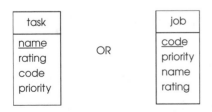

Fragment 10-12

it is a *not-to-be* relationship, your next instinct should be to learn whether it should evolve into a one-many relationship. (Remember, during controlled evolution, you should discuss the users' data in their own words. You should never use words like *not-to-be relationship* or *subordinate entity* in your discussions with users.)

Many-Many Shapes

Some shapes have a many-many relationship between two entities.

Shape: Plain Many-Many Relationship

Fragment 10-13 shows a plain many-many relationship, accompanied by some sample data. The LDS indicates that each product can contain several parts and each part can be contained in several products. Among other things,

- Product 45 has two parts.
- Product 52 has three parts.
- Product 18 has two parts.
- Part 8777 is in Product 45, Product 52, and Product 18.
- Part 2221 is in Product 52.
- Part 4321 is in no product.
- Part 5000 is in Product 45, Product 52, and Product 18.

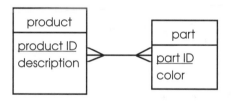

Fragment 10-13

	Part 2221	Part 8777	Part 4321	Part 5000
Product 45		X		X
Product 52	X	X		X
Product 18		X		X

Although legal, a many-many relationship rarely appears in a mature LDS. During controlled evolution (see Chapters 18 through 20), you will most likely evolve away from this shape, as the following example does.

Look at the sample data accompanying Fragment 10-14. Suppose that in each cell containing an X, the users want to write additional information. For example, suppose that Product 45 is a bicycle pump, but Product 52 is component of the space shuttle's climate control system. Although both products use Part 8777, they have different reliability and quality requirements. Thus users want to remember that Product 52 requires Part 8777 with a reliability of .99, whereas Product 45 requires Part 8777 with a reliability of .95. The modified sample data and the attendant LDS follow. The sample data shows that there are seven instances of the *product-assembly item* entity (because there are seven cells containing an X). Note that one instance of the entity has a null value for the reliability attribute: Product 18 requires Part 5000, but the reliability requirement is unknown or is not important.

	Part 2221	Part 8777	Part 4321	Part 5000
Product 45		X, .95		X, .95
Product 52	X, .99	X, .99		X, .99
Product 18		X, .95		X

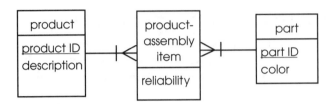

Fragment 10-14

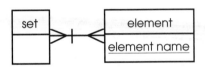

Fragment 10-15

Shape: Many-Many Relationship Making a Collection Entity

In Fragment 10-15, *set* is a collection entity. If a many-many relationship has a bar, it (probably[1]) makes a *collection entity*. This is very rare; it usually applies only to abstract situations.

To read more about this shape, see the section "Many-Many Collection Entities" in Chapter 8.

Two Entities, Two Relationships

Some shapes have two relationships between the same two entities.

If you illustrate sample data with instance diagrams (as in Figure 1-5 or as in the sample data accompanying Fragment 10-1), you need to use two different kinds of line for the instances of the different relationships.

Shape: Two One-One Relationships

Two entities can have two different one-one relationships. This is extremely rare; if you see this shape, you should expect it to evolve.

Only once in our data modeling have we seen this shape endure on an in-progress LDS. It is shown in Fragment 10-16.

---

[1] *Probably*, because there are some theoretically valid but unheard-of cases in which a multiple bar identifier includes a bar on a many-many relationship. See Chapter 13 for more information.

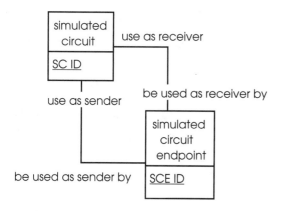

Fragment 10-16

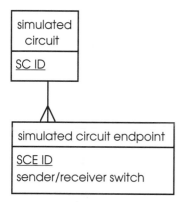

Fragment 10-17

In this case, we had to work to ensure that the users understood the instance data.

- Each instance of *simulated circuit endpoint* can be used as either the sender or the receiver of some simulated circuit, but not as both sender and receiver. In other words, no instance of the *simulated circuit endpoint* entity can have non-null values for both links.
- Each instance of *simulated circuit* must use one simulated circuit endpoint as a sender and another simulated circuit endpoint as a receiver.

It is worth noting that we considered replacing Fragment 10-16 with Fragment 10-17, which makes it clearer that each simulated circuit endpoint has at most one simulated circuit.

However, Fragment 10-17 forces the data modeler to make sure the users understand this aspect of the instance data:

- Each simulated circuit must have exactly two simulated circuit endpoints, and one of these two must be a sender and the other must be a receiver.

We rejected Fragment 10-17 for two reasons. First, we and the users agreed that the first shape was more helpful in reminding users about their data. Second, the users indicated that some simulated circuit endpoints can occasionally be unused by any simulated circuit. For such instances of simulated circuit endpoint, the sender/receiver switch is meaningless. That is, a simulated circuit endpoint is not inherently a sender or a receiver. It falls into one of those categories only when it is so employed by a simulated circuit.

Although we've never encountered it in our data models, it is valid for one of the relationships to be a *to-be* relationship, as in either Fragment 10-18 or Fragment 10-19. To stress the fact that we have never encountered either of these shapes in practice, Fragments 10-18 and 10-19 use meaningless names.

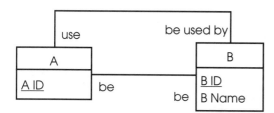

Fragment 10-18

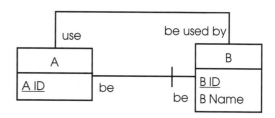

Fragment 10-19

One-One and One-Many Relationship

There are two ways in which two entities can have a one-one and a one-many relationship:

1. The one-one is a *not-to-be* relationship; this shape is called a *not-to-be* one-one relationship and a one-many relationship.
2. The one-one is a *to-be* relationship; this shape is called a *to-be* relationship and a one-many relationship.

Shape: *Not-to-be* One-One Relationship and One-Many Relationship

This shape is not unheard of, but it is uncommon merely because it uses a one-one relationship. Fragment 10-20 conforms to it.

When you design sample data for this shape, there are several noteworthy situations to explore. To explore these possibilities, consider these questions:

- Can an employee lead a department other than the department to which she belongs?

These are delayed-effect questions.

- Can an employee lead a department even if the employee belongs to no department?
- Can a department have an employee by whom it is led even if that department contains no employees?

We leave the exploration of these questions as an exercise for you.

Many database textbooks and user's guides for commercial database management systems illustrate one-one relationships with an example essentially equivalent to Fragment 10-20. The example is misleading. We have never encountered a moderate-sized business, organization, or institution whose data is accommodated by this fragment. Fragment 10-21 is much more realistic.

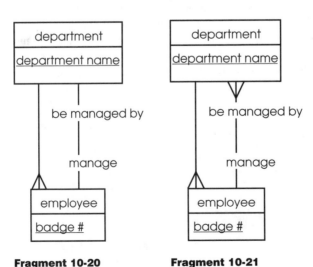

Fragment 10-20   **Fragment 10-21**

Shape: *To-be* Relationship and One-Many Relationship

An example of this shape is shown in Fragment 10-22. This shape is useful if there are descriptors that apply to managers but not to other employees.

Recognize the similarity between Fragment 10-22 and Fragment 10-23. Both shapes indicate that some employees can manage other employees and that each employee can be managed by one employee.

Also recognize the differences. Only Fragment 10-22 indicates that an employee can be considered a manager even if that employee does not manage any employees. (That is, Fragment 10-22 allows us to store an instance of the *manager* entity with a null value for the managed-employees link.)

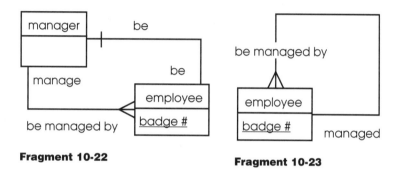

Fragment 10-22

Fragment 10-23

Two One-Many Relationships

There are two ways in which two entities can have two one-many relationships.

- If the chicken feet are at the same entity, this shape is called two same-direction one-many relationships.
- If the chicken feet are at different entities, this shape is called two opposite-direction one-many relationships.

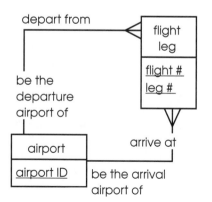

Fragment 10-24

Shape: Two Same-Direction One-Many Relationships

There are two uses for this shape. Because these two uses differ in so many respects, we discuss them separately in the next two sections.

Using Two Same-Direction One-Many Relationships for Directed Graphs

Fragment 10-24 accommodates data about an airline's flight schedule:

- Each airport can be the departure airport of flight legs and be the arrival airport of flight legs.
- Each flight leg can depart from one airport and arrive at one airport.

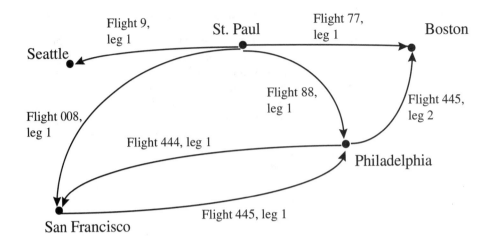

In the accompanying sample data, each dot represents an instance of the *airport* entity. Each arrow represents an instance of the *flight leg* entity.

This shape can evolve into other LDS fragments accommodating any of the following kinds of data:

- Multigraphs, in which each pair of points can have several same-direction directed arcs between them
- Forked-arc digraphs (directed graphs), in which each arc can terminate at more than one vertex
- Merging-arc digraphs, in which each arc can originate at more than one vertex
- Merging-and-forking-arc digraphs, in which each arc can have several originating vertices and several terminating vertices

This is a delayed-effect question.

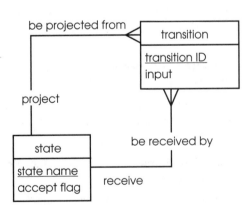

Fragment 10-25

When you design sample data or document this shape (see Chapter 17), be sure to consider the question *Can a flight leg arrive at the same airport from which it departs?* In the case of Fragment 10-24 the answer from users is probably no; no flight leg is scheduled to arrive at the same airport from which it departs. (But be careful about presuming too much. In a different context users might want to remember sight-seeing trips that do indeed land at the airport from which they take off.)

However, other applications of this shape might produce an affirmative answer to the corresponding question. For example, Fragment 10-25 accommodates data about

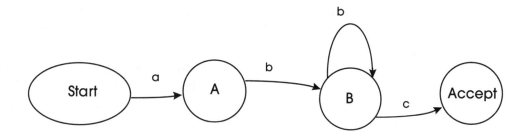

finite-state machines. The corresponding question to ask when designing sample data or when considering constraints is *Can an arrow be received by the same state from which it is projected?*

As the sample data shows, the answer to this question can be yes; there is a transition that starts and stops at state B.

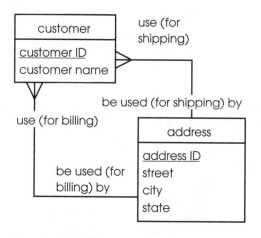

Fragment 10-26

This is a delayed-effect question.

Using Two Same-Direction One-Many Relationships for Nongraph Data

Fragment 10-26 accommodates data about customers and the various addresses customers use for various parts of their operations:

- Each address can be used by many customers for billing.
- Each address can be used by many customers for shipping.
- Each customer can use one address for billing.
- Each customer can use one address for shipping.

Do not try to visualize nongraph data as a graph. Although Fragments 10-24 and 10-26 have the same shape, only Fragment 10-24 accommodates graph data. If you try to visualize Fragment 10-26 as graph data, a confusing diagram will result. (In any such diagram, each arrow will correspond to a customer. But how would you represent customers who have no shipping address? And in which direction should the arrow point—toward the shipping address or toward the billing address?)

When you design sample data for this shape, be sure to consider the question *Can an address be used as a shipping address and a billing address by the same customer?*

The following shapes are similar to the shape called two same-direction one-many relationships:

- **Chicken feet in.** Notice that the entity near the chicken feet conforms to the chicken-feet-in shape. For example, in Fragment 10-26, the customer entity has two chicken feet in (see Chapter 11).

- **Multiple short paths.** Notice that the two relationships constitute two short (very short) paths between the two entities.

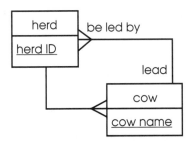

Fragment 10-27

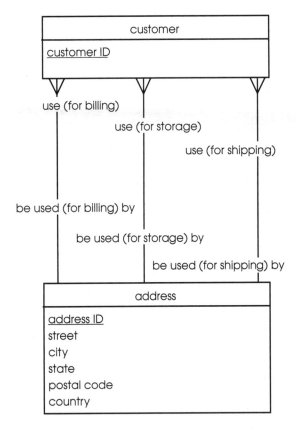

Fragment 10-28

Shape: Two Opposite-Direction One-Many Relationships

This shape is not uncommon; an example is shown in Fragment 10-27. This LDS fragment employs the same shape as Fragment 10-21.

Shape: Many-Many Relationship Plus Some Other Relationships

Two entities can be connected by two many-many relationships or by a many-many relationship plus a one-many or one-one relationship. However, such an LDS fragment does not endure for long on a typical LDS because many-many relationships quickly evolve into other shapes.

Two Entities, *n* Relationships

Two entities can have several relationships. Fragment 10-28 shows three one-many relationships between the same two entities. The fragment indicates that each customer can have up to three addresses: a billing address, a storage address, and a shipping address. It also indicates that each address can be used by many customers. What's more, each address can be used as a billing address, as a shipping address, as a storage address, or as any combination. For example, in the accompanying sample data, "200 Warehouse Rd." is used by two companies as their storage address; "10 Main St." is used by one company as both its shipping address and its billing address and by another company as its billing address.

Compare Fragment 10-28 with Fragment 10-29. They have identical shapes, but Fragment 10-29 constitutes an inappropriate use of the shape. To see why the fragment is wrong, compare the fragment's assertions to the users' understanding of their data.

Customer: **ACME**

Shipping	10 Main St.
Billing	10 Main St.
Storage	200 Warehouse Rd.

Customer: **EZPROJECTS**

Shipping	200 Warehouse Rd.
Billing	10 Main St.
Storage	202 Warehouse Rd.

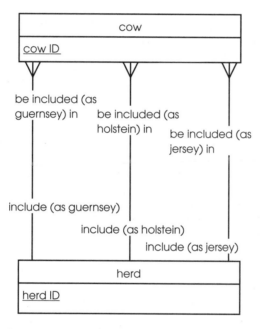

Fragment 10-29

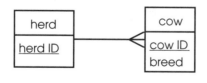

Fragment 10-30

- Users (dairy farmers) indicate that each herd can contain guernsey cows, holstein cows, and jersey cows. The fragment accommodates this understanding—so far, so good.

- Users indicate that each cow has only one breed. The LDS fragment falsely suggests that a cow can assume several breeds, provided that the cow is included in several herds. Here the LDS fragment is not faithful to the users' understanding of their data. (The LDS fragment also erroneously indicates that a cow can be in as many as three herds.)

- Users indicate that a cow can have a breed even if it does not belong to a herd. Here, too, the LDS is not faithful to the users; it falsely suggests that a cow has a breed only because it belongs to a herd.

Based on these user indications, Fragment 10-30 is more faithful to the dairy farmers' needs. Notice that a cow can have a breed even if it does not have a herd and that a cow has at most one breed.

On an in-progress LDS, you might find several many-many relationships between the same two entities, as in Fragment 10-31.

You might be tempted to replace this fragment with Fragment 10-32. You should make such a replacement only after careful consideration. More specifically, before making such a replacement, consider each many-many

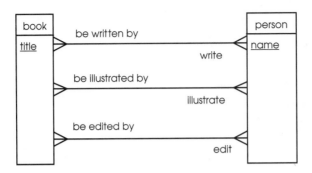

Fragment 10-31

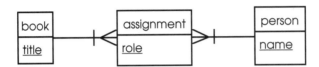

Fragment 10-32

relationship in turn to determine if that particular relationship should evolve into an intersection entity.

(For more information about intersection entities, see Chapter 8. For more information about replacing many-many relationships with intersection entities, see Chapter 18. For more information about shapes similar to Fragment 10-31, see the section "Multiple Short Paths" in Chapter 11.)

Exercises

1. For each two-entity shape,
   a. Create an example that fits the shape.
   b. Provide sample data.
   c. Determine what questions you would ask users about the shape.
2. Repeat question 1 until you are confident that you thoroughly know each shape.
3. For each state in Chapter 18, determine which two-entity shapes apply.

11
Chapter

Shapes with More Than Two Entities

Some shapes involve more than two entities and two or more relationships. This chapter describes them:

- Chicken feet in
- Chicken feet out
- Chicken feet across
- Subordinates out
- Subordinates across
- Multiple to-be relationships
- Multiple short paths

Shape: Chicken Feet In

If an entity has two or more degree-one links of one-many relationships, the entity participates in the chicken-feet-in shape—so named because there are many chicken feet touching the entity. The most common form of chicken feet in has three entities, as in Fragments 11-1 through 11-5.

From these fragments, notice the following:

- The presence or absence of bars does not affect whether a fragment exhibits the chicken-feet-in shape.
- Each fragment exhibits the characteristics of a state in The Flow (see Chapter 18).

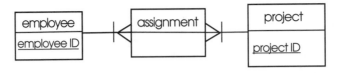

Fragment 11-1

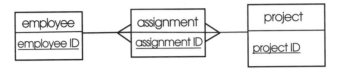

Fragment 11-2

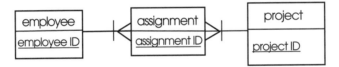

Fragment 11-3

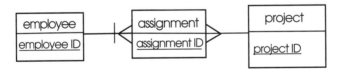

Fragment 11-4

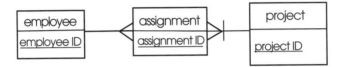

Fragment 11-5

- The chicken-feet-in shape consists of multiple occurrences of a smaller, more fundamental shape—the one-many relationship shape. Thus you can interpret chicken feet in merely by understanding all of its constituent parts.

The chicken-feet-in shape can have more than three entities. For example, Fragment 7-8 shows five entities that collectively exhibit the shape.

There are special cases of chicken feet in involving only two entities. For example, a fragment exhibits the chicken-feet-in shape if it exhibits either of these shapes:

- two same-direction one-many relationships shape (Fragments 10-24 through 10-26)
- two entities, *n* relationships shape with several one-many relationships in the same direction (Fragment 10-28)

Because the chicken-feet-in shape is composed of smaller, more fundamental shapes, all the fundamental LDS-reading skills apply to it. But there is an additional way to read the shape that is especially helpful to confused users. For an illustration of this reading technique, see the discussion of Fragments 7-6 through 7-8.

Shape: Chicken Feet Out

If an entity has two or more degree-many links of one-many relationships, the entity participates in the chicken-feet-out shape—so named because there are many chicken feet near the various describing entities. The simplest form of chicken feet out has three entities, as in Fragments 11-6 through 11-9.

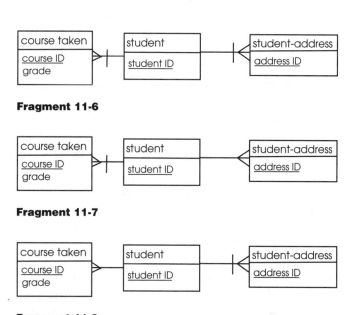

Fragment 11-6

Fragment 11-7

Fragment 11-8

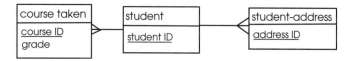

Fragment 11-9

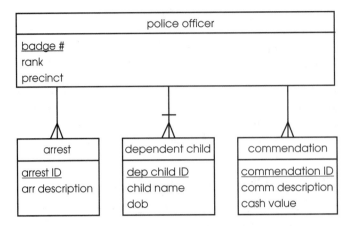

Fragment 11-10

In these fragments, notice the following:

- The presence or absence of bars does not affect whether a fragment exhibits the chicken-feet-out shape.
- The chicken-feet-out shape consists of multiple occurrences of a smaller, more fundamental shape—the one-many relationship shape. Thus you can interpret chicken feet out merely by understanding all of its constituent parts.

The chicken-feet-out shape can have more than three entities. For example, Fragment 11-10 shows four entities that collectively exhibit the shape.

There are special cases of chicken feet out involving only two entities. For example, a fragment exhibits the chicken-feet-out shape if it exhibits either of these shapes:

- two same-direction one-many relationships shape (e.g., Fragments 10-24 through 10-26)
- two entities, *n* relationships shape with several one-many relationships in the same direction (e.g., Fragment 10-28)

Because the chicken-feet-out shape is composed of smaller, more fundamental shapes, all the fundamental LDS-reading skills apply to it. But you should be able to recognize this shape anyway. Detecting this shape helps you recognize pivotal entities—entities that are of primary importance to the users' enterprise. In Fragment 11-10, a pivotal entity is *police officer*. Once you recognize a pivotal entity, you can anticipate how the LDS might evolve. For more information, see the section "Flow Investigation: Discover Relationship" in Chapter 18.

Avoid this error. Interpreting the chicken-feet-out shape, users (and novice modelers) sometimes overestimate the significance of the short path between the nonpivotal entities. For example, users encountering Fragment 11-10 might erroneously conclude that it accommodates some association between particular *arrests* and particular *commendations*. To make sure that users do not make such mistakes, you can do two things.

First, be sure to visualize sample data. Show how a particular <u>set</u> of *commendations* can have something in common (the police officer) with a particular <u>set</u> of *arrests*. Point out that there is no specific association between individual elements of the sets—between a specific arrest and a specific commendation.

Second, explicitly seek a relationship between *commendation* and *arrest*. See the section "Flow Investigation: Discover Relationship" in Chapter 18.

Shape: Chicken Feet Across

If an entity has a degree-many link of a one-many relationship and a degree-one link of a one-many relationship, the entity participates in the chicken-feet-across shape— so named because you can arrange the three entities on the diagram so that the chicken feet all face in the same direction. The simplest form of chicken feet across has three entities, as in Fragments 11-11 through 11-14.

From these fragments, notice the following:

• The presence or absence of bars does not affect whether a fragment exhibits the chicken-feet-across shape.

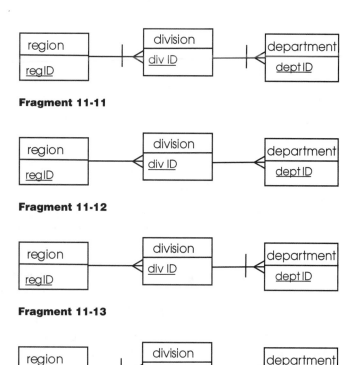

Fragment 11-11

Fragment 11-12

Fragment 11-13

Fragment 11-14

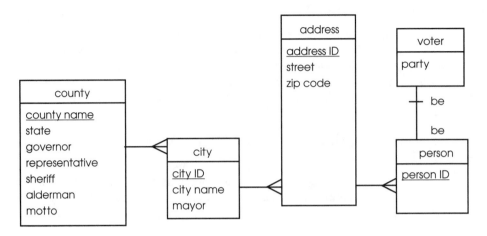

Fragment 11-15

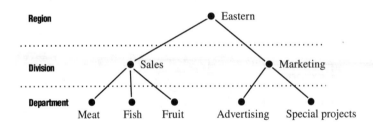

- The chicken-feet-across shape consists of multiple occurrences of a smaller, more fundamental shape—the one-many relationship shape. Thus you can interpret chicken feet across merely by understanding all of its constituent parts.

The chicken-feet-across shape can have more than three entities. For example, Fragment 11-15 shows four entities that collectively exhibit the shape. The four are *county, city, address,* and *person.*

Because the chicken-feet-across shape is composed of smaller, more fundamental shapes, all the fundamental LDS-reading skills apply to it. But you should be able to recognize this shape anyway, for several reasons. First, detecting this shape gives you a chance to discover and remedy LDS errors known as too-fine descriptor misplacement and too-coarse descriptor misplacement (see Chapter 19).

Second, detecting this shape gives you a chance to visualize data as a tree in which each level of the tree corresponds to instances of a particular entity. The accompanying figure shows instance data for Fragment 11-11.

Third, facility with this shape will help you model taxonomies, a form of data common to almost all enterprises. For more information, see Chapter 26.

Shape: Subordinates Out

If an entity has two to-be relationships with bars near the describing entities, the entity participates in the subordinates-out shape. Fragment 11-16 exhibits the subordinates-out shape.

The subordinates-out shape can have more than three entities, as in Fragment 11-17.

The subordinates-out shape consists of multiple occurrences of smaller, more fundamental shapes—the *to-be* relationship shape and the one-one relationship making a subordinate entity shape. Thus you can interpret subordinates out merely by understanding all of its constituent parts.

Shape: Subordinates Across

If an entity has a second entity subordinate to it and is itself subordinate to a third, it participates in the subordinates-across shape. Fragment 11-18 exhibits the subordinates-across shape.

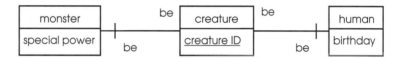

Fragment 11-16

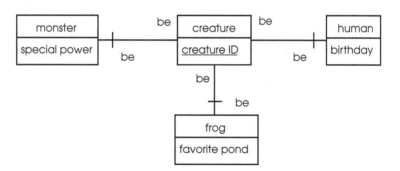

Fragment 11-17

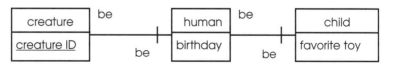

Fragment 11-18

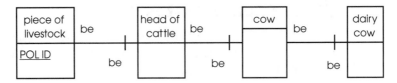

Fragment 11-19

The subordinates-across shape can have more than three entities, as in Fragment 11-19, which unrealistically includes few descriptors.

The subordinates-out shape consists of multiple occurrences of smaller, more fundamental shapes—the *to-be* relationship shape and the one-one relationship making a subordinate entity shape. Thus you can interpret subordinates out merely by understanding all of its constituent parts.

Shape: Multiple Plain *To-be* Relationships

If an entity has two plain *to-be* relationships, it participates in the multiple plain *to-be* relationships shape. Fragment 11-20 exhibits the shape.

The multiple plain *to-be* relationships shape can have more than three entities, as in Fragment 11-21.

The multiple plain *to-be* relationships shape consists of multiple occurrences of smaller, more fundamental shapes—the *to-be* relationship shape and the plain one-one relationship shape. Thus you can interpret it merely by understanding all of its constituent parts.

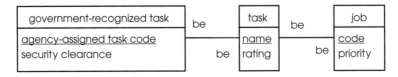

Fragment 11-20

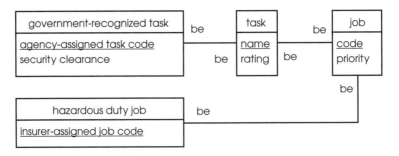

Fragment 11-21

Shape: Multiple *To-be* Relationships

The three preceding shapes—subordinates out, subordinates across, and multiple plain *to-be* relationships—are all special cases of a more generic shape: multiple *to-be* relationships. If an entity has any two *to-be* relationships, it participates in this shape. Fragments 11-16 through 11-22 all exhibit it.

Notice that Fragment 11-22 does not conform to any of the more specific shapes.

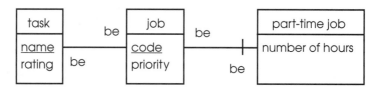

Fragment 11-22

It is worth recognizing these shapes for several reasons. First, detecting the shapes lets you visualize instances as overlapping sets. This visualization technique is shown in the two illustrations accompanying Fragment 10-5.

Second, detecting some of these shapes gives you a chance to anticipate how the LDS will evolve in a particular way. For more information, read the section "Collapsing Subordinates Out" in Chapter 20.

Third, detecting these shapes gives you a chance to assess the overall quality of the LDS. Remember, one-one relationships are rare. For more information, see the section "Assessing the Overall Style of an LDS" in Chapter 20.

Shape: Multiple Short Paths

If there is a set of entities *A, B, C, D, . . .* in which *A* is related to *B, B* is related to *C, C* is related to *D,* and so on, the entities and their intervening relationships are said to form a **path.** The length of a path is the number of relationships on it. For example, Fragment 11-1 shows a path of length 2 and Fragment 11-19 shows a path of length 3.

Sometimes it is useful to think of a path as a whole. For example, the chicken-feet-across shape can exist along a path. In Fragment 11-15, there is a chicken-feet-across path of length 3 (between *county* and *person*).

If several noteworthy paths exist between a given pair of entities, the entities are said to exhibit the multiple short paths shape. For example, Fragment 11-23 trivially exhibits the shape. (We say trivially because all the paths are identical and have length equal to one.)

The multiple short paths shape is especially interesting when the paths look very similar, as in Fragment 11-23. Such fragments let you anticipate how the LDS might evolve (see Chapter 20).

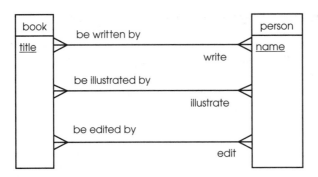

Fragment 11-23

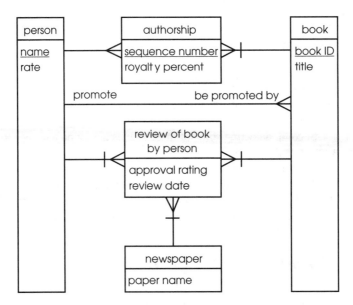

Fragment 11-24

Even when the paths do not look similar, there is some benefit to detecting the multiple short paths shape. For example, consider Fragment 11-24 containing three paths between *book* and *person*.

The fragment makes evident several ways that persons can contribute to or interact with books. Once you see so many paths, you know to seek more—to inquire of users, *What else can a person do to a book?* You might discover that persons can also edit, recommend, illustrate, and abridge books.

Detecting multiple short paths also lets you visualize the entire shape with a single illustration. For example, the table accompanying Fragment 7-14 would work here.

There is one more benefit to detecting this shape despite the differences among the various short paths. By comparing and contrasting the paths for the users, you can help the users understand the ramifications of the various decisions each individual path represents. For example, by comparing the top and bottom paths of Fragment 11-24, you can help the users grasp the difference between the two-part identifier of *authorship* and the three-part identifier of *review of book by person.*

Exercises

1. For each three-or-more-entities shape,
   a. Create an example that fits the shape.
   b. Provide sample data.
   c. Determine what questions you would ask users about the shape.
2. Repeat question 1 until you are confident that you thoroughly know each shape.

12 Chapter

Shapes with Reflexive Relationships

A reflexive relationship is a relationship connecting an entity to itself. A reflexive relationship can be one-one, one-many, or many-many.

Shape: One-One Reflexive Relationship

A reflexive relationship can be a one-one relationship. For example, LDS Fragment 12-1 indicates the following:

- Each student can tutor one student.
- Each student can be tutored by one student.

Whenever you see a reflexive one-one relationship on an LDS, your first instinct should be to see if it is missing a chicken foot. In most cases, the users will indicate that the reflexive one-one relationship should evolve into a one-many. When you first encounter Fragment 12-1 during controlled evolution, for example, you should ask the users the following questions:

- *Can a student tutor more than one student?*
- *Can a student be tutored by more than one student?*

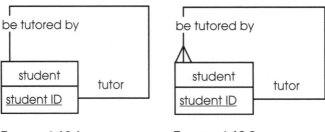

Fragment 12-1   **Fragment 12-2**

If the users say yes to the first question and no to the second, you should replace Fragment 12-1 with Fragment 12-2.

If they say yes to the second question only, you should add a chicken foot at the other end of the reflexive relationship. If they say yes to both questions, you should add two chicken feet.

Even if the users say no to both questions you ask during controlled evolution of a reflexive one-one relationship, you still have more work to do. Specifically, you must determine what the sample data looks like. To investigate the sample data, it is most helpful to visualize a graph in which each vertex represents an instance of the entity and each edge represents an instance of the reflexive relationship. For example, the following graph shows some sample data for Fragment 12-1.

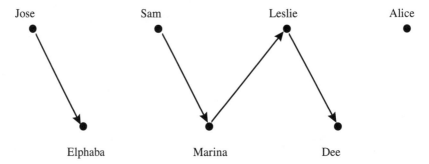

This diagram uses directed edges to indicate which student tutors the other. The arrows point from the tutoring student to the tutored student. In the diagram, notice that each student can tutor at most one student (because each vertex has at most one emerging arrow). Similarly, because each vertex has at most one incoming arrow, each student can be tutored by at most one student. Notice that a student can both tutor and be tutored. (Marina does both and Leslie does both.)

The data can take on several forms:

- Sequence data
- Cyclic sequence data
- Ordered pairs

These forms are described in the next sections.

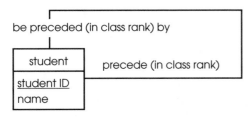

Fragment 12-3

ID	Name	Rank
111	Susan Smith	1
222	Leo Ursinus	2
555	Stanislau Wong	3
777	Ian Bhutto	4
888	Fred Alison	5

Sequence Data and Cyclic Sequence Data

When an entity has a one-one reflexive relationship, the data might be sequence data. For example, Fragment 12-3 accommodates data about students and their class rank (first in class, second in class, and so on). Typical sample data is given in the accompanying table.

As already stated, it helps to visualize data about reflexive relationships using graphs, so here is the same data in another format.

●――――――▶● ――――――▶● ――――――▶● ――――――▶●

Susan	Leo	Stanislau	Ian	Fred
Smith	Ursinis	Wong	Bhutto	Alison
(111)	(222)	(555)	(777)	(888)

Notice that the graph has no cycles. This is a characteristic of sequence data, but it is not a characteristic of the shape using a one-one reflexive relationship. In other words, you can use the shape to accommodate data that allows cycles.

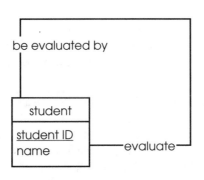

Fragment 12-4

For example, consider LDS Fragment 12-4. It indicates that each student can evaluate one student and be evaluated by one student. Following is some sample data using the same students as the preceding example:

- Susan evaluates Leo.
- Leo evaluates Stanislau.
- Stanislau evaluates Ian.
- Ian evaluates Fred.
- Fred evaluates Susan.

Once again, viewing the data as a graph makes the noteworthy characteristics (cycles) obvious.

When a one-one reflexive relationship accommodates data with cycles, the data is called *cyclic sequence data*. Notice that the sample data contains a single large cycle. However, multiple small cycles are possible.

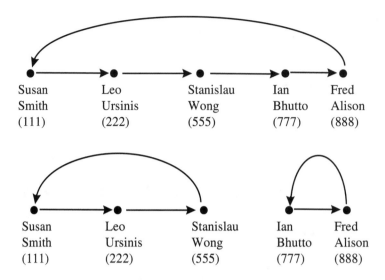

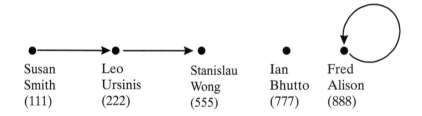

In fact, the one-one reflexive shape even accommodates cycles of length one (as in Fred, following). And, of course, either of the links in an instance can be null (as in Susan, evaluated by no one, and Stanislau, evaluating no one) or both of the links can be null (as in Ian, who neither evaluates nor is evaluated).

Because the one-one reflexive shape can accommodate all of these possibilities, you must ask the users the following questions to ensure that you and they understand the data fully:

These are delayed-effect questions.

- *Can an instance be related to itself?* For example, can a student evaluate himself or herself?
- *Can one of the links be null?* For example, can a student evaluate no one?
- *Can the other link be null?* For example, can a student be evaluated by no one?
- *Can both links be null?* For example, can a student neither evaluate nor be evaluated by anyone?

Just as cyclic sequence data can have multiple disjoint loops, sequence data can have multiple disjoint sequences. For example, consider Fragment 12-5. There can be several sequences because there are several classes, and students are ranked within their respective class. If there are three classes, there are three separate lists:

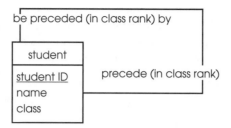

Fragment 12-5

- Sophomores: Susan, Leo, Stanislau, Ian, Fred
- Juniors: Pat, Lee, Leslie, Drake
- Seniors: Paul, Gloria, Drucinda, Chip

Once again, visualizing the data as a graph makes the noteworthy characteristic (multiple disjoint sequences) manifestly clear.

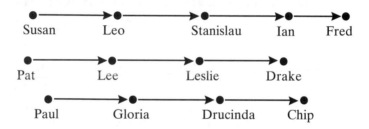

Compare Fragments 12-3 and 12-6. The shapes are quite similar in the data they can accommodate. However, there are differences.

A quick exercise: Write a paragraph describing the differences between the data accommodated by Fragments 12-3 and 12-6. Sketch out some sample data that is accommodated by Fragment 12-3 but not by Fragment 12-6. Sketch out some sample data that is accommodated by Fragment 12-6 but not by Fragment 12-3.

Fragment 12-6

Ordered Pairs

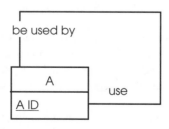

Fragment 12-7

When an entity has a one-one reflexive relationship, the data might be ordered pairs of entity instances (e.g., Fragment 12-7 and its accompanying sample data). However, we've never encountered any ordered-pair data for which a one-one reflexive relationship was the final shape.

In the sample data, each arrow points from the using item to the used item. For example, G uses H, but it is not the case that H uses G. To stress the fact that we have never seen this in practice, the LDS and sample data use meaningless names and data values. We have encountered ordered pairs in our data modeling, but we have never encountered a situation in which a one-one reflexive relationship was the most faithful way to represent the data. For more information about representing ordered pairs, see Chapter 26.

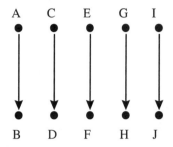

Shape: One-Many Reflexive Relationship

A reflexive relationship can be a one-many relationship. For example, Fragment 12-8 indicates the following:

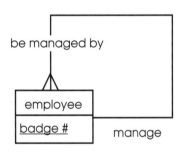

Fragment 12-8

- Each employee can manage employees.
- Each employee can be managed by one employee.

Whenever you see a reflexive one-many relationship on an LDS, your first instinct should be to see if it is missing a chicken foot. In some cases, the users will indicate that the reflexive one-many relationship should evolve into a many-many. When you first encounter Fragment 12-8 during controlled evolution, therefore, you should ask the users, *Can an employee be managed by several employees?*

If the users say yes, you should replace Fragment 12-8 with Fragment 12-9.

What if the users say neither yes nor no? That is, what if a user who is especially good at making distinctions says, *Not at any one time.* That is, the user indicates that at any one time, each employee has at most one managing employee, but throughout the course of an employee's entire career, that employee can have many different managers.

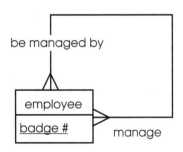

Fragment 12-9

Such a user is thinking hard about what is worth remembering. The user is making an effort to ensure that you understand the distinctions that are important to her. By providing such a detailed answer to a seemingly simply yes-or-no question, the user is helping you do your job.

But what if you do not have such a helpful user? Consider the worst-case scenario, in which each of the following facts holds:

- At any one time, each employee can be managed by one employee.
- The users indeed consider it worthwhile to remember the history of management within the company—including for each employee an indication of every person who managed that employee.
- When you ask the question *Can any employee have more than one manager?* the users say no.

When the users say no, they indicate that the one-many relationship (of Fragment 12-8) does not need to evolve into a many-many relationship. The users are not thinking about history, and you need to encourage them to do so. You need to ask a more probing question, to encourage the users to think about the finer distinctions—specifically the finer distinction that we call the "history problem."

We want to be especially clear. Your job is to ensure that the users consider the history problem. Ask a probing question to ensure that their answer reflects such consideration; your job is not to persuade users to deem history worth remembering. After you ask the probing question, if the users still indicate that about each employee they want to remember only one managing employee, then you have done your job.

Even if the users say no, indicating that the reflexive relationship should remain a one-many relationship, you still have more work to do. Specifically you must determine what the sample data looks like. As with reflexive relationships that are one-one, graphs can help you visualize the data. For example, the following graph shows some sample data for Fragment 12-8.

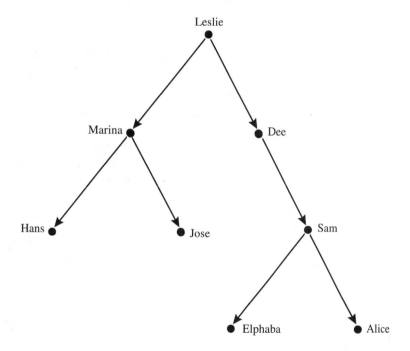

The arrows point from the managing employee to the managed employee. In the diagram, notice that each employee can be managed by at most one employee (because each vertex has at most one incoming edge). However, notice that a vertex can have several emerging edges—according to Fragment 12-8, each employee can manage many employees.

The graph makes it clear that the data is a tree with the vertex representing Leslie as the root. In our experience, users are comfortable thinking of their data as trees and visualizing it this way. However, we have noticed that users sometimes overlook these other possibilities:

- The data is a forest (of trees). That is, the data constitutes several separate trees. In other words, there are several persons with no manager. Notice that in the preceding diagram, only Leslie is unmanaged.
- The data is not a tree. That is, the data contains cycles.

This is a delayed-effect question.

Because a one-many reflexive relationship can accommodate trees, forests, and cyclic data and because users tend to overlook the latter two possibilities, you should be prepared to ask them questions to determine whether cycles are allowed and whether the data is a single, connected graph or several disconnected graphs.

A quick exercise: Suppose the users tell you the following about Fragment 12-8:

- Each employee <u>must</u> be managed by some employee.
- The graph of this data contains no cycles.

How do you respond?

Shape: Many-Many Reflexive Relationship

A reflexive relationship can be a many-many relationship. For example, LDS Fragment 12-10 shows a many-many reflexive relationship.

When you see a many-many reflexive relationship on an in-progress LDS, your first instinct should be to treat the relationship like any other many-many relationship: See if it should evolve into an intersection entity.

Remember, a many-many relationship evolves into an intersection entity when there are other descriptors that are worth remembering. Fragment 12-11 shows that each person's admiration of another person has an intensity, such as "great admiration" or "moderate admiration."

This is a very rare shape.

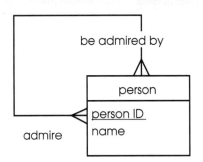

Fragment 12-10

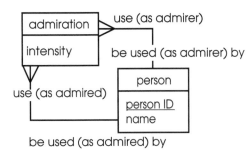

Fragment 12-11

For more information, see the section "Flow Stages: Initial Many-Many Relationship and New Intersection Entity" in Chapter 18.

Exercises

1. For each reflexive relationship shape,
    a. Create an example that fits the shape.
    b. Provide sample data.
    c. Determine what questions you would ask users about the shape.
2. Repeat question 1 until you are confident that you thoroughly know each shape.
3. In Chapter 26, determine which reflexive relationship shapes apply to each recipe.

Story Interlude

Real Users Will Surprise You

At a company X training session, I had just said, *Content-neutral data modelers can model just about anything.* Naturally the reaction was *Show me.* Right then some noise in the hallway got my attention. A man was filling the vending machines and writing on paper. I called a timeout and talked to him for a bit. He had to fill out a report for each stop on his route. When I asked him if I could copy his form, he offered me a blank form. I asked instead to copy the one he had just filled out.

As we reverse engineered, we found that the form had labeled regions filled in with text and numbers (28 cans of diet cola) plus a surprise. The surprise was handwritten text splashed diagonally across the form: "Refund: $1.75." The form was inadequate for his business so he sensibly augmented it as needed. Without talking to a real user doing real work we would have built a wrong-boundary LDS.

Moral: *Interview real users who do real work.*

Yes-and-No Answer 1

Here is a story with a moral you have seen before.

With a team of University X employees I was building a model for a system to track student progress toward degrees. I asked a shape-based question and heard yes and no from a pair of users (Claire and Patty). They dropped out of the conversation and began energetically whispering to each other. After a bit I called a timeout and asked them what was going on.

They had just discovered via data modeling that, although they had adjacent desks and performed the same job, they unknowingly had significantly different ideas about one part of the job. (The difference: See Patty and you graduate; see Claire and you don't.) They turned their chagrin into a positive attitude and became totally engaged users.

Moral: *Users learn a lot during data modeling.*

Yes-and-No Answer 2

I was at company X running an LDS meeting for a project with the task of supporting ab initio computing of molecule performance—heavy-duty science. I asked a shape-based question and got yes and no at the same time from two different research chemists. That was not a surprise, but what happened next was. They began fairly seriously mocking each other, saying, *You theorists never get anything done* and *Your kind are sloppy so we cannot trust your results.* They belonged to different camps that had strong, conflicting opinions about what it means to do good chemistry.

We worked out a way to model data that suited both, but if I had talked to just one of them, I would have produced a model that the other would have rejected.

This and similar yes/no experiences raise *Ask several users* to the level of a good habit.

Moral: *Talking to just one user is perilous.*

No Answer at All

Julia, a student in an industrial training class at company X, came to me during a break and said she had a problem. Her boss had told her that after the class was over she had to build a data model. Some high-level person in the funding agency had given the company money to begin this project, but there were no requirements and no users to talk to. Julia was supposed to figure it out on her own.

The content of the project was like another one I had been close to, so I put on my fake user hat and told her the least inclusive answers and the most inclusive answers she could have expected from users. We both felt like charlatans.

Julia left the company before she could be embarrassed by the project's certain failure.

Moral: *No users, no model.*

No Question, So No Answer

While visiting company X, I met a new consulting team, whose leader said, *We use a special programming paradigm called such-and-such; we do not need to talk to users; we'll give them what they need.* After several hundred thousand dollars was squandered, company X's management came to its senses and fired the consultants.

Moral: *Technologists can become so enamored of a programming technique that they assume it has mysterious powers, but the fact remains: No users, no model.*

Yes-and-No Answer 3

At company X, I was running an LDS meeting that was a resumption of one that had begun a day or so earlier. Two users began disagreeing on almost everything—lots of simultaneous yes/no answers. Finally, one of them said, *Well, what are we trying to do anyway?* At that point I realized that I had made a mistake of omission. I failed to reframe the meeting by reminding them that we were setting out to model the current system first. Only later would we determine what changes were needed for the future system. Once I did what should have been done, things settled down, and we began to get consensus decisions again.

Here is another story with the same moral.

Nancy, a graduate student, was doing some really cool research that I wanted to know more about. So we began to build an LDS. For a while things went well, but when I revisited an entity, trying to deepen my understanding, Nancy would decide to call it something else. After a while we both were frazzled and stopped. Only later did I realize that Nancy and I had different ideas about the purpose of our meeting. I was trying to build an LDS to understand how she saw her work. She thought I didn't understand what she said so she started paraphrasing and drawing analogies, neither of which made for good modeling.

She dumbed down the model so that I could understand it because I failed to make clear what the goal was.

Moral: *Clarify intent and be alert for shifting purpose.*

Yes-and-No Answer 4

At company X, I was running a training/consulting session. (Beforehand they sent me documentation of an existing system that the trainees knew—and were disenchanted with. I reverse engineered and produced a model and a list of questions. Then we examined my model as part of their training.) I asked a shape-based question: *Can an employee manage more than one department?* and got yes and no at the same time—not a surprise. Several of the students made faces at Leo, the one who said no. It turned out that Leo himself was the instance that led the others to say yes because right then Leo was managing two departments. While he was an energetic, caring manager, he did not see the importance of one versus many for data modeling.

Moral: *Users must learn the necessity of precision.*

Yes-and-No Answer 5

At company X, I was observing an LDS meeting. The modeler asked a shape-based question. Every user except Frank said no. Frank explained, *Well, it's not so simple,* and went to the board. In 10 minutes drew an example that made everyone realize that not only was he an expert, but he also could clearly describe the complexity of the model's content.

As time went on, the modelers formed the habit of going to Frank for a sanity check on the models they built with other users.

Moral: *Some users can make fine distinctions that improve an LDS's quality.*

13
Chapter

LDS Syntax Rules

This chapter gives the LDS syntax rules to which every LDS must conform. If an LDS fails to conform, it is meaningless and fails to communicate. As a data modeler, it is your responsibility to ensure that the in-progress LDS in syntactically valid. Master modelers do this instinctively.

Within Any LDS, Each Entity, Attribute, Relationship, and Link Has an Official Name That Is Unique

The things on an LDS have names, which are supplied by the users. It is through these names that the users confirm that the LDS accurately describes their information. If the names are wrong, the sentences you say will sound wrong to users.

Different things should have different names so that you and the users can tell them apart. The ability to distinguish between different things is so fundamental, we include this syntax rule.

Some ramifications of this rule are straightforward and have obvious merit. For example, an LDS cannot contain two different entities that have the same name.

Other ramifications are more subtle but have merits that you can appreciate after brief contemplation. For example, two attributes cannot have the same name, even if they exist in separate entities. Consider the syntactically invalid LDS Fragment 13-1. It contains two attributes named *endorsement contract;* this is a syntax violation. Because the two attributes have the same name, the LDS connotes that there is

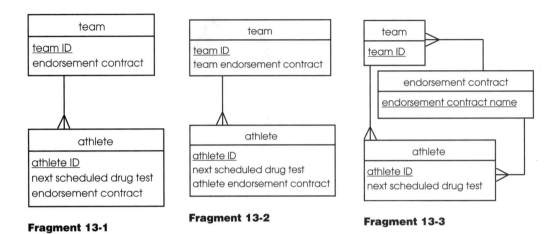

Fragment 13-1

Fragment 13-2

Fragment 13-3

one kind of thing called an endorsement contract. However, because there are two attributes, the LDS connotes that there are two kinds of things. In effect, the LDS contradicts itself.

When the LDS contains contradictory assertions like this, you and the users must decide which assertion is correct; then you must modify the LDS accordingly. If the users decide that there really are two different kinds of things whose names are, say, *team endorsement contract* and *athlete endorsement contract,* you replace the erroneous LDS with Fragment 13-2. If the users decide that there is one kind of thing called an endorsement contract (and it so happens that endorsement contracts can be held by individual athletes or by entire teams), you replace the erroneous LDS with Fragment 13-3. Note that in Fragment 13-3, the new relationships have chicken feet. You should not add chicken feet without the users' approval. For more information, see the section "Promoting Attributes" in Chapter 19. That section also contains information about helping the users choose between Fragments 13-2 and 13-3—that is, to choose whether there is one kind of thing or two different kinds of things.

Another subtle ramification of this syntax rule is that no entity name can be the same name as an attribute name. For example, consider the syntactically invalid LDS Fragment 13-4, in which the name *rating* applies to an attribute and to an entity. To appreciate why this is syntactically invalid, think about what you say when you read the *film* entity aloud:

- *Each film is identified by its title.*
- *About each film, we can remember its title, its rating, and its rating.*

The second sentence sounds peculiar because it reveals the syntactic error. Because the two things have the same name, the LDS connotes that there is one kind of thing called a rating. However, because there are two things called rating evident on the diagram, the LDS connotes that there are indeed two kinds of things. Once again, the LDS contradicts itself. And once again, you and the users must decide which of the two contradictory

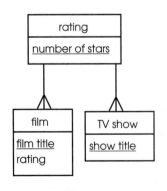

Fragment 13-4

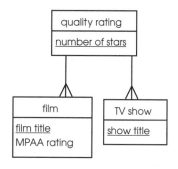

Fragment 13-5

assertions is correct. If the users decide that there really are two different kinds of things, you must secure, from users, names that can distinguish them.

For example, you can learn from users that there are two different kinds of ratings. One is a rating for quality (four stars, three stars, and so on); the other is an MPAA[1] rating for age appropriateness (G for general audiences admitted, PG for parental guidance suggested, R for restricted audiences only). Quality ratings apply to films and television, but MPAA ratings apply only to films. Fragment 13-5 contains the corrected names.

Be careful: It is syntactically correct for two or more links to have the same label. Remember, a link's label is not the same as its name.

No Reflexive Relationship Is a *To-be* Relationship

A *to-be* relationship must connect two distinct entities (rather than connecting an entity to itself).

This rule exists because any LDS containing a reflexive *to-be* relationship would contain a contradiction. More precisely, any instance of a reflexive *to-be* relationship would be a contradiction. Imagine such an instance of the relationship. It associates two distinct instances of the same category. Because there are two distinct instances of the category, the data suggests that there are two real-world things represented. But because an instance of a *to-be* relationship connects them, it suggests that there is only one real-world thing that merely has two interpretations.

Between Any Pair of Entities, There Is at Most One *To-be* Relationship

If you think about it, you will see that this rule has to exist. If there were two different *to-be* relationships between the same pair of entities, what would the second one mean that the first one didn't already mean?

Each Entity Has at Least One Identifier

By conforming to this rule, you keep the LDS meaningful.

An Entity Can Have Several Identifiers

Although it is extremely rare for an entity to have several identifiers, it is possible.

---

[1] Motion Picture Association of America.

No Identifier Can Be a Strict Subset of Another

If one identifier is a strict subset of another identifier, the identifiers contradict each other. Suppose that an entity[2] E has attributes A_1, A_2, A_3, and A_4. Suppose that the entity has two identifiers I_1 and I_2 such that $I_1 = \{A_1, A_2, A_3\}$ and $I_2 = \{A_1, A_2\}$. Note that I_2 is a subset of I_1. When you read the sentences for each identifier, you can see how they contradict each other:

Sentences about I_1:

1. *About each E, we must remember its A_1, its A_2, and its A_3.*
2. *No two Es can have the same A_1, A_2, and A_3.*
3. *Two Es could have the same A_1 and A_2 or the same A_1 and A_3 or the same A_2 and A_3.*

Sentences about I_2:

a. *About each E, we must remember its A_1 and its A_2.*
b. *No two Es can have the same A_1 and A_2.*
c. *Two Es could have the same A_1 or the same A_2.*

To recognize the contradiction, first notice that sentence 3 actually contains three separate assertions:

3.1 *Two Es could have the same A_1 and A_2.*

3.2 *Two Es could have the same A_1 and A_3.*

3.3 *Two Es could have the same A_2 and A_3.*

The contradiction exists between sentence 3.1 and sentence b; both sentences cannot be true.

The LDS Cannot Contain Any Cycles of Identification Dependency

When an identifier includes a link, an **identification dependency** exists. An identification dependency occurs when the identifier values of one entity rely on the instances of another entity. For example, in Fragment 13-6, an identification dependency exists from *line item* to *order*. That is, *line item* depends for its identity on *order*. To identify a particular instance of the *line item* entity, you must know the particular instance of the *order* entity to which that instance of *line item* applies.

Don't confuse identification dependency with other kinds of dependency. The users can tell you of an **existence dependency,** in which instances of one entity cannot exist without the related instances of some other entity also existing. For example, when discussing Fragment 13-6, the users can tell you, *Each line item must have a product.* In effect, the users are saying that an instance of *line item* cannot *exist* unless there is a corresponding instance of *product.* By contrast, the identification

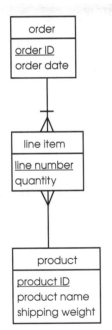

Fragment 13-6

---

[2]Contrary to our normal practice, we are using meaningless names during this discussion. It is impossible for us to use meaningful names for an illegal, meaningless construct.

dependency says that you cannot identify an instance of *line item* without also identifying the corresponding instance of *order.*

During data modeling, you care about identification dependencies, but you do not typically care about existence dependencies. There are many good reasons to ignore existence dependencies during data modeling, and we discuss them in Chapter 22.

On an LDS, there can be paths of identification dependencies. An *identification dependency path* is a sequence of entities $E_1, E_2, E_3, \ldots, E_n$ $(n > 1)$, in which each entity E_i $(i < n)$ depends for its identity on E_{i+1}. For example, in Fragment 13-7, there are six identification dependency paths:

> We borrow the words "path" and "cycle" from the mathematical field called graph theory.

- *row,matrix* (*row* depends on *matrix*)
- *column,matrix* (*column* depends on *matrix*)
- *cell,row* (*cell* depends on *row*)
- *cell,column* (*cell* depends on *column*)
- *cell,row,matrix* (*cell* depends on *row,* which depends on *matrix*)
- *cell,column,matrix* (*cell* depends on *row,* which depends on *matrix*)

Paths of identification dependency are legal, but cycles of identification dependency are not. An **identification dependency cycle** is a sequence of entities $E_1, E_2, E_3, \ldots, E_n$ $(n > 0)$, about which each of the following is true:

- Each entity E_i $(i < n)$ depends for its identity on E_{i+1}.
- The entity E_n depends for its identity on E_1.

For example, the syntactically invalid Fragment 13-8 contains an identification dependency cycle. *A* depends on *B,* which depends on *C,* which depends on *A.*

As we said in a footnote, when illustrating syntax errors, it is difficult or impossible to use meaningful names. Fragment 13-9, however, illustrates an exception. It calls to mind the famous philosophical conundrum *Which came first—the chicken or the egg?* If you appreciate the enigmatic characteristics of the question, then you can understand why cyclic identification dependencies are illegal.

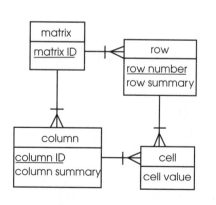

Fragment 13-7

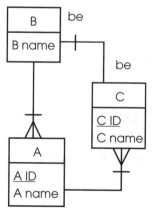

Fragment 13-8

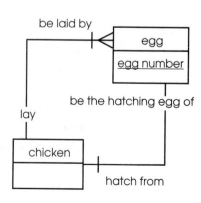

Fragment 13-9

No Link of a Reflexive Relationship Can Contribute to an Identifier

Anything that looks like this is illegal:

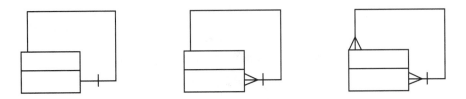

Note that this syntax rule is a special case of the rule prohibiting cyclic identification dependencies.

Both Links of a Relationship Cannot Contribute to Identifiers

Anything that looks like this is illegal:

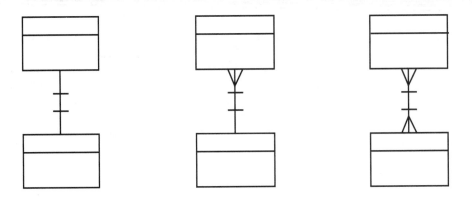

Note that this syntax rule is a special case of the rule prohibiting cyclic identification dependencies.

A Single-Descriptor Identifier Cannot Include the Degree-One Link of a One-Many Relationship

If an identifier includes a single descriptor that is the degree-one link of a one-many relationship, the LDS is syntactically invalid because it contains a contradiction. For example, consider the syntactically invalid Fragment 13-10. To appreciate the

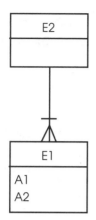

Fragment 13-10

contradiction, consider the various assertions the fragment contains. The identifier asserts

1. About each *E1,* we must remember its *E2.*
2. No two *E1*s can have the same *E2.*

The relationship asserts

a. About each *E1,* we can remember its *E2.*
b. About each *E2,* we can remember its *E1*s.

Sentence 2 and sentence b contradict each other. Sentence 2 indicates that there cannot be an instance of *E2* that is related to several instances of *E1.* Sentence b indicates that there can be an instance of *E2* that is related to several instances of *E1.*

A Multiple-Descriptor Identifier Cannot Include a Link of a One-One Relationship

If an identifier includes several descriptors, one of which is a link of a one-one relationship, the LDS is syntactically invalid because it contains a contradiction. For example, consider the syntactically invalid Fragment 13-11. To appreciate the contradiction, consider the various assertions the fragment contains. The multiple-descriptor identifier asserts

1. About each *E1,* we must remember its *E2* and its *A1.*
2. No two *E1*s can have the same *E2* and *A1.*
3. Two *E1*s could have the same *A1* or the same *E2.*

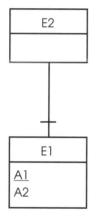

Fragment 13-11

The relationship asserts

a. About each *E1,* we can remember its *E2.*
b. About each *E2,* we can remember its *E1.*

To recognize the contradiction, first notice that sentence 3 actually is a shorthand for two separate assertions:

3.1. Two *E1*s could have the same *A1.*
3.2. Two *E1*s could have the same *E2.*

The contradiction exists between sentence 3.2 and sentence b; both sentences cannot be true. Suppose that sentence 3.2 is true. Then there can be two instances of *E1* that are related to the same instance of *E2.* Let *x* and *y* be two such instances of *E1* that are related to the same instance *z* of *E2.* But that means there is an instance (*z*) of *E2* about which we need to remember *two* different instances (*x* and *y*) of *E1.* This contradicts sentence b.

A Multiple-Descriptor Identifier Cannot Include the Degree-Many Link of a One-Many Relationship

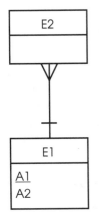

Fragment 13-12

If an identifier includes several descriptors, one of which is the degree-many link of a one-many relationship, the LDS is syntactically invalid because it contains a contradiction. For example, consider the syntactically invalid Fragment 13-12. To appreciate the contradiction, consider the various assertions contained in the fragment. The multiple-descriptor identifier asserts

1. About each *E1*, we must remember its (set of) *E2*s and its *A1*.
2. No two *E1*s can have the same (set of) *E2*s and *A1*.
3. Two *E1*s could have the same *A1* or the same (set of) *E2*s.

The relationship asserts

a. About each *E1*, we can remember its set of *E2*s.
b. About each *E2*, we can remember its *E1*.

With a little thought, you can detect the contradiction. First, recognize that sentence 3 is actually a conversational shorthand for these two sentences:

3.1. Two *E1*s could have the same *A1*.
3.2. Two *E1*s could have the same (set of) *E2*s.

The contradiction exists between sentence 3.2 and sentence b; both sentences cannot be true. Suppose that sentence 3.2 is true. Then there can be two instances of *E1* that are related to the exact same set *S* of *E2*s. Let *x* and *y* be two such instances of *E1*, and let *z* be a particular instance of *E2* that is in the set *S*. Then *z* is an instance of *E2* about which we need to remember two different instances (*x* and *y*) of *E1*. But this contradicts sentence b.

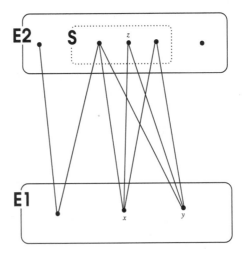

The sample data illustrates the contradiction. It shows *E1* (three instances including *x* and *y*), *E2* (five instances including *z*), and *S* (three elements including *z*). If *x* and *y* are related to the same set *S* of instances of *E2* (as allowed by sentence 3.2), then there is some instance *z* of *E2* that is related to two instances of *E1* (as disallowed by sentence b).

A Relationship Has Either Two Labels or Zero Labels

You cannot label one link of a relationship and leave the other link unlabeled. Either you label both or you label neither—helping users and other data modelers reading the LDS to remember to read each relationship in both directions.

All One-One Relationships Have Labels

Because it is so important to distinguish *to-be* relationships from *not-to-be* relationships, you must label every one-one relationship. (Note that when we say "label the relationship," we mean "label both of the relationship's links.")

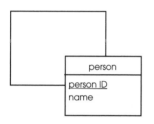

Fragment 13-13

All Reflexive Relationships Have Labels

If a reflexive relationship has no labels, it becomes possible for the two links to have identical names—which of course violates the first syntax rule in this chapter. Consider Fragment 13-13. Suppose the name of one of the links is *person of person*. What is the name of the other link? More to the point, what name besides *person of person* would be an accurate name for the link? Without link labels, you cannot distinguish one link from the other. Both links seem to be about the same thing.

Between Any Pair of Entities, There Is at Most One Unlabeled Relationship

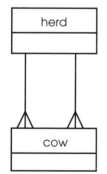

Fragment 13-14

Recall from Chapter 3 that some relationships are not labeled. You can omit the labels when the meaning of the relationship is obvious to you and to the users. Also recall that when you read an unlabeled degree-one link aloud to users, you say, *About each <described-entity-name>, we can remember its <describing-entity-name>.*

To appreciate why there can be at most one unlabeled relationship between any pair of entities, consider the ambiguity that would arise if there were two unlabeled relationships between *cow* and *herd*.

To read the left relationship from the syntactically invalid Fragment 13-14, you would say:

- *About each herd, we can remember its cows.*
- *About each cow, we can remember its herd.*

To read the right relationship, you would say:

- *About each herd, we can remember its cows.*
- *About each cow, we can remember its herd.*

Notice that the two pairs of sentences are identical. Without labels on one of the relationships, there is no way to differentiate what the relationships mean.

Valid Relationships

You can ask yourself six questions about each relationship:

1. Is it one-one, one-many, or many-many?
2. *To-be* or *not to-be?*
3. Reflexive or not reflexive?
4. Labeled or unlabeled?
5. Is there a bar or no bar?
6. Does it form a collection entity or not?

Question 1 has three possible answers; each of the other questions has two. Thus there are $3 \times 2^5 = 96$ possible sets of answers to these questions. Of these 96 possibilities, only 17 are valid. They are shown in the accompanying table.

The 17 valid possibilities follow.

1. *To-be* relationship making a subordinate entity
2. Plain *to-be* relationship
3. Reflexive one-one relationship
4. *Not-to-be* relationship making a subordinate entity
5. Plain *not-to-be* one-one relationship
6. Reflexive one-many relationship
7. Labeled one-many relationship making a collection entity
8. Labeled one-many relationship making a dependent or intersection entity
9. Plain labeled one-many relationship
10. Unlabeled one-many relationship making a collection entity
11. Unlabeled one-many relationship making a dependent or intersection entity
12. Plain unlabeled one-many relationship
13. Reflexive many-many relationship
14. Labeled many-many relationship making a collection entity
15. Plain labeled many-many relationship
16. Unlabeled many-many relationship making a collection entity
17. Plain unlabeled many-many relationship

| | | | Labeled | | | | Unlabeled | | | |
| | | | Bar | | No bar | | Bar | | No bar | |
			Collection entity	Not collection entity	Collection entity	Not collection entity	Collection entity	Not collection entity	Collection entity	Not collection entity
One-one	*To-be*	Reflexive								
		Not reflexive		1		2				
	Not-to-be	Reflexive				3				
		Not reflexive		4		5				
One-many	*To-be*	Reflexive								
		Not reflexive								
	Not-to-be	Reflexive				6				
		Not reflexive	7	8		9	10	11		12
Many-many	*To-be*	Reflexive								
		Not reflexive								
	Not-to-be	Reflexive				13				
		Not reflexive	14			15	16			17

Exercises

1. For each valid kind of relationship,
   a. Create an example that fits it.
   b. Provide sample data.
   c. Determine what questions you would ask users about it.
2. Repeat question 1 until you are confident that you have mastered each shape.
3. For each invalid kind of relationship—that is, for each empty cell of the table—determine what syntax rule or rules it violates.
4. Chapter 3 contains several fragments with this label: *Warning: This fragment shows a syntactically invalid LDS.* For each such fragment, indicate what syntax rule or rules it violates.

14
Chapter

Getting the Names Right

In data modeling, you succeed by getting the names right. Remember, you use the names of entities, attributes, and links when you read the sentences aloud to users. When the names are incorrect, users will tell you that the sentences—the assertions of the LDS—are inaccurate. When the names are correct, users will hear the sentences and confirm the correctness of the LDS.

Entity Names

Although all the names on an LDS are important, the entity names are especially so. The entity name is important because the entity is so often the focus of the discussion. (Recall from Chapter 3 how prominently the entity name figures in the sentences you say.) After you get a little experience working on real data models with real users, you will grow to appreciate the importance of entity names because you will surely, at one time or another, suffer the high cost of getting an entity name wrong. When an entity has the wrong name, virtually every sentence you say about the entity will be wrong. This will confuse the users and significantly retard the evolution of the LDS.

There are several ways that an entity name (call it *XYZ*) can be wrong.

1. The name *XYZ* can be too exclusive. That is, the name can suggest the exclusion of instances that are present. If the name is too exclusive, then the entity has some instances to which the name *XYZ* does not apply.

2. The name *XYZ* can be too inclusive. That is, the name can suggest the inclusion of instances that are not present. If the name is too inclusive, then there are some things that are not instances of the entity, even though the name *XYZ* applies to each of those things.
3. The name *XYZ* can be too coarse. That is, entire groups of the instances can describe one *XYZ*.
4. The name *XYZ* can be too fine. That is, each instance can describe an entire group of *XYZ*s.
5. The name *XYZ* can be completely inaccurate. That is, the name can grossly abuse or ignore the users' vocabulary.
6. The name *XYZ* can be an overloaded word. That is, the word "XYZ" can mean different things to different users.
7. The name *XYZ* can violate LDS syntax. That is, the name can be something other than a singular noun or singular noun phrase.

The following sections describe the first six of these potential errors. The seventh potential error is described in Chapter 13.

Too-Exclusive and Too-Inclusive Entity Names

If an entity name is too exclusive, the name applies only to some of the entity's instances. That is, it wrongly connotes the exclusion of some possible instances from the set of allowable instances. Consider the sample data and corresponding LDS Fragment 14-1.

As a name for the unnamed entity, *authorship* is too exclusive; it fails to connote the possibility for instances describing M. White's editing of "Throwing Curves" and M. Black's illustration of "A Secret of Fame."

On the other hand, if an entity name is too inclusive, it wrongly connotes that some unimportant instances are worth remembering. In Fragment 14-1, *person-document pair* is a too-inclusive name; it wrongly connotes that each and every combination of one person and one document is worth remembering as an instance of the entity. The sample data reveals otherwise: Only certain noteworthy combinations of one person and one document are worth remembering. Specifically, the memorable combinations are those combinations in which the person contributed in a role

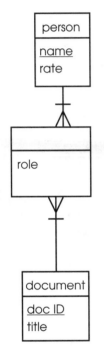

Fragment 14-1

Person	Rate	Doc ID	Title	Role
M. Black	33	rrt4y	Lessons in Music	Author
M. Blue	44	888	Throwing Curves	Author
M. White	77	888	Throwing Curves	Editor
M. Brown	11	43241	History of Soccer	Author
M. Black	33	twdw	A Secret of Fame	Illustrator

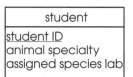

Fragment 14-2

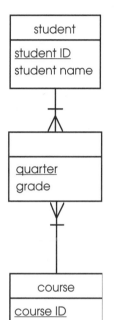

Fragment 14-3

specific to the document. Any name for this entity should connote what makes the instances memorable. A more accurate name for this entity is *contribution by person to document,* which the users might shorten to *contribution.*

In Fragment 14-2 is another example of a too-inclusive entity name. The users (office workers at Acme University) indicate that each instance of the entity describes a veterinary student. The users also indicate that there are other schools in the Acme University system, including schools of law, medicine, dentistry, and public policy. The entity name is too inclusive; it connotes that each and every Acme University student is remembered as an instance. A more accurate name is *veterinary school student.*

Too-Coarse Entity Names

If an entity name is too coarse, the name applies not to individual instances of the entity but to entire groups of instances. That is, it fails to connote the fine detail that each instance of the entity provides.

For example, during a conversation with users, you have developed an LDS fragment like Fragment 14-3. Along the way, you have learned the following:

- A *registration* is an event that occurs once per quarter, administered by the registrar's office.
- A *student registration* is the set of courses a particular student selects during a particular quarter. During any quarter, a student can select up to four courses.

The users provide the following sample data.

Stu ID	Name	Doc ID	Title	Quarter	Grade
55555	Fred	Mat45	Algebra	1996, Fall	F
55555	Fred	Mat45	Algebra	1997, Spring	A
55555	Fred	Mat62	Calculus	1997, Spring	B
44444	Ethel	Lit04	Shakespeare	1997, Spring	B
44444	Ethel	Lit05	Faulkner	1997, Fall	
44444	Ethel	Mat45	Algebra	1997, Spring	B

As a name for the intersection entity, *registration* is too coarse; it wrongly suggests that each instance describes a registration, whereas each instance describes a detail about a registration. You can tell that the name is too coarse because it takes *six* instances of the entity to describe *three* registrations. If *registration* were the correct name, the number of described registrations would equal the number of instances.

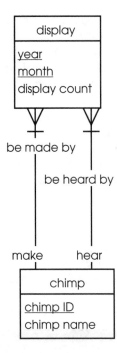

Fragment 14-4

As a name for the intersection entity, *student registration* is also too coarse. Once again, you know the name is too coarse because it takes more than one instance to describe one so-named thing. For example, there are two instances that together describe Fred's registration for Spring 1997.

A more accurate name for this entity is *selection of course by student,* which the users might shorten to *selection.*

Too-Fine Entity Names

If an entity name is too fine, each instance describes an entire set of so-named things. The entity name wrongly connotes that the instances contain more detail than they actually contain.

For example, working from the schema for a legacy system,[1] you develop an LDS fragment like Fragment 14-4. As a first guess for entity names, you use the names evident in the legacy system.

Along the way, you have learned from users that a *display* is a vocal and physical demonstration (chest thumping, roaring, and so on) performed by one chimpanzee for another chimpanzee.

From the legacy system, you gather the following sample data.

Displayer		Displayee			
ID	**Name**	**ID**	**Name**	**Year & Month**	**Count**
L333	Lee	S444	Sam	1996, October	12
L333	Lee	M888	Mel	1997, April	14
L333	Lee	L777	Leslie	1997, April	13
S444	Sam	L333	Lee	1997, April	5
S444	Sam	L777	Leslie	1997, October	2
S444	Sam	L777	Leslie	1997, May	3

---

[1] Inspecting legacy systems is one way to start a brand-new LDS. See the section "Discovering Entities" in Chapter 19.

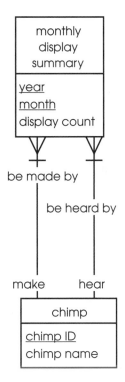

year
month
display count

be made by

be heard by

make   hear

chimp

chimp ID
chimp name

Fragment 14-5

As an entity name, *display* is too fine, because the data in the so-named entity actually provides a coarser view. Each instance describes not one display but a summary of displays. For example, the first instance summarizes 12 displays that Lee made to Sam in October 1996.

Better names for this entity are *display summary* (a fair name), *monthly display summary* (a better name), or *monthly displayer-displayee summary* (a slightly awkward but very accurate name).

After you replace a too-fine entity name with a better name, you might need to relabel some links or change some attribute names. For example, the descriptor labels in Fragment 14-5 are not correct; a chimp does not make monthly display summaries.

In fact any time you change the name of an entity, you should reread the entire entity to ensure that all the associated names (of attributes and related entities) and labels (of links) remain valid.

For more information see Chapter 16.

Completely Inaccurate Names

If an entity name is completely inaccurate, it is meaningless to the users. When you discuss an LDS fragment that includes an inaccurate name, confusion will surely ensue.

A user can choose a name that he or she thinks is good but that others think is bad—because of their differing provincial views of the data. For example, in a university one user might choose the name *registration* because a student registers for a course and then gets a grade. However, another user might object, claiming that nobody gets a grade when registering, so *registration* is bad. A third user might claim that registration is the entire session during which a student registers for all of his or her courses. Still another user might claim that registration is an office where registering occurs.

In our experience, inaccurate names also arise when you or the users take shortcuts. During controlled evolution, there are certain times when the need for an entity arises before you know the entity's name. At such times, you draw the new entity and ask the users to name it. If the users have difficulty naming the entity, you help them by suggesting some possible names. If you or the users are tired from an arduous data-modeling session, you may be tempted simply to choose a name without letting the users accept or reject it. This is a dangerous shortcut. We have made this mistake ourselves, and it has led to serious, time-wasting confusion. The confusion abated when we finally revisited the entity and secured a correct name from the users.

Choosing the correct name can be difficult for the users too. If they are tired, they might casually choose an inaccurate name or accept an inaccurate name that you suggest.

Overloaded Names

When one word has several meanings, we say that the word is overloaded. Although English has many overloaded words, overloading is usually not a problem because people typically use words in a context that provides enough clues to determine which meaning of a word applies. For example, two different meanings of the word "pride" are "arrogance" and "herd" (of lions). In the following sentences, context helps us decide how to interpret the word "pride":

- A humble man is afraid of pride.
- A sensible zebra is afraid of the pride.

Some contextual clues are based on knowledge (we know that "humble" is the opposite of "proud"; we know that lions eat zebras). Other contextual clues are based purely on syntax ("of pride" is syntactically different from "of the pride").

Relying on context is not infallible. For example, the following sentence lacks sufficient contextual clues to help us choose what the word "pride" means in this case:

- Any sensible, humble zebra is afraid of any pride.

Because context is not reliable, an LDS cannot use overloaded words for names. It is especially important to avoid overloaded words as entity names.

In data modeling, overloading can be easy to detect provided that the two meanings of an overloaded word are vastly different. For example, suppose you are data modeling for a client that tests and manufacturers medical prosthetic devices and equipment for physical therapy. Government regulations require that the company conduct extensive testing of its products. Users from the manufacturing department use the word "cast" to mean "form, mold." To them, a cast is a part of the manufacturing process. Users from the product testing department use the word "cast" to refer to a specific prosthetic device worn by a specific human test subject to repair a specific broken bone. As you work with these users, either separately or simultaneously, it will be obvious that there are two different meanings of the one word. (It will be obvious to you because the word "cast" will have two completely different, unrelated sets of descriptors.)

Not all overloading is easy to detect. Sometimes the users themselves are not aware that a word has two (or more) different meanings—particularly if the various meanings differ in only subtle ways. For example, suppose you are data modeling for a mail order retailer. Users in the sales department use the word "shipment" to refer to the transmission of a customer's order. Users in the shipping/receiving department use the same word to refer to any set of boxes mailed to any customer on the same truck as part of the same order. Users in the accounts payable department use the word "shipment" to refer to any single box that was shipped.

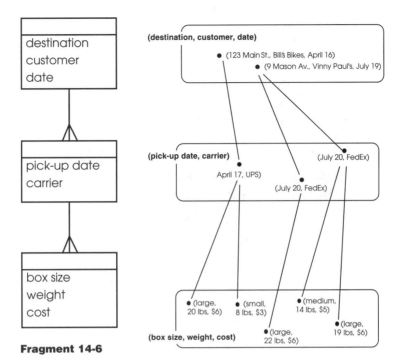

Fragment 14-6

Fragment 14-6 and its sample data illustrate the naming problem.

Besides omitting the entity names, the LDS fragment omits the identifiers, stressing the fact that if you do not know what to call each entity, you probably do not know how to distinguish their instances from each other.

The sample data shows that there are two instances of the top entity, three instances of the middle entity, and five instances of the bottom entity. If you ask how many shipments are evident, you get different answers from different users. Salespeople say two shipments because there are two instances of the top entity. Shipping clerks say three shipments. Users from accounts payable say five shipments.

When the users have subtly different overloaded words, a data visualization like the one with Fragment 14-6 will help them appreciate the differences in their respective vocabularies. As presented, the preceding data visualization is a bit contrived— we've made the problem seem easy by providing the illustration. When you actually encounter a subtly overloaded word while working with users, the major difficulties are realizing that the word is overloaded and drawing the instance data. Once the instance data is drawn, it is relatively easy to ask the various users how many shipments are evident. But drawing the instance data can be so challenging, you might not even be able to do it.

Although that sounds like a bleak state of affairs, you can overcome it. When you find yourself so confused that you cannot begin to draw instance data, ask the users to draw it. First ask the users to write down one shipment (or whatever word you do not understand). Then ask the users to write down a second instance. It is in drawing the second instance that the users must decide for themselves what the word ("shipment," in this case) means. Don't be surprised if the users struggle to draw the second instance, or if one user draws a second instance and the other users immediately disagree. This disagreement can be a sign that the users are confronting the problem of overloading.

After you help the users discover overloading, you must insist that they choose unique names for each of the entities.

Working with Users to Get the Entity Names Right

To name an entity correctly, you must rely on the users. After all, the noun (or noun phrase) that becomes the entity name is part of their vocabulary. Any name you come up with is probably wrong. Even when you become an expert data modeler with much experience, you must remember that you are never the final arbiter of entity names. You might believe that a name you suggest is absolutely accurate. But if the users do understand the name you suggest but still disapprove of it, then you must accede to their judgment. Remember, when the users choose the name, they claim ownership of that portion of the LDS, and they tacitly accept responsibility for the correctness of the name. When you choose the name, you effectively absolve the users from accepting responsibility for that part of the LDS. And if the users do not accept the responsibility for a portion of the LDS, you can be certain that that portion of the LDS will never be very good.

Since you cannot choose the name yourself, you help primarily by turning a critical eye on the entity names users suggest. When you assess a user-suggested entity name, keep the possible naming errors in mind. When you suspect that a name is bad, don't immediately suggest another name to the users. Instead, explain to the users why the name they suggested might be wrong (too coarse, too fine, and so on), and then ask them for an improved name. In this way, you help the users understand their responsibility to name the entity accurately, and you help them understand all the ways a name can be inaccurate.

Notice how carefully you manage the shared responsibility. As data modeler, you are responsible for ensuring that the names are accurate and syntactically correct. But the responsibility for coming up with the names belongs with the users. The process of naming entities is a bit like the Socratic method—and you get to be Socrates. Recall that Socrates enlightened his Athenian neighbors, not by directly revealing the truth to them but by encouraging them to refine further their own understanding. He did this by asking probing questions or by making sure the citizens of Athens grasped the ramifications of their asserted opinions. You do the same thing here.[2]

---

[2] Careful, this analogy has its limitations. When we discuss what information is worth remembering, the whole notion of revealing the truth is misguided. A mature LDS does not represent an absolute truth that has been revealed by the process of controlled evolution. A mature LDS represents a set of deliberate decisions made by the users about what is worth remembering.

```
┌─────────────────────┐
│      chapter        │
├─────────────────────┤
│ name                │
│ author              │
│ due date            │
│ page count          │
│                     │
└─────────────────────┘
```

Fragment 14-7

```
┌─────────────────────┐
│    book portion     │
├─────────────────────┤
│ name                │
│ author              │
│ due date            │
│ page count          │
│                     │
└─────────────────────┘
```

Fragment 14-8

Here's how it happens. The users suggest a name (say, *chapter* in Fragment 14-7). You think about a particular naming error (say, the too-exclusive error), and you help the users to check that the name avoids this error. You induce such user scrutiny by asking a probing question, such as *Is it possible for a thing to have an author, a due date, and a number of pages even though that thing is not a chapter?* Or you can induce the users to think hard about the name in other ways, such as by helping them visualize sample data. In some cases, the user scrutiny will confirm that the name avoids the error. In other cases, the scrutiny reveals that the name is indeed erroneous. Thereupon the users sometimes suggest an improved name that avoids the error—but if they don't immediately volunteer an accurate name, you explicitly ask for one. If the users cannot suggest another name (or if they suggest only names that are no better than the original), it probably means that they do not truly understand what is wrong with the original name. You can cautiously suggest an improved name. You shouldn't expect the users to accept the name you suggest. Rather, you should expect the name you suggest to help the users understand why the original name is wrong. And once they understand why the original name is wrong, they will be able to give you an accurate name.

Fragment 14-7 modified to use a less exclusive name is shown in Fragment 14-8. The new entity name in this fragment represents a more refined understanding of the data. Because you forced the users to scrutinize the entity name *chapter,* the users revealed to you that there are some things that are not chapters but have all the same descriptors as chapters. For example, there are appendixes and prefaces and epilogues. *Book portion* is a correct name for this entity because each instance describes what the users call a book portion—a chapter, appendix, preface, or epilogue.

Expect to Work Hard on Naming Entities

Finding the right name for an entity can be hard and can sometimes take a long time. (If it were easy, the users wouldn't need your help.) Don't be surprised if occasionally you and the users spend 30 minutes trying to name a single entity accurately. There are several reasons why it is so difficult. One common reason is the sixth kind of naming error, overloading. When an entity name is incorrect because it is an overloaded word, it can take a long time to come up with the correct name because it can take a long time for you and the users to realize with absolute certainty that the existing entity name is actually wrong. Some users will insist that the name is right, while other users will insist with equal conviction that the name is wrong. It can take a while for you and these two sets of users to sort things out.

There are other, more general reasons why it can take users a long time to name an entity accurately. Of course, it can take a long time whenever the users don't really understand what it is they are trying to remember. Don't forget, the entity name conveys what kind of memorable thing each instance of the entity describes. If the users are vague about what the memorable things are, they will struggle to name the entity.

But even if the users know exactly what kinds of things they want to remember, they can still struggle to come up with names. That's because users typically use their vocabulary orally, which accommodates a certain casualness that written vocabulary does not accommodate. When users speak to each other as they go about their jobs, they can use shortcuts like pronouns ("that one") and pointing ("the one over there") that they cannot use in written vocabulary. The names on an LDS constitute written vocabulary—official vocabulary that retains its meaning even in the absence of external cues like context and physical gestures. Establishing official vocabulary can take time, even for people who are perfectly lucid during their oral discourse. And in any serious data modeling effort, you will eventually encounter some entities describing things users have only talked (rather than written) about.

Be Willing to Work Hard Because It's Worth It

Despite the high cost of keeping the entity names accurate, you should be especially vigilant about doing so for several reasons. First, an inaccurate entity name can exact a terribly high cost in user confusion. The eventual cost of a bad name is much higher than the (admittedly significant) immediate cost of maintaining good names. Second, a good entity name can "go bad." That is, as an entity evolves during controlled evolution, its name can become inaccurate—even if you and the users have already confirmed the accuracy of the name. Thus you need to reexamine entity names often.

This might seem discouraging. But there is nothing silly about frequently reexamining entity names. For the following reasons, you should not be discouraged:

- Not every entity will be difficult to name or will have an unstable name. Users will be able to name most entities accurately on the first or second try because most entities will be part of the users' written vocabulary.
- Remember, you succeed in data modeling by getting the names right. Reexamining the names is not a tangential part of data modeling—it is an essential part.
- Reexamining a name is not a sign of duplicated effort or wasted effort. Rather, it is a sign of progress. By replacing a name with a more accurate name, you and the users make finer and finer distinctions. In effect, the LDS matures. This is consistent with theories of learning.[3] As your awareness grows, you revisit old material that you had understood and develop a more mature understanding of it.
- Gradually, the frequency with which you must reexamine an entity's name shrinks. Admittedly, when an LDS is very immature, you spend a great deal of time revisiting entity names. But that just means that in the early stages, you can make a great deal of progress quickly. As any portion of the LDS matures, you need to reexamine the entity names less and less often.

Manage the Difficulty: Choose the Right Moments to Work Hard

There's one more reason for encouragement. Beyond merely saying "frequently," we can be a bit more specific about when you should reexamine entity names. Obviously, when you first create an entity, you should try hard to get the name right. Thereafter,

---

[3] See R. Caine and G. Caine, *Making Connections: Teaching and the Human Brain,* Addison-Wesley, Reading, MA, 1994.

you should reexamine the name any time you make a substantial change to the entity. And in most cases, the kind of change you make to the entity correlates with the kind of naming error you should suspect.

- After you enlarge an entity's identifier, check that the entity name is not too coarse.
- After you shrink an entity's identifier, check that the entity name is not too fine.
- After you add to or remove from an entity a descriptor of a *to-be* relationship, check that the entity name is not too inclusive or too exclusive
- Whenever you detect systemic confusion (perhaps leading to user disputes, impatience, or bickering) about an entity, check that the entity name is not grossly erroneous or overloaded.
- Whenever the discussion of an entity leads to factional disputes among the users, check that the entity name is not overloaded. (Remember, "overloaded" means "having several definitions." In such a dispute, each "faction" is a set of users employing a particular definition of the overloaded word.)

Manage the Difficulty: Use the Expertise at Your Disposal

Let the users do the work they're best suited for. Let them shoulder as much entity-naming responsibility as possible. In practical terms during the search for an entity name, this means that you sometimes sit back and let the users discuss the entity; you don't intercede. Sitting back and watching the users have a prolonged discussion can make you anxious, worrying about whether you should jump into the conversational fray. But sitting back doesn't mean that you stop working. As the users discuss the entity name, you listen intently, trying to decide whether the users need your help.

Sometimes it is best to stay out of it. Just because the users struggle to name an entity doesn't necessarily mean that they need your immediate help. If they struggle because they don't understand the entity, then yes, you should help. But some struggles have nothing to do with a lack of understanding. Remember, there are many things for which the users do not have official written vocabulary, even though the users understand the things perfectly well. When the time comes to name an entity whose instances describe such things, the users are in for a struggle because they have to compose a name for the entity, right there on the spot. As long as you remain convinced that the users really do understand the entity, there is no need for you to jump in. Let them compose an entity name, and then you can help out by reacting to it.

On the other hand, it is sometimes best to jump into the conversation immediately.

- If the users become angry with each other, jump in, perhaps suggesting a brief break.
- If the users lose focus, discussing topics other than the unnamed entity, jump in, reminding them of the problem at hand.
- If the users show persistent disagreement over seemingly trivial naming differences, jump in. You need to investigate why the users care about such trivial differences. Your investigations can reveal a lot.

- You are ignorant about the data. The differences are not trivial; they only seem trivial to you because the users are making a distinction you do not understand. You need to learn more from the users.
- You are ignorant about naming standards. The differences seem trivial to you because the competing names are synonymous (e.g., *employment episode* and *episode of employment*), but the users have strong preferences based on their awareness of competing naming standards used in their organization.
- The differences are truly trivial, and the users are wasting time over something unimportant.
- If the users show persistent disagreement or confusion about what the entity means, jump in. If the users do not understand the entity, they will not compose an accurate name.

Sometimes you have some leeway. If some users understand the entity well, but others remain confused, you can jump in to enlighten the confused users. But when we're data modeling, we like to stay quiet in these situations. We give the aware users a chance to explain the entity to their confused colleagues. The informed, aware users are probably more helpful than we are, and they often create real, telling instances that we record and reuse with other users. Only if the confusion persists do we jump in.

Manage the Difficulty: Teach the Users a Helpful Basic Principle

As you work with a group of users on an LDS, they will gradually get a feel for what makes an entity name good or bad. Users who take seriously their entity-naming responsibility will come to understand why an overloaded name is bad and why a syntactically invalid name is bad and why a grossly erroneous name is bad. Astute users might even grow to appreciate each of the other four types of error (too coarse, too fine, too inclusive, and too exclusive) as distinct, but that is not absolutely necessary. Instead of teaching the users about each of these four types of error, you can teach them this rule of thumb:

Rule of thumb for entity names

Short version: One entity instance per one *<entity-name>*.

Long version: Each *<entity-name>* is described by one entity instance, and each entity instance describes a whole *<entity-name>* exclusively.

Suppose the users tell you that the name of an entity should be *widget*. In effect, the users assert that <u>each widget is described by one entity instance and each entity instance describes a whole widget exclusively.</u> The underlined portion of the preceding sentence confirms that the name *widget* avoids the first four types of naming error. Here's how:

- **Each widget is described by one entity instance.** In other words, there is no widget that is not described by some instance of this entity. Thus the name *widget* avoids the too-inclusive naming error.

- **Each entity instance describes a widget.** In other words, there is no instance of this entity describing something other than a widget. Thus the name *widget* avoids the too-exclusive naming error.
- **Each entity instance describes a <u>whole</u> widget.** In other words, the instance does not describe merely a part of a widget, requiring you to examine an entire group of instances for a description of the whole widget. Thus the name *widget* avoids the too-coarse naming error.
- **Each entity instance describes a widget <u>exclusively</u>.** In other words, there is no group of widgets described by some individual instance; an instance describes one and only one widget. Thus the name *widget* avoids the too-fine naming error.

There's one other very quick way to help the users understand the rule of thumb for entity names. If the users recommend *widget* as the name of the entity, you say: *That means that if there are, say, seven widgets, there will be exactly seven instances of this entity, and if there are, say, four instances of this entity, that means there are four widgets.*

Example: Checking a Name That You Suspect Is Too Coarse

When you enlarge an identifier, the entity name can become too coarse. For example, while working on LDS Fragment 14-9, the users provide the accompanying sample data.

employee
<u>badge #</u>
name
hire date
sign-on bonus

Fragment 14-9

Badge	Name	Hire date	Sign-on bonus
7777	A. Wottle	06 July 1982	2,500
9090	S. Gushikin	06 July 1982	
1122	J. Viren	06 July 1982	3,000
1122	J. Viren	22 Feb 1970	500
9090	S. Gushikin	14 May 1996	10,000

The sample data convinces you that the identifier of the *employee* entity is incorrect. After a brief discussion with the users (see the section "Fixing identifiers" in Chapter 19), you add *hire date* to the identifier, yielding Fragment 14-10.

Because you have just enlarged the identifier, you suspect that the entity name might be too coarse—that there can be entire groups of instances that describe a single employee.

employee
<u>badge #</u>
name
<u>hire date</u>
sign-on bonus

Fragment 14-10

You ask the users how many employees are evident in the sample data. The users indicate that there are three (Wottle, Gushikin, and Viren). Since there are five instances containing data about only three employees, the name *employee* is too coarse.

Using the sample data, you explain the problem to the users. You say: *Employee is not the right name for this entity because the purpose of each instance is not to describe some employee. Each instance might describe something about an employee, but we know that each instance has some other purpose. Look, if each instance* *described an employee, we wouldn't need two different instances to describe "J. Viren." We need a name for what each <u>one</u> of these instances is. The sample data shows five instances. Tell me, what do we have five of here? Five <u>what</u>?"*

Some users seem to get your point, but others do not; they do not understand why the entity name *employee* is wrong. You give the aware users a few moments to explain the problem to the confused users. The explanations do not work, so you decide to explain the problem yourself.

You focus the attention of the confused users onto a single group of instances pertaining to one employee. For example, erase all instances except the following two. Say: *It is wrong to say that we have two employees shown here; there is only one. But we have two somethings. Two <u>what</u>? What do we have two of here?*

Badge	Name	Hire date	Sign-on bonus
9090	S. Gushikin	06 July 1982	
9090	S. Gushikin	14 May 1996	10,000

At this point, the users understand and say: *We have two occasions on which an employee worked for the company.* You say: *So one possible name for this entity is "occasion on which an employee worked for the company."* The users immediately recognize this as a cumbersome name and begin discussing alternatives. You listen quietly as they consider several possible names, including *employment episode, employment event, episode of employment, work stint,* and *work episode.*

The users quickly agree on *employment episode,* and you draw LDS Fragment 14-11.

```
┌─────────────────────┐
│  employment         │
│  episode            │
├─────────────────────┤
│  badge #            │
│  name               │
│  hire date          │
│  sign-on bonus      │
└─────────────────────┘
```

Fragment 14-11

Naming Attributes

An attribute name should indicate what each value of the attribute constitutes. Here are a rule and two guidelines for naming attributes:

- **Rule:** An attribute name should be a singular noun or noun phrase: *Singular* because each attribute value is a scalar; *noun* or *noun phrase* because each attribute value is a thing.
- **Guideline:** An attribute name should suggest the attribute's scale. For example, it is wrong to name an attribute *rating number* if the possible values are "good," "fair," and "poor." This is a guideline rather than a rule because the existing user vocabulary sometimes violates this principle. For example, airline companies use an attribute called *confirmation number* whose values can contain letters.
- **Guideline:** An attribute name should not suggest the attribute's encoding. For example, it is wrong to name an attribute *skill_description_var_char* if your intent is to indicate that the skill description will be implemented as a variable-length character string. Such naming subjects the LDS to premature obsolescence and unnecessarily brings implementation into the logical modeling discussion.

Naming Relationships and Links

Although every relationship and link have an official name, you do not expend any effort to name these things. Instead, you work to label links accurately. Once a relationship has accurate labels (or once you and the users have determined that a relationship does not need labels because the relationship's meaning is obvious), you can speak about the relationship and its links clearly and accurately. And if you can do that, you will be able to derive the official names of the relationship and its links at those rare moments when you need to use them.

For more information, see Chapter 16.

Exercises

1. For each way that an entity name can be wrong,
   a. Create an example entity that makes that error.
   b. Provide sample data that illustrates the error.
   c. Determine what questions you would ask users to help correct the error.
2. Repeat question 1 until you are confident that you thoroughly know how to handle each wrong way.
3. Find a real database schema, and look for errors in names. (Note: This exercise is smaller than the reverse engineering exercises in the Appendix.)

15
Chapter

Official Names

ecall from Chapter 13 that every entity, descriptor, and relationship has a name that is guaranteed to be unique throughout the scope of the entire LDS. These unique names are official names. We call them official because they can sometimes become so unwieldy that users naturally employ more casual, unofficial names during their discourse.

Official Names Can Be Awkward

Because official names are so important, you should be willing to cope with some unavoidable awkwardness. The awkwardness is tolerable because official names satisfy an absolutely essential need—the need to distinguish things on the LDS from each other. In fact, the occasional awkwardness is a consequence of the need to ensure that each official name is unique. To make a fine distinction between two things that differ only slightly, it sometimes takes a lot of words or a cumbersome turn of phrase.

The awkwardness is tolerable also because it is limited; it rarely affects the official names of entities and attributes; it more commonly affects relationships and links.

The official names of entities and attributes are simply the words as they appear directly on the diagram. For example, on LDS Fragment 15-1, the entities have official names, *department* and *employee,* and the attributes have official names, *department name* and *badge #.*

For links, however, awkward names crop up frequently. For example, in Fragment 15-1, there is one degree-one link. Its official name cannot be *department* because another thing—an entity—already has that name. The descriptor's official name is *department of employee.*

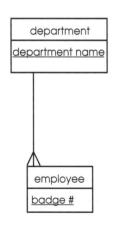

Fragment 15-1

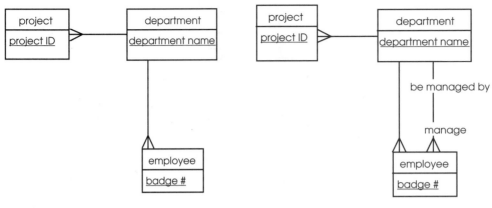

Fragment 15-2   **Fragment 15-3**

Similarly, Fragment 15-2 includes another degree-one link. Its official name is *department of project.*

And Fragment 15-3 contains yet another degree-one descriptor. Its official name cannot be *department of employee* because another thing on the LDS already has that name. Its official name is *managed department of employee.*

So far, we've only talked about the degree-one links. But there are three other links, and they have names, too. In Fragment 15-3, they are *employees of department, projects of department,* and *managing employees of department.*

So the official names of the six links are somewhat cumbersome, but they do their job; they distinguish among the various things on the LDS.

Coping with Awkwardness in Official Names of Links

An awkward official name is tolerable because its very awkwardness is a sign that the LDS is probably quite accurate—that it makes fine, user-approved, worthwhile distinctions between things that are similar but not identical. Even though the users themselves make these fine distinctions, they still can need your help coping with the clumsy names. Specifically, they need you to read the LDS in a way that minimizes the confusion potentially caused by clumsy names.

You minimize this confusion by using unofficial names when you read the LDS. Unofficial names are not vague (absolutely not!), but they are a bit more conversational than official names. When you read an LDS, you use unofficial names only for links; you do not need to use unofficial names for other things.

The following table italicizes the unofficial names you use when reading the links from the preceding LDS.

Notice that in rows 1 and 3, the unofficial name is simply the name of the describing entity. Notice also that the two descriptors use the same unofficial name; unofficial names need not be unique. Notice that in rows 2 and 4, the unofficial names

Look familiar?
This reviews stuff
you know.

	Official name	Sentence you say
1	*Department of employee*	About each employee, we can remember its *department.*
2	*Employees of department*	About each department, we can remember its *employees.*
3	*Department of project*	About each project, we can remember its *department.*
4	*Projects of department*	About each department, we can remember its *projects.*
5	*Managed department of employee*	About each employee, we can remember *the department he or she manages.*
6	*Managing employees of department*	About each department, we can remember *the employees who manage it.*

are the plural of the describing entity. Notice that in rows 5 and 6, the unofficial name is a more complex noun phrase.

Coping with Awkwardness in Official Names of Relationships[1]

Every relationship has an official name. Some relationships can have names that are quite pithy, but for other relationships, it seems that the only possible names are quite awkward. Once again, what's most important is to find a name that uniquely and completely distinguishes the relationship from every other named thing on the LDS. If the name is accurate and brief, great. But if the name must be long or awkward to be accurate, well, so be it. And as it turns out, many relationships have awkward names.

Once again, as you read the LDS aloud, you can work to ensure that the awkwardness of the names does not make what you say sound stilted. To avoid the awkwardness of relationship names, you don't need to rely on unofficial names. In fact, the rather surprising way to cope with this awkwardness is to avoid talking about relationships altogether! If you review Chapter 3, you'll notice that as you read an LDS,

---

[1] Sometimes it takes a lot of words to say something not very important. This whole section about relationship names is one of those times. We include this section "in the spirit of full disclosure." Yes, a relationship does have a name, and yes, the name, however awkward, should be meaningful. But no, you do not need to spend very much time agonizing over this material. In fact, we recommend that you read this section casually at first. The time to come back and study this section closely is when you tackle Chapter 23.

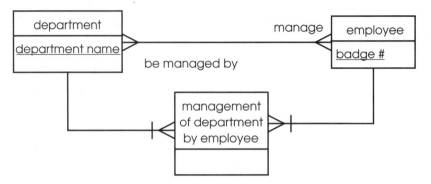

Fragment 15-4

you never actually read a relationship in its entirety. Instead, you read each of the relationship's individual links. Regardless of the grace or clumsiness of the names, this is the preferred way to read an LDS. So it is rather easy to avoid mentioning an awkward name for a relationship—you naturally and appropriately focus not on the relationship but on its two links. (And if one of the links has an awkward name, well, you use the more conversational unofficial name.)

Throughout this entire textbook, there is only one situation in which the name of a relationship arises at a predictable moment (see Chapter 18, especially the section "Flow Stages: Initial Many-Many Relationship and New Intersection Entity"). Besides preparedness for the aforementioned moment, there is only one other reason even to know that a relationship has an official name. You must ensure that you do not create a relationship that shares an official name with an entity. For example, Fragment 15-4 contains just such an error. In this LDS, the problem is that the intersection entity and the many-many relationship have the same official name.

Merely changing one of the names in some trivial way does not solve the problem. Admittedly, if you change the name of the intersection entity to *management episode,* that might eliminate the syntax error. But the syntax error is merely evidence of the real problem. The real problem is that you cannot tell what the relationship means that the intersection entity doesn't already mean. Suppose you know that employee # 45678 manages the sales department. Should you represent that fact as an instance of the many-many relationship or as an instance of the intersection entity? The question is hard to answer because the names do not adequately distinguish the relationship from the intersection entity.

The point is, relationship names are not arbitrary; rather they indicate what the relationship means. What's more, relationship names are meaningful in the same way entity names are meaningful. Specifically, each name connotes what one instance is. For example, consider Fragment 15-5 and its sample data.

Herd is a good official name of the entity on the left because each individual instance of the entity describes *one* herd—not more than one herd, not less than one herd, and not something other than one herd. Similarly, a good official name for the

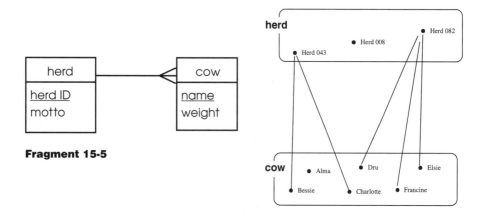

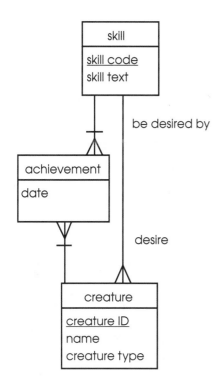

Fragment 15-5

Fragment 15-6

relationship is *membership of a cow in a herd*. What makes this name good is that it describes each individual instance of the relationship. That is, each instance really does indicate the membership of a cow in a herd. The leftmost instance, for example, indicates the membership of Bessie in Herd 043.

Creating accurate names for relationships is not a very important skill because, as we have said before, it is almost always preferable to discuss links rather than relationships. However, creating accurate names for entities is a very important skill, and we say quite a bit more about it in Chapter 14.

We've said that relationship names can be awkward, but so far, the examples have been relatively straightforward: *management of department by employee* and *membership of cow in herd*. Now we present some relationships that have very awkward names. As you look at these examples, notice that the LDS fragments are not especially abstract or otherwise unusual.

In Fragment 15-6, the relationship between *creature* and *achievement* could have any of these names:

- *creature-achievement pair in which the creature makes the achievement*. This name is awkward merely because it is so long.
- *achievement of an achievement by a creature*. This name is awkward because it is redundant: "the achievement of an achievement"?

Similarly, the relationship between *skill* and *achievement* could have any of these names:

- *skill-achievement pair in which the skill applies to the achievement*
- *skill-achievement pair in which the skill is the skill of the achievement*

Don't be discouraged by the awkwardness of these names. There is no reason to be discouraged; what's important is that the LDS is easy to read. In fact, this LDS is so easy to read, it was one of the first examples we presented—many chapters ago. We revisit this LDS now for several reasons. First, we want to convince you that an awkward relationship name is not a strange phenomenon—even the simplest LDS can contain one. Second, we want to convince you that you can read any LDS, no matter how awkward the relationship names are. Third, we want to remind you that as you read an LDS, you truly do not need to think about relationship names. Remember that when you first learned how to read this LDS so many chapters ago, we had not even defined the words "entity" and "relationship."

A Few Notes About Official Names and *To-be* Relationships

To-be relationships require some special thought with regard to both relationship names and link names.

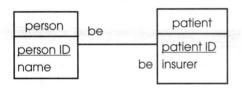

Fragment 15-7

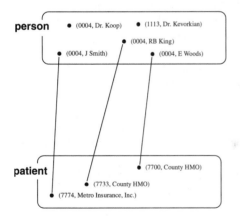

The name of a *to-be* relationship will never arise unless a user explicitly asks about it. We've already mentioned the two very specific reasons why you must be aware of a relationship name: (1) to ensure that the relationship does not share an official name with an entity, and (2) to ensure that you correctly handle the flow stages called *initial many-many relationship* and *new intersection entity* (see Chapter 18). As it turns out, these reasons never involve *to-be* relationships. When you're dealing with a *to-be* relationship, the name just won't come up in typical discourse.

Nevertheless, in the unlikely event that an inquisitive user does ask about the name, you need to be able to answer intelligently. What's more, the name of a *to-be* relationship is less awkward than you might expect, so the name can actually help you appreciate what a *to-be* relationship means. For example, in Fragment 15-7, the official name of the relationship is *equivalence of a person and a patient.*

The name is accurate and meaningful because it characterizes each individual instance of the relationship. In the sample data, for example, the leftmost relationship indicates the equivalence of a person (J Smith) with a patient (#7774).

Although the names of *to-be* relationships rarely arise as you talk with users, the names of the individual links can come up. After all, the preferred way to discuss relationship is to discuss each of the two links in turn. Chapter 3 shows you how to read a *to-be* relationship. For the *to-be* relationship in Fragment 15-7, you say: *About each patient, we can remember its interpretation as person* and *About each person, we can remember its interpretation as a patient.* In those sentences, you use unofficial names "interpretation as a person" and "interpretation as a patient." The official names are

- *person that is equivalent to a patient.*
- *patient that is equivalent to a person.*

Exercise

A number of things in the recipes in Chapter 26 have awkward official names. For each of those recipes,

a. Read its fragment aloud.

b. Determine the official name of each relationship.

c. Create instances that help you explain the fragment.

16 Chapter

Labeling Links

Remember, an LDS is a vehicle for communication. If it is not clear what the entities, attributes, and relationships mean, the LDS fails to communicate. This chapter discusses how to add link labels to relationships whose meaning is not obvious without them.

Each relationship's official name conveys most of the relationship's meaning. Equivalent to the relationship name, a single sentence conveys the same meaning. For example, for the relationship named *desire for a skill by a creature,* the equivalent sentence is "Creature desires skill."

The relationship name and the equivalent sentence convey most but not all of the relationship's meaning. They do convey what each instance of the relationship means. They do not convey the degrees of the two individual links. To convey that, you can use the two link names, which you learned about in Chapter 13. Or you can use the two sentences that are equivalent (and in many ways preferable) to the individual link names. You learned how to say these sentences in Chapter 3. For example, these are the official names and equivalent sentences of the two links in LDS Fragment 16-1:

- Link name: *desired skill of creature*
  Equivalent sentence: *Each creature can desire a skill.*
- Link name: *desiring creatures of skill*
  Equivalent sentence: *Each skill can be desired by creatures.*

As you can see, the sentences are somewhat clearer than the link names. Thus, when you need to label two links, you should choose labels that yield clear, accurate sentences. When labeling, don't worry so much about the names of the links; worry

Fragment 16-1

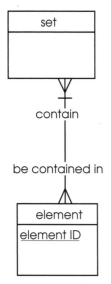

Fragment 16-2

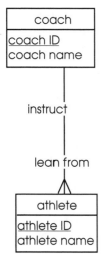

Fragment 16-3

about the sentences. And as you worry about the sentences, worry about the two per-link sentences, not the one per-relationship sentence. Once you say either of the per-link sentences, the single, per-relationship sentence becomes obvious—actually saying it would be redundant. Taken together, the two per-link sentences say everything you need to say about the relationship.

"Make a good sentence for each link," then, is the primary principle for labeling links. There are other, secondary principles, but these are merely devices to help you satisfy the primary principle. In the following examples, we present some good and some bad link labels. Along the way, we mention some of the secondary principles. But we mention them only briefly, because any serious discussion of them quickly deteriorates into a rather technical discussion of English grammar. We believe that such discussions are not necessary because most students who create excellent labels are not experts in the technical details of English grammar. Such students are typically quite articulate, but they are not grammarians.

LDS Fragment 16-2 contains a well-labeled relationship. The labels generate clear sentences, and what's most important, the users indicate that the sentences are accurate:

- *Each set can contain elements.*
- *Each element can be contained in sets.*

You know the labels are good because the sentences are clear and accurate. But beyond that, what makes them good? Do the labels have some special characteristics? The answer is yes. These characteristics illustrate a secondary principle of link labeling:

Principle: Good link labels use verbs. A good link label should be a verb because each label becomes the predicate of a sentence. The verbs in this example are "contain" and "be contained."

Principle: Good link labels use the same verb for each link of a relationship. The relationship has only one meaning, as revealed by its official name—or by the sentence that is equivalent to the official name. When you use the same verb for each link label, you reinforce for the users that the relationship has only one basic meaning. Note that you use two different forms[1] of the verb, which ensures that the resulting sentences sound good.

Although there are times when you have no choice but to violate this principle, you should do so grudgingly. (Some later examples show legitimate violations of this principle.) When you use two different verbs, you invite confusion, and you create work. For example, consider Fragment 16-3, which uses two different verbs. At first glance, everything seems fine because the labels yield clear sentences:

- *Each coach can instruct athletes.*
- *Each athlete can learn from a coach.*

---

[1] If you know your English grammar, you will recognize that the two forms are the *active* voice and the *passive* voice. Refer to any decent grammar book.

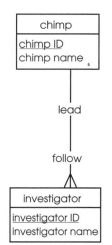

Fragment 16-4

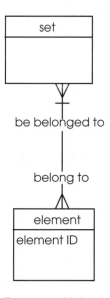

Fragment 16-5

But there's a problem. The sentences, taken together, do not re-inforce each other's meaning. The first sentence indicates that the name of the relationship is *instruction of athlete by coach* and that the equivalent sentence is *coach instructs athlete*. The second sentence indicates that the name of the relationship is *learning by athlete from coach* and that the equivalent sentence is *athlete learns from coach*. Are these relationship names equivalent? You cannot say, because only the users can say whether "instruct" and "learn from" are symmetrically oppo-site. So you need to ask the users, which takes time. When you use two different verbs for the same relationship, you're mak-ing more work for you and the users.

Besides creating work, you invite confusion. Users can attach surprising connotations to words—connotations that defy even your worst expectations. To you, it might seem ob-vious that "lead" is the opposite of "follow," so the labels in Fragment 16-4 might seem perfectly reasonable to you. But your vocabulary is immaterial; the users' vocabulary is what's important. In fact, our users did reject these labels. To them, "lead" is not the opposite of "follow." To them, the correct la-bels are "follow" and "be followed by." Because the two verbs have different meanings, the fragment contains two contradic-tory assertions about what the relationship as a whole means. Such contradictions inevitably yield confusion.

Principle: Good labels use transitive verbs. A transitive verb is a verb that imparts its action directly onto something. The acted-on thing is known (grammatically) as the direct ob-ject. In the sentence *Each set can contain elements,* "contain" is a transitive verb whose direct object is "elements."

An intransitive verb is a verb that imparts its action only in-directly. The link labels in Fragment 16-5 use an intransitive verb. "Belong" is an intransitive verb because you cannot "be-long something." You can "belong <u>to</u> something or belong <u>near</u> something or belong <u>above</u> something, but you cannot belong something. If a verb is intransitive, you use it with a preposi-tion, such as "to," "near," or "above."[2]

---

[2] Other prepositions are from, to, into, under, over, above, below, within, before, after, and by. For a com-plete list, refer to any grammar book. A good rule of thumb: If you cannot put a noun immediately after the verb but must use an interceding preposition, then the verb is intransitive. Note that merely using a preposition is not a sign of intransitivity. For example, the sentence *Each element can be contained in sets* uses the preposition *in*. But that is a passive-voice sentence. The test for transitivity/intransitivity is best applied to active-voice sentences, such as *Each set can contain elements*. Because a noun (*elements*) immediately follows the verb, you can conclude that the verb is transitive. (Even here, we're simplifying things a bit. We warned you that the grammar discussions could quickly become esoteric.)

An intransitive verb is undesirable because it yields awkward sentences and particularly awkward link names:

- *Each element can belong to sets.*
  Associated link name: *Belonged to sets of elements*
- *Each set can be belonged to by elements.*
  Associated link name: *Elements that belong to it of sets*

It is the second sentence and link name pair that is awkward.

If the users find the two labeling options equally accurate, you should use "contained/be contained by" rather than "belong to/be belonged to by," because "contain" is a transitive verb.

In rare cases, you will not be able to find a transitive verb that the users deem accurate. In such cases, you should use whatever intransitive verb the users suggest. Later, whenever you read that portion of the LDS, you should proceed with caution to ensure that the users understand the somewhat awkward sentences.

Even if you do find a transitive verb, things might still seem awkward. For example, the link labels in Fragment 16-6 use a transitive verb (*deliver*), yet the resulting sentences are somewhat awkward:

- *Each doctor can deliver treatment to patients.*
- *Each patient can be delivered treatment by a doctor.*

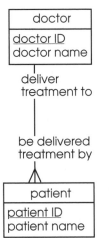

Fragment 16-6

Worse than the sentences, the labels themselves are quite cumbersome. The problem is that although "deliver" is a transitive verb, the direct object is neither of the entity names but some other noun altogether ("treatment"). The labels themselves seem cumbersome because it takes a lot of words to indicate what the relationship means. This leads us to the next principle.

Principle: Transitive-verb labels work best when one of the entity names can serve as the direct object. For example, Fragment 16-7 uses a transitive verb and yields very good sentences:

- *Each doctor can treat patients.*
- *Each patient can be treated by a doctor.*

The transitive verb is "treat"; the labels are good because an entity name (patient) serves as the direct object (the directly acted-on thing).

The longer labels (e.g., *deliver treatment to*), although accurate, are awkward. Happily, the awkwardness is avoidable; a better labeling alternative (e.g., *treat*) is available. In some cases, however, no better alternative will be available; you will have to accept labels that are long and cumbersome but accurate. If that's the price you have to pay for accuracy, so be it.

Principle: Use powerful verbs. What makes *treat* a better label than *deliver treatment to?* It is better because it uses the verb to convey most of the meaning.[3] The

Fragment 16-7

---

[3] Experienced and thoughtful writers employ this principle to make their prose forceful and direct. *John loves Mary* is a more powerful sentence than *John feels love for Mary* because the first sentence uses a powerful verb (*loves*) whereas the second sentence uses a weak verb (*feels*) and relies on a noun (*love*) to convey much of the meaning.

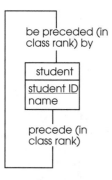

Fragment 16-8

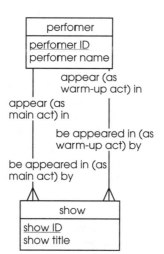

Fragment 16-9

inferior label relies on a noun (treatment) to convey the essence of the relationship's meaning.

For some relationships, you cannot find such a powerful, content-rich verb. For example, in Fragment 16-8, the verb "precede" provides some but not all of the content. What's important is that the relationship establishes a precedence according to class rank.

Principle: Use parentheses judiciously. Fragment 16-8 also illustrates the use of parentheses to help you and the users construct the sentences. The parentheses set off portions of the link label that can appear in several places in the sentence. For example, the following two sentences are equally valid:

- *Each student can be preceded in class rank by one other student.*
- *Each student can be preceded by one other student in class rank.*

The words "in class rank" can appear in several different places in the sentence, so you set them off in parentheses when you label the link.

When a relationship defies good labeling, there are sometimes several alternatives. For example, consider the two relationships in Fragment 16-9. One possibility for labeling is shown in the diagram. It yields these quite awkward sentences:

- *Each performer can appear as warm-up act in shows.*
- *Each show can be appeared in by one performer as warm-up act.*
- *Each performer can appear as main act in shows.*
- *Each show can be appeared in by one performer as main act.*

An alternative scheme employs the labels *use (as warm-up)*, *be used (as warm-up by)*, *use (as main)*, and *be used (as main) by*. This scheme yields these sentences:

- *Each show can use one performer as its warm-up performer.*
- *Each performer can be used as the warm-up performer of shows.*
- *Each show can use one performer as its main performer.*
- *Each performer can be used as the main performer of shows.*

These sentences are pretty awkward, too.

Because no excellent labels appear possible in this case, you and the users must choose between these two slightly awkward but accurate possibilities. Try both schemes and choose whichever one seems clearer to the users.

When you have "parallel" relationships like the ones in Fragment 16-9, use the same labeling scheme for both relationships. That is, don't use one labeling scheme for one relationship and another scheme for the other relationship. That misguided

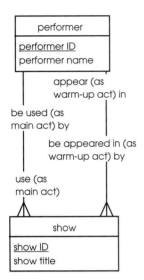

Fragment 16-10

approach (shown in Fragment 16-10) shrouds the parallelism; it makes the users work too hard to recognize the similarities between the two relationships.

When two less-than-ideal labeling alternatives are equally appealing, you cannot predict which one the users will prefer. On the one hand, the verb "appear" is appealing because it is relatively powerful—it conveys some meaning. But its drawback is that it is an intransitive verb. A performer appears <u>in</u> a show. On the other hand, the verb "use" is appealing because it is a transitive verb. But its drawback is that it is a very weak verb—it conveys little meaning. The essence of the relationship's meaning is contained in the other words: *use as main act* or *use as warm-up act*. Nevertheless, "use" can help you solve some thorny labeling problems.

Principle: Employ "use" as a catch-all transitive verb. Sometimes you won't be so lucky: Rather than having two or more moderately appealing labeling alternatives, you will have trouble coming up with even one reasonable alternative. In such a case, try to employ the word *use* as a weak verb with additional words to convey the essence of the relationship's meaning. For example, LDS Fragment 16-11 employs the word *use* to solve a difficult labeling problem. It yields the sentences

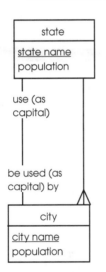

Fragment 16-11

- *Each state can use a city as capital.*
- *Each city can be used as capital by a state.*

As you can see, "use" is a weak verb; other words convey the essence of the relationship's meaning. But there is no better alternative—the users have no verb in their vocabulary to indicate what a capital city "does" to its state.

In particularly thorny problems, even the clever deployment of the word "use" doesn't work. It seems that nothing works. Although you and the users agree on what the relationship means, there seems to be no way to find a verb that works in both directions. In such cases, which will be very rare, you can violate the principle about using the same verb in both directions.

For example, the relationship in Fragment 16-12 uses two different verbs for its two labels. The verbs are "depart" and "be." These labels work, even though they conform to absolutely none of the secondary labeling principles. They do, however, satisfy the primary labeling principle because they generate clear, accurate, user-approved sentences:

- *Each airport can be the departure airport of flight legs.*
- *Each flight can depart from an airport.*

Don't forget that the secondary labeling principles are truly secondary and that what's important is that the users approve of the labels. As an alternative to the labels in Fragment 16-12, those in Fragment 16-13 conform to the secondary labeling prin-

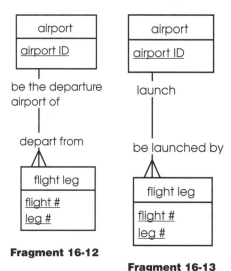

Fragment 16-12

Fragment 16-13

ciples. The labels use a transitive verb, they use the same verb in each direction, they use one of the entity names as the direct object of the verb, and they use a powerful verb. However, the users reject these labels because they do not conform to user vocabulary. The users never say that an airport "launches" a flight leg.

Taken together, Fragments 16-12 and 16-13 illustrate the relative importance of the primary and secondary labeling principles. The seemingly inferior labels are actually better because, despite their awkwardness, they more accurately reflect how the users understand their data.

Nevertheless, the secondary principles remain important. They can help you to generate good labels for most relationships that need labeling.

Exercises

1. For each labeling principle, make up a new example that illustrates it.
2. Repeat question 1 until you are confident that you can correctly apply the principle.
3. Try to come up with better labels for the one-one links of Fragment 16-11. For each label you devise, assess its quality, both in terms of the labeling principles and from the perspective of an imaginary user.

17
Chapter

Documenting
an LDS

As an LDS matures and stabilizes, you should create
a document describing its contents. This document
is helpful for several reasons. First, the act of writing the document will force you to
scrutinize the LDS with a critical eye; if you took shortcuts while creating the LDS,
the act of writing about it will reveal the errors lurking within it.

Second, if the LDS is good, a supporting document can help it become an enduring resource for the culture whose information it describes. That is, the document
helps ensure that the culture can continue to use the LDS even if you are no longer
present to read it aloud or design sample data about it.

Third, a document can help its users leverage as broadly as possible their investment in the LDS. For example, a document can make the LDS a valuable resource
for virtually any members of the organization: process designers, managers, software
professionals, and end users alike.

Fourth, a document can protect the LDS from fragment oscillation. An oscil-
lating fragment is a portion of the LDS that continuously changes back and forth
between two shapes as the LDS evolves. This phenomenon can occur when two
shapes seem equally compelling for the task at hand (for an example, see the discussion of Fragments 10-4 and 10-5). You can waste time repeatedly covering the same
ground—repeatedly asking the users the same questions. This is especially likely if
there are multiple data modelers working on the same large LDS. By documenting

the decision and the reasoning behind it (as in our description of why we chose Fragment 10-4), you can prevent other modelers from wasting the users' time covering the same territory.

Of course, for a document to realize any of these lofty goals, you need to put some thought and effort into it. With this chapter, we're trying to give you a head start.

The Audience

Know your audience. There are two primary audiences for the document you write:

• **Users.** This is the most important audience for the document because users are the most important constituents of the LDS and the entire data-modeling effort. Users are interested in the assertions contained on the LDS and the justifications for those decisions.
• **You and other data modelers.** Modelers are interested in the assertions, but for some portions of the LDS they are also interested in a detailed history of the LDSs evolution.

In addition, you can serve other, secondary audiences. But be careful that you do not create a document that tries to be all things to all people. The various audiences have varying interests, and no one document will be of interest to everyone. A later section of this chapter describes these secondary audiences and the information they are interested in.

Front Matter

The front matter can include any or all of the following:

• **Naming conventions.** There are two sources of naming conventions. The first is the book you are now reading—containing the conventions that Carlis and Maguire recommend for entity names, descriptor names, relationship names, and link labels. The second is the culture. The business or organization for whom you are creating the LDS might have conventions for product names, department names, or any other kind of name. These conventions typically predate the data-modeling effort and supersede the LDS naming conventions whenever there is a clash.
• **Target audiences.** The front matter should explicitly indicate who should read the document. If the document has several audiences, the front matter should instruct each audience about what portions of the document apply and what portions can be ignored.
• **How to read an LDS.** It wouldn't hurt to include a brief primer on how to read an LDS diagram. You can include some simple examples—as simple as the examples we used in Chapter 3. However, you should use examples taken directly from the LDS you are documenting.
• **Table of contents.** No document is complete without one.

Entity Documentation

You should document each entity. The most important part of the message is this: *What do we mean by one of these?* That is, what precisely constitutes a single instance of the category represented by the entity? Toward that end, you should consider including the following information:

- **Explanation of the entity name.** Why is the entity name accurate? What other entity names were considered and rejected as inaccurate? For each rejected entity name, was it rejected for a particular reason? Was the rejected name too coarse? Too fine? Too inclusive? Too exclusive? (See Chapter 14.) What words (if any) does the culture use as synonyms of the entity name? If the LDS is the result of an effort to integrate data from separately developed systems, what words from those systems correspond to this entity name? (The correspondence might not be exact.) Note that it is especially important to justify the entity name if the identifier is an arbitrary identifier.
- **Explanation of the entity's identifier (or in rare cases, identifiers).** If the identifier is an arbitrary identifier, why? Why were other, more meaningful identifiers rejected? If the identifier has multiple descriptors, why? Give examples of pairs of entity instances in which a subset of the identifier's descriptor values are equal.
- **Sample instances.** You must give sample instances of the entity, but you need not give them here. You can refer to a per-shape section of the document that contains sample instances of this entity. Wherever you give sample instances, be sure to annotate them with a count of how many instances are present. Remember, being able to count the instances is an excellent way to solidify the users' understanding of *What do we mean by one of these?* Where an entity has no more than a few dozen instances (you might call it a look-up table), you might decide to include all its instances so that they can be readily referenced.
- **Cross references.** You should add **pointers to the per-attribute and per-link sections for each of the entity's descriptors.**

Attribute Documentation

You should document the following information about each attribute:

- **Explanation of its name.** Is the name accurate? What other possible attribute names were rejected as inaccurate?
- **Its scale.** Be sure to point out if the attribute's name connotes the wrong scale. Remember, this can happen if the user's existing vocabulary gives the attribute a name suggesting the wrong scale. For example, the *PhoneNumber* attribute accommodates values whose scale is nominal, not numeric. (See Chapter 9.)
- **Domain of values.** It's the set of legal or expected values for the attribute.
- **Sample values.** You should give sample values of the attribute, but you probably should not give them here. Instead, you should give them where you give sample instances of the entity containing the attribute.

Link Documentation

You should document each link. Consider including the following information:

- **Link name.** Remember, the link name does not appear on the diagram; only selected link labels appear. You rarely or never say a link name when reading an LDS to users. But a good link name can help the users understand the attendant relationship. A word of warning: A bad link name is confusing; it does more harm than good. If you are not going make an accurate link name, don't bother documenting a link name at all. (See the end of Chapter 14.)
- **Explanation of the chicken foot.** If the link is a degree-many link, it might have a finite maximum degree. For example, in Fragment 10-5, the maximum degree is 2. It is worth mentioning this in the documentation.

Relationship Documentation

For each relationship, you should consider including the following documentation:

- **Official name of the relationship.** Remember, the relationship name does not appear on the diagram and is likely to be awkward. But an accurate name for the relationship can, despite its awkwardness, help the users understand what the relationship means.
- **Sample data.** You should give sample values of the relationship, but you should probably not give them in each per-relationship section. Instead, you should give them as part of the sample data about a larger shape in which the relationship participates.

Fragment Documentation

Some small portions of the LDS will deserve elucidation. For each such LDS fragment, you should document it as a unit (in addition to documenting each of its entities, relationships, and descriptors). You need to use your judgment about which fragments deserve this documentation, but we can give two hints to help you decide. First, keep track of which fragments confused the users during the modeling sessions. For which fragments did you find yourself frequently drawing sample data? Which fragments did the users argue about? Which fragments did the users spend the most time discussing? Such fragments deserve special documentation.

Second, consider documenting any fragment exhibiting any of these shapes:

- Multiple short paths
- Chicken feet in with a high number of chicken feet. For example, Fragment 7-8 deserves documentation.
- Any fragment resulting from increasing the level of abstraction. For example, Fragment 7-15 requires documentation more urgently than Fragment 7-14 does.
- Subordinates across
- Subordinates out

Documenting a fragment is a bit more freewheeling than documenting an individual entity, descriptor, or relationship. You may user whatever rhetorical devices you can think of to explain the fragment. But as you work to document the fragment, keep the following hints in mind. First, use sample data liberally. Use realistic sample data, and keep in mind what we told you about annotating sample data in Chapter 5.

Second, if a fragment has been the subject of many user conversations, consider explicitly documenting the decisions reflected in the fragment. Show alternative fragments that were considered but rejected, and tell why they were rejected.

Constraint Documentation

As the LDS matures and stabilizes, you will become aware of candidate constraints, which you can document. Your documentation of candidate constraints will fall into three categories:

- **Worthy constraints about user categories.** On rare occasions, a fundamental aspect of a user-recognized category will not be expressed on the LDS diagram. In such cases, a constraint is necessary, and you should document any such constraint.
- **True constraints about instance data.** More often, a candidate constraint does not refine the definition of a user-recognized category but instead simply restricts what instances are possible. Typically, these constraints are short-lived because they become invalid when the users decide to change the way they process data. (Remember what Chapter 2 says: Processing needs change more frequently than data needs do.)
- **False constraints.** In the most common case of all, a candidate constraint is false. Surprisingly, even some of these false constraints deserve documentation because they reflect what the users expect from a "normal" or "complete" set of instance data. If you document any of these constraints, be sure to tell the whole story: that this candidate constraint is actually false. To illustrate the invalidity of one of these constraints, you can show some valid instance data for which the candidate constraint does not hold.

For a more thorough discussion about these three categories of candidate constraints, see Chapter 22.

Issues List

Keep track of the outstanding issues, questions, and concerns you have about an in-progress model. As models grow more and more complex, such a list will make sure that nothing falls through the cracks. Virtually anything can go on an issues list. For example, our issues lists have included the following:

- **Questions that need to be asked.** Many questions will occur to you while you are studying an in-progress model without users present. Keep these questions in the open issues list so that you don't forget them.

- **Questions to ask a particular user.** Sometimes during a modeling meeting, the users cannot answer a question but give the name of the expert who can. Keep track of such questions and the users who can answer them.
- **Nouns deserving investigation.** Sometimes a noun can come up during a meeting while you are focused on a particular problem. Use the issues list to keep track of these nouns so that you or your data-modeling colleagues know to investigate this noun later. (For example, see the mention of the word "work" in the discussion of Fragment 6-12.)

Don't limit yourself to these types of issues. The issues list is for you and the other data modelers; keep track of whatever you need to.

Also, don't limit yourself to unresolved issues. We separate our issues lists into two parts: open issues and closed issues. If an issue is closed, we keep track of who closed it and why. For closed issues, it is especially important to record details about which user answered the question. Remember, you will surely encounter the provincial view of data (see Chapters 1 and 2) in which different users perceive their data needs differently. This provincial view can manifest itself when two different users give different answers to a question you ask. When you encounter this phenomenon, you need to mediate a discussion between the two users to determine why they disagree. If your closed issue does not indicate who answered the question, you will not be able to bring the disagreeing parties together.

Supplemental Material for Secondary Audiences

A stable, high-fidelity LDS can support many tasks performed by the members of an organization. In the supplemental material we write about an LDS, we have found it useful to include information supporting two communities in particular: software professionals and business designers.

Software Professionals

This should come as no surprise: Software professionals such as database designers and programmers are interested in the LDS. You can supplement the document you write to include information of particular interest to the software professionals. You can include any information your audience needs, but we have found the following especially useful:

- **Names of database tables and columns.** The DBMS you use to store the data users want remembered will probably restrict the length of table names and column names. Thus the names of the tables and columns might not be obvious from the corresponding names on the LDS.
- **Deviations from the "default" database schema.** Remember, the LDS constitutes WHAT the categories of data are; the database schema constitutes HOW the instances of those categories will be stored. Because there are so many possible

HOWs, it is useful to write down the precise mapping between the categories on the LDS and the tables and columns in the database schema.

If you choose to include this information, be careful to keep it well segregated from the nontechnological information so that the document's primary audience (the users) can ignore it easily. If you force the users to wade through a bunch of technical material of no interest to them, you will effectively squander your efforts to create a data model that is purely logical.

Business Designers

In most organizations, certain people make recommendations about how the business should operate. In a manufacturing organization, industrial engineers design the process by which products are manufactured. In catalog sales organizations, process specialists design the sequence of steps through which a customer's order is taken over the phone, assembled at the warehouse, and shipped. In an automotive service shop, managers dictate the policies by which reception clerks accept customer vehicles, interview them about the repair or diagnostic work required, arrange short-term rentals of replacement vehicles, and convey the work orders to the staff of automotive mechanics.

Different businesses use different names for this function; we call it "business design." The people who are responsible for business design might do any or all of the following:

- Create policies and procedures manuals
- Create process models
- Create paper forms or data-entry screens to be filled out during individual steps of a process

The business designers care about the LDS because what they create depends on it. For example, the paper forms they create are used to collect instance data. The individual steps of the process models they create describe the process of data collection and manipulation.

You can work with these business designers to supplement the document you write about the LDS. Working together, you can achieve the following:

- Make sure that the policies and procedures manuals use the same vocabulary as the LDS.
- Make sure that the process models are described according to how their individual steps manipulate instance data of the LDS.
- Make sure that the paper forms or data-entry screens correspond appropriately to the categories of data on the LDS.

Exercise

Reread Chapter 6 and document the LDS (as of the final fragment in the chapter).

Story Interlude

Panic

Company X was panicking. They called me to help reverse-engineer an application before it was too late. The only person who really understood the application was retiring soon and the company needed to record what only he knew.

Moral: *Document now, before it is too late.*

Grateful users

After building an LDS, users often express gratitude to modelers. At company X, I observed users shaking modelers' hands and saying how wonderful it was to be able to talk about their business and not have to feel overwhelmed by technology. They said that they had been in previous requirements sessions that made them feel stupid. With LDS they felt empowered.

Moral: *Users appreciate being asked to make decisions about their realm, not about technology.*

Modelers as Story Tellers

At company X, several modelers began to take on LDS tour-guide duties. Users would bring in visitors (off-site users, potential customers, or senior management) and ask a modeler to tell the data's story. The modeler would read portions of the LDS, peppering the story with real instances (learned from users, of course).

Modelers can quickly and broadly learn a lot about the company. Their content-neutral way of working allows them, in effect, to be tutored by expert users. Their duties prevent them from having a provincial view of data. Their LDS-reading skills enable them to present succinctly what the company remembers about itself.

Moral: *Modelers become a knowledgeable resource for users.*

Not My Fault

Here is a surprise: Some data modelers are not perfect.

At company X, I was observing an LDS session. Roy, the modeler, began by reviewing the in-progress LDS and then asked a shape-based question. Based on the users' response he modified the LDS appropriately. Then Roy started behaving defensively. He spent several minutes yammering about how it was not his fault that the model changed and he could not be deemed a failure when the users were the ones who were changing their minds. The users were puzzled and did not know what to say. The meeting went downhill and fizzled to a stop. Roy had interpreted change and struggle as signs of failure and not merely as how things normally progress.

Roy's defensive behavior persisted, and he eventually was shifted to other duties.

Moral: *Relax—struggle is normal.*

Smaller Is Not Better

At company X, I was running an LDS session, and at first things were going great. But then I started to get no to my shape-based questions when I expected yes. Eventually I called a timeout and found a way to indicate my concern about the answers—not any one in particular, but about the preponderance of *No, do not remember that.* User Cate, one of the nay-sayers, piped up with *Well, the LDS is big enough.* She was trying to get closure.

I had failed to remind them that an LDS reflects their burden-shifting decisions and that it reflects those exceptional instances that they decided exist and must be accommodated.

After my reminder they, by consensus vote, revised many noes into yeses. Cate acquiesced but persisted in thinking *Smaller means better* instead of *Smaller means different.*

Moral: *The LDS is as big as user decisions make it.*

Bigger Is Not Better

At company X, Kathleen, a novice modeler, misbehaved. She lost sight of *Do what is worth doing.* As she modeled with users she pressured them to include more on the model. Part of her motivation was her realization that, if the users said yes to her questions, then she could use one of the more intricate shapes she had just learned.

She acted as if a bigger, fancier model is a better model.

Moral: *Let the users decide.*

Small Can Be Good

At company X, I led a modeling session where the users (software developers) wanted to build an LDS to understand one of their main software products. Although the product was a success, its innards were a mystery (these users had widely differing views of it), and maintaining and enhancing it caused significant pain. To jump start the session, I had built a preliminary model from the product's manuals and produced a long list of questions. We quickly concluded that the manual was, at best, too vague, and decided to start with a blank board. In order to reconcile points of view and to stress the model, we tried many variations.

At the end of the day-and-a-half-long session, even though the LDS had only about a dozen entities, the users were tired and happy—tired because they had worked very hard, happy because they had learned a lot in coming to their consensus view of the product's data.

Moral: *Users can measure progress by quality, not quantity.*

Take a Field Trip

At Company X, I was helping a team of modelers who were struggling with a model of various mechanical and electronic components connected in a dizzying array of ways. The instances that the users gave did not make sense to the modelers. The modelers all thought that the users were well-informed and articulate, but unlike most modeling adventures, the modelers' normal, initial fogginess about the users' alien culture was not clearing up. (I was in no better shape.)

Then one user, Wendy, called a timeout and took us all on a field trip. We went elsewhere in the company complex where Wendy pointed to real, physical instances of the model's categories. These things had mass, shape, color, and place. They were juxtaposed with each other in meaningful ways. They had labels, warnings, and instruction sheets.

Because of the field trip, the fog lifted and sunny smiles appeared. Moreover, modelers had a new kind of approach to the model content. They said, for example, *I saw variously colored cables; tell me about them.*

The team continued to struggle—after all the system was inherently complex and intricate—but they successfully completed the model.

Moral: *Anchor your understanding with real instances.*

18
Chapter

Script for
Controlled
Evolution:
The Flow

During controlled evolution, you and the users discuss the LDS, the users make decisions about what is worth remembering, and you modify the LDS accordingly. These step-wise refinements are easy for you to make and for the users to follow. Because many of these refining steps occur in a predictable order, you can prepare for these discussions by studying The Flow.

The Flow is a loose script for discussing LDSs. It is only a loose script because some steps occur at almost any time during the discussion.

Script for The Flow

In The Flow, you help the users articulate the relationship or short path between two entities. Figure 18-1 illustrates The Flow in detail. The diagram reflects the question-and-answer nature of the conversation with users. It contains ovals (representing the questions you ask) and rectangles (representing the various stages the in-progress

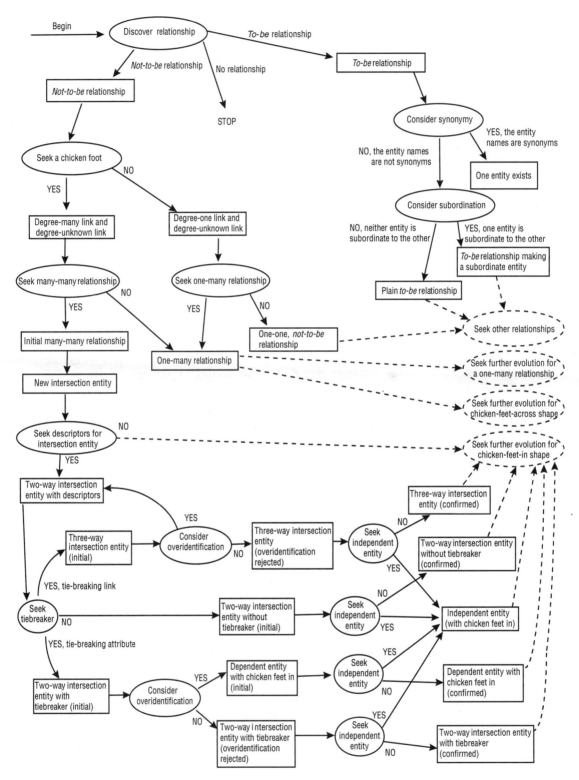

Figure 18-1. The Flow

LDS fragment can be in based on the answers the users provide). In addition, the diagram uses these other conventions:

- An arrow pointing from a rectangle to an oval indicates that when an LDS fragment reaches a particular stage, you should initiate a particular investigation (that is, you should ask a particular question).
- An arrow from an oval to a rectangle indicates that for a particular answer to a question, you should modify the LDS accordingly.
- An arrow from an oval to another oval indicates that for a particular answer to a question, you should immediately ask a follow-up question.
- An arrow between two rectangles indicates that when an LDS fragment reaches a particular stage, you should immediately transform the fragment into another shape.
- Dotted ovals represent large-scale investigations that you can initiate when you reach a natural stopping point in The Flow. These large-scale investigations can involve reinitiating The Flow.
- A dotted arrow points from a natural stopping point in The Flow to a large-scale investigation you perform after reaching a natural stopping point.

For example, consider the portion of The Flow shown in Figure 18-2. The top arrow indicates that when the LDS fragment includes an evolving relationship with one degree-many link and another link whose degree is not yet known, you should proceed to ask a question determining whether the other link's degree is many. The arrow labeled NO indicates that if the answer to the question is no, you should make the evolving relationship a one-many relationship. Similarly, the arrow labeled YES indicates that if the answer is yes, the evolving relationship becomes a many-many relationship.

The arrow pointing to the new intersection entity rectangle indicates that when the fragment evolves to include a many-many relationship, you should replace the relationship with an intersection entity between the other two entities immediately, before asking any other questions of the users.

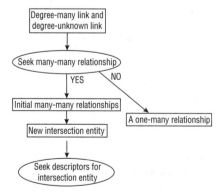

Figure 18-2.   Portion of The Flow

Discussing a *Not-to-Be* Relationship

This section describes the portion of The Flow during which you and the users discuss and develop a *not-to-be* relationship. It corresponds to the upper left portion of Figure 18-1.

Flow Investigation: Discover Relationship

You begin The Flow when you discover a relationship that exists between two entities. You can discover a relationship in any of the following ways:

- By listening to the users talk about their data
- By discovering hidden relationships expressed on the LDS
- By explicitly asking the users if a relationship exists between two entities

Listening to Users

You discover most relationships simply by listening to users. For example, when discussing circuits, users in the telephony industry can hardly avoid mentioning that circuits are sold to customers. In effect, the users are indicating a relationship between the entities *circuit* and *customer.* All you have to do is pay attention.

Discovering Hidden Relationships

As you study an in-progress LDS, you can discover "hidden" relationships—relationships that are implied with attributes. When you discover such a relationship, you should remove the attributes and draw the relationship explicitly on the diagram. Then for each new relationship you draw, you should proceed with The Flow to learn its details.

There are several ways an LDS can contain hidden relationships:

- An entity can include descriptors that replicate the identifying descriptors of some other entity. For example, in Fragment 18-1, herd's identifier is replicated in the cow entity.
- An entity can include a descriptor (or set of descriptors) whose value (or set of values) specifies a unique instance of some other entity. For example, in Fragment 18-1, each value of the attribute *leading cow name* uniquely specifies a cow.
- Two entities can include attributes that have the same name. For example, in Fragment 18-1, both entities have an attribute named *farm.*

Fragment 18-2 shows the improved LDS. The remedy for the third problem (multiple attributes named *farm*) deserves special attention. Notice that the remedy includes creating a new entity called *farm.* For more information about remedying like-named attributes, see the section "Promoting Attributes" in Chapter 19.

Notice the question marks in Fragment 18-2. Each question mark indicates that the degree of a link is not known. We say more about these question marks soon.

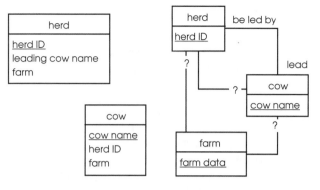

Fragment 18-1   **Fragment 18-2**

Explicitly Asking for Relationships

During controlled evolution, there are certain times when you should seek a relationship between two entities:

- When two entities have names you cannot distinguish on the LDS. For example, if the LDS contains *job* and *task* entities and you suspect these words might be synonyms, you should seek a relationship between the entities.
- When a relationship or short path already exists between two entities. For example, in Fragment 18-3, you should seek a relationship between *course* and *student.*
- When two entities were created to replace a single entity whose name used an overloaded word whose various definitions differed only subtly. For an example of this, see the creation of the *agribusiness industry* and *agribusiness company* entities in Chapter 21.
- When two entities are pivotal to the users' enterprise. It is easy to recognize a pivotal entity, although it is hard to formalize exactly how this recognition happens. Pivotal entities are among the first ones you discover when working on a new LDS. Pivotal entities tend to be common, independent entities, and they tend to exhibit the *chicken feet out* shape.

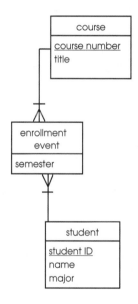

Fragment 18-3

Be cautious about the last item in the list. Seeking relationships between pivotal entities is somewhat speculative, and if you resort to it too much, the conversation is probably not inducing users to be forthcoming with details about their information, or you are not recognizing the existence of relationships when the users allude to them.

Securing an Answer to the Question

You want to find out if there is a relationship between two entities, and if there is a relationship, you want to know what it means. Lacking any other indication of the relationship, you find out by asking a question, and as usual, you should phrase the question in the users' words. This is a little tricky, because until you know what the relationship means, you are missing a key piece of vocabulary. For example, suppose you are seeking a relationship between *course* and *student* in Fragment 18-3. You can ask either of the following questions:

* *Can a student be associated with a course in some way besides enrollment?*
* *Is there some association between student and course beyond the enrollment of students in courses?*

These sentences include the vocabulary ("course," "enrollment," and "student") that you already know about the users' data. But the sentences are necessarily indistinct ("some association") in referring to the speculated relationship.[1]

This vagueness is even more evident when you seek a relationship between two entities between which there is no existing relationship or short path. For example, suppose on an in-progress LDS, you suspect that a relationship exists between two pivotal entities, *protein* and *scientist*.

* *Can a protein be associated with a scientist?*
* *Is there some association between protein and scientist?*

There is no way to avoid this vagueness. However, you can be sure to use the vocabulary you already do know ("course," "student," "enrollment," "protein," "scientist") to help the users understand your questions. And as soon as the users answer the question, the vagueness disappears because their answer provides you with new vocabulary.

Possible Answers to the Question

When you seek a relationship, there can be three possible results:

* **No relationship.** For example, users can say *No, there is no other association between students and courses.* If no relationship exists, you are finished with The Flow.
* ***To-be* relationship.** If you ask the question *Can jobs be associated with tasks?* users can indicate that a job can be a task or a task can be a job. They'll typically say *They're the same thing* or *There's no difference between jobs and tasks.* Such answers indicate a *to-be* relationship. If a *to-be* relationship exists, you must continue by investigating whether the related entities are synonyms, whether one

---

[1] If you know what the speculated relationship means, you could ask about it directly: *Can a student tutor a course?* But if you know enough to use the word "tutor," you already know about the relationship, and you don't have to ask this question at all. Don't try to eliminate the vagueness by guessing what the relationship might mean—that will only falsely restrict the scope of the users' answer. If the vagueness of your question baffles the users, you can offer them some examples. That is, you can speculate aloud about the possible meanings such a relationship might take. But make it clear to the users that you are speculating and that you are interested in any relationship whatsoever, not just in the accuracy of your own speculations.

of the entities is subordinate to the other, or if they are both subordinate to a third entity. As this answer occurs infrequently, we defer its discussion until later in this chapter.

- *Not-to-be* **relationship.** For example, users can respond to your question by saying *Yes, students can tutor courses.* Notice that with such an answer, the users have provided you with a new piece of vocabulary: "tutor." As this answer is quite common, we discuss it next.

Flow Stage: *Not-to-be* Relationship

Immediately after you discover that a *not-to-be* relationship exists between two entities, you should draw a line connecting the two entities. When the LDS is in this state, you should realize two things:

- At this point, the LDS fragment is syntactically invalid because you have not asserted a degree (one or many) for either of the links. The newly added relationship in Fragment 18-4 uses question marks to indicate that the degrees are not yet known. Each question mark reminds you to ask the users about the degree of the link. If you don't use question marks, you cannot distinguish between degree-one links and degree-unknown links.
- At this point, you should know what the relationship means. That is, you should be able to label the links. The decision actually to add the labels can come now or later, but you should be able to say now what the labels would be. Indeed, in some situations, you can decide to add link labels immediately. Specifically, you can add the labels immediately if the newly added relationship constitutes a second short path between the entities. Fragment 18-4 shows a newly added relationship, including link labels. You add this relationship when the users respond to your question about an additional relationship with *Yes, students can tutor courses.*

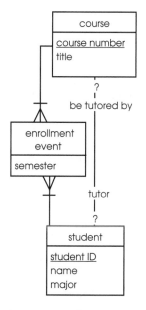

Fragment 18-4

Flow Investigation: Seek a Chicken Foot

After you discover a *not-to-be* relationship and after you have added any necessary link labels, you should choose one of the two links and secure from the users a decision about whether its degree is one or many.

Securing an Answer to the Question

To learn the degree of a link, you can ask the users a direct question. The questions are deceptively simple. For example, you can use either of the following questions to investigate the top question mark of Fragment 18-4:

- *Can any student tutor more than one course?*
- *Is there such a thing as a student with several courses that he or she tutors?*

The simplicity of these questions belies their carefully constructed phrasing. This phrasing ensures the following:

- The sentences use singular form of the described entity—in this case, the word "student." Remember, you are asking a question about a particular link, and each value of the link serves to describe an entity instance. So when you ask the question, you want the users to think about an instance of the entity. (In fact, you want the users to think of an arbitrary[2] instance of the described[3] entity.) In effect, you want to learn whether there can be an *individual* entity instance whose link value can be plural. Thus the sentences take care to use the singular form of the name of the described entity.

    Consider the alternative: using the plural form of the described entity. For example, if you ask *Can students tutor more than one course?* you might get a false affirmative. A user can say yes, meaning *Yes, there are several courses eligible for tutoring by students.* You, as data modeler, would be misled[4] by this affirmative response into adding a chicken foot to the diagram.

- The sentences correctly employ the user vocabulary. Most notably in this case, the sentences correctly use the word "tutor." They do not use a near-synonym (like "teach," "coach," or "assist"). What's more, the sentences do not confuse active voice with passive voice. That is, they do not erroneously use the wrong link label, as in *Can any student be tutored by more than one course?*

Possible Answers to the Question

The question has two possible answers. For example, consider the top question mark in Fragment 18-4. There are two possibilities:

- If the users say yes, replace the question mark with a chicken foot. Such a chicken foot would indicate that there is a link whose name is *tutored courses of student* and whose degree is many.

---

[2] "Arbitrary" does not mean "typical." As you put this question to the users, you do not want them to think about the typical instance of the entity. Rather, you want to characterize the question this way: *If I arbitrarily select an instance of the entity, could the attendant descriptor value be plural?* For the top question mark of Fragment 18-2, you want users to consider *If I arbitrarily select a student, could the set of courses tutored by that student contain two or more elements?*

[3] Remember, when you think about a link, there are two entities, the <u>described</u> entity and the describing entity. The described entity is so called because each of its instances is described by the attendant descriptor value. For example, the cow Alma is part of the description of Herd 083 because we can describe Herd 083—at least in part—by calling it a herd containing Alma.

[4] By the way, such a misinterpretation is not the user's fault; it's your fault. As the data modeler, you must articulate your questions to eliminate misinterpretation. Although we're belaboring a rather simple point, we want to be sure you learn well this simple trick (using singulars, not plurals) for clarity—so that when you are working on an LDS with busy, highly paid, perhaps impatient users who have a limited amount of time to spend answering your questions, you won't have to fumble for the right words. What's more, the users will grow more willing to answer your questions as you earn their respect with your confident, direct, and effective use of language.

- If the users say no, replace the question mark with a line endpoint with no chicken foot. Such an endpoint would indicate that there is a link whose name is *tutored course of student* and whose degree is one.

Flow Investigation: Seek a One-Many Relationship

When an evolving relationship has a degree-one link and a degree-unknown link, you should secure from the users a decision whether the unknown degree is one or many.

Securing an Answer to the Question

By the way, the right-most relationship in Fragment 18-5 corresponds to the stage of The Flow known as "Degree-one link and degree-unknown link."

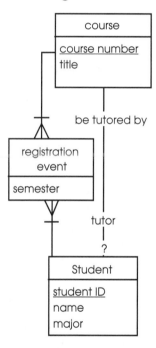

Fragment 18-5

As when you sought the degree of the first link, you learn the degree of this link by asking the users a direct question. You can use either of the following questions to investigate the question mark of Fragment 18-5.

- *Can any course be tutored by more than one student?*
- *Is there such a thing as a course with several students tutoring it?*

Once again, the questions deserve scrutiny despite their apparent simplicity. Notice that the questions use the singular form of the described entity, *course.* It would be wrong to phrase the question as *Can courses be tutored by several students?*

Notice also that the questions correctly employ the user vocabulary. They employ the user word "tutor," and they use the correct form with the subject *course.* The first sentence, for example, uses the link label *be tutored by* because it is the label near the described entity *course.* It would be wrong to ask *Can any course tutor more than one student?*

Possible Answers to the Question

The question has two possible answers:

- If the users say yes, replace the question mark with a chicken foot. Such a chicken foot would indicate that there is a link whose name is *tutoring students of course* and whose degree is many. Then, because the relationship is a one-many relationship, you should pursue further evolution. (See the section of this chapter called "Flow Continuation: Seek Further Evolution for a One-Many Relationship.")

- If the users say no, replace the question mark with a line endpoint with no chicken foot. Such an endpoint would indicate that there is a link whose name is *tutoring student of course* and whose degree is one. Then, because the relationship is a one-one, *not-to-be* relationship, you should reinvestigate. (See the section of this chapter called "Flow Stage: One-One, *Not-to-be* Relationship.)

Flow Investigation: Seek a Many-Many Relationship

When an evolving relationship has a degree-many link and a degree-unknown link, you should secure from the users a decision whether the unknown degree is one or many.

Securing an Answer to the Question

By the way, the rightmost relationship in Fragment 18-6 corresponds to the stage of The Flow known as "Degree-many link and degree-unknown link."

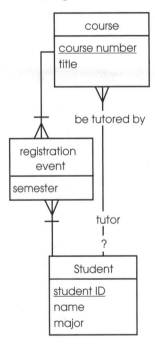

Fragment 18-6

As when you sought the degree of the first link, you learn the degree of this link by asking the users a direct question. You can use either of the following questions to investigate the question mark of Fragment 18-6:

- *Can any course be tutored by more than one student?*
- *Is there such a thing as a course with several students tutoring it?*

Once again, the questions deserve scrutiny despite their apparent simplicity. Notice that the questions use the singular form of the described entity. In this case, the described entity is *course*. It would be wrong to phrase the question as *Can courses be tutored by several students?*

Notice also that the questions correctly employ the user vocabulary. They employ the user word "tutor," and they use the correct form with the subject *course*. The first sentence, for example, uses the link label *be tutored by* because it is the label near the described entity *course*. It would be wrong to ask *Can any course tutor more than one student?*

Important: Notice that the questions in this section are identical to the questions we describe in the preceding section. It does not matter whether the degree of the link you already understand is one or many; the questions you ask are identical, because the questions you ask are about the link whose degree is unknown. The details of the other link (the one whose degree you already know) are immaterial to the questions you ask or to the possible answers you can get from the users.

Possible Answers to the Question

The question has two possible answers.

- If the users say yes, replace the question mark with a chicken foot. Such a chicken foot would indicate that there is a link whose name is *tutoring students of course* and whose degree is many. Then, because the relationship is a many-many relationship, you should immediately replace it with an intersection entity. (See the section of this chapter called "Flow Stages: Initial Many-Many Relationship and New Intersection Entity.")
- If the users say no, replace the question mark with a line endpoint with no chicken foot. Such an endpoint would indicate that there is a link whose name is *tutoring student of course* and whose degree is one. Then, because the relationship is a one-many relationship, pursue further evolution. (See the section of this chapter called "Flow Continuation: Seek Further Evolution for a One-Many Relationship.")

Flow Stage: One-One, *Not-to-be* Relationship

If the evolving relationship is a *not-to-be* relationship, yet the users indicate that both links have degree one, you should pause to investigate. Such relationships are so rare, you should doubt your own progress. Recheck each link in turn—is the degree truly one? Are the users oversimplifying when they answer your questions? Sometimes users oversimplify by considering only the typical instances of the described entity *("Typically, a course has at most[5] one tutor")* without considering the legitimate atypical instances *("Some interdepartmental courses can have a tutor from each department, so I guess one of those courses could have several tutors")*.

After reinvestigating, if the relationship remains a one-one *not-to-be* relationship, you should be sure to add labels to the links, if you haven't already.

When you have a labeled one-one *not-to-be* relationship on the LDS and you are convinced that the users are faithfully describing their (atypical as well as typical) instances to you, you have reached the end of The Flow. You should then seek other relationships between the two entities. (See the section of this chapter called "Flow Continuation: Seek Other Relationships.")

---

[5] Notice the ambiguity of the user's language. "Typically" suggests that the user is articulating a rule of thumb, not a hard-and-fast rule. On the other hand, "at most" connotes a hard-and-fast rule. It is unclear what the user is trying to say. When listening to users, you must ask follow-up questions to make sure you understand them. When you ask follow-up questions, you should not be persnickety or legalistic with the users. Don't scold them because their language is imprecise. Everyone speaks ambiguously, and you are not there to embarrass or shame the users into speaking accurately. You are there to make sure that you and everyone else in the room understands the decisions about what is worth remembering— but you don't have to irritate everybody to reach that goal. Your probing questions will eventually make everyone aware of the value of speaking accurately.

Flow Stage: One-Many Relationship

When a relationship evolves to a one-many relationship, you reach the end of The Flow. The end of The Flow is a good place to pause, collect your thoughts, and review the in-progress LDS. Specifically, you should consider the following actions:

- Reexamine the names and the identifiers of the two entities that are associated through the one-many relationship. Does each entity name apply to a single instance of the entity? For each entity, do the descriptors that contribute to its identifier suffice to distinguish each instance from every other instance? Is the entity overidentified?
- Read the LDS fragment to users to confirm that you understand the data and that the LDS expresses their decisions about what's worth remembering. (In addition, each time you read the LDS to users, they grow more comfortable reading LDS diagrams themselves.)
- Pursue further evolution. (See the section of this chapter called "Flow Continuation: Seek Further Evolution for a One-Many Relationship.")

Flow Stages: Initial Many-Many Relationship and New Intersection Entity

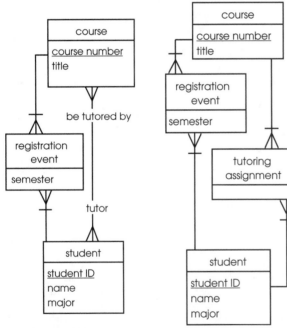

Fragment 18-7

Fragment 18-8

When an evolving relationship becomes a many-many relationship, you should take the following steps:

1. Aloud to the users, read the relationship in both directions; that is, read each link in turn. For example, read the many-many relationship in Fragment 18-7 by saying, *Each student can tutor several courses* and *Each course can be tutored by several students.* As you read each link, you can point to the appropriate portions of the diagram to help users follow along.
2. Replace the many-many relationship with an intersection entity. Fragment 18-8 shows the result when you replace the many-many relationship of Fragment 18-7.
3. Aloud to the users, read the newly added short path between *course* and *student.*

Steps 1 and 3 help the users understand why the short path, including the intersection entity, is equivalent to the replaced many-many

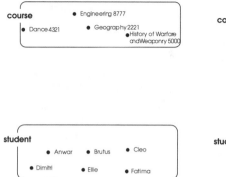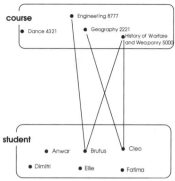

relationship. If users do not understand why they are equivalent, you can help them by drawing some sample data. After you read the many-many relationship aloud, draw a figure like the left side of the figure above. To this figure, gradually add lines, as in the figure at right. After you add each line, describe it. For example, after you add the leftmost line, point to it and say, *This indicates that Brutus tutors Engineering 8777.*

Add enough lines to illustrate that a course can have several tutoring students and that a student can tutor several courses. Then point out the ramifications. For example, point out that *Brutus tutors several courses* and that *History of Warfare and Weaponry has several tutors.*

At this point, the users should understand how the LDS (with the many-many relationship) accommodates the sample data. Now you must lead them through the conversion of the many-many relationship into a short path including an intersection entity. You must make the users realize the following:

- In the illustration of the sample data, each line constitutes a memorable thing.
- Each line is an instance of the same kind of memorable thing.
- This kind of memorable thing must have some name. Ask the users to supply the name. You can suggest names, but remember that the final decision is the users'. In the example you might suggest these names:[6]
    - *Indication of tutoring*
    - *Tutoring of course by student*
    - *Tutoring responsibility*

Make sure the name you suggest is a noun or noun phrase. Note that when you suggest names, you can use the official name of the relationship, provided it is not too awkward. This is one of the rare situations in which you explicitly consider the official name of a relationship. Read about names of relationships in Chapter 15.

---

[6] You can suggest these names because you have some sense of what the relationship means, based on the words the users employed when they first told you about the relationship.

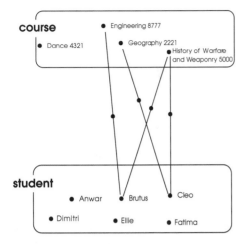

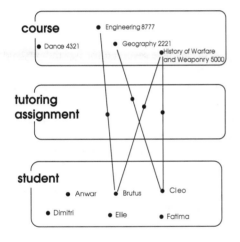

Now you can replace the many-many relationship with the short path including the intersection entity. For the name of the intersection entity, use the name the users supplied.

Point out that the new LDS accommodates the same sample data as the old LDS does.

On the same set of sample data you used to visualize the many-many relationship, draw a dot atop each line, as shown in the figure at the top left.

Then say, *By replacing the many-many relationship with an intersection entity, we are not changing what we can remember. We are merely choosing to think of those lines as instances of this new box, rather than as instances of the line we just replaced. Since this new box has a name that we can see on the diagram, we can put that name on the sample data.*

Then modify the drawing of the sample data so that it looks like the figure at the bottom left.

When you finish modifying the illustration of the sample data, point out that you did not add any sample data whatsoever. There were four lines in the middle of the sample illustration; now there are four dots. The meaning of the illustration has not changed.

Before continuing we need to address a learning issue: Some novice modelers object to immediately replacing a many-many relationship with an intersection entity. The objection goes something like this:

In my opinion there is no need to replace the many-many relationship. Look, if that intersection entity has no other descriptors then it clutters the diagram. I will put an intersection entity there, but only when the users want to remember other descriptors.

Such students sometimes mistakenly think a smaller LDS is better than a larger one. While working on an early, simple exercise (such as the first one in the Appendix) where the students must be both modeler and user, such students make self-serving, unrealistic, burden-shifting decisions to keep their answer small.

However, for several reasons this argument is flawed. First, real users make different burden-shifting decisions that place more burden on the system. So many-many relationships are rare (see Chapter 10) because real users ask the system to remember more. Second, when you make the intersection entity, then you can seek more descriptors just as you do with any entity. Third, as you will see in the section "Flow Continuation: Seek Further Evolution for Chicken-Feet-In Shape," you can, in the rare cases when it is appropriate, reestablish a many-many relationship.

Developing a Chicken-Feet-In Shape

This section describes the portion of The Flow during which you and the users discuss and develop a chicken-feet-in shape, beginning with an initial intersection entity. It corresponds to the bottom portion of Figure 18-1, replicated in Figure 18-3.

Preview of Working on a New Intersection Entity

Immediately after you add a new intersection entity to an in-progress LDS, a lot can happen fast. The new entity can get new descriptors, its identifier can change, and its name can change several times in succession as the users refine their understanding of the entity. The next few sections describe some of these changes.

As you read these next few sections, you should realize a few things. First, realize that the users might proceed through a number of Flow steps as if they were a single step. Specifically, the users might realize that the set of steps "Seek tiebreaker," "Consider overidentification," and "Seek independent entity" are all part of a single effort to establish an accurate identifier for the new entity. In effect, the users can recognize the portion of The Flow shown in Figure 18-3 as a single initiative. For example, experienced users can immediately offer an identifier that changes the entity from an intersection entity to a dependent entity.

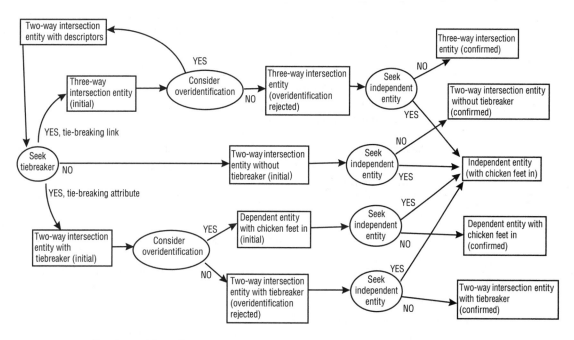

Figure 18-3. Portion of The Flow

Second, you should realize that whenever you change the identifier of the entity, you should revisit the entity name. Figure 18-3 presents a somewhat simplified picture; it excludes these entity-naming steps. For more information, see the section "Working with Users to Get the Entity Names Right" in Chapter 14.

Third, you should realize that the users might lead you to take the steps of the flow in an order other than the order presented here. Specifically, the users might first struggle to name and identify the entity accurately and only then tell you about the entity's descriptors. You can ask users for new descriptors at any time, and users can tell you about them at any time. The Flow explicitly suggests that you ask for new descriptors immediately after you create a new intersection entity because whenever a brand-new entity appears on an in-progress LDS, that's an especially good time to ask. (It is a good time to ask because a new entity is more likely to be misinterpreted by users, and accurately placed descriptors can help users interpret what an entity means. See the section "Relocating Misplaced Descriptors" in Chapter 19.) But there really is no bad time to ask for new descriptors, and The Flow diagram does not show all the various times you could ask.

Fourth, you should realize that although many user conversations about newly added intersection entities do not follow The Flow exactly as scripted, many conversations will indeed follow The Flow exactly as scripted. In other words, the script is not arbitrary—it makes sense to seek a tiebreaker before considering overidentification, and it makes sense to consider overidentification before seeking an independent entity.

Finally, you should realize that the flow is iterative, even as it applies to the evolution of an individual entity. Look carefully at the names of the stages. Notice that certain sets of stages have very similar names:

- Three-way intersection entity (initial)
  Three-way intersection entity (overidentification rejected)
  Three-way intersection entity (confirmed)
- Two-way intersection entity without tiebreaker (initial)
  Two-way intersection entity without tiebreaker (confirmed)
- Two-way intersection entity with tiebreaker (initial)
  Two-way intersection entity with tiebreaker (overidentification rejected)
  Two-way intersection entity with tiebreaker (confirmed)
- Dependent entity (initial)
  Dependent entity (confirmed)

The names differ only slightly because the stages differ only subtly. Consider the two stages "Dependent entity (initial)" and "Dependent entity (confirmed)." Between these two stages, the evolving entity does not change. The only difference is how many questions you have asked about the entity. In one case, you have asked whether the entity should become an independent entity. Because the users said no, the entity itself remained unchanged. But at some later time, you might want to ask the same question again. For example, you might later discover (perhaps by looking at sample data) that an identifying descriptor has null values. You again need to consider whether the entity should become an independent entity. (Indeed, something about the entity has to change because nulls are not allowed as values of identifying descriptors.)

Flow Investigation: Seek Descriptors for Intersection Entity

When an in-progress LDS includes an initial intersection entity, you should expect to add descriptors to the entity. You add descriptors to the entity for either of two reasons: (1) there is an additional kind of thing worth remembering about each instance of the entity; (2) the initial entity needs a tiebreaker. This section describes the first of these additions; the next section describes the second.

We mention the second of these investigations here because during controlled evolution the users can initiate the search for a tiebreaker first, before seeking any other descriptors. As the previous section mentions, The Flow diagram shows a slightly simplified view in which you must first seek other descriptors and only then seek a tiebreaker.[7]

Remember that in practice, these two investigations can happen in either order. In some situations, users immediately recognize the need for a tiebreaker because the name of the intersection entity demands one. For an example illustrating the immediate, user-induced search for a tiebreaker, see the next section. For more information about seeking descriptors, see the section "Seeking Descriptors" in Chapter 19.

Flow Investigation: Seek Tiebreaker

When an evolving short path includes a two-way intersection entity (with or without additional descriptors), you should investigate whether the identifier needs a tiebreaker and what descriptor should serve as the tiebreaker.

In some cases, you don't need to seek a tiebreaker because users tell you about the needed tiebreaker without any prompting. Consider again Fragment 18-8 with the newly added intersection entity *tutoring assignment*. As soon as you read the new short path to the users, one user says: *Sure, there is such a thing as a tutoring assignment, but the assignments are not permanent. Tutoring assignments are revisited every year.* This user is (perhaps[8]) indicating the need for a tiebreaker.

---

[7]There is some justification for this simplified view. When you seek a tiebreaker for an initial intersection entity, you seek to enlarge the identifier by adding a tie-breaking descriptor to it. So, strictly speaking, even an immediate search for a tiebreaker includes a search for a new descriptor. However, the user motivation for seeking a tiebreaker and the user motivation for seeking additional descriptors differ significantly. These differences are reflected in the way you converse with users during the two different investigations. You will only irritate the users with your pedantry if you insist on stressing the similarities between (1) searching for an additional descriptor (because there are additional kinds of things to remember about each instance), and (2) searching for an additional descriptor (because the identifier needs to be enlarged).

[8]We say "perhaps" because strictly speaking, the users have not yet said that they need to remember tutoring assignments from earlier years. Remember, the LDS expresses the users' decisions about what

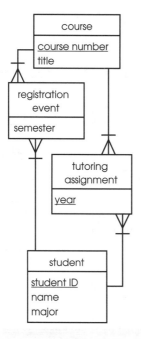

Fragment 18-9

Fragment 18-9 shows your response. After you draw Fragment 18-9, you should discuss it thoroughly with users. Read it aloud and draw some sample data. You want to confirm that the new identifier of *tutoring assignment* is correct. Note that this discussion can lead you to consider immediately whether the new identifier is too large. (See "Flow Investigation: Consider Overidentification.")

As you discuss Fragment 18-9 with users, you want to confirm that the entity name is correct.

For more information about seeking tiebreakers, see the section "Underidentification" in Chapter 19.

Flow Investigation: Consider Overidentification

After you add a tiebreaker to an intersection entity, you should immediately consider whether the entity is overidentified. Specifically, you should consider removing one of the original descriptors from the identifier. For an example of removing a descriptor from an intersection immediately after adding a tiebreaker to it, see the evolution of the *achievement* entity in Chapter 6. For more information about remedying overidentification, see the section "Fixing Identifiers" in Chapter 19.

Flow Investigation: Seek Independent Entity

An entity that is not an independent entity can evolve to become an independent entity—particularly if you discover that null values are allowed for the link or links contributing to the entity's identifier.

For an example of converting a dependent entity into an independent entity, see the evolution of the *head of cattle* entity in Chapter 6.

---

things are worth remembering. And sometimes the users will know about some things and still decide that those things (like last year's tutoring assignments) are not worth remembering. Some of the hardest decisions the users will make occur at the "boundaries" of the LDS—the places where the users decide to exclude certain known, well-understood things. In this particular situation, you can reasonably suspect that last year's tutoring assignments are indeed worth remembering because one user brought it up without any prompting from you. But even if the users later contract the scope of the database—deciding that last year's assignments are not worth remembering after all—there is no harm in having the in-progress LDS reflect this more expansive boundary decision. In fact, most boundary decisions are made by stepping slightly over the boundary, then pulling back.

Discussing a *To-be* Relationship

This section describes the portion of The Flow during which you and the users discuss and develop a *to-be* relationship. It corresponds to the upper right portion of Figure 18-1.

Flow Investigation: Consider Synonymy

When you first encounter a *to-be* relationship between two entities, you should wonder whether the two entity names are synonyms. That is, you should wonder whether every instance of either entity is related to an instance of the other entity.

Securing an Answer to the Question

Suppose you discover a *to-be* relationship between entities called *politician* and *elected official*. You need to ask the users two questions:

- *Is there such a thing as a politician who is not an elected official?*
- *Is there such a thing as an elected official who is not a politician?*

Possible Answers to the Question

There are several possible answers to this pair of questions.

- The users say no to both questions. In effect, the users say that every politician is an elected official and every elected official is a politician. You should take the following steps:
    1. Delete the *to-be* relationship.
    2. Merge the entities—that is, create a new entity with all the descriptors from both of the two original entities.
    3. Allow the users to choose a name for the resulting entity—the name will typically be one of the names of the original two entities.
  An example using entities named *task* and *job* illustrates the performance of these steps. Refer to the section "*To-be* One-One Relationships" in Chapter 10.
- The users say no to one question and yes to the other. In this case, you should consider subordination. See the next section.
- The users say yes to both questions. In this case, you should leave the *to-be* relationship unchanged. In fact, you can skip the test for subordination and move directly to The Flow stage called "Plain *To-be* relationship."

Flow Investigation: Consider Subordination

If one of the links of a plain *to-be* relationship can be null but the other cannot, you should wonder whether the relationship should evolve to become a *to-be* relationship making a subordinate entity.

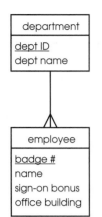

Fragment 18-10

Fragment 18-11

"Fat spot" is defined here.

Note that by asking this question, you are effectively revisiting the identifier of one of the entities. That is, you want to know whether the entity's existing identifier should be changed to consist only of the link of the *to-be* relationship. See "Fixing Identifiers" in Chapter 19.

Continuing the Discussion

This section describes the portion of The Flow occurring after you reach a natural stopping point, when you encourage users to reassess the existing fragment for additional opportunities to improve it. This section corresponds to the dotted ovals in Figure 18-1.

Flow Continuation: Seek Other Relationships

When you reach the end of The Flow, you should seek another relationship between the two original entities. For example, suppose you and the users follow The Flow to explore the enrollment of students in courses. When you are satisfied that the in-progress LDS expresses the phenomenon of enrollment of students in courses, you should seek another relationship between the entities *student* and *course*.

In effect, you are beginning The Flow again.

Flow Continuation: Seek Further Evolution for a One-Many Relationship

When The Flow produces a one-many relationship, you will sometimes need to replace the relationship with a more complex taxonomic structure.

For example, consider Fragments 18-10 and 18-11. Fragment 18-10 shows a one-many relationship, but Fragment 18-11 shows a more complex structure.

Generally, you do not explicitly ask the users whether to make this change. Rather, as you add more and more descriptors to the two entities, you consider whether each descriptor suffers from too-coarse or too-fine misplacement. More specifically, you consider whether descriptors near the chicken foot suffer from too-fine misplacement and whether descriptors of the other entity suffer from too-coarse misplacement. In Fragment 18-10, the *office building* attribute suffers from too-fine misplacement. However, moving it to the coarser entity (*department*) is not correct because users indicate that each department can have many office buildings. As possible locations for the attribute, one entity is too coarse and the other is too fine. The attribute rightly belongs somewhere in between, in some other entity. We call the in-between entity a **fat spot**.

For more information about too-coarse and too-fine misplacement of descriptors, see the section "Relocating Misplaced Descriptors" in Chapter 19.

After you replace the one-many relationship with a more complex structure, don't forget about subsequent evolution. Specifically, remember these possibilities:

- The more complex shape includes two one-many relationships. Could either of these relationships evolve to become a many-many relationship? For example, could the relationship between *employee* and *group* become a many-many relationship? Could either of these relationships be replaced by a more complex structure involving a fat spot? For example, is there a fat spot (perhaps an entity called *team*) on the relationship between *group* and *employee?*
- The two original entities (*department* and *employee*) might have still other relationships between them. Don't forget that when you reach the end of The Flow, you seek other relationships between the two original entities, as described in the preceding section.
- The entity at the fat spot might have other descriptors or other relationships to either of the two original entities. For example, there might be a relationship indicating that each employee can lead a group.

Flow Continuation: Seek Further Evolution for the Chicken-Feet-Across Shape

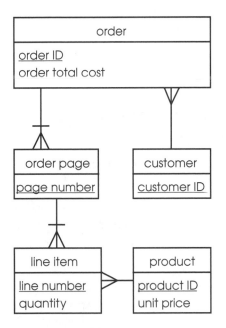

Fragment 18-12

When The Flow produces a one-many relationship, that relationship might be part of a fragment exhibiting the chicken-feet-across shape. In such cases, you should investigate whether the fragment includes a spurious entity. Specifically, you should look for a spurious fat spot.

For example, consider Fragment 18-12. The path of entities *customer, order, order page, line item* exhibits the chicken-feet-across shape.

Pay special attention to the entity *order page,* which is a fat spot between *order* and *line item.* You should work with the users to determine whether *order page* is necessary—whether they truly consider it worthwhile to remember which line items appear on the first page of an order and which line items appear on each subsequent page.

You should suspect that the entity is a spurious fat spot because its name alludes to a physical data container (the page). Remember, a logical data model should not be concerned with physical data representation. Some other words to watch out for are screen, form, report, record, folder.

To express your concerns to the users, you should speculate what the LDS would look like without the spurious fat spot, draw it, and read it aloud. Then, let the users decide whether they prefer the fragment that excludes the fat spot. For example, you should draw Fragment 18-13 and let the users choose between it and Fragment 18-12.

If the users have trouble choosing, you can ask them questions that will force them to indicate whether the fat spot matters—whether it has any real significance. For example, you can ask them how their business would change if they got a new

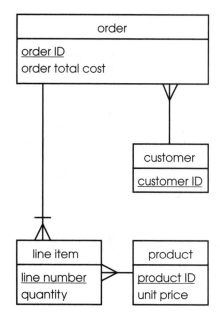

Fragment 18-13

printer capable of fitting more line items on each page of an order. Would that make any difference? Or you could ask them any of the following other questions:

- *Suppose a customer places an order requiring two pages. Then, the customer calls back and reduces his purchases significantly, so the order can be printed on one page. Would that make a difference? Besides modifying the database to remove the line items the customer no longer wants to purchase, would there be any other work to do? Does it really matter what page a line item is on?*
- *Suppose that each page of an order can contain ten line items. An order entry clerk enters an order with fifteen line items. Then, because of a power failure, the clerk must reenter the same order. While reentering the order, the clerk reverses the sequence of line items. If the power had not failed, some line items would have ended up on the second page of the order, but now those line items are on the first page. Does this matter?*

Remember, not all fat spots are spurious. For example, in Fragment 18-13, *order* is a fat spot between *customer* and *line item*.

Flow Continuation: Seek Further Evolution for the Chicken-Feet-In Shape

When The Flow produces an intersection entity (or any entity with chicken feet in), you should consider further evolution. Specifically, consider these possibilities:

- The evolving fragment includes several one-many relationships. Might one or more of these relationships evolve to become a many-many relationship? For example, look at what happens to the one-many relationship between *achievement* and *creature* in Chapter 6.
- Could the one-many relationships require fat spots?
- Could there be additional relationships between the new entity and the original entities? For example, in Chapter 6, a relationship eventually arises between *achievement* (the new chicken-feet-in entity) and *creature* (an original entity). Each instance of the new relationship indicates that a creature witnesses an achievement.
- The two original entities might have still other relationships between them.
- If the initial intersection entity has not changed (same identifier, no other descriptors), you might choose to revert to a many-many relationship. However, we caution against doing so because, over time or with other users, that bare intersection entity is likely to evolve. (Remember, many-many relationships are rare.)

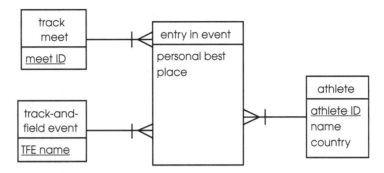

Fragment 18-14

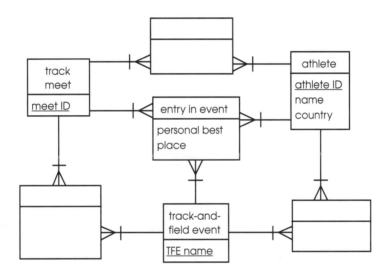

Fragment 18-15

- If there are more than two relationships in the chicken-feet-in shape, you should investigate whether the entity can be decomposed into simpler manifestations of the shape. The remainder of this chapter elaborates.

Suppose that controlled evolution yields Fragment 18-14. Because the *entry in event* entity exhibits chicken-feet-in with more than two relationships, you should investigate whether it should be decomposed into one or more simpler entities exhibiting chicken feet in. That is, you investigate whether one or more of the unnamed entities shown in Fragment 18-15 should be added.

There are three reasons why you should add such an entity. First, you can discover that a descriptor of the existing chicken-feet-in entity should be moved to one of the speculated entities. For example, the *personal best* attribute belongs on the intersection entity between *athlete* and *track-and-field event*. (You learn from the users that

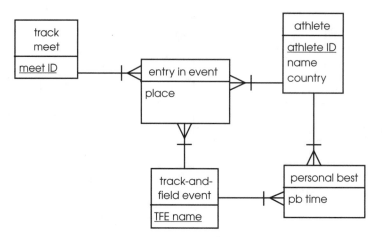

Fragment 18-16

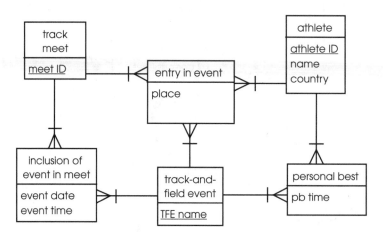

Fragment 18-17

each athlete has a personal best time for each event.) Fragment 18-16 shows the resulting LDS.

Second, you can discover a previously unknown descriptor that belongs on one of the speculated entities. For example, you can learn that users need to remember the scheduled time of each *track-and-field event* for each *track meet*. Fragment 18-17 shows the resulting LDS.

Third, you can discover that the speculated entity needs to exist merely because the users need to remember noteworthy pairs of instances of the other entities. For example, the users can indicate that they need to remember noteworthy (*athlete, track meet*) pairs. Each noteworthy pair indicates that an athlete has committed to attend-

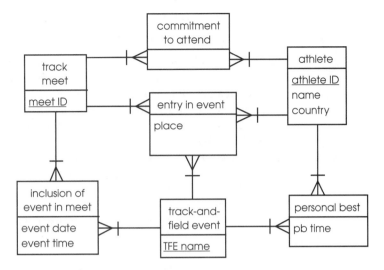

Fragment 18-18

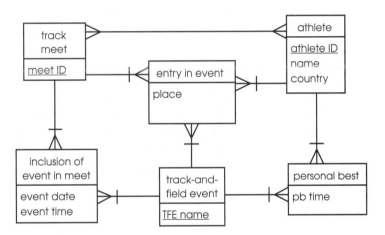

Fragment 18-19

ing the meet and competing in it. (Users indicate that an athlete can commit to a track meet before choosing which events he or she will compete in.) Fragment 18-18 shows the result.

Of course, you can choose to replace *commitment to appear* with a many-many relationship (see Fragment 18-19), but we recommend that you leave the intersection entity on the diagram to remind you and the users to seek descriptors for it. (One possible descriptor is *appearance fee,* because some star athletes are paid a fee merely for appearing in track meets.)

At the end of all this, the original chicken-feet-in entity (e.g., *entry in event*) might or might not remain. It can remain for any of the following reasons:

- A descriptor you already knew about belongs there. For example, the attribute *place* belongs in *entry in event* because it indicates what place (first, second, and so on) a particular athlete finished in a particular event at a particular track meet.
- A previously undiscovered descriptor belongs there. For example, the attribute *finish time* belongs in *entry in event* because it indicates an athlete's time in a particular event at a particular track meet.
- The three-way association is worth remembering even if it has no other descriptors. For example, suppose the users make a boundary decision that the attributes *finish time* and *place* are not worth remembering because the users are responsible for organizing track meets. They are not responsible for actually administering the meets or timing the races or determining the order of finish. (Responsibility for those tasks rests with an international sport governing body.) Even in this case, the users can indicate that the *entry in event* entity is necessary because they want to remember which athletes plan to compete in which particular races.

There is a useful guideline for predicting whether the original chicken-feet-in entity will remain at the end of these investigations. If it has a name the users like, it will probably survive. If it has a contrived name the users dislike, it will probably not survive. For example, consider Fragment 18-20, in which the chicken-feet-in entity has a contrived name. The entity (*PWF*) is not likely to remain on the LDS.

It is worth realizing that if you follow controlled evolution, you are not likely to end up with such a poor name or with such a questionable entity. However, you can encounter such entities if you produce an initial draft of the LDS through reverse engineering—the process of generating a logical model based on a previously implemented system.

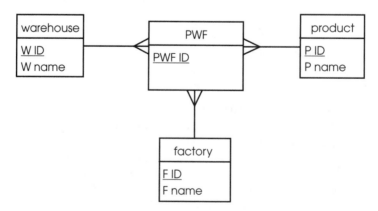

Fragment 18-20

For example, if you generate the in-progress LDS, Fragment 18-20 can result from an implemented system that includes the following four tables.

Product		Warehouse		Factory	
ID	Name	ID	Name	ID	Name
P1	Paper	W1	Williamstown	F1	Fridley
P2	Plutonium	W2	Waltham	F2	Fredericksburg

PWF

ID	Product	Warehouse	Factory
1		W1	F1
2		W1	F2
3		W2	F2
4	P1		F1
5	P1		F2
6	P2		F2
7	P1	W1	
8	P2	W2	

The table PWF contains three kinds of relationships: a relationship between warehouses and factories (rows 1 through 3), a relationship between products and factories (4 through 6), and a relationship between products and warehouses (7 and 8). But there is no row of the table indicating a three-way association among a product, a warehouse, and a factory. This, combined with the awkward name for the table, is strong evidence that the original chicken-feet-in entity of Fragment 18-20 is probably unnecessary.

But be careful here; strong evidence does not constitute proof. You must confirm with the users that *PWF* is not necessary. Just because the existing data does not include a three-way association does not mean that such an association is impossible. You must ask the users if there is any reason to remember particular (*product, warehouse, factory*) combinations.

If the original chicken-feet-in entity has more than three relationships, things can get a bit trickier. For example, consider Fragment 12-21, in which *shipment* is a four-way intersection entity. As you attempt to decompose *shipment* into simpler

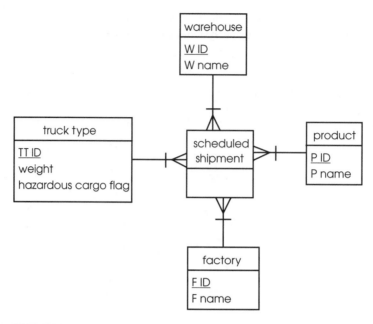

Fragment 18-21

chicken-feet-in entities, realize that some of the resulting simpler entities might be only marginally simpler. That is, some of the entities might be three-way intersection entities.

Exercises

1. For each stage of The Flow,
   a. Create an example that fits the stage.
   b. Provide sample data.
   c. Determine what questions you would ask users about the example in the investigation that follows the stage.
2. Repeat question 1 until you are confident that you thoroughly know each part of The Flow.
3. For each stage of The Flow, determine which shapes apply.
4. Suppose you are helping users to develop an LDS accommodating information about the administration of track-and-field meets. Fragment 18-19 represents the in-progress LDS. An astute user points out that not all track-and-field performances are measured in time. For example, the long jump, pole vault, and discus are measured in distance. Using the same format we used in Chapters 6 and 21, describe how the ensuing conversation between you and the users transpires. For each change in the LDS, draw the result.

19
Chapter

Local, Anytime Steps of Controlled Evolution

U sers do not care about The Flow. It doesn't matter to them that you are following a script. What's important to users are the consequences of The Flow—that you always seem to know what question to ask, that you keep the data-modeling meeting moving forward, and that you ask specific, direct questions that help the users maintain their focus.

The Flow is important because it is important to you; it helps you remember some of the many questions you need to ask users. By learning The Flow, you prepare yourself for data-modeling meetings, which can be nerve-wracking (if you're not confident of your data-modeling skill), confusing (if you don't know how to encourage the users to be explicit and retain their focus), and generally useless (if you are not able to preserve each user decision on the LDS quickly).

But learning the script of The Flow is not all there is. You must prepare to ask the users other questions. To the users, these other questions are just like the questions in The Flow because (1) they focus on small details, (2) they help the users retain their focus, and (3) they use direct, concrete language.

These questions differ from the questions of The Flow in one regard only: They arise at many different times, so no Flow-like script can help you know when to ask them. Although these questions can crop up at various times, this chapter advises you about especially useful times to ask them.

Discovering Entities

Where do entities come from? From users, of course. In the section "Flow Investigation: Discover Relationship" in Chapter 18, we said that you discover relationships by listening to users. You discover new entities the same way, both at the beginning of data modeling and in the midst of controlled evolution. You listen to the users for a while and then say, *I heard you say . . .* and write something on the board.

But what should you listen for? What should you do next? Here are two things that master modelers do: Keep grounded and notice unnamed data.

Keep Grounded

Suppose you have a blank board, and you have heard the users say, essentially, *Creature achieve skill.* If you first focus on "achieve," the conversation will be fraught with uncertainty. It will be up in the air, not grounded, because achieving occurs in the grounding context of creature and skill. Without that context already on the model, users will be hard pressed to articulate just what one "achieve" is. (And "achieve" is the wrong part of speech—entity names are nouns, not verbs.) While we cannot give you an algorithm to follow, we can give you the rough guidelines.

To stay grounded, you should focus users, attention on the following:

a. Nouns before verbs: *creature* and *skill* before *achieve.*
b. Nouns and verbs before modifiers: *achieve* before *proficiency.*
c. Things with mass before things that occur: *victim* before *crime, committee* before *meeting, cow* before *milking event.*
d. Discrete things before things with vague or changing boundaries: *cow* before *herd, cow* before *milk.*
e. Things before connections between things: *graph node* before *edge, airport* before *flight.*
f. Thing and place before thing in place: *chimp* and *map coordinate* before *chimp at map coordinate; movie* and *theater* before *show* (*on a date, at a time,* perhaps *on a screen*).
g. Place before connected places before connected places in time: *flight route* before *flight schedule* before *itinerary* (before *reservation* before *special meal*).
h. Thing before state or event or interval: *player* before *current event; player* before *trade; player* before *major-league stint; drama, theater,* and *show* before *reservation.*

Notice Unnamed Data

Often you do not begin a data model de novo but instead first reverse engineer an existing manual or computerized application before deciding on the new model. You may have manuals, forms, file formats, code, and real data to work with. In each place you may find unnamed data.

You can see some data in a place or a place where some data could go or even data scrawled in any old place. You then ask users, *What do you call this?* or *What do you mean by one of these?* Users may be able to give you a name quickly, or they may need to invent a name that they chew on for a while before coming to a consensus. (Perhaps you and they will use the other steps in this chapter.)

Fixing Identifiers

At various moments during controlled evolution, the conversation will naturally focus on a particular entity. At such times, you should ensure that the entity's identifier includes the right descriptors. An entity's identifier can be incorrect by including too many descriptors, not enough descriptors, or the wrong descriptors.

Underidentification

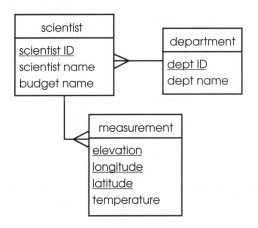

Fragment 19-1

If an entity's identifier includes too few descriptors, the entity is said to be **underidentified.** You can discover underidentification by studying sample data or by asking the users a direct question.

Asking the Question

When an entity is underidentified, the identifier is not sufficient to distinguish among all the various potential instances of the entity. That is, there are several potential instances that share a value for the identifier. By adding additional descriptors to the identifier, you can "break the tie" among these instances. So when you ask users a question about underidentification, you simply want them to consider the possibility of "ties." For example, about Fragment 19-1, you can ask, *Can two measurements have the same elevation, longitude, and latitude?*[1]

Possible Answers to the Question

Users can respond in any of several ways:

- They can confirm that the existing identifier does not underidentify the entity.
- They can immediately offer a tiebreaking descriptor. For example, they can say, *Two measurements can occur at the same location, latitude, and longitude, provided that they occur on different dates.* The users have effectively indicated that a *date* descriptor should be added to the identifier.

---

[1] You'll notice that in forming this question, you merely convert an assertion of the LDS from a declarative sentence to an interrogative sentence. The existing identifier asserts (among other things) that no two measurements can have the same elevation, longitude, and latitude. The question merely asks, *Is that really so?* Remember, you're testing whether the existing identifier is correct; that naturally means that you confirm that its attendant English-language assertions are true.

- They can admit the potential for ties without offering a tiebreaking descriptor. In this case, you must ask a follow-up question explicitly seeking the tiebreaking descriptor. For example, you can say, *How do you distinguish between two measurements occurring at the same latitude, longitude, and elevation?*
- They can disagree with each other. For example, some users will insist no, while others insist that *Yes, two measurements can have the same longitude and latitude.* This could be a sign that *measurement* is an overloaded word; it means different things to different people (see "Overloaded Names" in Chapter 14).

Overidentification

If an entity's identifier includes too many descriptors, the entity is said to be **overidentified.** You can discover overidentification by asking the users a direct question.

Asking the Question

When an entity is overidentified, some subset of the identifier's descriptors will suffice to distinguish each instance from every other instance. Your question needs to ask the users to consider each of the possible subsets in turn. If the identifier has n descriptors, you ask n questions, each of which suggests the removal of one of the descriptors from the identifier.

For example, if you suspect that *measurement* is overidentified, you ask these questions:

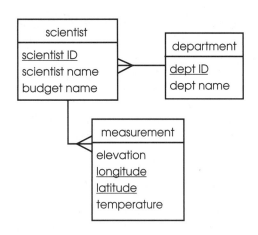

Fragment 19-2

- *Can two measurements have the same elevation and longitude?*
- *Can two measurements have the same elevation and latitude?*
- *Can two measurements have the same latitude and longitude?*

Suppose the users say yes, yes, and *No, two measurements cannot have the same longitude and latitude.* You replace Fragment 19-1 with Fragment 19-2.

Be careful here. The users have merely said that *elevation* is not part of the identifier. They have not said that elevation is not worth remembering. You should not delete the descriptor; just remove it from the identifier. Suppose the users know that every measurement occurs on the ground—not at the top of a tall building, not in a weather balloon—so at a particular latitude and longitude, there is only one possible elevation at which a measurement could take place. That means that *elevation* is not part of the identifier. But it does not mean that elevation is no longer worth remembering.

Ask all the questions. Of the set of identifying descriptors, there may be several subsets that suffice as an identifier. You need to discover each of these subsets so the users can choose among them.

Possible Answers to the Question

Users can respond (to the entire set of questions) in any of several ways:

- They can say yes to each of your questions. That is, they can confirm that the existing identifier does not overidentify the entity.
- They can say no to exactly one of your questions. That is, they can immediately suggest the correct identifier.
- They can say no to two or more of your questions. In this case, there are two possible situations:
  1. The users are indicating that there are two possible smaller (coarser) identifiers, and you must determine which one is better.
  2. The users are indicating that there is a much coarser identifier—that you should correct the existing identifier by removing more than one descriptor from it.
- They can disagree with each other. For example, some users will insist that the existing identifier is correct, while others will insist that some descriptors can be removed from it. This could be a sign that the entity name is an overloaded word—that it means different things to different people (see "Overloaded Names" in Chapter 14).

General Misidentification

Besides having too few or too many descriptors, an identifier can simply have the wrong descriptors. There are several noteworthy cases:

- The identifier includes an extraneous descriptor—wrongly included in the identifier merely because the descriptor cannot have null values. You can create an identifier with too many descriptors if you misunderstand the users. For example, about an in-progress LDS including an entity called *achievement,* a user says, *An achievement must have a creature, a skill, and a proficiency.* You might mistakenly promote these constraints into an identifier.
- The identifier works for almost all possible instances of the entity, but there are some instances for which the identifier does not work. For example, an in-progress LDS includes an entity called *billable account.* The identifier is an attribute called *billable account number.* The *billable account* entity exists in this state through many drafts of the LDS. Eventually, the users realize that a new billable account is created by the members of one department, then a form is sent to another department, which assigns the new billable account a number. It sometimes takes two days for the account to receive its number. During that two-day interval, the billable account exists even though it does not have a billable account number. Thus *billable account number* cannot serve as the identifier.

Extraneous Identifiers

While you are examining an identifier to ensure that it does not overidentify or underidentify the entity, it is a good idea to ensure that the entity does not have too many identifiers. Remember, it is very rare for users to choose to have more than one identifier for an entity.

Seeking Descriptors

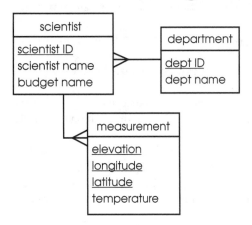

Fragment 19-3

At various moments during controlled evolution, the conversation will naturally focus on a particular entity. At such times, you should seek descriptors for the entity. You can seek descriptors by listening to users, by explicitly asking users for them, and by studying sample data the users provide.

Asking the Question

When you explicitly ask users for additional descriptors, it's best to remind users what you already can remember about each instance of an entity, then ask what else they want to remember. For example, when seeking descriptors for the measurement entity (Fragment 19-3), say, *About each measurement, we can remember its elevation, its latitude, its longitude, its temperature, and its scientist. What else should we remember about it?*

Possible Answers to the Question

In answering this question, users can tell you of links or attributes.

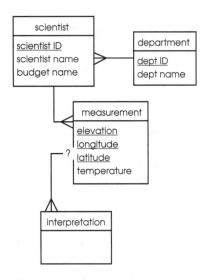

Fragment 19-4

- The users can tell you about a link—and the attendant describing entity—by clearly using a plural form of a noun in their response. For example, the users can tell you that each measurement *can have interpretations.* Even if the users have never before used the word "interpretation" (that is, even if the in-progress LDS contains no entity or attribute whose name is *interpretation*), you know to add an entity called *interpretation,* a relationship between it and *measurement,* a chicken foot near *interpretation,* and a question mark near *measurement.* You know to do all this because the users employed the plural form of the word "interpretation." You don't yet know what an interpretation is—you don't even know what the identifier of *interpretation* is—but you know that each measurement can have many interpretations. The new entity and evolving relationship of Fragment 19-4 reflect the state of your knowledge.

- The users can tell you about a link by using the name of an existing entity in their response. For example, the users can tell you that each measurement *can have a department that pays for it.* Fragment 19-5 shows your response.

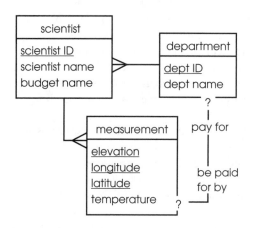

Fragment 19-5

- The users can tell you about an attribute, but the descriptor has the same name as some other attribute already on the LDS. For example, the users can tell you that each measurement *can have a budget name*. Notice that the in-progress LDS (Fragment 19-3) already contains an attribute whose name is *budget name*. Thus, when you add an attribute called *budget name* to the *measurement* entity, you create an invalid LDS; it contains a nonunique name. You can remedy this problem by promoting the like-named attributes or by changing one or both of the attribute names. (See the section of this chapter called "Promoting Attributes.")
- The users can tell you about a new attribute. For example, the users can tell you that each measurement can have a reliability rating.

Giving the Users Extra Help

Sometimes users will have difficulty realizing that they want new descriptors because your question is so general (*What else do you want to remember?*) that it fails to direct their thinking. In this situation, you can help them by reminding them of the kinds of questions for which they might need new descriptors:

Questions about *who*
- Is there a person you want to remember?
- Is there a group or department or people you want to remember?
- Is there a role or function you want to remember?

Questions about *where*
- Is there a place you want to remember?
- Is there a region or area you want to remember?

Questions about *when*
- Is there a moment in time you want to remember?
- Is there a period of time you want to remember?

Questions about *why*
- Is there a reason, motivation, or justification you want to remember?

Questions about *how*
- Is there a method, technique, or script you want to remember?

Questions about *what*
- Is there a thing, a part of a thing, or a group of things you want to remember?

Questions of measurement
- How much?
- How many?
- How fast?
- How long?
- How far?
- How high?
- How hot?

Be careful here; these questions are speculative. The vocabulary you use might not match the vocabulary the users recognize. For example, consider the questions about *why.* In trying to stir the users' imagination, you use several synonyms: "reason," "motivation," and "justification." But the users might prefer the word *cause,* and it is impossible for you to anticipate this preference. In highly specialized cultures, the mismatch between the vocabulary you use and the vocabulary users would recognize can be substantial. Be prepared to ask these speculative questions in several different ways, with different sets of words.

There are several other reasons for you to be careful. First, the list of possible questions of measurement has no limit. As specialists in their particular field, your users will have metrics that you cannot anticipate. (If your users are jewelers, for example, they will have ways to measure the quality of a diamond that are probably unknown to you. Rather than *how long* or *how far,* the users might need to answer questions like *how lustrous* or *how pure*).

Second, the *What* questions are especially open-ended. Here, you need to rely on the users' ability to be forthcoming.

Third, you need to recognize the subtle distinctions between the kinds of questions for which users might require descriptors. For example, consider the following kinds of questions, which are all about time:

- At what moment?
- During what period?
- For how long?

If the users do not readily suggest names for such descriptors, you should suggest names that make these fine distinctions clear. For example, consider an attribute named *visit time.* Based on this name alone, it is hard to determine whether the attribute's values denote the time of day when the visit occurred or the duration of the visit. If the users do not insist on the name *visit time,* you can choose one of these other names to make the attribute's meaning clear: *visit time of day* or *visit duration.*

Promoting Attributes

During controlled evolution, you sometimes need to replace an attribute with a more complex structure.

Promoting a Plural Attribute

In the most obvious case, you promote an attribute that is plural. For example, if the *class* entity includes a *students* descriptor,[2] you should promote the attribute into a more complex structure that includes a relationship and an entity named *student.* Fragments 19-6 and 19-7 illustrate.

---

[2] It is worth stopping to consider how the LDS might have gotten into this illegal state—how it got a plural attribute name. In the most typical case, the users were quickly rattling off descriptors, and you

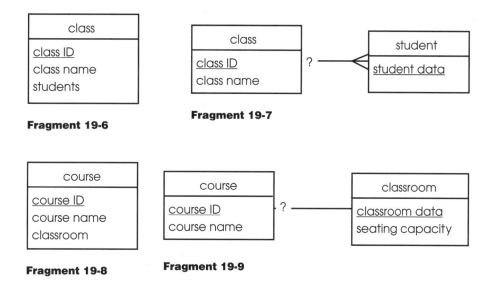

Fragment 19-6

Fragment 19-7

Fragment 19-8

Fragment 19-9

In Fragment 19-6, when you try to read the plural attribute, you say, *Each class can have students.* There is nothing wrong with this sentence—indeed the users might confirm its correctness. But the plural attribute constitutes illegal LDS syntax. In Fragment 19-7, when you read the link, you say the same user-approved sentence, but this time the LDS contains no invalid plural attributes.

Promoting a Singular Attribute

In a less obvious case, you promote an attribute that is singular. There are three motivations:

Motivation: The attribute has descriptors. For example, if the *course* entity has a *classroom* descriptor and the users indicate that they want to remember each classroom's seating capacity, you promote the *classroom* attribute. Fragments 19-8 and 19-9 illustrate the in-progress LDS before and after the promotion and consequent addition of the *seating capacity* attribute.

Notice that the sentences you say about *course* are unaffected by the promotion. Most notably, the following sentence applies to both fragments: *Each course can have a classroom.*

Motivation: There are two like-named attributes in two different entities. For example, if both the *county* and *city* entities have an attribute called *election monitor,* you should consider replacing the attributes with a more complex structure. Fragments 19-10 and 19-11 illustrate.

---

were writing them down as quickly as possible. In your rush to keep up, you might have quickly included a plural noun as a descriptor. You might have knowingly written down the plural noun, intending to remedy the problem later.

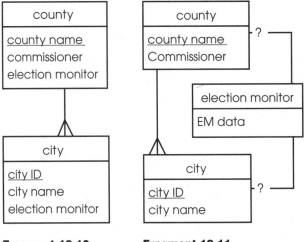

Fragment 19-10   **Fragment 19-11**

Notice that the sentences you say about *county* and *city* are unaffected by the promotion. Most notably, the following sentences apply to both LDS fragments: *Each county can have an election monitor* and *Each city can have an election monitor.*

When you see like-named attributes, you have to do something because, as it stands, the LDS is syntactically invalid. However, you do not necessarily promote the attributes. In some cases, merely renaming one attribute will suffice. In other cases, you rename both attributes.

If the attributes are not alike at all, they should not have like names. If the attributes are alike, you should promote them. With the users, you should investigate which of these situations applies. Have the users think about two instances of the respective entities in which the like-named attributes have equal values.

- If the values' equality is meaningful, the attributes truly are alike. For example, consider an instance of *county* and an instance of *city.* According to the instances, the election monitor of Orange County is League of Women Voters, and the election monitor of the City of Los Angeles is League of Women Voters. The values' equality is meaningful; they both refer to the same thing. You should promote the attributes.
- If the values' equality is merely coincidental, the attributes are not alike. For example, consider an instance of *county* and an instance of *company*, and suppose that each entity includes a descriptor called *name.* According to the instances, there is a county named Northwest and a company named Northwest. The values' equality is meaningless to the users; it is a mere coincidence. You should rename one or both of the attributes.

Motivation: The attribute's possible values are worth remembering in their own right. Consider LDS Fragments 19-12 and 19-13. The fragments differ only in that Fragment 19-13 lets us remember the list of valid eye colors, whereas Fragment

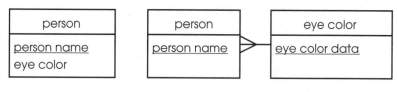

Fragment 19-12   **Fragment 19-13**

19-12 lets us remember only those eye colors that actually apply to particular persons. By choosing Fragment 19-13, the users indicate that they want to remember eye colors in their own right. Notice that the promotion of the attribute in Fragment 19-12 into the more complex structure in Fragment 19-13 leaves this sentence unchanged: *Each person can have an eye color.*

You use this motivation only for promoting nominal-scale, cyclic-scale, or interval-scale attributes.

Relocating Misplaced Descriptors

A descriptor can be misplaced—it belongs in another entity. As an LDS evolves, you must occasionally work to discover and relocate misplaced descriptors. There are three techniques for discovering misplaced descriptors: (1) relying on names, (2) studying sample data for patterns of descriptor values, and (3) studying sample data for correlations between descriptor values and identifier values.

You should know all three techniques because no one of them is perfect. Each technique has weaknesses; each one applies better or worse to certain circumstances. Therefore, before we describe each technique, we describe some circumstances in which descriptors can be misplaced. Then, when we describe each technique, we tell you how well it suits the various circumstances.

Factors for Characterizing Descriptor Misplacement

The possible circumstances of descriptor misplacement are determined by four factors:

- **Type** of misplacement
- **Existence or nonexistence of the correct entity**—the entity where the misplaced descriptor really belongs
- **Length of path** between the erroneous entity and the correct entity
- **Number** of descriptors to be moved from the erroneous entity to the correct entity

The remainder of this section describes these circumstances, describes two techniques for diagnosing descriptor misplacement, presents some examples of descriptor misplacement and relocation, and lists some steps of The Flow after which you should investigate descriptor misplacement.

Type of Descriptor Misplacement

Following are several types of descriptor misplacement:

- Gross misplacement—the descriptor belongs in a completely unrelated entity.
- Too-fine misplacement—the descriptor belongs in a related but coarser entity. That is, the descriptor describes things that are coarser than the instances of the entity.
- Too-coarse misplacement—the descriptor belongs in a finer entity. That is, the descriptor describes things that are finer than the instances of the entity.
- Too-inclusive misplacement—the descriptor belongs in a more exclusive entity. That is, the descriptor describes only some of the instances of the entity.
- Too-exclusive misplacement—the descriptor belongs in a more inclusive entity. That is, the descriptor applies to every instance of the entity, plus some other instances.

LDS fragment 19-14 illustrates some of these errors. To understand why some descriptors are misplaced, recall these facts about federal, state, and local governments:

- Each state has a governor. Thus the *governor* descriptor within the *county* entity is misplaced; it belongs in a coarser *state* entity. This is too-fine misplacement.
- Each city can have a mayor. Thus the *mayor* descriptor within the *county* entity is misplaced; it belongs in the finer *city* entity. This is too-coarse misplacement.
- When a person registers to vote, he or she can claim affiliation with a political party. Thus the *party* descriptor within the *person* entity is misplaced; it belongs in the more exclusive *voter* entity. This is too-inclusive misplacement.
- Each address can contain persons, both registered voters and other persons too young or too apathetic to vote. Thus the *address of voter* descriptor is misplaced;

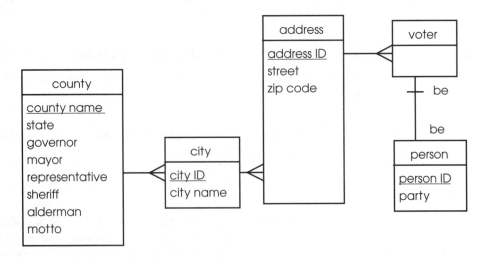

Fragment 19-14

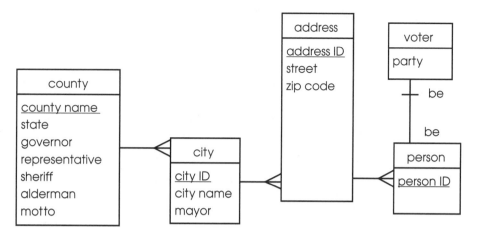

Fragment 19-15

it belongs in the more inclusive *person* entity (with the name *address of person*). This is too-exclusive misplacement.

- Each member of the U.S. House of Representatives serves a particular legislative district. Thus the *representative* descriptor is misplaced; it belongs in the *district* entity. This is gross misplacement.

Important!

Notice that either kind of descriptor (link or attribute) can be misplaced. Fragment 19-15 shows some of the descriptors relocated correctly. The relocated descriptors are *mayor, party,* and *address of person.* Fragment 19-17 shows the relocation of the remaining misplaced descriptors.

When you know the type of descriptor misplacement, you (typically) know what shape you're dealing with. (We say "typically" because gross misplacement corresponds to no particular shape. But the other types of misplacement correspond to specific shapes.) The table on page 260 summarizes.

At the beginning of descriptor relocation, the shape that you're dealing with might not be visible on the diagram. If the misplaced descriptor belongs in an entity that doesn't exist, you have to create the entity; only then is the shape evident on the LDS. The next section elaborates.

Existence or Nonexistence of the Correct Entity

The correct entity for a misplaced descriptor might not exist on the LDS. For example, Fragment 19-14 contains no entity named *state* or *district,* although the *governor* and *representative* descriptors properly belong in such entities. As you work to relocate misplaced descriptors, be prepared to create new entities. Fragment 19-16 shows the relocated descriptors. Notice that the needed entities have been added and that the LDS has subsequently evolved to include relationships between *district* and *state* and between *district* and *address.* Notice also that we added *state* entity merely by promoting an attribute.

Type of misplacement	Shape	Relocation	Example of misplacement
Too coarse	One-many relationship	A descriptor moves toward the chicken foot, stopping at the related entity.	cow — herd / cow name
	Chicken feet across	A descriptor moves toward the chicken foot, perhaps along several consecutive relationships.	cow — herd — farm / cow name
	Chicken feet in	A descriptor moves from a chicken-feet-in entity of a few relationships to one or more relationships.	The relocation of a descriptor from *authorship* to *review of book by person* in Fragment 11-24.
Too fine	One-many relationship	A descriptor moves away from the chicken foot to the related entity.	county / governor — state
	Chicken feet across	A descriptor moves away from the chicken foot, perhaps along several consecutive relationships.	city / governor — county — state
	Chicken feet in	A descriptor moves from a chicken-feet-in entity of many relationship to one of fewer relationships.	The relocation of the *personal best* attribute in Fragments 18-14 through 18-16.
Too inclusive	*To-be* relationship	A descriptor moves along a *to-be* relationship, perhaps toward a subordinate entity.	child — be — human / favorite toy — be
	To-be's across	A descriptor moves along one or several consecutive *to-be* relationships, perhaps toward subordinate entities.	child — be — human — be — be — creature / favorite toy
Too exclusive	*To-be* relationship	A descriptor moves along a *to-be* relationship, perhaps away from a subordinate entity.	human / creature name — be — be — creature
	To-be's across	A descriptor moves along one or several consecutive *to-be* relationships, perhaps away from subordinate entities.	child / creature name — be — human — be — be — creature — be

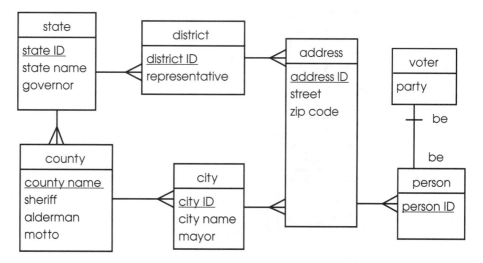

Fragment 19-16

Path Length from the Misplacement Entity to the Relocation Entity

For any type of misplacement other than gross misplacement, you can think of descriptor relocation as the act of sliding the descriptor along one or more relationships.

If the relocation entity does not exist, you can think of the path length as fractional. For example, suppose you learn that the *alderman* descriptor is misplaced. You learn that the *county* entity is too coarse for the descriptor, so you slide the descriptor to *city*. (The path length is now 1.) Then you learn that the *city* entity is too coarse, so you slide the descriptor to *address*. (The path length is 2.) Then you learn that you've gone too far; *address* is too fine. You need to slide the descriptor back toward *city* but not all the way. The path length is between 1 and 2. Between *city* and *address,* the one-many relationship evolves into the chicken-feet-across shape. (See Fragment 19-17.) Now you need to secure from the users a name and an identifier for this new entity.

Number of Descriptors to be Relocated

Within an entity you can sometimes find several descriptors that are equally misplaced—they all belong in some other entity. It is useful to recognize this as a single situation rather than as several individual cases of descriptor misplacement. Why? Because in very specific circumstances, finding a single misplaced descriptor might not induce you to relocate it, whereas finding several equally misplaced descriptors can induce you to perform the relocation.

The number of misplaced descriptors becomes important only in a very specific set of circumstances—when the type of misplacement is too inclusive and the correct entity does not yet exist. Remember that the remedy for too-inclusive misplacement involves sliding the descriptor along a *to-be* relationship. Remember also that

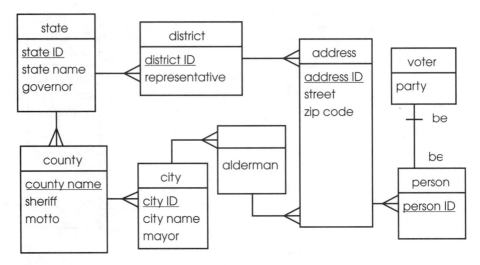

Fragment 19-17

when an LDS has too many one-one relationships, it can become difficult to read; the LDS loses its effectiveness as a medium of communication. As we've said before, you should think carefully before accepting any LDS fragment that includes a one-one relationship. But to create a new entity to remedy too-inclusive misplacement, you must also create a *to-be* relationship between it and the misplacement entity.

You have to use your judgment. On the one hand, because the descriptor is misplaced, you feel compelled to relocate it. On the other hand, every *to-be* relationship you add to the diagram exacts a price in simplicity. One factor that can help you decide is the number of misplaced descriptors. If there are several misplaced descriptors, the gain in accuracy probably outweighs the loss in simplicity; you'd make the relocation. If there is only one misplaced descriptor, the loss in simplicity probably outweighs the potential gain clarity; you probably would not make the relocation.

Ways to Detect Descriptor Misplacement

There are two techniques for discovering misplaced descriptors: (1) relying on names and (2) studying sample data for patterns of descriptor values.

Relying on the Names

We say "usually" but read the next paragraphs.

If an accurately named descriptor is misplaced within an accurately named entity, the misplacement will (usually) be obvious to anyone who knows the vocabulary. In the previous examples, the descriptors and entities have accurate names. Thus each misplacement becomes obvious when you read the corresponding sentence. For example, when you read the sentence, *Each county can have a mayor*, to a user who knows what the words *county* and *mayor* mean, the user will contradict your sentence. In effect, the user says *No, mayor is not a descriptor of county.*

Accurate names do not guarantee that you will detect all misplaced descriptors. The names reveal misplacement only when you avoid each of these pitfalls.

- If you fail to read the appropriate sentence to the users, you deny them a chance to disclaim the assertion. You want to give the users every opportunity to tell you that a descriptor is misplaced. In fact, if you suspect misplaced descriptors, there is a specific diction you should use because this diction makes the misplacement of a descriptor especially noticeable. You point to each descriptor in turn, saying, *Each instance of this descriptor contains a <entity-name>'s <descriptor-name>.* For example, to read the individual descriptors of the *county* entity, you say:
    - *Each instance of this* (point to county name) *contains a county's county name.*
    - *Each instance of this* (point to governor) *contains a county's governor.*
    - *Each instance of this* (point to governor) *contains a county's state.*
    - *Each instance of this* (point to mayor) *contains a county's mayor.*
    - *Each instance of this* (point to representative) *contains a county's representative.*
    - *Each instance of this* (point to sheriff) *contains a county's sheriff.*
    - *Each instance of this* (point to alderman) *contains a county's alderman.*
    - *Each instance of this* (point to motto) *contains a county's motto.*
    - *Each instance of this* (point to state) *contains a county's state.*
    - *Each instance of this* (point to cities) *contains a county's cities.*

  As you say each of these sentences, users will balk at certain phrases. For example, the following phrases cause users to hesitate: *a county's governor, a county's mayor, a county's representative.*

- If the descriptor is an attribute that should be promoted into an entity, the users might not balk when you read it. For example, when you point to the *state* descriptor and say, *Each instance of this contains a county's state,* users might not balk because there's nothing wrong with what you just said—state really *is* a descriptor of county. Strictly speaking, the problem is not descriptor misplacement but that an attribute should be promoted.

  This pitfall is usually not a serious problem because the need for a new entity soon becomes evident for other reasons. For example, when you and the users inspect the *governor* attribute, you quickly realize that governor is misplaced and that governor is a descriptor of state. This induces you to create a *state* entity and to realize that the *state* attribute deserves promotion.

- The users can employ a certain idiomatic speech pattern that can conceal a descriptor's misplacement. For example, suppose that the *person* entity contains the *representative* descriptor, which ought to be in the *district* entity. While pointing to the descriptor, you say, *Each instance of this contains a person's representative.* Ideally, the users would balk at this sentence—at the words *a person's representative.* After all, representative is not a descriptor of person. However, in common usage, American voters frequently say things like *I am going to write a letter to my representative* or *Who is your representative?* This idiomatic speech

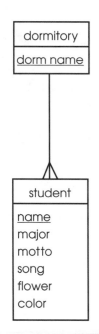

Fragment 19-18

pattern is a shorthand—*my representative* is a shorthand for *the representative of the district of my address*. If the users are accustomed to this idiomatic shorthand, they will not balk at the expression *a person's representative*. You can still discover the descriptor's misplacement by studying sample data.

Studying Sample Data

You and the users can study sample data to confirm that descriptors are not misplaced. Within the data, different patterns reveal different types of misplacement. Studying sample data is especially effective for detecting too-fine and too-inclusive misplacement. We show some examples next.

Too-fine misplacement. If a descriptor belongs in a coarser entity, the sample data will show that for entire groups of instances, the descriptor value remains constant. For example, consider the sample data for Fragment 19-18.

Dorm	Motto	Song	Flower	Color	Name	Major
Wilson	Truth	Fun	Rose	Green	E Mulderry	Math
Wilson	Truth	Fun	Rose	Green	A Jones	Math
Byner	Honor	ABC	Rose	Red	A Castro	History
Byner	Honor	ABC	Rose	Red	E Gale	History
Byner	Honor	ABC	Tulip		I Wilson	History
Tesla		Fun	Tulip	Blue	J Johnson	French
Tesla		Fun	Tulip	Blue	L Mandell	French
Frankel	Try		Tulip		K Conway	Physics
Frankel	Try		Tulip		A Kowalski	Physics

This data should make you suspect that the descriptors *motto* and *major* belong in the *dormitory* entity. You cannot relocate either descriptor without first asking the users to confirm your suspicion. For example, you ask, *Can I always know a student's motto merely by knowing what dormitory that student lives in?* If the users say yes, you can move the descriptor.

There are two reasons why the users might say no to such a question, even though the data suggests yes. First, the data might mislead you by pure coincidence. When you ask about the *major* descriptor, for example, the users can indicate that there is absolutely no correlation between dormitories and majors; the students in the sample data have elected to live with their classmates. If you frequently encounter such coincidences in the sample data, you are looking at too-small data sets or at carelessly concocted data. You should insist that the users let you inspect real data, and plenty of it.

Second, the sample data can mislead you because a strong but not absolutely reliable correlation exists. For example, the users can explain that at the beginning of each year, students with like interests and like majors are housed together. However, a student can change her major midyear without moving to a different dormitory.

The sample data also suggests that the *song* descriptor might be misplaced. The fact that two dormitories use the same song ("Fun") is immaterial. What's important and suggested by the sample data is that no dormitory uses two different songs.

Notice that the sample data does not suggest that *flower* belongs in *dormitory*. There is a dormitory (Byner) that has two different flowers. Similarly, *color* does not belong in *dormitory* because there is a dormitory that has two different values (red and null) for *color.*

thoroughbred horse
horse name
winnings
sex
trainer name
weight
birthday
date of next ovulation

Fragment 19-19

Too-inclusive misplacement. If a descriptor belongs in a more exclusive entity, the sample data will show a particular pattern of null values.

Sometimes null values indicate descriptor misplacement, but most often they do not. For example, consider the sample data for LDS Fragment 19-19. There are five columns with null values. But only one column (date of next ovulation) corresponds to a misplaced descriptor. The descriptor *date of next ovulation* is misplaced because it does not describe all horses; it describes only female horses. So null values alone are not a certain indication of too-inclusive misplacement. For certain indication, you must detect a specific kind of null value.

Thoroughbred horse name	Winnings	Sex	Trainer name	Weight	Birthday	Date of next ovulation
Mustang Sally	836,232	F	Jones	1500	95jan14	97may14
Sir Edward	747,233	M	Jones		95jan23	
Fast Eddie	8,484	M		1700		
Lady Jane	74,999	F	Smith	1620		97may18
Punchy Judy		F	Smith	1578	95jun11	

There are many kinds of null values. That is, null values can be interpreted in many ways. Some research papers in database systems distinguish among 14 different interpretations for null values! Here, we need not make such fine distinctions. We can concern ourselves with only two general kinds of null values: the answer-unknown null value and the question-invalid null value.

Remember, each value represents an answer to a specific question. For example, in the sample data there is a value (1500) that answers the question *What does Mustang Sally weigh?* Each null value indicates that the database does not contain the

thoroughbred horse
<u>horse name</u>
winnings
sex
trainer name
weight
birthday
date of next ovulation
sperm count
sperm motility rating
stud fee

Fragment 19-20

answer to a specific question. But there are reasons why the database might not contain an answer:

- Sometimes the users lack knowledge. For example, one null value in the sample data indicates that we do not know Lady Jane's birthday. This is an answer-unknown null value.
- Sometimes the question itself is invalid. For example, one null value in the sample data indicates the Sir Edward has no date of next ovulation—because Sir Edward is male and no male ovulates. This is a question-invalid null value.

When you study sample data for too-inclusive misplacement, you must look for question-invalid null values.

As we said earlier in this chapter (see the subsection "Number of Descriptors to Be Relocated"), when you encounter a solitary descriptor suffering from too-inclusive misplacement and the correct entity does not yet exist on the LDS, you and the users might decide not to relocate the descriptor. But when you find many descriptors in that situation, the gain in accuracy can be worth the increased complexity on the diagram. For example in Fragment 19-20, there are a number of descriptors that apply only to male horses—sperm count, sperm motility rating, and stud fee. In this case, you might choose to relocate the descriptors.

Exercises

1. For each grounding guideline,
   a. Create an example that fits the guideline.
   b. Provide sample data that explains it.
   c. Determine what questions you would ask users about that example.
2. For each kind of identifier error,
   a. Create an example that fits the error.
   b. Provide sample data that explains it.
   c. Determine what questions you would ask users about that error.
3. Repeat questions 1 and 2 until you are confident that you thoroughly know each grounding guideline and identifier error.
4. Look at forms that you use in your everyday world and find unnamed data.
5. Explain the consequences of failing to promote an attribute.
6. Explain the consequences of failing to correct misplaced descriptors.
7. Look again at Fragment 18-9. Suppose a user says the following: *A student can tutor a course, but a student does not register for a course. A student registers for a particular section of a course. For example, a student does not register for Chinese history but for Chinese history taught Mondays at 10:00 A.M. (rather than say, Chinese history taught Thursdays at 3:00 P.M.).* What do you do? Of the four

descriptors of the *course* entity in Fragment 18-9, which do you suspect is misplaced? Write a description of how the conversation between you and the users would transpire as you work to eliminate misplaced descriptors, and show how the LDS would evolve as the users answer your questions. Have a classmate or colleague play the role of user while you play the role of data modeler. To transcribe your conversation, use a format like the format of Chapters 6 and 21.

20
Chapter

Global, Anytime Steps of Controlled Evolution

Controlled evolution works because the users can follow along. They can see how their decisions affect the LDS because each specific question you ask yields a specific and small-scale change (or no change at all). Users have little difficulty understanding the evolution of the LDS.

Sometimes, however, you must perform the following modifications that the users perceive as drastic because the modifications affect large portions of the diagram:

- Redrawing the diagram
- Altering the overall style of an LDS
- Changing a fragment's level of abstraction

Redrawing the Diagram

During a modeling meeting, you typically work at an erasable board with a marker. After the meeting, you use data modeling software to maintain an electronic copy of your work. In the effort to develop a large system or set of systems, this electronic copy of a data model can become quite large and quite important to the organization.

This electronic copy is the master copy of the in-progress LDS. As it grows, it can become quite messy. Merely by moving its entities around, you can make it more legible. This is a mundane task, and for large models it can be quite difficult. But the effort is worth it; a needlessly messy diagram makes life difficult for both you and the users. A messy model actually impedes controlled evolution.

There are a few rules of thumb for improving a model's layout.

(1) **Try to minimize crossing lines.** This can be quite difficult, and on any model of moderate size, you will not be able to eliminate all of them. (Only trivial LDSs completely avoid crossing lines.) But if you can rearrange entities to reduce the number of crossing lines by, say, 50 percent, you will notice a marked increase in the diagram's clarity.

(2) **Use color judiciously.** There are good and bad ways to use color. We do not recommend using color to represent anything meaningful. For example, do not assign a different color to each division of the company and then try to color the entities according to which division is responsible for that entity. (We have seen this tried.) This approach needlessly complicates the process of controlled evolution. You and the users will waste time discussing unimportant things rather than working on refining the database-boundary decisions expressed on the LDS.

On a complex LDS, you can use color to help people keep things straight. One LDS we worked on was so large, it could fit on a 10-foot-wide, 6-foot-tall sheet only if we reduced it to 60 percent of its original size. Most of the approximately 2000 relationships connected entities no more than a few inches apart; the lines representing these relationships were short and easy to follow. But several hundred lines were longer than 4 feet! We drew some of these long lines in color to help the observer's eye trace the relationship.

(3) **Stay ahead of things.** Don't let the diagram get too messy. The messier the diagram becomes, the more profoundly it will change when you eventually get around to fixing it. Profound changes will make its redrawn version especially disorienting to users and other modelers who had grown accustomed to the existing layout. Users will eventually prefer the improved, tidier diagram, but if everything on the diagram has moved, people will initially be annoyed. (*The customer entity was always in the top left; where did it go?*)

Altering the Overall Style of an LDS

As you become a master data modeler, you gradually develop automatic behaviors that help you produce good LDSs. These automatic behaviors operate at a microscopic scale. For example, you automatically check that your entity names are accurate (see Chapter 14) and that your identifiers are appropriate to the users' needs. You make these microscopic-scale checks frequently. Until you become a master data modeler, you must discipline yourself to stick to these behaviors. You must follow The Flow consciously.

You will also develop instincts that prevent you from producing bad LDSs. You will still make mistakes, but you will not allow them to linger on an in-progress LDS for days and weeks at a time, because when you work on an LDS containing a mistake, your instincts will tell you that something is wrong.

Until you develop these instincts, you need to seek out such mistakes on your in-progress LDSs explicitly. This effort operates at a macroscopic scale because the mistakes you are trying to perceive are bad stylistic trends rather than localized errors like bad syntax or inappropriate identifiers. To find a bad trend, you need to look at the LDS as a whole.

A bad trend occurs when a supposedly rare construction occurs frequently on the in-progress LDS. Most rare constructions are rare shapes. (In the descriptions of individual shapes in Chapters 8 through 12, we mention which shapes are rare.) Following are the bad trends you might find:

- Too many labeled relationships. Remember, if you and the users understand the unlabeled relationship, don't bother labeling its links.
- Too many many-many relationships. If you detect this, you are probably skipping the step of The Flow called *Flow investigation: Seek descriptors for intersection entity.*
- Too many one-one relationships. If you detect this, you might be neglecting to investigate both links of each relationship.
- Entities with multiple identifiers. If you find many entities with two (or more) identifiers, check your work. Are there really two (or more) entities, and one identifier applies to each of them? Is there really only one identifier, and the other identifier is merely a set of descriptors, each of whose values cannot be null? If you find entities with multiple identifiers, make sure you really understand the concept of identifier. This is a truly rare construction; we have built a 1000-entity LDS in which no entity had multiple identifiers.
- Collection entities. If you detect the one-many collection entity shape or the many-many collection entity shape, your first instinct should be a deep, abiding suspicion that you have erred. Anchor your understanding with instances. These shapes are so very rare, you can spend an entire career as a commercial data modeler without ever encountering them.

When you find a bad stylistic trend, you won't be able to fix it without more input from the users. But before you seek further input from them, work hard without them to understand why the trend is bad, why the existing LDS is poor. Discovering a bad trend is not an entirely negative experience; it is a chance for you to become a better modeler. But you should capitalize on that chance before your next encounter with users. Otherwise, you will just make similar mistakes again, wasting more of the users' time.

Changing the Level of Abstraction

Some LDS fragments can change drastically in one fell swoop. These drastic modifications can disorient users, who expect the LDS to evolve gradually. These changes involve altering the level of abstraction present on the LDS.

This notion of abstractness is worth a few words. An LDS is considered **abstract** if it has relatively few user words present as entity names and descriptor

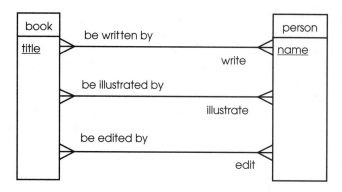

Fragment 20-1

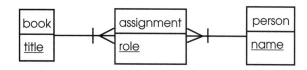

Fragment 20-2

names. Conversely, an LDS with many user words present is considered **concrete.** For example, compare LDS Fragments 20-1 and 20-2 about the same user phenomenon.

Fragment 20-1 is concrete; it contains user words like *write, illustrate,* and *edit.*

Fragment 20-2, on the other hand, is abstract; the user words *write, illustrate,* and *edit* do not appear. Fragment 20-1 can evolve into Fragment 20-2; the user words have been relegated into instance data (they become possible values of the *role* attribute).

When you modify the LDS in a way that relegates user words from the diagram to instance data, you are said to increase the level of abstraction in the LDS. There are three typical ways to do this:

- Combining multiple short paths
- Collapsing the chicken-feet-across shape representing a taxonomy
- Collapsing the subordinates-out shape

Combining Multiple Short Paths

Fragment 20-1 contains the *multiple short paths* shape. By replacing it with Fragment 20-2, you effectively combine the short paths into a single short path.

Note that to combine multiple short paths, you do not ask the users a specific yes-or-no question. Rather, you use your judgment about whether it <u>could be</u> worth making this change; then you talk with users to determine whether it <u>is</u> worth making the change. Draw the before and after fragments, read them both aloud, draw a single set of sample data, and make sure the users realize that either fragment accommodates that data.

Above all, respect the users' wishes. If they do not unequivocally impel you to combine the short paths, don't.

Collapsing a Taxonomy

Fragment 20-3 uses the chicken-feet-across shape to express a three-level taxonomy. The levels are *state, county,* and *city.* (Ignore for the moment the syntax error—the three attributes all named *population.*)

In some situations, you can express a taxonomy with a single entity and a reflexive relationship. For example, you can replace Fragment 20-3 with Fragment 20-4.

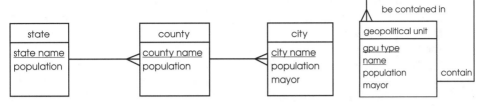

Fragment 20-3   **Fragment 20-4**

(Note the two-part identifier. The possible values of *gpu type* are "state," "county," and "city.")

In deciding whether to collapse a taxonomy, you do not ask a specific question of the users. Rather, you use your judgment to determine whether it <u>could be</u> worth collapsing it, then talk with users to see if it actually <u>is</u> worth it.

In most situations, it will not be worth collapsing. Collapse it only if the users unequivocally demand it. But there is a middle ground; you can partially collapse a taxonomy. Fragment 20-5 illustrates. The taxonomy is partially collapsed because only some of the descriptors have been moved to the generic entity *geopolitical unit*. The two *city*-specific nonidentifying descriptors remain in the *city* entity, and the one *state*-specific nonidentifying descriptor remains in the *state* entity.

As a compromise that tries to capture the strengths of Fragments 20-3 and 20-4, this LDS is a bit clumsy and introduces some shortcomings of its own. First, look at the *county* entity. Should it appear in Fragment 20-5 or not? Perhaps not, because it has no nonidentifying descriptors. Nevertheless, users might like to see it there to remind them that "county" is one type of geopolitical unit. As a modeler responsible for controlled evolution, you might want to retain the *county* entity to remind you to seek descriptors for it.

Second, the diagram does not show the hierarchy of taxonomic levels. That is, the diagram does not show that *state* is the coarsest level and *city* is the finest.

Third, the diagram does not explicitly show that the possible values of *gpu type* are "state," "city," and "county." That is, it does not explicitly indicate the correlation between the names of the subordinate entities and the possible values of *gpu type*.

Because of these shortcomings, you must gauge the users' perceptions before choosing to employ a partially collapsed taxonomy. Do the users really

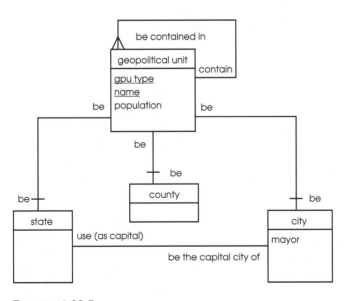

Fragment 20-5

understand the fragment? Can they readily suggest a meaningful name (e.g., *geopolitical unit*) for the entity representing the collapsed taxonomy? Does the impetus for collapsing the taxonomy come from the users, or do you find yourself lobbying for the partially collapsed shape? (You should never lobby for shapes.)

There's one more thing to notice about Fragment 20-5: It exhibits the subordinates-out shape. Moving from a partially collapsed taxonomy to a fully collapsed taxonomy means collapsing the subordinates-out shape. This step is described in the next section.

Collapsing Subordinates Out

Like Fragment 20-5, Fragment 20-6 exhibits the subordinates-out shape. You can collapse the shape into a single entity, yielding a shape like Fragment 20-7.

Notice the addition of the attribute *compensation type.* The possible values of this attribute are "salary" and "wage."

Make special note of the attribute name: not merely *type* or *employee type,* but *compensation type.* This is a good name because it allows the very real possibility that there will be other attributes accommodating other ways to classify employees:

- full-time vs. part-time (call the attribute *time status*)
- domestic vs. foreign (*country type*)
- top secret vs. secret vs. clearance pending (*security clearance type*)
- permanent vs. temporary vs. summer intern (*employment type*)

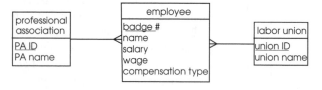

Fragment 20-6

Fragment 20-7

Guidelines for Increasing or Decreasing Abstractness

Making an LDS more abstract is a risky business; ordinarily you should not do it unless the users demand it. There are some advantages to making an LDS more abstract, but they are almost always outweighed by the disadvantages.

Advantage: An abstract LDS can become more enduring because it can allow users to extend their categories without adding entities or descriptors. That is, it allows users to extend their categories merely by adding instances of a generic (highly abstract) category. For example, if the users decide they want to remember that some persons *review* books or *create indexes for* books, Fragment 20-2 accommodates these decisions without modification. The more concrete Fragment 20-1 requires alteration. Similarly, Fragment 20-4 easily accommodates the addition of the *nation* level to the taxonomy, but Fragment 20-3 would require the addition of a *nation* entity and a one-many relationship from *nation* to *state.*

Disadvantage: The LDS becomes simpler. That sounds as if it should be considered advantageous, but wait. The problem is that it becomes simpler than the user-modeler conversation requires. The putatively simpler LDS conceals detail from you and the users. It is less effective at fostering communication. Abstract entities are likely to have names that are generic (like *assignment*) or contrived (like *geopolitical unit*). Such names do a poor job of reminding users what the LDS is about. By comparison, the LDS that shows many user words (e.g., *county* or *illustrate*) is more effective.

Disadvantage: An abstract LDS conceals opportunities to perform The Flow. For example, Fragments 20-1 and 20-8 present many opportunities to convert a many-many relationship into an intersection entity for which you can seek further descriptors. The more abstract Fragment 20-2 conceals those opportunities.

Similarly, using Fragment 20-3, you can perform the Flow continuation "Seek other relationships" between *state* and *city.* This effort might reveal a relationship between state and city indicating that a city is the capital of a state (see Fragment 16-11). Fragment 20-4 makes it very difficult to discover this relationship.

Disadvantage: Abstract models conceal subtle distinctions that concrete models reveal. For example, Fragment 20-2 cannot express differences between short paths that are similar but not identical. In contrast, consider Fragment 20-8. It has many short paths between the entities. Combining these paths can make the LDS

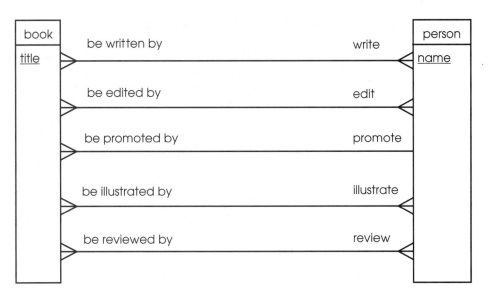

Fragment 20-8

considerably smaller. (If there were dozens of short paths, you might seriously consider using Fragment 20-2.) But look at the third relationship. It is not a many-many relationship; it is a one-many. Using Fragment 20-2 conceals this noteworthy aspect of book promotion.

When You Can and Cannot Use Abstract Shapes

Despite the many disadvantages of abstract fragments, there are times when increasing abstractness makes sense:

- If the multiple-short-paths shape contains dozens or hundreds of short, very similar paths, you can become more willing to combine the paths.
- If the taxonomy contains many levels, many level-independent descriptors, and few level-specific descriptors, you can become more willing to collapse it.
- If an entity participates in many different subordinates-out shapes (because there are many orthogonal ways to classify its instances), you become more willing to collapse each of the subordinates-out shapes and add a classification attribute (such as *compensation type, time status, country type, security clearance type,* or *employment type*).

As we create models and watch our students and colleagues create models, we notice some trends. Novice modelers tend to use the subordinates-out shape too often; they put themselves in the awkward position of having to perform a global, disorienting modification to the model to make it more manageable.

Modelers trained in object-oriented implementation tend to combine multiple short paths. Such modelers are inappropriately thinking ahead to the implementation phase, during which a small set of general, highly abstract classes can maximize the reuse of code. During the logical modeling phase, such tendencies toward the abstract serve the users poorly.

Object-oriented modelers also tend to use subordinates out too often. They tend to think of all data as existing in class hierarchies in which specific classes inherit their properties from general ones. You should not force users to think of their data as conforming to class hierarchies any more than you should force them to think of their data as existing in relations or tables. If the users tell you about a truly hierarchical set of categories, model it appropriately and accurately, but do not set out looking for class hierarchies. (Remember, you should not lobby for particular shapes!)

Object-oriented modelers tend to use partially collapsed taxonomies. A partially collapsed taxonomy contains a generic entity (like *geopolitical unit*) that can correspond to an implemented class that is highly reusable. It also contains the subordinates-out shape that can correspond to a class hierarchy in an implemented system.

Exercises

1. Extend Chapter 6 in such a way that you find yourself (as a modeler) driven to change the level of abstraction.
2. Write an essay stating the pros and cons of this statement: *You should not lobby for particular shapes.*

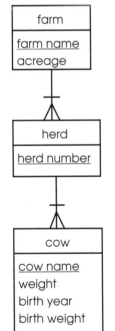

Fragment 21-1

21
Chapter

Conversations About Dairy Farming

This chapter presents a typical conversation with users and shows the gradual improvement to an LDS. Your users are members of a governmental body regulating the dairy industry in a small New England state.

Meeting with Users from the General Offices

You begin by meeting with users from the general offices. After a brief discussion, the LDS includes Fragment 21-1.

You have asked the users to bring printouts of their data. You ask the users to show you some data about farms, herds, and cows. You briefly scan the data the users provide, selecting some data and writing it down on page 278.

Aloud to the users, you begin talking about this data. Among other things, you say, *Six cows are described here.* One astute user says, *No. Leo is not a cow; he's a bull.*

At this point, you must decide between two alternatives:

• The LDS includes one entity named *cow* and another entity called *bull.*
• The LDS contains an entity whose instances describe both cows and bulls.

Farm name	Herd number	Cow name	Weight	Birth year	Birth weight
Yagar's	22	Alma	600	1994	65
Yagar's	22	Bess	656		64
Yagar's	44	Alma		1993	55
Ned	22	Leo	655	1994	52
Ned	33	Amy	656	1993	
Ned	34	Pat	703	1992	55

You look again at the sample data. In particular, you notice that each descriptor applies equally well to Leo as to the cows. Thus you conclude that so far, there is no need for two separate entities. To be sure, you ask the users *Is there anything you want to remember about each bull that you do not need to remember about each cow? Is there anything about each cow that you do not want to remember about each bull?* To each question, the users say no.

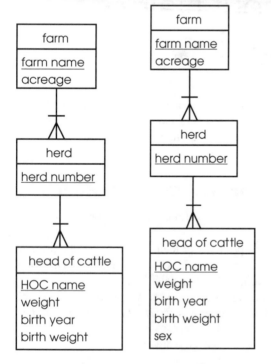

Fragment 21-2   **Fragment 21-3**

You ask the users what the new name of the cow entity should be, explaining to them that "cow" is not an accurate name because some instances are not cows.

The users say that a correct name for the entity is *head of cattle,* so you change the LDS accordingly. (Fragment 21-2).

You also ask the users whether they need to remember the sex of each head of cattle. Initially, the users say that they can tell the sex by looking at the name. You recognize that this decision shifts the burden (the burden of remembering the sex of a head of cattle) from the database to the users. You want to make sure that the users understand this consequence of the decision. You ask the following questions:

- *Can you always determine the sex of a head of cattle merely from the name? What about the head of cattle named Pat? Is Pat a bull or a cow?* The users admit that sometimes the name does not indicate the sex.
- *If you do not know the sex of a head of cattle, is that a problem? Do you really need to remember the sex?* The users say yes, they do need to remember the sex.

As a result of this discussion, you change the LDS accordingly (Fragment 21-3).

Farm name	Herd number	Cow name	Weight	Birth year	Birth weight
Yagar's	22	Alma	600	1994	65
Yagar's	22	Bess	656		64
Yagar's		Lisa	150	1997	55
Yagar's		Ella	135	1997	54
Yagar's	44	Alma		1993	55
Ned	22	Leo	655	1994	52
Ned	33	Amy	656	1993	
Ned	34	Pat	703	1992	55

With the users' guidance, you continue to look at the sample data. You notice that some cattle do not belong to a herd.

You ask users if this is a typographical error, and they say no. They indicate that some dairy farmers have "at-large" cows, belonging to no herd. Some farmers separate calves from their herds until the calves reach maturity. Other farmers keep their newly purchased cows away from their herds until the new cows pass a thorough veterinary screening for communicable bovine diseases.

You realize that the identifier of *head of cattle* is wrong; its link allows nulls. Before[1] mentioning this to users, you scan the data, looking for other possible identifiers. You see no candidates. Most of the descriptors allow nulls; they cannot contribute to the identifier. The only two descriptors that show no null values are, taken together, insufficient to distinguish the cows from each other. That is, two cows share values for *farm* and *cow name*.

You point out that *head of cattle* needs a different identifier. You explain that because not every instance has a herd, users cannot be assured that every instance will be distinguishable from every other instance. You say *Suppose you have two cows that do not have a herd. How do you distinguish those cows from each other?*

Users grapple with the question, offering different opinions, debating the various possibilities. During the discussion, one user points out that some cows do not even have names—some farmers do not name their calves until they reach a certain minimum age.

You listen for a while, hoping that you might hear the users mention a new descriptor that could contribute to the identifier of *head of cattle*. When you are convinced that the discussion will yield no new identifier, you interrupt.

---

[1] Why do you scan the data before asking the users for the identifier of *head of cattle?* Not because you are trying to do their work for them, but because you want to be fully aware of the situation before asking the users any questions.

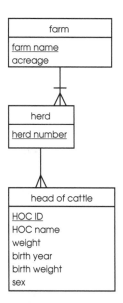

Fragment 21-4

Here you are using your expertise with the recipe for taxonomies.

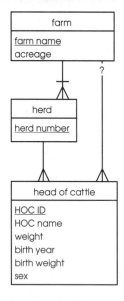

Here you are using your expertise with the recipes for history.

Fragment 21-5

You recap the situation, including the facts that are evident on the LDS and the important facts you just overheard. You say: *The diagram needs to say how you distinguish head of cattle from each other. As it stands now, the diagram is wrong. It says that you can use the combination of the herd and the head of cattle name. But we know that this is unreliable because some head of cattle have no name and some head of cattle have no herd. It appears that you will need to use an arbitrary identifier—a meaningless number or piece of text—to identify each head of cattle. If we carefully assign an identifier value to each head of cattle, we can use that value forevermore to refer to that head of cattle.*

With the users' approval, you modify the LDS to include an arbitrary identifier for *head of cattle* (Fragment 21-4). Then you reread the *head of cattle* entity aloud to ensure that the users still agree with the assertions on the LDS.

Once again, you call the users' attention to the sample data showing some head of cattle (Lisa and Ella) that have no herd. You point out that according to the sample data, Lisa and Ella do have a farm. The in-progress LDS is wrong—it cannot accommodate instances like Lisa and Ella—because there is no way to remember a head of cattle's farm. You draw Fragment 21-5.

Notice that you draw the relationship with one degree-many descriptor (see the chicken foot?) and one degree-unknown descriptor (see the question mark?). You use a degree-many descriptor because you have already seen sample data indicating that each farm can have many head of cattle. Indeed, Ella and Lisa are from the same farm.

Although it appears from the sample data that each head of cattle can have only one farm, you use a degree-unknown descriptor anyway. In effect, you are forcing yourself to ask the users a question. You ask: *Can a head of cattle have more than one farm?* Users say no. To double-check the users' answer, you say, *I believe you that, <u>at any one time</u>, a head of cattle has at most one farm. But is it possible for a head of cattle to have several farms at different times during its lifetime?* Users say that while some farmers do sell cows and bulls to each other, they are not interested in keeping track of the history of cattle ownership.

As a result of this discussion, you replace the question mark with a degree-one descriptor, as shown in Fragment 21-6.

You realize the potential for confusion from your expertise with the shape called "Multiple Short Paths."

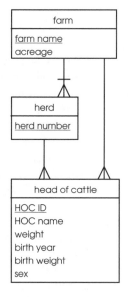

Fragment 21-6

You realize that there is a potential for confusion, so you stop to read a portion of the LDS. You want the users to understand that for any individual head of cattle, that head's farm is equivalent to that head's herd's farm. Pointing to the appropriate pieces of the diagram, you say:

- *When you focus attention on a particular head of cattle—a particular instance of this* (point to *head of cattle*) . . .
- *. . . you can determine what particular farm that head of cattle comes from. That is, you can focus your attention on a particular instance of this.* (From *head of cattle,* point along the relationship leading to *farm,* stopping at that entity.)
- *From the same instance of head of cattle* (again point to *head of cattle*) *you can determine a particular instance of herd* (point along the relationship leading to *herd,* pausing there) . . .
- *. . . from which you can determine a particular instance of farm* (point along the relationship leading from *herd* to *farm,* stopping at *farm*), *and that farm is the same farm you determined by following this shorter path* (point again to the relationship between head of cattle and farm.)

To make sure the users understand, you ask them to paraphrase what you just said. Some users get it, but others don't. One user paraphrases it especially clearly, so you let her explain it to the confused users.

You ask the users if there are any other associations between *head of cattle* and *farm.* They say no.

Your meeting with the users is running out of time. Although you have many other questions to ask, you scan your written notes to see if there are any especially important questions. (In some respects, all questions are equally important, but since the meeting is ending, you are looking for the questions that might uncover research you can do without users. Research can help you prepare for the next meeting.)

You say, *You mentioned something called communicable bovine diseases. Is it important to remember something about communicable bovine diseases?* The users say no.

You read the LDS one last time and thank the users for their time. You and they agree to meet again in three days.

Meeting with Veterinary Epidemiologists

The next day, you meet with a different set of users; these users are from the veterinary epidemiology department of the state governing body.

Congratulations! Because the users are not impressed, you can suspect that they can find no reason to disagree with the assertions on the LDS.[2]

Before the users arrive, you draw the existing LDS on the board at the front of the room. When they arrive, you say, *We have time to talk about farms, herds, and head of cattle. Specifically, I want you to tell me what you need to remember about these things. So far, I know the following: About each farm, we can remember its . . .*

You continue to read the portion of the LDS pertaining to farms, herds, and head of cattle. You read that entire portion through once. On finishing, you ask the users if they have any questions, and they do not. In fact, the users do not seem terribly impressed with what you have read; they simply say something like, *Yeah, that seems right.*

After reading the portion of the LDS to users, you begin to inquire about each entity. You say, *About each head of cattle, we can remember its HOC ID, its HOC name, its weight, birth year, birth weight, and sex. Is there anything else you want to remember about it?*

The users immediately offer many suggestions. They say, *Yes, a head of cattle can have a c435 immunization, a c482 immunization, a steering date, a c840 exposure, a urine ph level . . .*

You interrupt, only to slow them down. You ask about each of these things in turn, starting with c435 immunization. The users say, *We need to know whether a head of cattle has been immunized for the c435 virus.* You modify the *head of cattle* entity as shown in Fragment 21-7.

head of cattle
HOC ID
HOC name
weight
birth year
birth weight
sex
c435 immunization

Fragment 21-7

You are thinking about the scale of the attribute.

You say, *What exactly do you want to remember? Is it just a yes-or-no question—yes, the head of cattle has been immunized, or no, it has not? Or do you perhaps want to remember the date of the immunization?*

Users say that they want to remember the date of the immunization, so you modify the entity as shown in Fragment 21-8.

One user, a newcomer to the department of veterinary epidemiology, asks the other users a clarifying question. During the ensuing discussion, you overhear the experienced users say that each cow must receive a c435 immunization every three years.

head of cattle
HOC ID
HOC name
weight
birth year
birth weight
sex
c435 immunization date

Fragment 21-8

---

[2] This effect can be frustrating, but you should recognize it as a favorable occasion. With one group of users, you have been working very hard on an LDS, eventually achieving a data model that they endorse. Later, when you show the LDS to another group of users, they endorse it without fanfare—without recognizing just what an achievement the LDS is. The new users practically shrug at it. Such seeming indifference on the part of users is not evidence that the new users are dismissive of your hard work. Rather, it is a sign that you have done such a good job securing and recording decisions from one set of users, the other users can agree effortlessly with the LDS's clear, pithy expression of the decisions.

You're considering promoting the attribute.

head of cattle
HOC ID
HOC name
weight
birth year
birth weight
sex
date of last c435 immunization

Fragment 21-9

head of cattle
HOC ID
HOC name
weight
birth year
birth weight
sex
date of last c435 immunization
c482 immunization flag

Fragment 21-10

Smart users will eventually understand the goals of the data modeling effort and subsequently will speak more clearly and more carefully.

head of cattle
HOC ID
HOC name
weight
birth year
birth weight
sex
date of last c435 immunization
c482 immunization flag
c777 immunization date

Fragment 21-11

Based on what you overheard, you say, *So a head of cattle can have more than one c435 immunization? Do you want to remember all of these various immunizations?*

Users say no, they just need to remember the date of the most recent immunization. You suggest a name you think is more accurate: *Date of last c435 immunization.* The users accept your suggestion, so you draw Fragment 21-9.

You read the *head of cattle* entity aloud. Then you say, *That takes care of c435 immunizations. But didn't you mention some other immunizations? What are they?*

One user (Catherine) says, *There is a c482 immunization. It is a bit different from c435 immunizations because a cow gets at most one c482 immunization during her lifetime. So all we need to remember is the date of the immunization, period. Not the date of the <u>last</u> immunization.*

You say, *Do you really need to remember the date at all? Will it suffice to remember merely some indication of whether the immunization has occurred?*

Catherine says, *Yes, you're right.* You modify the *head of cattle* entity, as shown in Fragment 21-10. The users quickly accept the name you recommend for the new attribute.

You ask, *What else is worth remembering about each head of cattle?*

Catherine says, *There is another kind of immunization, c770 immunization. This one is different from the other two. A head of cattle can have at most one c770 immunization during its lifetime, but we need more than just a flag. We need to remember the date on which the immunization occurred because we care how old the cow was when the immunization was administered.*

You suggest that the name of the resulting attribute should be *c777 immunization date.* Catherine and the other users agree, so you modify the *head of cattle* entity as shown in Fragment 21-11.

Your meeting with the users from the department of veterinary epidemiology is drawing to a close. One last time, you read the portion of the LDS on which you have been focusing.

You ask the users if there are any questions. They say no. You ask the users what other areas deserve attention, and they say that they keep very careful watch over the types of food that are eaten by cattle. You ask if there are any documents that you can read to learn about this. They suggest several, and you arrange to get copies of these documents for your study.

Meeting with Economic Analysts

The next day you meet with yet a different set of users—those who analyze the economic trends of the dairy industry.

To prepare for the meeting, you look at a policies and procedures manual. You have only 30 minutes to examine it, so you simply scan it for important words—words that appear prominently in the table of contents or words that have many entries in the manual's index. You find several seemingly important words, including "agribusiness," "crop," and "regulator." You plan to ask the users about these words when you meet with them.

When you finally meet with the users, you start by reading the existing LDS to them. Then you ask the users if they have any questions, to which they say no. Then, you say, *What is an agribusiness?* One user responds:

It is a corporation that grows, cultivates, or raises agricultural products and by-products, including livestock, grain, vegetables, fruits. The state recognizes certain tax statuses that apply to agribusinesses and enacts legislation for tax purposes and to create subsidies for agribusinesses. Regulatory agencies exist for certain agribusinesses, and some agribusinesses deal directly with retail customers. Others, however, provide raw materials to manufacturers who use those raw materials to create consumer and industrial products. The state also is interested in the tax base of agribusiness and in enacting legislation that fosters the success of certain agribusinesses and in legislation that establishes guidelines and regulations for health and safety in various areas of agribusinesses.

The users are rambling. Rambling is not unusual, and you should be prepared to control it.

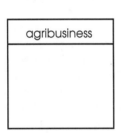

Fragment 21-12

You recognize that the user is rambling through a stream-of-consciousness rendering of whatever is known about agribusiness. You cannot follow everything he said, but you jot down some of the nouns you hear: "subsidy," "tax," "tax status," "tax base," "product," "legislation," and "regulation."

You interrupt the rambling user, saying, *Wait, I cannot keep up, and I want to get everything you are saying. First of all, there is such a thing as an agribusiness.* You draw Fragment 21-12.

You say, *Now, I heard you say many things, but I want to take them one at a time. You said something about an agribusiness having a subsidy. Did I get that right? Can an agribusiness have a subsidy?*

Here you are making a mistake, and in a few moments, you will see the high cost of that mistake.

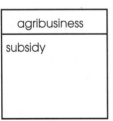

Fragment 21-13

The users say yes, so you draw Fragment 21-13.

Anticipating that you might want to promote the new attribute, you ask, *Can an agribusiness have more than one subsidy?*

One user says yes, but two others say no.

Hoping that the users will settle the dispute themselves, you let them discuss their disagreement. But they cannot resolve it, and they begin to lose patience with each other.

To shed light on the confusion, you ask another question: *What is a subsidy?* You hope to discover that they are using two different meanings of the word "subsidy." But the users quickly agree on a definition: A subsidy is a government grant. Pressing further, you ask the users for examples of subsidies; you hope that this will uncover the different definitions. One user (Pedro) offers these examples of subsidies:

- Small-farmers' goat-cheese subsidy
- Solar-powered, ecosensitive, and appropriate technologies' agricultural program of 1989

Other users disagree. Laura says, *No, those are not subsidies; they are subsidy programs. A subsidy is a specific award—a grant of a certain dollar amount to a particular farm.*

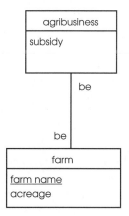

Fragment 21-14

You say, *To a farm? I thought subsidies went to agribusinesses.*

Users say, *A farm is an agribusiness.*

You make a note of this on the LDS, as in Fragment 21-14. But you do not immediately distract the users from the more immediate problem about subsidies. Getting back to that, you say, *OK, so you were saying that there are these things called subsidy programs.* Laura says, *Yes, a subsidy is a specific grant awarded to a specific farm (or agribusiness) for a specific dollar amount. Those dollars come from a larger budget that pertains to a particular subsidy program.*

Pedro then says, *OK, I understand what Laura is saying. But she's not using the words right. A subsidy is a legislated program from whose budget individual grants are given to particular agribusinesses. A subsidy award is one such grant.*

Laura and Pedro continue to disagree about the vocabulary, so you intercede. You explain that you need two names—a name for those things that have budgets from which individual awards come, and a name for those things that are awarded to particular agribusinesses. You offer four naming options. The first option uses the words as Pedro uses them (naming option 1 in the table on page 286). The second option uses Laura's words. The third and fourth options use names you suggest.

The users eventually agree to use naming option 4.

So now you go back to the LDS to reask the question that originally caused so much confusion. You are convinced that you have now conquered the confusion by settling the dispute about the meaning of "subsidy." So you ask, *Can an agribusiness*

	Thing awarded to a particular agribusiness	Thing with a budget from which award money comes
Naming option 1:	subsidy grant	subsidy
Naming option 2:	subsidy	subsidy program
Naming option 3:	subsidy grant	subsidy program
Naming option 4:	subsidy award	subsidy program

have more than one subsidy program? Once again, some users say yes and other users say no.

The persistent disagreement discourages you and the users. Together, you and they have worked hard to resolve the dispute involving the word "subsidy." And yet the resolution of the dispute has not solved the original problem. Insisting that the users define the word "subsidy" was a good instinct. As you can see, the ambiguity of the word "subsidy" was not the problem.

What's more, you are becoming anxious because during the prolonged discussion about "subsidy," the users have not seen the LDS evolving or improving, and you know that one important way to help the users retain their focus is to direct their attention to the evolution of the LDS.

The users are very frustrated—they snap at each other about the question you just asked. Quite testy, Pedro says, *It is ridiculous to think that an agribusiness has only one subsidy program. I can give you dozens of examples of agribusinesses that have several subsidy programs. The dairy industry has (1) the School Milk Packaging Subsidy Program, (2) the Cheddar Manufacturer's Assistance Program, and (3) the Family-Owned Dairy Protection Act of 1972.*

Laura rebuts: *That's not the point. No agribusiness can have more than one subsidy program because there's a state law that disallows it. If Ethan's Country Orchard gets a subsidy award from the State Council of Cider Bottlers, then that's the only subsidy award Ethan's can get. And that one award Ethan gets must come from one subsidy program, so that's the only subsidy program Ethan's can have. An agribusiness can have only one subsidy program.*

Pedro continues to disagree: *No. Let me explain . . .*

At this point, Pedro and Laura simply take turns repeating their earlier arguments; they have stopped listening to each other. And you cannot follow the argument anymore because it is so heated and the users are no longer talking about the LDS at it is drawn on the board at the front of the room. You have lost control of the meeting.

You give everyone a 20-minute break so that they can cool off and you can collect your thoughts and determine why the meeting is proceeding so awkwardly.

During the break, you examine the in-progress LDS, focusing on the recently discussed portion shown in Fragment 21-15. Then, away from the pressure and intensity of an in-progress meeting with testy users, you see a glaring omission—a syntax

You still haven't found your mistake, and that is why problems persist.

You finally detect the error that caused the meeting to go awry.

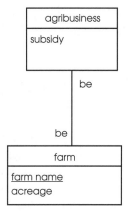

Fragment 21-15

Notice that when you remedy your mistake, the users' mood improves.

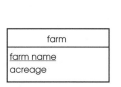

Fragment 21-16

error. The entity *agribusiness* has no identifier. You realize that this is almost certainly the cause of the misunderstanding.

When the meeting resumes, you ask Laura and Pedro separately to write down some examples of *agribusiness*. Pedro writes:

- Dairy industry
- Apple products industry
- Maple syrup and sugaring industry

Laura writes:

- Wilson Farms
- Riverside Farms and Stables
- Ethan's Country Orchard

Now you tell Pedro to imagine that his list is complete, and you ask how to distinguish each item in the list from every other item. Pedro says that every item has a unique name.

Similarly, you tell Laura to imagine that her list is complete, and you ask how to distinguish each item in the list from every other item. Laura says that every item has a state-assigned company number.

Pedro, becalmed by the 20-minute break, now recognizes the problem. He says, *Aha! I'm talking about whole industries, but Laura is talking about individual companies.* Laura quickly agrees with Pedro's assessment.

You erase the *agribusiness* entity from the in-progress LDS. In its place, you draw Fragment 21-16. You read the LDS to the users:

There is such a thing as an agribusiness company. About each agribusiness company we can remember its company number, which we use to distinguish agribusiness companies from each other.

There is another kind of thing called an agribusiness industry. About each one of those, we can remember its agribusiness industry name. We use each agribusiness industry's name to distinguish it from all the other agribusiness industries.

You ask the users to approve of the words you have just spoken. They do, without comment but with obvious relief.

Before forgetting what you just erased, you ask the users about something they said earlier. You say, *Before I understood the distinction between agribusiness companies and agribusiness industries, someone said something about a farm being an agribusiness. Is a farm an agribusiness company or an agribusiness industry?*

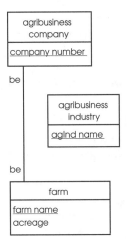

Fragment 21-17

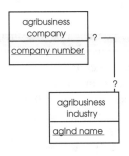

Fragment 21-18

Here you are using your expertise with overloaded words.

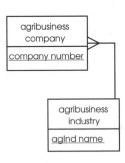

Fragment 21-19

Here you are performing the step of The Flow called "consider synonymy."

As you expect, the users say that a farm is an agribusiness company, so you add the *to-be* relationship, as shown in Fragment 21-17.

Now you have a choice. You can investigate the *to-be* relationship (performing steps of The Flow called "consider synonymy" and "consider subordination"), or you can seek a relationship between *agribusiness company* and *agribusiness industry*. It doesn't matter which you choose because you'll have to do both of them eventually. You decide to postpone the investigation of the *to-be* relationship, since the users have already been thinking hard about agribusiness (and since the topic no longer seems to be inducing rancorous arguments).

You ask the users if there is some association between agribusiness industries and agribusiness companies. You know that when the various meanings of a word differ only subtly, there is often a relationship between the resulting entities. They say yes, because each agribusiness company can have a particular agribusiness industry. You modify the LDS as shown in Fragment 21-18.

You ask if any agribusiness company can have more than one agribusiness industry. The users say no. You also ask if any agribusiness industry can have several agribusiness companies, to which the users say yes. You modify the LDS as shown in Fragment 21-19.

You ask the users if there are other relationships between agribusiness companies and agribusiness industries. They say no.

You ask the users for other descriptors of *agribusiness industry,* and they cannot come up with any. At this point, you begin to wonder whether the LDS should include the entity called *agribusiness industry*. You wonder because it is a lonely-attribute independent entity with one non-identifying descriptor that is the degree-many link of a one-many relationship. You ask the users for sample data about agribusiness companies and agribusiness industries, and they make arrangements to give you some printouts the next day. You agree, and for the time being, you stop the conversation about agribusiness and move on to other things.

Getting back to the *to-be* relationship, you ask: *Is there such a thing as a farm that is not an agribusiness company?* The users say no.

You ask: *Is there such a thing as an agribusiness company that is not a farm?* The users say yes. Some agribusiness companies take farm products as raw materials to make consumer products, but these companies are not farms.

You say: *Suppose you have a list of agribusiness companies; the list includes some farms and some other companies. The list might look something like this.* You sketch out the following data.

Farm name	Acreage	Agribusiness company number	Agribusiness industry name
Wilson Farms	1000	789ser	Dairy
Riverside	7000	fd9s9f	Maple sugaring
Ethan's	3400	i23i1i2	Apple products
		h34h3h	Maple sugaring
		z9z9z9z	Dairy
		77qser	Dairy

Remember, the pursuit of descriptors can arise any time you focus attention on a particular entity.

You want to ask the users a question about one of the bottom three instances—the instances that are not farms. As you try to phrase the question, you realize how awkward it is to talk about any of these three instances because there are so few meaningful descriptors. Although you can refer to the last instance as *the company whose number is 77qser,* you know that users probably have some other, more convenient way of discussing companies. So you postpone your question and instead begin to seek descriptors for the *agribusiness company* entity. You say: *About each agribusiness company, we can remember its company number and its agribusiness industry. An agribusiness company can be a farm. What else do you want to remember?*

To your surprise, the users say there is nothing else they want to remember. You say, *Nothing else? This sample data I've drawn is faithful to the existing diagram, and it shows that some agribusiness companies have nothing but a number and an industry. Isn't there anything else you want to remember about a company, like its name, perhaps?*

The users indicate that your sample data is unrealistic; you should not have left the farm name column blank for the rows near the bottom of the sample data. You point out that those rows describe companies that are not farms—that's why they also leave the acreage column blank. Users say, *Well, every company has a name.*

You think of two possible ways to fix the evolving LDS:

1. Add an attribute (perhaps called *company name*) to the entity called *agribusiness company,* and remove the *farm name* attribute. In effect, you are relocating the *farm name* descriptor (because it suffers from too-exclusive misplacement), and then you are renaming the relocated descriptor.
2. Add an attribute (perhaps called *company name*) to the entity called *agribusiness company.* This option makes sense if a farm can have a farm name that is different from its company name.

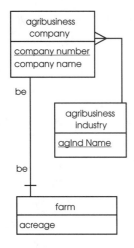

Fragment 21-20

Since you have finished (for now) seeking descriptors, you can resume The Flow where you left off—at the *consider subordination* step.

Pointing to the first row of the sample data, you ask if the company name is Wilson Farms. Users say yes, so you ask a follow-up question: *Is every farm's name its company name?* Again, users say yes, so you choose option 1.

Before making the change, you realize that by relocating the *farm name* attribute, you will leave the *farm* entity without an identifier. You suspect that the entity will become a subordinate entity. You modify the sample data to make it look like the following table; then you ask the users how they distinguish the farms—the top three rows in the sample data—from each other. You point out that the agribusiness company number will suffice. You say, *Once you know what company you're talking about, you surely know what farm you're talking about (if that company happens to be a farm). Right?* The users agree, so you modify the LDS to make *Farm* a subordinate entity (Fragment 21-20).

Agribusiness company name	Acreage	Agribusiness company number	Agribusiness industry name
Wilson Farms	1000	789ser	Dairy
Riverside	7000	fd9s9f	Maple sugaring
Ethan's	3400	i23i1i2	Apple products
Perrin Candy		h34h3h	Maple sugaring
Acme Foods		z9z9z9z	Dairy
Jane's Foods		77qser	Dairy

At this point, your meeting with the economic analysts is drawing to a close. You remind the users of the printouts of real data you want to inspect, you arrange another meeting at their convenience, and you read the recently changed portions of the LDS to them one last time.

Exercises

1. For each part of the conversation decide
   a. which step or part of controlled evolution pertains.
   b. which shapes apply.
   c. what other ways you could represent allowed and disallowed instances.

2. Extend this chapter by writing a section entitled "Meeting About Milk." Find two or more other people who can play the role of users.
3. Extend this chapter by writing a section entitled "Meeting About Farm Machinery." Find two or more other people who can play the role of users.

Story Interlude

Let Users Express Themselves

At company X, I was observing an LDS session. Jim, a novice modeler, was struggling. At one point he snapped at the users, saying, *Tell me about your data, not about what you do.* The users were unhappy about being chastised, and little progress was made. At a break, as planned, another modeler took over, and Jim became the scribe.

A few months later I observed Jim again. He had cured his problem and had become a competent modeler. When users talked, he listened and then said, *I heard you say. . . .*

Moral: *Allow users to express themselves however they want.*

Talk to the Sky

I was late getting to company X, and I walked into an LDS meeting that had been going on for an hour or so. Two novice modelers, Mary-Ruth and Vince, were sitting at a table talking with several bored users. I thought they were taking a break, since there was an LDS fragment on the board but nobody was looking at it. I was wrong. They had just been talking—trying to model without using a model. I reminded them to use the LDS as a vehicle of communication. Vince went to the board, erased the LDS (it was a leftover from another meeting), and began to focus the users' attention on shape-based questions. Mary-Ruth became the scribe, and the users became engaged in the process.

Moral: *Master modelers talk via the LDS; novices talk to the sky.*

Skipping Steps

At company X, I observed Jim, a modeler, showing off. He and the users were at the beginning of The Flow, in the discover relationship investigation. After the users talked for a bit, Jim gleefully said, *I know where you are going,* and put a two-way intersection entity with tiebreaker on the board, turned around, and preened. The users were lost, and the meeting fizzled. Jim pouted because nobody appreciated his brilliant shortcut.

Jim misbehaved. Building an LDS is about users making decisions, and his showing off got them lost. Even if he guessed right about the destination, his task, which he ignored, was to guide them.

Here another story with the same moral.

At company Y, I made a mistake when I promoted an attribute. I removed the attribute, created an entity with an identifying attribute, drew a relationship, and—here comes the error—put a chicken foot at the end of the box-to-box line where the attribute had been. My error was that I failed to ask about the degree of the link. In most cases of attribute promotion, that degree will be many, but I should not have made this decision for the users. Fortunately, the users were alert enough to correct me.

Moral: *Do not skip steps in controlled evolution.*

Misusing Power

At company X, Susan, an intermediate modeler, misbehaved. She called a timeout, said she had an idea that she needed to work on, and sent the users and observing modelers away for an hour. When they returned, she displayed a quite small LDS. It was small because she had raised the level of abstraction.

Unfortunately, only Susan understood it. The users were openly perplexed because none of the more generic names came from them. The other modelers nodded sagely, but they were lost too.

Susan had misused the power she had as the controlling modeler. She decided, not the users.

Moral: *Do not prematurely move to a higher level of abstraction.*

Too Many Cooks

At company X, Colleen ran a modeling meeting that went terribly awry. Four users and three modelers (Maureen, Eileen, and Kevin) attended. Things went well for a while. Then Maureen asked a user a question. This was acceptable because it clarified a point. Eileen asked a follow-up question about what a different user had said 10 minutes earlier. Before the user was done replying, Kevin stopped scribing and got a third user's attention and talked about something else. In short, order nobody was looking at the model or at Colleen, and the users felt themselves being tugged in several directions at once.

This meeting induced an explicit policy within the data modeling group: One modeler controls the meeting, a scribe scribes, and other modelers observe but do not disrupt. When a novice modeler is running a meeting, a mentoring modeler who observes must not disrupt but can call a timeout to meet with the novice.

Moral: *One data modeler controls a data modeling meeting.*

Rare Shapes

In a company X training class, I gave the students a small reverse engineering exercise using X data. One team of students had labels for every relationship, despite their knowing that a model should have few labeled relationships. When I asked why they used so many labels, all but one shrugged their shoulders. Jeff, however, said, *Well, without the labels, we did not understand what we meant.*

Jeff's team used a weak, general name for a key entity (*robot*), while other teams used a more focused name (*controller*). Jeff's team chose a weak entity name and then was impelled to put the notion of control in each label.

I asked Jeff's team, *Should we change the entity name and remove the labels?* They replied yes, so they modified the name and resumed making progress.

Moral: *A stylistic mistake can induce other stylistic mistakes.*

22
Chapter

Constraints

A constraint is a rule or restriction about what constitutes valid instance data of the categories on the data model. The LDS notation does not accommodate constraints, and the process of controlled evolution discourages you from discussing most constraints. This is by design; we think premature discussion of constraints is a bad idea. This chapter describes why.

Postponing the consideration of constraints makes economic sense. (We are invoking the "Do what's worth doing" principle articulated in the beginning of this book book.) You postpone discussing constraints for the following reasons:

- Constraint definition requires a mature, stabilized data model.
- Many candidate constraints turn out to be false.
- Many constraints subject a data model to premature obsolescence.

Constraint Definition Requires a Stabilized Data Model

Remember, a constraint is a rule restricting what instances are possible. You might ask, *Instances of what?* You would do well to realize that we're talking about instances of the user-recognized categories. The point is, until you understand a category thoroughly, there is no point struggling to constrain its instances.

Most of controlled evolution is about altering the fundamental definitions of categories. For example, any time you alter the identifier of an entity, you change your fundamental understanding of the corresponding category. If you tried to perform The

Flow on an in-progress model that included constraints, you would need to revise (or discard altogether) each applicable constraint any time you modified the LDS diagram. The process would become unwieldy and each incremental step of The Flow would take too long. A primary purpose of The Flow—to retain the users' attention and participation—would be defeated. And you would find yourself discarding virtually all of the constraints you "discovered" during the early stages of the modeling effort when your appreciation of the users' categories was unrealistically simple.

Many Candidate Constraints Turn Out to Be False

Even after the data model has stabilized, you should remain skeptical of constraints that the users describe. Users overreport constraints. This phenomenon occurs for two reasons:

- **The provincial view of data.** A user in a particular department might never encounter data during its early, necessarily incomplete stages of collection. For example, a clerk in the discharge office of a hospital might report a constraint: *Every patient has at least one diagnosis code.* This user has never seen any patient data that fails to satisfy such a constraint, because this user never encounters patient information immediately after admittance to the emergency room, before doctors know what is wrong with the patient.
- **Users fail to appreciate their own flexibility.** Put another way, users fail to appreciate the inflexibility of software systems. For example, a user can report, *Any company vice president must have a college degree.* Of course, you can find sample data to contradict this: There is an employee with 35 years seniority who became vice president 10 years ago, before the new policy requiring degrees was instituted.

In a case like this, the users might be able to refine the constraint, to accommodate the known exceptions: *No one without a college degree can be hired as or promoted to vice president.*

Of course, even these refined constraints can eventually turn out to be false, as when the chief executive concocts a vice-presidential role for his college-dropout nephew.

Many Constraints Subject a Data Model to Premature Obsolescence

Even if a constraint is true, it can become false in the future. We are not talking about situations deserving cynicism, such as the nepotistic rule breaking of the preceding paragraph. Rather, we are describing a legitimate phenomenon common to all organizations: previously valid constraints become invalid when the users change their processing habits.

Put another way, many constraints are about processing, not data. Many people overlook this fact, perhaps because constraints are often referred to as "data constraints."

customer
customer ID
billing account number
credit limit

Fragment 22-1

In some cases, it is easy to see that a constraint is entirely about processing. For example, consider the refined constraint of the previous section: *No one without a college degree can be hired as or promoted to vice president.* This rule constrains a particular process: the act of promoting an employee to vice president. In other cases, it is more difficult to see. For example, consider Fragment 22-1 and the constraint *Each customer must have a billing account number.* This constraint holds because the organization's current policies dictate the procedure for adding new customers to the system:

1. The Customer Accounts Group maintains a pool of available, valid billing account numbers.
2. The Customer Accounts Group adds new customers to the system as necessary.
3. When a new customer is added, the Customer Accounts Group assigns that customer a billing account number.

The constraint is a function of processing (not data) because you can invalidate it merely by changing the processing without changing the categories of data. For example, suppose that policy 2 is changed so that new customers are added to the system by the Operations Group. Accordingly, policy 3 is changed slightly to "*After* a new customer is added, the Customer Accounts Group . . . ." The constraint has become invalid; it does not hold immediately after the Operations Group adds a new customer but before the Customer Accounts Group assigns a billing account number.

Worthy Constraints

As you can see, there are several reasons why a particular constraint should be excluded from a data model: (1) the model is not yet a stable expression of the to-be-constrained categories, (2) the constraint is false, and (3) the constraint is about process, not data.

A small percentage of candidate constraints do not suffer from these shortcomings. These are the constraints that refine the definitions of the user-recognized categories. Such constraints are not really about what instances are possible; they are about what categories are possible. These constraints will be few because both the LDS notation and the process of controlled evolution assure that most category-defining details appear on the LDS diagram.

During controlled evolution, you will sometimes choose a shape that moves some category-defining information off the diagram. In such a case, a **worthy constraint** results.

For example, consider LDS Fragment 22-2 (and ignore for a moment its syntax error: three identically named attributes). Suppose you decide to increase the level of abstraction (see the section "Collapsing a Taxonomy" in Chapter 20). The resulting LDS is

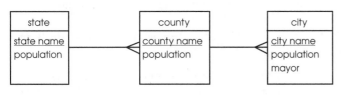

Fragment 22-2

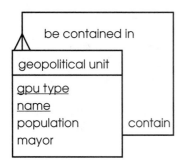

Fragment 22-3

shown in Fragment 22-3. This LDS conceals the fact that *mayor* applies only to *city*. This fact is a fundamental part of the definition of the *city, county,* and *state* categories—it is not a function of processing or of the users' overzealous reporting of constraints. Yet this fact about the *mayor* attribute must be expressed as a constraint restricting the valid instances of the *geopolitical unit* category.

As it turns out, whenever you increase the level of abstraction, you run the risk of moving some category-defining information off the LDS diagram. This is why we caution you in Chapter 20 about too casually increasing the level of abstraction on an in-progress diagram.

There are several other situations when you explicitly discuss potential constraints because you know they are worthy. These are the situations in which you ask a delayed-effect question. For example,

- When discussing a fragment like Fragment 10-25, you inquire whether the arc of a directed graph can connect a vertex to itself. (*Can an arrow be received by the same state from which it is projected?*)
- When choosing Fragment 10-16 over Fragment 10-17, you should discuss the bulleted items listed alongside Fragment 10-16.

Recognizing that a candidate constraint is "worthy" has practical implications. First, worthy constraints should be documented (see Chapter 17).

Second, a worthy constraint can affect how you visualize data for that fragment. For example, Fragments 10-24 and 10-26 use the same shape, but because 10-24 is about graph data, you can visualize its sample data as dots and arrows. (Recognizing that 10-24 is about graph data is equivalent to recognizing that it has a worthy candidate constraint: *Each flight leg must have a departure airport and an arrival airport.*)

Third, a worthy constraint can affect how you anticipate the evolution of the LDS. For example, Fragments 10-24 and 10-26 have different evolutionary potential because one of them is constrained to contain graph data and the other is not.

Fourth, a worthy constraint is a candidate for aggressive enforcement in an implemented system. The next section discusses this in detail.

Constraints and Shifting the Burden

As you move into the implementation phase of your software effort, thinking about constraints becomes more worthwhile. About each candidate constraint, you ask the following questions:

- Is this constraint worth enforcing at all? That is, is this truly a hard-and-fast rule, or is it merely a guideline?
- Where should you shift the burden? If a constraint is worth enforcing, which component of the system should enforce it?

As a rule, the worthy constraints deserve aggressive enforcement by the data-storage component of the implemented system. For example the constraint on Fragment 22-3 states *Only cities have mayors* deserves such aggressive enforcement. But remember, there will be few such constraints. Definitions of user-recognized categories do not generally induce off-diagram constraints; they induce on-diagram shapes.

Surprisingly, some false constraints deserve enforcement, albeit a less aggressive, occasional enforcement. A large set of user-reported constraints will be false merely because in an implemented system, you want to let users save data in an incomplete state. For example, you want to allow users to save a partially completed sales order, even if the order includes no delivery address. But just before printing the mailing label, the delivery address must be present. The constraint requiring a delivery address for each order is enforceable but only by the processing component and only at the stage of the process that prints out the mailing labels.

Between the constraints enforced continuously by the storage component and those enforced occasionally by the processing component, there is a wide gulf of constraints that can be enforced by any component. Technological and architectural issues beyond the scope of this book come into play here. Depending on a host of factors, you can choose to enforce constraints in the data storage component, the processing component, or the user-interface component. Or you can shift the burden onto the users and not enforce the constraint at all.

Summary and Final Thoughts

There are three types of information users want to tell you: (1) information defining categories, (2) rules defining what constitutes a valid instance of a category, and (3) information defining processing. The LDS notation and technique focuses on the first of the three.

During the data modeling phase, the mechanism of "constraints" is available to supplement the assertions contained on an LDS. For the most part, this mechanism should be ignored during the data-modeling phase because most constraints are directly or indirectly about the second (instances) or third (processing) types of user information, because many constraints turn out to be false, and because constraint articulation requires a mature, stabilized LDS.

Because constraint notation would impede the users' ability to read LDSs and because so few constraints are worthy of attention during the data-modeling phase, the LDS notation does not include any conventions for expressing constraints. In the rare cases when you encounter a worthy constraint, you should document it.

Later, during the implementation stages of a software project, candidate constraints deserve scrutiny to determine whether and how aggressively they should be enforced. A few constraints will obviously deserve aggressive, continuous enforcement by the data-storage component because they define or refine user categories. Because they are true only at certain stages of processing many constraints will obviously deserve occasional enforcement only. Some constraints will qualify for continuous enforcement, although the decision about how aggressively to enforce them and which architectural component should enforce them depends on factors beyond the scope of this book.

The fact that these constraints are enforceable during various stages of the processing and by various components of the implemented system does not change the essential messages of this chapter:

- On a Logical <u>Data</u> Structure, constraints expressing rules about *processing* do not belong.
- On a Logical Data <u>Structure</u>, constraints expressing rules about *instances* do not belong.

Exercise

Suppose for Fragment 1-1 your users said, *An achievement has a proficiency between 1 and 3.* Make up a scenario where that statement

a. becomes void because the LDS changed.
b. turns out to be false.
c. turns out to be about processing.

23 Chapter

LDS for LDS

f you've made it this far, you have signaled your determination to become a member of the culture of data modelers. Because that culture is like any other, we can make an LDS articulating the kinds of things its members want to remember.

The Meta-LDS

Recall Chapter 3, "Reading an LDS with Sentences." It introduced most of the fundamental concepts of LDS in a particular order. We will build up an LDS for the culture of data modelers in the same order. This LDS will contain names that by now are familiar to you, names like *relationship, link, attribute, descriptor, identifier,* and *entity.*

Entities and Attributes

There are entities and attributes. An entity is a kind of thing. Every attribute is a descriptor, which is in turn a kind of thing. Every kind of thing has a name distinguishing it from every other kind of thing. Fragment 23-1 corresponds to what we've just said.

Entities Have Descriptors

An entity is a kind of thing that can have descriptors; each descriptor applies to one entity. An attribute is a descriptor whose values are singletons (scalars); each attribute has a scale. Fragment 23-2 reflects these additional assertions.

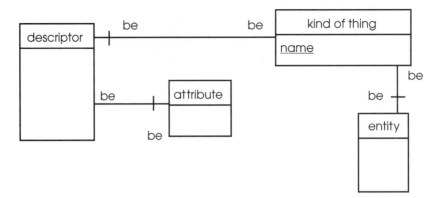

Fragment 23-1

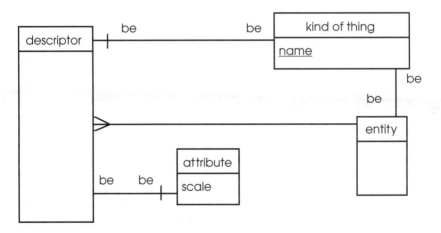

Fragment 23-2

Relationships and Links

Another kind of thing is a relationship. Each relationship is either a *to-be* or a *not-to-be* relationship. Each relationship consists of two links; each link is part of one relationship. Each link has a maximum degree and can have a label that appears on the diagram. Each link is a descriptor. See Fragment 23-3.

Identifiers

There are identifiers. Each identifier consists of a set of descriptors. A descriptor can contribute to several different identifiers, but two identifiers cannot have exactly the same set of descriptors. In fact, it is accurate to say that each identifier is a set of descriptors. (That's why *identifier* is a collection entity.) Each identifier marks its contributing descriptors with a graphical symbol (typically a bar). Each entity can have many identifiers (although most entities have only one). Each identifier has one entity. See the meta-LDS in Fragment 23-4.

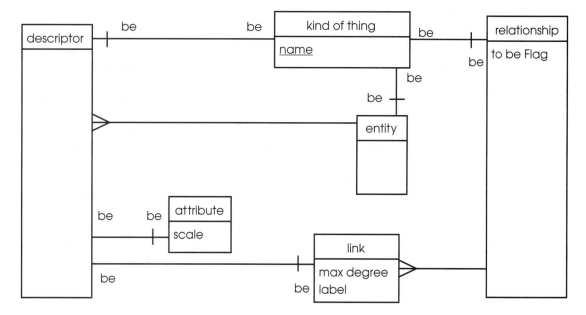

Fragment 23-3

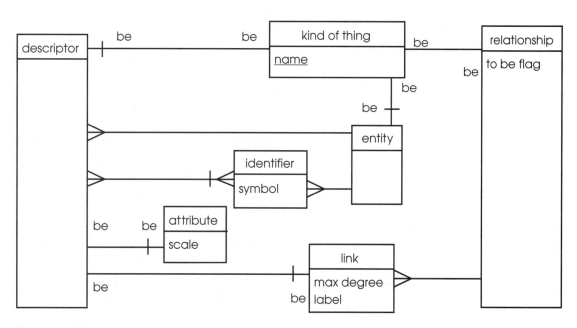

Fragment 23-4

Discussion

Fragment 23-4 has a name: **meta-LDS.** In some respects, the meta-LDS is unusual. Specifically, it has several traits that are signposts of highly abstract data models: (1) it has more entities than attributes; (2) it has more one-one relationships than any other kind of relationship; (3) it has a collection entity.

But in most respects, this LDS is like any other. Thus you can analyze it by anchoring your understanding with instances. You can anticipate how it might evolve. You can enumerate several constraints that might apply to its instances, then realize that most of these constraints are excessive and would not be enforced by any automated system.

Of course, this discourse can get confusing because the very words we use to talk about LDSs appear as entity names on the LDS we want to discuss. To minimize the confusion, we will resurrect the informal vocabulary we used in Chapter 3. It will be easier to discuss the "entity box" than the "entity entity."

Anchoring Your Understanding with Instances

You can understand the meta-LDS by seeing that it accommodates LDSs. For example, you can use Fragment 23-5 as sample data for the meta-LDS.

Now is a good time to remember the counting exercises you did in Chapter 3:

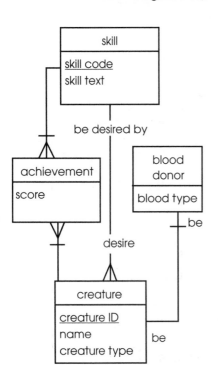

Fragment 23-5

- By counting entities, you were counting instances of the *entity* box. The sample LDS has four entities, so the *entity* box would have four instances.
- By counting attributes, you were counting instances of the *attribute* box. This sample data shows seven instances.
- By counting chicken feet, you were counting instances of the *link* box whose *max degree* equals "many." This sample data shows three such instances.
- By counting labeled lines, you were counting instances of the *relationship* box whose corresponding two instances of the *link* box had nonnull values for *label*. This sample data would have two such instances of the *relationship* box.

Strictly speaking, Fragment 23-5 suffices as a way to visualize instance data for the meta-LDS. (Remember, you can visualize instance data in any format that is instructive.) But to help you understand the meta-LDS, we also present the instance data in a purely typographical format. (Notice that, for instances made up of several words, we formed them into one string with each word capitalized.)

Kinds of Thing

Name	Type
Skill	Entity
Achievement	Entity
BloodDonor	Entity
Creature	Entity
SkillCode	Attribute
SkillText	Attribute
Score	Attribute
BloodType	Attribute
CreatureID	Attribute
Name	Attribute
CreatureType	Attribute
AchievementsOfSkill	Link
SkillOfAchievement	Link
AchievementsOfCreature	Link
CreatureOfAchievement	Link
DesiringCreaturesOfSkill	Link
DesiredSkillOfCreature	Link
InterpretationOfCreatureAsBloodDonor	Link
InterpretationOfBloodDonorAsCreature	Link
InclusionOfSkillInAchievement	Relationship
InclusionOfCreatureInAchievement	Relationship
DesireOfSkillByCreature	Relationship
EquivalenceOfCreatureAndBloodDonor	Relationship

Links

Name	Max degree	Label
AchievementsOfSkill	Many	
SkillOfAchievement	One	
AchievementsOfCreature	Many	
CreatureOfAchievement	One	
DesiringCreaturesOfSkill	Many	be desired by
DesiredSkillOfCreature	One	desire
InterpretationOfCreatureAsBloodDonor	One	be
InterpretationOfBloodDonorAsCreature	One	be

Attributes

Name	Scale
SkillCode	Nominal
SkillText	Nominal
Score	Numeric
BloodType	Nominal
CreatureID	Nominal
Name	Nominal
CreatureType	Nominal

Descriptors

Name	Described entity
SkillCode	Skill
SkillText	Skill
AchievementsOfSkill	Skill
DesiringCreaturesOfSkill	Skill
Score	Achievement

CreatureOfAchievement	Achievement
SkillOfAchievement	Achievement
DesiredSkillOfCreature	Creature
AchievementsOfCreature	Creature
CreatureID	Creature
Name	Creature
CreatureType	Creature
InterpretationOfCreatureAsBloodDonor	Creature
BloodType	BloodDonor
InterpretationOfBloodDonorAsCreature	BloodDonor

Relationships

Name	Links
InclusionOfSkillInAchievement	AchievementsOfSkill
	SkillOfAchievement
InclusionOfCreatureInAchievement	AchievementsOfCreature
	CreatureOfAchievement
DesireOfSkillByCreature	DesiringCreaturesOfSkill
	DesiredSkillOfCreature
EquivalenceOfCreatureAndBlood Donor	InterpretationOfCreatureAsBloodDonor
	InterpretationOfBloodDonorAsCreature

Identifiers

Identified entity	Set of descriptors	Symbol
Skill	{ SkillCode }	bar
Achievement	{ CreatureOfAchievement, SkillOfAchievement }	bar
Creature	{ CreatureID }	bar
BloodDonor	{ InterpretationOfBloodDonorAsCreature)	bar

Notes About the Instance Data

From the meta-LDS and the accompanying instance data, notice that there are three kinds of *kind of thing: entity, relationship,* and *descriptor.* Likewise, there are two kinds of *descriptor: attribute* and *link.*

Look at the inside-the-box text called *name.* It is worth thinking about the values of this as you think about the various kinds of *kind of thing.*

- If the *kind of thing* is an entity, the name is the entity name, which would appear on an in-progress LDS as top-of-the-box text. You would say this name when you say the sentences described in Chapter 3. In the instance data, one such value of *name* is "BloodDonor."
- If the *kind of thing* is an attribute, the name is the attribute name, which would appear on an LDS as inside-the-box text. You would say this name when you say the sentences. In the instance data, one such value of *name* is "Score."
- If the *kind of thing* is a link, the name is a noun phrase that does not appear on an LDS. Remember, links might have visible labels, but their names are not visible on the diagram. But you do say an abbreviated form of this noun phrase when you read the sentences. The value of *name* might be something like "cows of herd." When you are saying the sentence about the *herd,* entity, you say, "We can remember its cows." In the instance data, one such value of *name* is "DesiringCreaturesOfSkill."
- If the *kind of thing* is a relationship, the value of *name* is the relationship's official name, a noun phrase that you almost never say, even in abbreviated form. But remember, this noun phrase exists and is meaningful. The two reasons you never say it are (1) It is typically awkward, and (2) You don't talk about relationships that often; you talk about the links (see Chapter 15). In the instance data, one such value of *name* is "DesireOfSkillByCreature."

Anticipating How the Meta-LDS Might Evolve

Like any LDS, the meta-LDS can change as the members of the data-modeling community decide to remember different kinds of data. To illustrate, we discuss two potential additions to the meta-LDS.

Suppose you wanted to remember the minimum degree for a descriptor. In such a case, you would add to the *descriptor* box the following inside-the-box text: *min degree.* The resulting LDS contains two attributes with similar names: *max degree* and *min degree.* These attributes would induce us to consider promoting the attributes into an entity (see Chapter 19). Fragment 23-6 shows the result of the promotion and subsequent evolution.

Fragment 23-6 also contains another change, resulting from an enlargement of the database boundary. Specifically, it allows the database to store multiple separate LDSs. Each instance of the *data model* box describes a complete LDS. Notice that the identifier of the *kind of thing* box has changed because in the new, broader-scope instance data, *name* does not suffice to distinguish instances of *kind of thing* from each other. For example, two entities named "Person" could coexist, provided they were part of different LDSs.

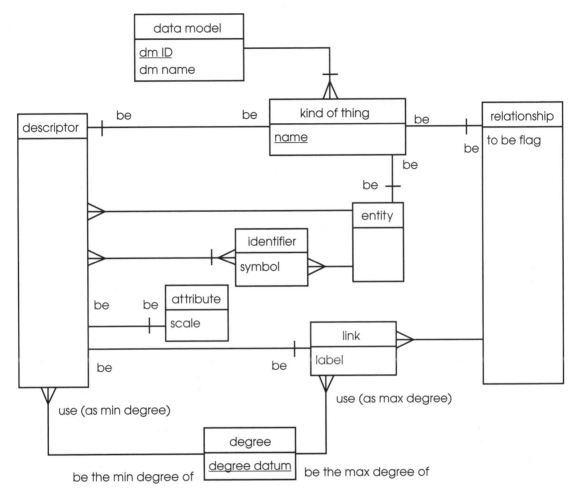

Fragment 23-6

Constraints on the Meta-LDS

The meta-LDS gives us an excellent chance to illustrate some of the points we made about constaints in Chapter 22. Applying the lessons of that chapter to the meta-LDS, you would expect to find the following:

- There is a small set of candidate constraints refining the categories evident on the meta-LDS.
- There is a larger set of candidate constraints restricting what instances of the meta-LDS categories are possible.
- The act of implementing an automated software system based on the meta-LDS will induce you to relax many candidate constraints.

Category-Refining Constraints

You can find a likely set of category-refining constraints in Chapter 4. You find that most definitions do not need constraints because the definitions are manifest on the meta-LDS itself. For example, consider the definition of *entity:* "a kind of memorable thing that has descriptors." In large measure, the LDS asserts as much. The only constraint you might add is this:

1. Each instance of the *entity* box must have a nonnull value for the Descriptors-OfEntity link. (That is, every entity must have at least one descriptor.)

Other definitions suggest other candidate constraints:

2. For each instance of the *relationship* box, the value of the LinksOfRelationship descriptor must be a set containing exactly two elements. (That is, each relationship must have exactly two links.)
3. Each instance of the *kind of thing* box must have an interpretation as exactly one of {Descriptor, Entity, Relationship}. (That is, a kind of thing is either an entity, a relationship, or a descriptor.)
4. Each instance of the *descriptor* box must have an interpretation as exactly one of {Attribute, Link}. (That is, a descriptor is either an attribute or a link.)

But it remains true that generally, the definitions do not induce constraints because the definitions are explicitly asserted by the meta-LDS itself.

Instance-Restricting Constraints

You can find a likely set of instance-restricting constraints in Chapter 13. Virtually every syntax rule suggests a candidate constraint.

5. For each instance of the *entity* box, the value of the link whose name is Identifiers-OfEntity cannot be the null set. (That is, each entity must have an identifier.)
6. Each instance of the *relationship* box both of whose links have *max degree* equal to one, must have nonnull labels for the links. (That is, every one-one relationship must have labels.)
7. For each instance of the *relationship* box, both corresponding instances of the *link* box have a nonnull value of *label* or both corresponding instances of the *link* box have a null value of *label*. (That is, every relationship has either two labels or zero labels.)

The only syntax rules that do not suggest candidate constraints are those made manifest by the LDS itself. For example, consider the syntax rule stating, "Within any LDS, each entity, attribute, relationship, and link has a name that is unique." This rule is expressed by the LDS itself—by the bars on the *kind of thing, entity, relationship, descriptor, attribute,* and *link* boxes.

Implemented Systems

If you try to build software for creating LDSs, you use the meta-LDS to assess what kinds of things the software must store. As customary when thinking about implementation, you scrutinize each candidate constraint with a skeptical eye. In particular, you ask the following questions about each constraint:

- Is this constraint worth enforcing at all? That is, is this truly a hard-and-fast rule, or is it merely a guideline?
- Where should you shift the burden? That is, is this constraint so fundamental that it should be enforced by the data storage component of the implemented system, or should the responsibility for enforcing it be moved to another, more transient part of the system?

As a rule, the constraints that stem from definitions survive this scrutiny, and you remain willing to enforce them aggressively, perhaps in the data-storage component. In our example of implementation of LDS-building software, candidates 2, 3, and 4 remain worthy of aggressive enforcement.

Note, however, that not every definition-induced constraint will survive. For example, candidate 1 does not. It is easy to imagine a usage pattern in which a data modeler creates several entities and then saves the file before taking a break. After the break, the modeler reopens the file to enter the descriptors for each entity. If the data-storage component enforced candidate constraint 1, the initial file save operation would fail.

Although definition-induced constraints tend to survive this scrutiny, remember that there will be few such constraints. Definitions of user-recognized categories do not generally induce constraints; they induce shapes on the LDS.

The rule-induced constraints tend not to survive this scrutiny quite so well. That's because in general, you want software that lets users save their work in intermediate stages. In this example, you want the LDS-building software to save in-progress work, even if the work constitutes a syntactically invalid LDS. (Note: This relaxation of the syntax rules is a concession to the way people use software, but it does not authorize data modelers to employ syntactically invalid LDSs in conversations with users.) For example, candidate constraints 5, 6, and 7 could be relaxed in an implemented system.

Remember, "relaxing" a constraint does not necessarily mean discarding it. Often, it means enforcing it only at particular moments during the user's interaction with the software. In our speculated LDS-building software, you would enforce most syntax rules during a particular stage of the LDS-building process. It is easy to imagine the software including a "Check LDS syntax" command that inspects the contents of the file and reports on the violations.

Summary

The meta-LDS (Fragment 23-4) describes the kinds of thing that users of the LDS notation consider worth remembering. The meta-LDS is highly abstract and is difficult to talk about because it contains the words we ordinarily reserve for discussing LDSs. But it is an LDS like any other in the following respects:

- It can evolve.
- It is best understood by anchoring your understanding with instances.
- It is intended to serve a particular set of users, in this case the culture of data modelers using the LDS notation.

- It induces a few candidate constraints worthy of aggressive enforcement because they define or refine categories the users (data modelers who the use LDS technique and notation) recognize.
- It induces many candidate constraints not worthy of aggressive enforcement because they are false or are true only at certain times during the process of entering an LDS into data-modeling software.
- It reflects boundary decisions. An especially noteworthy decision is that which places instance-restricting constraints outside the boundary of the meta-LDS. (That's why Fragment 23-4 includes no box named *constraint*.) There are other boundary decisions we made in the meta-LDS. The next chapter describes them in more detail.

Exercises

1. Using Fragment 7-14, create instance data for the meta-LDS (Fragment 23-4) in the format used in this chapter.
2. Do the same thing for Fragment 7-15.
3. Do the same thing for the meta-LDS itself.
4. Document the meta-LDS according to the guidelines in Chapter 17.

24
Chapter

Decisions: Designing a Data-Modeling Notation

This chapter compares decisions we made while designing the LDS technique and notation with decisions made by the designers of other techniques and notations for data modeling. We present these decisions as a series of answers to specific questions. The differences among various data-modeling notations and techniques stem from the different answers chosen by their respective designers.

This chapter is not for novices, but it can be useful to you if any of the following situations applies:

- You are an incipient master of the LDS technique, and you want to solidify your understanding of the LDS technique.
- You are an expert in another notation, and you want to compare it to the LDS notation.
- You are an expert in several other notations, and you want a framework for comparing them with each other.

We do not presume to offer the last word on data-modeling notation. After all, database experts, philosophers, cognitive scientists, neuroscientists, and others have debated for decades or centuries about categorization in the contexts of databases, linguistics, anthropology, and so on. Much has already been said, and much more will be said. If you want to explore the substantial literature on categorization, start with the following book:

- G. Lakoff, *Women, Fire and Dangerous Things: What Categories Reveal about the Mind,* University of Chicago Press, Chicago, 1987.

Quite a few works on databases present general discussions of DBMS and, in particular, various modeling techniques and notations. We like the following:

- R. Elmasri and S. Navathe, *Fundamentals of Database Systems,* Third Edition, Addison-Wesley, Reading, MA, 2000.
- C. Date, *An Introduction to Database Systems,* Seventh Edition, Addison-Wesley, Reading, MA, 2000 (particularly Chapters 24 and 25).
- G. Koch and K. Loney, *ORACLE8i: The Complete Reference,* Osborne, Berkeley, CA, 2000.
- G. Booch, J. Rumbaugh, and I. Jacobson, *The Unified Modeling Language User Guide,* Addison-Wesley, Reading, MA, 1999.
- D. Hay, *Data Model Patterns: Conventions of Thought,* Dorset House, New York, NY, 1996.
- T. Halpin, *Conceptual Schema and Relational Database Design,* Prentice Hall, Upper Saddle River, NJ, 1995.
- T. Bruce, *Designing Quality Databases with IDEF1X Information Models,* Dorset House, New York, NY, 1992.
- R. Barker, *Case*Method: Entity Relationship Modeling,* Addison-Wesley, Reading, MA, 1990.
- R. Hull and R. King, "Semantic Database Modeling: Survey, Applications and Research Issues," *ACM Computing Surveys* (19, 3), 1987.
- D. Tsichritzis and F. Lochovsky, *Data Models,* Prentice-Hall, Upper Saddle River, NJ, 1982.
- W. Kent, *Data and Reality,* North-Holland, Amsterdam, Netherlands, 1978.

We also recommend Michael Senko's seminal works:

- M. Senko et al., "Data Structures and Accessing in Data-Base Systems," *IBM Systems Journal* (12, 1), 1973.
- M. Senko, "Specification of Stored Data Structures and Desired Output Results in DIAM II with FORAL," *Proceedings of the International Conference on Very Large Data Bases,* Framingham, MA, 1975.

In addition to reading about other notations, you should try software products that support data modeling and other phases of system design and implementation. Experiment with each product's display options, seeking a set of options that best promote the good habits described in Chapter 2. Each of the following four products supports more than one notation system and gives users some control over displays. The first two are specifically for database work; the second two are more general drawing tools with special database stencils, or palettes:

- ER*win* (www.platinum.com),
- Silverrun/RDM (www.silverrun.com)
- Visio (www.visio.com),
- Visual Thought (www.confluent.com)

To make your comparison of modeling techniques and tools realistic, you should study real models (not the simplified sample models presented in textbooks and product documentation). A real model is likely to have hundreds of entities, twice as many relationships, and five to ten times as many attributes. Look at a model expressed in one notation system and try to convert it to another system.

Of course, the acid test for any system purporting to support the process of logical data modeling is how well it supports the conversation with users. You should observe experts modeling with users, continuously assessing how well the conversation transpires. Do the users remain engaged? Are technology issues pushed to the background? Can the users read the in-progress model with little or no help from the modeling expert? Does the model evolve piecemeal so that the users can follow along? Does the notation encourage the modeler to recognize when two fragments exhibit the same shape? Does the modeling notation encourage the modeler to "do what's worth doing"? For example, does it postpone the pursuit of constraints? Does it create a model that resists premature obsolescence?

Overall Decisions

What Is the Purpose?

This question accounts for most of the differences between modeling notations. Different creators of notation systems have decided to serve somewhat different audiences and purposes. For our part, we designed the LDS notation to help modelers and users name the memorable types of data and indicate what distinguishes among the instances of the types.

Other designers design their notations to serve other purposes. Unfortunately, many of these notations try to serve too many distinct purposes, such as logical modeling and relational database design or logical modeling and component-based software design. Such notations include information of no interest to users. If you try to use one of these notations for logical modeling with users, the conversation will be impeded by a notation that is too intricate for the job.

What Concepts Are Modeled?

Notation systems vary in the concepts they contain. That is, creators make different decisions about what users must specify. In doing so, creators must balance two opposing forces: content and complexity. They should remember that data modelers and users need appropriate notation, as complex as necessary but as simple as possible.

By creating "rich" notations, designers allow users and modelers to express more on the diagram. But richer is not necessarily better.

- As you capture more concepts, the model gets more cluttered, and clutter impedes communication. Since everything need not be represented in one display and you want to focus on important decisions, you may choose to omit (or postpone the discussion of) details that don't improve communication.
- People need more training to read richer notations. A notation might be so intricate that the users reject it.
- Some designers create richer notations to accommodate implementation details. Using such a notation as a vehicle for communication with users is not advisable. Users will recognize the technological flavor of the discussion and presume that they cannot contribute to the discussion. Remember, keeping the users engaged is of paramount importance.

Some designers err in the other direction, creating "poor" notations. These notations are excessively simple and do not have the expressive power to define the user-recognized categories. (The most common mistake that results in a too-poor notation is omitting identifiers.)

What Are the Names of the Modeled Concepts?

Designers differ on what they call concepts. The differences are immaterial to users because a disciplined modeler will not impose his or her vocabulary on users. But these differences become important to modelers when they try to communicate with each other.

When you try to communicate with an expert in another system or when you try to compare different notations, naming variations will cause several kinds of problems:

- **Synonymy.** A concept has more than one name. For example, some designers use the term "association role" to refer to links.
- **Overloading.** A name means entirely different things in different notation systems. (This is sometimes called the homonym problem.) For example, some designers use the word "object" to refer to class.
- **Near synonymy.** Different designers can recognize concepts that are similar but not identical. If you do not recognize the subtle distinctions between these concepts, the respective names will appear to be synonyms to you. For example, in the Unified Modeling Language (UML), an association is very similar to the LDS concept of relationship. But the concepts are not synonymous because LDS relationships are binary and UML associations are not necessarily binary.

Should a Model Include Behavior?

In some systems, names of behaviors are added. For example, operations, which are the allowed activities on a entity, can appear in a separate lower section of that entity's box. Behaviors also include collaborations, which specify entities (classes) working together, and interfaces, which are collections of operations. Each concept has some acceptable graphical symbol such as a box or circle supplemented by various kinds of arrows.

Because we believe it makes economic sense to perform logical data modeling unfettered by issues of processing, we emphatically say *No, our models do not include behaviors.*

Do not misunderstand us. We applaud graphical techniques for process modeling, and we use them ourselves. However, we think capturing process should not be intermingled with data modeling; it should come later.

What Graphical Notations Should Be Used?

Different notation systems depict concepts differently. Often surface variations have little substantive differences, but they can cause three problems:

- **Shift.** If you learned one notation system and then shift to another, you can be forced to use different symbols or to assign different meanings to the symbols you use in the original system. For example, in LDS a bar on a relationship line means "part of identifier," but in other notations it can mean "minimum degree of one."
- **Dogma.** Adherents of different notation systems might be at loggerheads over seemingly minor matters. For example, one reviewer of this book chastised us for using "chicken foot" over "crow foot," which he said was "the standard." (We cried "fowl.")
- **Unrealistic simplicity.** Notational devices that work well for toy-size models can be awkward or impossible to use for realistic cases. This does-not-scale characteristic occurs with some notational choices that require fortuitous drawing (not content) decisions or with notations that do not spare[1] ink. We prefer those notations that honor Tufte's principle: Keep to a minimum both nondata ink and redundant-data ink.

Decisions About Entities

Every notation system includes the concept of entity. The words, however, vary. Other notation designers have used these words to mean entity: *entity type, class, object, object type, table, relationship, fact table, dimension table, record,* and *record type.*

When experts in separate notations confer, things can be especially confusing because of overloaded words. For example, some notation designers use the word "entity" the way we use "entity instance." To us, "DOG" is an entity, and "LASSIE" is an entity instance. To some other notation designers, "DOG" is an entity type, and "LASSIE" is an entity.

---

[1] See E. Tufte, *The Visual Display of Quantitative Information,* Graphics Press, Cheshire, CT, 1983. This is a terrific book. Read it even if you have no interest in data models. We also recommend G. Read, *Source Book of Proposed Music Notation Reforms,* Greenwood Press, New York, 1987. It is a thoughtful and entertaining compendium of variations that failed.

Should an Entity Name Characterize One Instance or Many?

The LDS technique requires that each entity name characterizes one instance of that entity. Other techniques are less explicit about this, allowing plural nouns. (They also allow verbs on some entities, such as two-way intersection entities.) A plural noun does not work in the LDS technique because it interferes with the graceful reading of the sentences described in Chapter 3.

We think that designers should be explicit about how entities should be named because many practicing data modelers need guidance. In one case, we encountered an entity named *newspaper*. Each instance of the entity described an article, feature story, editorial, or column appearing in the newspaper. The putative rationale for this unusual name? Taken as a whole, the contents of the entity described a newspaper, which, after all, consists of articles, features stories, editorials, and columns. This is a very confusing naming standard, and we reject it unequivocally. The name should characterize each instance, not the collection of all instances.

Should There Be Different Notations for Different Kinds of Entity?

In some systems different kinds of entities have different symbols. For example, a subordinate entity could have a differently lined box. Similarly, the line connecting the subordinate entity to its "superordinate" entity could have special styling (dashes, say) to indicate that it is a *to-be* relationship.

Two factors lead us to answer no for this question. One factor is our desire to create a notation that supports the process of controlled evolution. As an entity evolves, its identifier can change—meaning that the entity's "kind" changes. If the data modeler is constantly redrawing the entity in a different style whenever the identifier changes, The Flow is interrupted.

The second factor is our desire for an appropriate notation—leading us to seek a simple notation rather than a "rich" one.

Should Each Entity Have an Identifier?

We emphatically answer yes, because without identifiers, you don't know what you are talking about. (Without identifiers, you can never be sure for any particular entity "what is meant by one of these.")

Object-oriented modelers often say no, dismissing this problem by pointing out that object-persistence systems give each object a systemwide unique object identifier (OID) or a globally unique identifier (GUID). But this does not solve the problem at all. You need to get the users to think about identifiers. Automatically generated systemwide identifiers cause as many problems as they create. Whenever you create a new instance of the PERSON class—say, an instance to describe Ben Franklin—the instance gets a unique identifier. But what if you already created an instance of that class to describe Ben Franklin? Now the system contains two objects, both instances of the PERSON class, both purporting to describe Ben Franklin. When it comes time to update some information about Ben Franklin, which object should you modify? Both?

Perversely, some conceptual modeling notations do not include identifiers. Some computer scientists think that identifiers do not even exist at the conceptual level. They maintain that identifiers are an invention of the information age, necessitated by the technological landscape of electronic information processing. This opinion ignores much historical evidence to the contrary. There are many examples of arbitrary identifiers whose invention preceded the invention of the first computer (for example, the Dewey Decimal System, the one-letter or two-letter abbreviations for the chemical elements found in the periodic table, and automobile license plates).

In discussions[2] about identifiers, there is often an unfortunate commingling of separable problems—the existence of a particular identifier and where that identifier's values come from. The second problem is noteworthy—humans sometimes find it taxing to generate identifier values at the moment they are needed. However, this is a processing problem—at what stage of the process is an identifier value created? We can and do preassign identifiers in manual applications (preprinted order forms often come with an order number on them), or we use computer systems to issue identifiers. (A new student at the University of Minnesota gets the next-higher unused integer-valued student ID.)

Because generating identifier values is often difficult, some notation designers choose to avoid the problem altogether by excluding identifiers from their notations.

But bad things happen when you do not express an identifier for an entity. You violate a good habit ("Be rigorous") described in Chapter 2, and you more easily become vague about what you mean by one instance of an entity.

Our experience teaching data modeling to several thousand students and colleagues supports this opinion. When looking at the in-progress models of teams that are struggling, almost always their struggles stem from a failure to express identifiers. Often teammates appear to be disagreeing, but they really just differently understand the meaning of the model's words. When they choose identifiers (and anchor their understanding with instances), the disagreements evaporate.

Good things happen when you do express an identifier for an entity. You foster communication three ways. First, a good portion of the controlled evolution in The Flow comes by considering different choices for an entity's identifier. Without identifiers, there is much less available to guide you. Second, many shapes are partly named by their identifier. Without identifiers, modeling would become harder because there would be fewer shapes to draw upon. Third, the name you choose for an entity must be congruent with its identifier. You solidify your confidence in an entity name by thinking about exceptional instances and those that cannot be accommodated with the chosen identifier. Without identifiers, you would have fewer means to validate your understanding of "what you mean by one of these."

Review the good habit "Be rigorous."

---

[2] This issue was a concern before today's object-oriented paradigms. C. Date (in *An Introduction to Database Systems,* Volume II, Addison-Wesley, Reading, MA, 1983) wrote about the even-then-ongoing issue of identifiers versus surrogates, an older term for OID.

Decisions About Identifiers

We answered the previous question emphatically: *Yes, identifiers are necessary.* But there are follow-up questions.

Should All Identifiers Be Arbitrary?

We say no. Arbitrary identifiers should be used only when absolutely necessary. Review our answer to the previous question, particularly the discussion of object-oriented designers' use of OIDs and GUIDs. The shortcomings of OIDs and GUIDs apply to all arbitrary identifiers.

How Should Identifiers Be Annotated?

An attribute that is part of an identifier has been annotated by a symbol (e.g., _, *, @) under or next to the attribute name and by appearing in the top part of an entity rectangle. We think that these alternatives are equally effective.

An identifying link has been annotated by a bar (as in the LDS notation) and a line pattern different from what is used for a nonidentifying link—for example, a solid, dashed, or double line or a solid half line, perhaps with the same pattern used for the entity box. In some systems, no bar or other identifying notation appears on the line, but the relation's identifying foreign key attributes appear in the identifier portion of the entity's rectangle. This technique mixes WHAT and HOW.

Can Identifiers Include Links?

We conclude yes, because an entity has descriptors and some of them form the entity's identifier.

Can an Entity Have Multiple Identifiers?

We conclude yes, although this is an especially rare phenomenon.

Must an Entity Have Multiple Identifiers?

An entity never needs to have more than one identifier, but it can if the users say so. It makes economic sense that an entity rarely has more than one identifier. There is little worth in distinguishing among the instances in several ways simultaneously—any one way will suffice.

How Are Multiple Identifiers Annotated?

In the rare case where an entity has more than one identifier, some acceptable alternate symbol, such as a dashed line, is used.

Decisions About Attributes

All notation systems include the concept of attribute. The terms, however, vary. Other notation designers have used these words for attribute: column, field, entity, non-stored entity, characteristic, variable, and property.

Is There a Difference Between Entities and Attributes?

We say yes; some modeling experts say no. By saying no, there are notational ramifications: Everything looks the same and is represented by a box (or an oval). This has one drawback and one advantage. The drawback is that large models become very unwieldy. We have worked on models with 1200 entities and approximately 6000 attributes. Using the LDS notation that distinguishes between attributes and entities, this diagram is merely difficult to manage—it has 1200 boxes on it. But using a notation that expresses both entities and attributes as boxes creates a diagram with 7200 boxes. It also multiplies the number of lines (every attribute is connected to an entity; such connections are shown by lines).

The advantage is that because there is no distinction between attributes and entities, users never need to experience the noticeable diagrammatic modification that occurs when you promote an attribute (see Chapter 19).

In some no-distinction notation systems, the name "attribute" is not used. There are instead two kinds of entity, "stored" entity and "nonstored" entity. Since these correspond to what we mean by attribute and entity, we chose the shorter names.

Do Attributes Belong on the Diagram?

In some systems entities and relationships are displayed graphically but attributes are not. For several reasons our answer to the question is yes. If you think "an entity has descriptors," then you conclude yes. If you choose yes for *Should an entity have an identifier?* then you easily conclude yes, because attributes can be part of identifiers. You might justify no by claiming that the model is simpler, but we would counter that by claiming that without attributes the model fails to communicate—readers do not understand it.[3]

Do Data Types Belong on the Diagram?

In some systems an attribute's encoding, or data type, is displayed graphically. We think that this variation is fine for implementation-level viewing. But this detail is not needed for modeling with users. So we say no and note that some data-modeling software lets you toggle on/off a "physical" model that shows data types and other easy-to-display implementation details.

---

[3] A manager of a data-modeling group has told us that for presentation to executives, he puts what he can on a transparency (about 20 entities and 40 relationships but no attributes) and waves his hands at it. He does not try to get them to understand, just to be reassured.

Do Scales Belong on the Diagram?

We know of no notation system that supports scale directly. Our decision is yes, *but not directly.* Instead, in practice we indicate the scale of an attribute by judiciously choosing its name so that its scale is apparent. We also describe each attribute's scale in documentation.

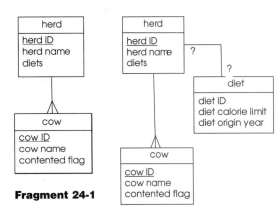

Fragment 24-1

Fragment 24-2

Are Plural Attributes Allowed?

In some systems an attribute can be multivalued. In Fragment 24-1, *diets* is such an attribute. This notation is compact, but there are issues that lead us to deem it inferior. We answer this question no.

You might argue *yes, diets is acceptable and perhaps even desirable* because it saves space (by using a variable-length character encoding for diets) or reduces query execution time or conserves screen space. However, such reasoning mixes WHAT and HOW. Remember from Chapter 1 the WHAT-not-HOW faith that, given an LDS, you can choose physical level structures yielding both efficient operation and surface forms convenient for the users. Notice that *diet* and *herd* are like Figures 1-3 and 1-4, which show multivalued implementations. You will lose flexibility and get a lower-quality LDS by prematurely choosing multivalued attributes.

You might argue yes, *diets is better* because Fragment 24-1 is simpler than Fragment 24-2, where *diet* is an entity. Well, it is simpler, but there is a problem. The only way to detect that *diets* is multivalue is to recognize that the word is plural. There is no symbolic notation equivalent to a chicken foot to indicate "multivalued." So you added a notion without adding a supporting symbol to catch the eye. The "s" in diets is the only clue. But not all plurals end in s ("alumni"), some singular terms do end in s ("miss"), and some nouns have indistinguishable singular and plural forms ("sheep"). This convention moves away from graphical data modeling and toward textual modeling. It is hard to recognize a shape on a textual model, so it is hard to anticipate how a model might evolve.

Are Foreign Key Attributes on the Model?

In some modeling systems geared toward relational implementations, a foreign-key[4] link is redundantly represented by placing the one or several attributes that form the identifier of the describing entity (e.g., ID of *creature*) with the described entity's own attributes (e.g., *proficiency of achievement*). If identifying attributes are separated from nonidentifying ones, then they are placed appropriately. They might each

---

[4]Foreign key is defined in Chapter 25.

be labeled "FK" for foreign key. If an entity has several foreign keys, the attributes might be labeled with FK1, FK2, and so on. You might think of this variation as showing a relational schema with lines indicating which relations are associated with each other.

We see two problems. First, while each box contains the names of a relation's columns and taken together the boxes form a schema, there is no direct diagrammatic link between foreign key columns and their relationship line incident to the box. Second, the foreign key columns add no logical content but merely indicate how the links will be implemented. Thus they clutter the diagram for no gain. (We do find a schema diagram with those columns useful when working with an RDBMS for designing queries but not when modeling with users.)

So our answer to this question is no, because we are trying to support logical data modeling, not schema design.

Are Type-Level Attributes Allowed?

Some systems support a different kind of attribute, called a "type-level attribute" to distinguish it from an ordinary "instance-level attribute." For example, the collection of instances of the entity achievement could have "type-level attribute" "expected score," where the expected score describes achievement (the type), not any particular instance. A type-level attribute can be annotated in a special portion of the entity box or hidden in a pop-up box.

For several reasons we think the question's answer should be no. One reason is that such "attributes" might actually describe some hidden entity, which, when it is visible, is analyzed just like any other entity. When such analysis occurs you might discover, for example, that users really want to remember an expected score for each type of creature and a different expected score for each skill. Another reason is that such "attributes" often are details, such as default values for attributes, so they can be captured elsewhere; they are not important enough to clutter the diagram.

Decisions About Relationships

All notation systems include the concept of relationship. The words, however, vary. Other notation designers have used these words for relationship: relationship type, association, association type, connector, and link.

Are All Relationships Binary?

We think that an *n*-ary relationship should be replaced with *n* binary relationships to a new entity exhibiting the chicken-feet-in shape. Our reasons include the ones we give in Chapter 18 for converting a many-many relationship into an intersection entity and then looking for other descriptors, and so on. In addition, since plain *n*-ary relationships occur rarely, we think it too much of a burden to learn special notation for content that can be adequately depicted with simpler notation. Finally, if *n*-ary relationships are allowed, then users and modelers must choose between equally valid alternatives.[5]

Is There a Difference Between Relationships and Entities?

Your answer to this question depends on your answer to the following three smaller questions. This makes sense because the question really amounts to this: What have entities got that relationships don't, and vice versa? Entities have identifiers. Should relationship also have identifiers? Entities can have attributes. Should relationships also have them? Entities have links. Should relationships?

Can a Relationship Have Attributes?

In some systems, where a relationship name appears inside a diamond or oval, a relationship can have descriptors. The descriptors are annotated in some convenient way, for example, with attributes in a rectangle hanging from the relationship line and with each attribute in an oval with a line drawn to the relationship diamond.

We say no, because this variation forces users and modelers to choose between equally valid alternatives, for example, between "achieve" relationship with relationship attribute "proficiency" and "achievement" entity with attribute "proficiency." So modelers and users have more notation to learn for no added content.

Can a Relationship Have Links?

We say no. Some notation systems allow a relationship to have links to entities or to other relationships. We find models with such variations to be much harder to read than an equivalent-content LDS. Models expressed in such a notation can get confusing. For example, imagine a model containing a relationship that has a relationship to another relationship.

Can a Relationship Have an ID? Must a Relationship Have an ID?

No notation system we know of has a yes for this question. We also conclude no, but we think that if a relationship has descriptors, then it should also have an identifier.

Is There a Difference Between Relationships and Entities? Revisited

We conclude yes, there are differences. A relationship does not have attributes, links, or an ID. If you allow a relationship to have any one of these things, you must allow all three, in which case, there is no practical difference between relationships and en-

---

[5] William Kent in *Data and Reality*, North-Holland, Amsterdam, 1978, thoroughly examines *n*-ary relationships. He concludes yes, restrict relationships to binary ones.

tities. In such a situation, the only difference between relationships and entities is how you draw them, which is a content-free difference that wrongly burdens users.

Some designers of notations for conceptual modeling say that you should give users the opportunity to think of things as relationships or entities, as they see fit, that it is wrong to force users to think of something as an entity if they prefer to think of it as a relationship. We agree. We don't force users to think of anything other than categories. As soon as something has descriptors, we make it an entity; before it has descriptors, we make it an attribute or a relationship. But we never use the words *entity, attribute,* or *relationship* with the users. Recall from Chapter 3 that we read LDSs to users without using any data-modeling vocabulary. We just read what it says. And recall also that for intersection entities and other *chicken-feet-in* shapes, we advise supplemental diction to call attention to the fact that an intersection entity expresses an association between the other two entities.

Do Relationships Have Names?

We say yes, because on rare occasions, users will ask a question whose answer requires a relationship name. For example, an inquisitive user might look at the sample data accompanying Fragment 10-1 and say the following:

> *Each of these dots* (pointing at the top of the diagram) *represents a herd; there are three herds. Each of these dots* (pointing at the bottom of the diagram) *represents a cow; there are six cows. But* (pointing at the middle of the diagram) *what does each of these lines represent?*

You need to be able to say, *Each of these lines represents <u>the membership of a cow in a herd</u>.* (The underlined part is the relationship name.)

However, we say that relationship names are of secondary importance during the process of controlled evolution. Users rarely ask questions like this.

Review Chapter 15, which discusses relationship names in detail.

Should There Be Different Notations for Different Kinds of Relationships?

We say no merely because we prefer simpler notations.

During controlled evolution, it is rare for a *to-be* relationship to become a *not-to-be* relationship, and vice versa. Thus there is a certain appeal to having different line styles for these two kinds of relationship. We acknowledge that this is a valid alternative, and our objections to it are not vehement.

Should Relationship Names Be Verbs?

We say no, and we think there are lots of problems with saying yes. First, people tend to design their notations for the simple case in which the verb can be a transitive verb whose subject is one of the related entities and whose direct object is the other. As Chapter 16 shows, this is frequently not the case.

Second, because the relationship is just a category of thing, its official name should be a noun or noun phrase, just like every other category name.

Third, a verb deceives because, while something occurs ("creature achieves skill"), the data model should not connote activity per se. With the data model you are not depicting the process itself; you are saying what users have decided to remember about the process. You do not remember achieving; you remember achievement—a noun.

What Does a Relationship Look Like on the Diagram?

In some systems a relationship line is plain, while in others it is interrupted by an oval or diamond.

Ovals or diamonds are needed for things like the relationship's name or its attributes or to be the focal point of an *n*-way relationship. However, because we believe that relationship names should not appear on a diagram, that relationships should not have attributes or identifiers or links, and that relationships should be binary, we see no reason to waste ink making a relationship look like anything other than a line connecting two boxes.

Decisions About Links

All notation systems include the concept of link. The words, however, vary. Other notation designers have used these words for link: role, direction, relationship descriptor, and foreign key.

Do Links Have Names?

We say yes, links have names, because you need link names when you help users understand the LDS. Admittedly, you do not say link names when you read the sentences described in Chapter 3. But when users are confused by an LDS and you look for different ways to read it to them, link names can be helpful. Review the section "Similarities Between Sentences" in Chapter 3.

Are Link Names on the Diagram?

Although links have names, they do not appear on the diagram. Instead, we put link labels on the diagram because link labels help the users read the LDS better than link names would.

How Should a Link Label Be Annotated?

Link labels have been placed near the described entity, near the describing entity, and inside a domino or oval that bisects the relationship line. We find each of these variations to be acceptable. But we prefer decisions that honor Tufte's principle: Minimize both nondata ink and redundant-data ink. We find that placing the labels near the described entity works well.

Which Links Get Labeled?

In some systems every link must be explicitly labeled. In other systems with binary relationships, exactly one link of each relationship is labeled.

We believe the following:

- A relationship should be labeled only if its meaning is not obvious to the users and the data modelers. This honors Tufte's principle of not using ink unless it is needed. The eye-catching labels are then reserved for relationships that deserve special attention because their meaning is not obvious.
- If a relationship is labeled, both of its links should be labeled. This reinforces the principle that each relationship has two links. It discourages users and modelers from erroneously concluding that a relationship has a "primary direction." At the conceptual or logical level, relationships do not have primary directions. It is just as legitimate to ask about the *cows-of-herd* link as it is to ask about the *herd-of-cow* link.
- The links of certain relationships must be labeled. These are syntax rules (see Chapter 13).

What Does Maximum Degree Look Like?

In every system, a link maximum degree can be either one or many. In some systems, it can be a specific integer. (Degree has also been called cardinality.)

The following symbols show several ways that a relationship with link maximum degree many has been annotated (the right end of each line).

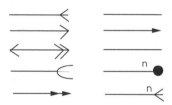

(In some systems, as in LDS, a link minimum degree is not expressed on the data model. In others it must be specified and can have a value of zero (null allowed) or 1 (nonnull) or perhaps a specific integer. Link minimum degree (0 or 1) has been annotated several ways: a number, an open oval, a small diamond, a bar, and a double bar (all at the end of or across the relationship line).

Decisions About Descriptors

Most notation systems include the concepts of attribute and link, but few explicitly recognize the similarities between them. That is, few systems explicitly discuss the concept of descriptor. Among the systems that do recognize the category of descriptor, the terms vary. Other notation designers have used these words to mean descriptor: data member and property.

Should Entities and Descriptors Share a Namespace?

This is another way of asking if data model names should be unique. We say yes for reasons already given in the "Promoting Attributes" section in Chapter 19 and in Chapter 23.

Notice that yes does not apply at implementation levels. For example, in an implemented relational schema, it is acceptable to have identically named columns in different tables.

However, at the logical level, duplicate names on an LDS will cause uncertainty. And remember, a data model should communicate precisely.

Decisions About Constraints

Many notation systems include the concept of constraint; the terms, however, vary. Other notation designers have used these words for constraint: rule, business rule, and data constraint.

In designing the LDS notation, we have chosen to exclude constraints: Chapter 22 explains why. In that chapter, we present the questions we think are important:

- Does a candidate constraint refine the definition of a user-recognized category?
- Is a candidate constraint actually false because the users are overlooking exceptional situations?
- Is a candidate constraint false some of the time but true at certain moments during data processing?
- Is a legitimately true constraint a function of processing—can it become false when the users change their policies and procedures?

We categorize constraints this way because it helps us distinguish worthy constraints (those deserving aggressive, continuous enforcement by an implemented system) from marginally worthy constraints (those deserving occasional enforcement) and from false constraints (those that should never be enforced).

Designers of other notations ask different questions about constraints. These questions categorize constraints according to their syntactic complexity. For example, designers of other notations can recognize the following categories of constraints:

1. Minimum-degree constraints for links. For example, "Each *flight leg* must have an arrival airport." (See Fragment 24-3.)
2. Minimum-degree constraints for attributes. For example, "Each *plane type* must have a *minimum crew size*."
3. Intrainstance, intraattribute constraints. For example, "salary cannot exceed $100,000."
4. Intrainstance, interattribute constraints. For example, "salary + bonus cannot exceed $130,000."
5. Intrainstance, intralink constraints. For example, "No *flight* can have more than five *flight legs*."

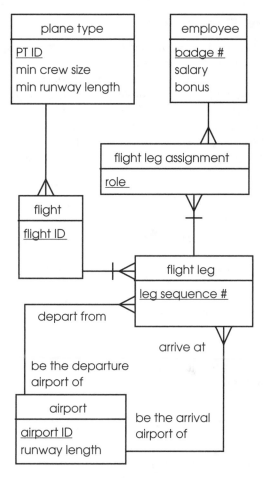

Fragment 24-3

6. Intrainstance, interlink constraints. For example, "*flight leg.departure airport* cannot equal *flight leg.arrival airport.*" (That is, *Each flight leg must arrive at a different airport than it departs from.*)

7. Interinstance, intradescriptor constraints. For example, "Max(salary) cannot exceed Min(salary) * 5." (That is, *The highest-paid employee can receive no more than five times the salary of the lowest-paid employee.*)

8. Interentity constraints. For example, "For each *flight leg,* the *minimum runway length* of the *plane type* of the *flight* must not exceed the *runway length* of the arrival *airport* and must not exceed the *runway length* of the departure *airport.*"

Generally, constraints in the low-numbered categories are easy to express on a diagram, and constraints in the high-numbered categories are difficult to express on a diagram. It should not surprise you, then, that some notations accommodate the easily expressed constraints, but no notation accommodates the hard-to-express ones.

That's unfortunate, because there is little or no correlation between a constraint's syntactic complexity and its worthiness. For example, the following worthy constraint is somewhat complex —certainly too complex to be represented graphically on a data model diagram:

The departure airport of a flight's first flight leg cannot be the arrival airport of any of that flight's flight legs.

Conversely, the following easily expressed constraint is not especially worthy:

Each flight must have a plane type.

The constraint is not worthy because the user who reported it as a constraint had a provincial view of the data—the user had never participated in the early stages of the flight-scheduling process, when flight paths and preliminary schedules are laid out before the plane types are chosen for each flight. This constraint is not true at all times and deserves at best occasional enforcement. More probably, this "rule" should not be considered a constraint at all. Rather, the system should include a built-in capability to report on all flights that do not have a plane type.

Should the Diagram Capture Minimum Degree?

We say no, because minimum-degree constraints are so often false or are a function of processing. Other notation designers are inconsistent about this answer. Many notations require minimum degree for links but do not even allow minimum degree for attributes (i.e., not null constraints). We think this inconsistency is a disservice to users because it conceals from them one of the similarities between attributes and links. (Attributes and links are different, but too much is made of their differences and not enough is made of their similarities. Minimum degree applies to all descriptors; see the section "Anticipating How the Meta-LDS Might Evolve" in Chapter 23).

Should the Diagram Capture Intrainstance, Intraattribute Constraints?

We say no, because these constraints are so often false or are a function of processing. No notations express these constraints on the diagram, although some have well-defined languages for declaring them in text.

Should the Diagram Capture Intrainstance, Interattribute Constraints?

We say no, because these constraints are so often false or are a function of processing. No notations express these constraints on the diagram, although some have well-defined languages for declaring them in text.

Should the Diagram Capture Intrainstance, Intralink Constraints?

We say no, because these constraints are so often false or are a function of processing. No notations express these constraints on the diagram, although some have well-defined languages for declaring them in text.

Should the Diagram Capture Intrainstance, Interdescriptor Constraints?

We say no, because these constraints are so often false or are a function of processing and because expressing such constraints would require a user-hostile notation. In general, no notations express these constraints on the diagram, although some have well-defined languages for declaring them in text. However, some notations can express a particular class of intrainstance, interdescriptor constraints called triangle relationships. The next section elaborates.

Should the Diagram Capture Triangle Relationships?

We say no, but it is a close call. An entity can have a set of *to-be* links that are mutually exclusive or perhaps mutually exclusive and exhaustive.

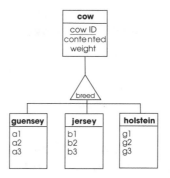

Some systems express such constraints with a special notation. For example, the accompanying figure uses a triangle to indicate that each cow must be exactly one of the breeds *guernsey, jersey,* or *holstein.* We call these relationships **triangle relationships.** In some systems, the triangle is replaced with some other symbol. (We have seen circles and horseshoes).

In some systems the triangle has a name in it, while in others it is blank. We prefer a named triangle because it fosters precise reading. In some systems lines also have labels. We dislike such labels because they add no content.

Some systems use a special notation to distinguish a set of mutually exclusive *to-be* links from a set of mutually exclusive and exhaustive *to-be* links. That is, some graphical convention (say, a dotted triangle) would indicate that each cow <u>can</u> have a breed, whereas some other convention (a solid triangle) would indicate that each cow <u>must</u> have a breed.

No notation we have seen gives the modeler the flexibility to use triangle relationships yet explicitly declare identifiers for all the entities involved. We do not like this inflexibility. It is easy to imagine a situation in which a subordinate entity has an alternate identifier.

For example, an entity called *employee* can have a triangle relationship to the entities *USA employee* and *Asia employee. Employee* has an identifying attribute, *badge #.* In addition, *USA employee* has an identifying attribute: *social security #.*

Although we find merit in triangle relationships, we prefer to exclude them from the LDS notation. We find the cost of increased diagrammatic complexity to exceed the value in increased expressiveness. Remember that in logical data modeling, the bellwether of success is getting the correct names for the user-recognized categories. Excluding triangle relationships does not interfere with the discovery of those names.

Should the Diagram Capture Interinstance, Intradescriptor Constraints?

We say no, because these constraints are so often false or are a function of processing and because expressing such constraints would require a user-hostile notation. No notations express these constraints on the diagram, although some have well-defined languages for declaring them in text.

Should the Diagram Capture Interinstance, Interdescriptor, Intraentity Constraints?

We say no, because these constraints are so often false or are a function of processing and because expressing such constraints would require a user-hostile notation. No notations express these constraints on the diagram, although some have well-defined languages for declaring them in text.

Should the Diagram Capture Interinstance, Interentity Constraints?

We say no, because these constraints are so often false or are a function of processing and because expressing such constraints would require a byzantine, user-hostile notation. No notations express these constraints on the diagram, although some have well-defined languages for declaring them in text.

Summary and Final Thoughts

The choice of whether to express a concept on the model comes down to a judgment about whether the concept is valuable enough semantically to tip the balance between content and complexity. A concept must suit a specified audience and its purposes. It must be named reasonably. Its notation must enhance, not impede, your work.

From our point of view, enriching the notation is easy, but we resist doing so. Additions should occur to LDS only if they are likely to yield better data models. A rich notation might theoretically accommodate more than a spare notation, but if the richness of the notation interferes with controlled evolution, it can effectively yield less accurate models. All the decisions we have made about the LDS notation and technique are intended to honor what we know about humans, about data, about software technology, and about how these three things interact. Reread Chapters 1 and 2 and see if you agree with our decisions.

Exercises

1. Read the data-modeling sources given in the beginning of this chapter, and judge how each notation system supports each good habit from Chapter 2.
2. Take a real data model, convert it into several notation systems, and compare them.

25
Chapter

LDS and the Relational Model

Chapter 1 presents an example intended, in part, to plant a seed of faith—faith that you can implement an LDS in many ways. One of those ways (Figure 1-2) was in simple tables. In this chapter we nourish that faith by looking more closely at connecting the LDS with the relational realm, where many implementations occur.

The relational realm is complex. For three decades database researchers have devoted considerable time and space in conferences and journals to developing solid theoretical underpinnings for various database topics, with the relational model a prominent topic. During that same period, a standard, SQL, and an entire industry have arisen. Vendors (Oracle, IBM, Sybase, and Microsoft are prominent ones) have built large, complex software products. These products all support the SQL language, and all approximate the relational model.

Unfortunately, it is often said that these products are faithful manifestations of the relational model. This is false. They are SQL implementations, which makes them fairly good approximations of the relational model. So you need to be careful as you read about the relational model and these SQL products.[1]

---

[1] A strength of R. Elmasri and S. Navathe's book, *Fundamentals of Database Systems,* Third Edition (Addison-Wesley, 2000), is how it points to the database literature. The end of each chapter compactly describes what has been written on the subject. We recommend their book as a starting point for reading about the database realm.

In this chapter, we

- define **relational database** and differentiate relational databases from SQL databases.
- define **relational schema.**
- delineate both a simple way to map from an LDS to a relational schema and some not-so-simple ways.
- examine **normal form,** a significant notion in the relational world, and describe how it jibes with LDS.

Relational Databases

A relational database consists of a set of relations. A relation has

- a name, which is unique within the database.
- a set of distinct column[2] names. The same column name can appear in more than one relation, but it is unique within each relation. Each column may have a datatype (integer, etc.) in which it is implemented.
- a set of distinct rows, where each row[3] contains a single (or atomic[4]) value for a column. A relation with all single-valued columns is said to be **normalized.**
- no order; that is, the order of both columns and rows is irrelevant since they are distinguishable by names and values, respectively.
- A primary key, a subset of a relation's columns. A relation's primary key distinguishes between its rows. Although you may choose to declare more than one primary key, you rarely do.

A relation can connect to another relation only through data; there are no direct pointers. When one or more columns in one relation correspond to identifying columns in another relation, they can be declared a **foreign key.** The paired columns in the different relations may or may not have the same names.

This is important.   A relational database can differ from an SQL database in an important way: SQL databases do not realize the relational model. They fail to implement the relational model by permitting you to omit primary keys and therefore permitting you to have duplicate rows.

An SQL database consists of **tables,** which are like relations but do not necessarily have primary keys. To be explicit, each table has

- a name, which is unique within the database.
- a set of distinct column names. The same column name can appear in more than

---

[2] In the relational literature, a column is also called an attribute. We use "column" because we use "attribute" for something else.

[3] Similarly, a row is also called a **tuple.** We use "row" because it is shorter and because "row" and "column" go together nicely. As you will see shortly, a row is not the same thing as an entity instance.

[4] A relation cannot look like Figures 1-3 or 1-4 unless you tell the DBMS to treat a nonsimple thing, such as "(A,1),(E,3),(Z,3)," as a singleton. So be careful—"atomic" is your decision, not some global truth.

one table, but it is unique within each relation. Each column can have a datatype in which its values are stored.

- a set of not necessarily distinct rows. Two rows of a table are considered distinct if there is at least one column for which the rows have different values. If two table rows are indistinct—if they have identical values for every column—you can differentiate them only by position (because each row is necessarily stored in a different place within the database file).

Working with tables instead of relations changes the way you think. In this chapter we show you mappings from LDS to relations rather than to tables.

A relational DBMS must remember much more than we show here. For example, it must remember column datatype, user characteristics, views, indices, and constraints. To understand a DBMS's meta-data, you should study (and draw an LDS for) its "dictionary" or "catalog"—the tables that exist before any user or database designer enters anything.

Finally, there is one more definition. A relational **schema** is a relational database that contains no rows. During the software implementation phase, database designers create relational schemas. Later, during the lifetime of the deployed application, users add rows as they work with the system.[5]

Mapping an LDS to a Relational Schema

In this section we show you how to map from an LDS to a relational schema, that is, to relation names, column names, and primary keys.

We use this form:

> *<relation name>:* [*<list of primary-key column names>*],
> *<list of nonprimary-key column names>*.

For example,

> Achievement: [C_id, S_code], proficiency.

In general there are many possible ways to map from an LDS (WHAT) to a DBMS schema (a partial HOW) or to a collection of record structures.[6] However, the procedure we present here is simple. It is so simple that you should expect data-modeling software, except for a few cases, to accomplish it for you automatically.

---

[5] People differ in exactly what they think a schema consists of. You might see these things included: column datatypes, foreign keys, and indices.

[6] A relationship can have up to 17 possible mappings to a schema or record structure. See J. Carlis and S. March, "Multilevel Model of Physical Database Design Problems and Solutions," IEEE COMPDEC Conference (now ICDE), 1984; J. Carlis and S. March, "On the Interdependencies between Record Structure and Access Path Design," *Journal of MIS,* June 1989; and C. Dabrowski, J. Carlis, S. March, and D. Jefferson, "Integrating a Knowledge-Based Component into a Physical Database Design System," *Information and Management,* March 1989.

The first two steps of the procedure need no explanation:

- **Step 1.** Each entity maps to a relation with the same name. For example, *skill* maps to Skill.[7]
- **Step 2.** Each attribute of an entity becomes a like-named column of a relation. If the attribute contributes to the entity's identifier, then its corresponding column becomes part of the relations's primary key. For example, *C_name* maps to C_name.

This is important.

Since the column values of a relation must be atomic, you cannot represent any degree-many link of the LDS in one column. Remember, the value of a degree-many link can be an entire set of values, and relational columns can contain only scalar values. (Since most relationships are one-many, only one link of most relationships is mapped via this procedure.) Therefore a row in a relation will not correspond to an entity instance if the entity has any degree-many links.

Each degree-one link, via steps 3 through 5, maps to one or several columns that correspond to the primary key of the relation corresponding to the describing entity.

- **Step 3.** Map each degree-one link where the describing entity is an independent entity. A degree-one link maps to one column when the describing entity is a lonely-attribute independent entity, or it maps to one or several columns when the describing entity is a common independent entity (review Chapter 8). For example, (a) *skill* from Fragment 1-1 is a common independent entity with just *C_id* identifying it, so the link *skill of achievement* maps to a single column with the name C_id, and (b) *course* from Fragment 3-18 is a common independent entity with two identifying attributes, so the link *course of registration item* maps to two columns named Course Name and Department.

    If the mapped link was part of the entity's identifier, then each column it maps to becomes part of the relation's identifier.
- **Step 4.** Examine each unmapped degree-one link in turn and map it if possible.

    If a degree-one link's describing entity has had all of its identifying descriptors mapped into primary key columns, then map that link. In the schema of the described relation, include a column for each column of the primary key of the describing relation.

    Prepend those columns with link labels and relation names as needed.

    If the mapped link was part of the entity's identifier, then each column it maps to becomes part of the relation's identifier.
- **Step 5.** Repeat step 4 until all degree-one links are mapped.

Here are some example mappings:

The relational schema for Fragment 25-1 is

Skill: [S_code], S_description

Region: [R_ID], R_remark

---

[7] Notice that in this chapter LDS names are italicized, but relation and column names are not.

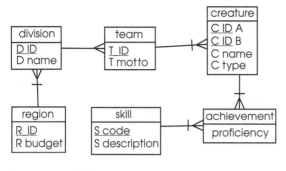

Fragment 25-1

Division: [R_ID, D_ID], D_Name

Team: [T_ID], R_ID, D_ID, T_motto

Creature: [T_ID, C_ID_A, C_ID_B], C_name, C_type

Achievement: [T_ID, C_ID_A, C_ID_B, S_code], proficiency

Notice that R_id is a column in Team but not in Creature.

To test your understanding of the procedure, change the identifier of *team* in Fragment 25-1 to *T_ID* and *division of team,* then determine the schema. You should end up with R_ID as a column in the Achievement relation.

When one link is barred in a one-one relationship, only the barred link is mapped. For example, the schema for Fragment 25-2 is

Legal parameter value: [String]

Scoring matrix: [Indicating_Legal_parameter_Value_String], Sensitivity

In this situation, as you would expect from step 4, the barred link maps to a primary key column. However, the nonbarred link maps to nothing, even though it is degree one. (Try to map that link; you will conclude that you cannot.)

This procedure works when two entities have two or more relationships. For example, the schema for Fragment 25-3 is

State: [state name]

City: [city_ID], state name, state capital of

The City relation has two foreign keys: State Name and State Capital of. For each foreign key, there is one instance of foreign column–home column pair: state name in

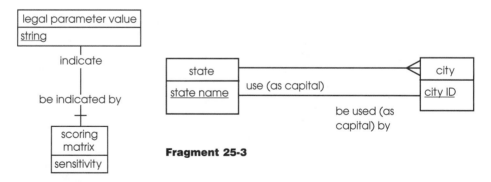

Fragment 25-3

Fragment 25-2

state paired with state name in city and state name in state paired with state capital of in city.

Here is a test of your understanding of foreign key:

- Assume for expository purposes that you replaced the solely identifying attribute state name with an admittedly unlikely compound identifier having the identifying attributes state first name and state last name.
- STOP! Before you read further, write down all the detail about each foreign key.
- There still is one identifier in the relation state and two foreign keys in the relation city, but now city has five columns, and each foreign key has two pairs of columns. We emphasize two because if you do not see that there are two pairs for each foreign key then you do not understand foreign keys.

This is important.

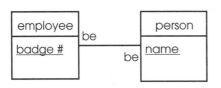

Fragment 25-4

This simple mapping procedure works, except in the following four LDS cases.

Case 1: When both links are degree one (either *to-be* or *not-to-be*) and neither is barred, then you must choose from three options. You can map one link, the other link, or both links. For example, Fragment 25-4 has three correct schemas:

Employee:[Badge #], Name
Person:[Name]

Employee: [Badge #]
Person:[Name], Badge #

Employee: [Badge #], Name
Person:[Name], Badge #

How should you choose? Well, you will need to use information other than what is on the LDS. You could consider how the data will be used or stored, but that information may not be available (and it might change rapidly, leaving you with an inconvenient schema).

Now that you know about this first case, you can answer this question: *How many schemas* (HOWs) *must you choose from when you use this simple mapping for an LDS* (WHAT)? The answer is at least 3^n, where n is the number of nonbarred one-one relationships.

Case 2: If you have a collection entity, you cannot convert it directly into a relation. You must give the entity an arbitrary identifier, remove the identifier that makes the entity a collection entity, and proceed to convert the entity to a relation.

Case 3: If the LDS contains any many-many relationships, you must convert each of them to an intersection entity. Then you create a relation corresponding to the intersection entity.

Case 4: If an entity has several identifiers (a rare but possible situation), you should create a primary key corresponding to one of the identifiers. For each other identifier you similarly can make a list of columns and declare that it should have a "unique" index built for it.

Nonsimple mappings are possible. They do not conform to the guideline that "one entity maps to one relation," and they come at a price: DBMSs do not take up the burden of keeping track of things.

Here are three not-so-simple mappings:

Split. You can split (or fragment) a relation vertically or horizontally. Vertical splitting means that you put some of the relation's columns in one relation and some in another relation, perhaps duplicating nonprimary-key columns, but definitely duplicating primary-key columns. In both relations you include all rows. Horizontal splitting means that you include all columns but split the rows into different relations. (You can choose to duplicate some rows.)

Denormalize. You can denormalize, for example,

Creature: [C_ID], C_type, C_name
Achievement: [C_ID, S_code], proficiency, C_name
Skill: [S_code], S_description

where C_name is duplicated.

Absorb. You can completely absorb relations, for example,

Achievement: [C_ID], S_code, proficiency, C_name, C_type, S_description

Note: All of the Creature and Skill data has been absorbed into the Achievement relation—and Creature and Skill relations do not exist at all. This mapping doesn't work if any Creature or Skill has no Achievements.[8] (Review the example in Chapter 1.)

These three mappings may make some database activities faster, but they also may cause expensive updates and engender the possibility of update anomalies.[9]

LDS and Normal Forms

Normal forms have been intensely studied by database researchers.[10] Here are the key points you need to know in relating an LDS to normal forms:

- A relation has a "normal form." Basically, normal form is a number from 1 to 5, written as 1NF to 5NF and read as "first normal form" to "fifth normal form." A relation's normal form tells you if the relation can have duplicate data and therefore if update anomalies can occur. To get simpler or faster querying, you might decide to risk update anomalies.

- Generally, high normal forms are desirable. For example, 3NF is in most situations preferable to 2NF.

- You can determine a relation's normal form using the mathematical notion called **functional determinant** (or its mirror image, **functional dependency**). $X \rightarrow y$ is

---

[8] Here Creature is absorbed into Achievement. Achievement cannot be absorbed into Creature because of the "normalized" requirement. When mapping to nonrelational systems, you are not so restricted.

[9] See the next section, "LDS and Normal Forms."

[10] Look elsewhere for lengthy expositions, including Chapters 14 and 15 of Elmasri and Navathe, and William Kent, "A Simple Guide to Five Normal Forms in Relational Database Theory," *Communications of the ACM* (25, 2), February 1983.

read as "*X* functionally determines *y*" (or "*y* is functionally dependent on *X*"). *X* is a set of columns; *y* is generally one column but can be a set of columns.

- The simple mapping from a good LDS yields high normal form relations. The nonsimple mappings from a good LDS yield lower normal form relations. This amounts to a "denormalization."
- There is a process called "normalization" by which database designers can improve the normal form for a set of relations. The process converts relations from lower to higher normal forms.
- If you start with a good LDS, the procedure given earlier in this chapter will yield a schema whose relations are in high normal forms. That is, normalization is not necessary because relations of low normal forms cannot result from a good LDS.

The next sections show you how normal forms relate to LDS.

First Normal Form

A relation is in first normal form (1NF) if each of its columns contains singleton (scalar) values. Obviously, for the default procedure to generate a relation that is not in 1NF, the initial LDS would have to contain a plural attribute. But such an LDS (see Fragment 19-6) is a poor LDS, and only a very inexperienced data modeler would attempt to generate a relational schema from it.

lecture
<u>speaker_ID</u>
<u>date</u>
<u>time</u>
topic
speaker name
location
company name
company location
speaker job title
company ID

Fragment 25-5

Second Normal Form

A relation is in second normal form (2NF) if it is in first normal form and if every nonprimary key column is dependent on the entire primary key.

If you generate the default schema for Fragment 25-5, you will produce a relation that is in 1NF but not in 2NF. The resulting relation would include a nonkey column called SpeakerName and a primary key consisting of the columns SpeakerID, Date, and Time. But the column SpeakerName does not depend on the entire key; it depends on a subset of the primary key—the individual column SpeakerID.

It is worth noting that an experienced modeler would never attempt to generate a relational schema from Fragment 25-5 because an experienced modeler would recognize further opportunities to perform The Flow. That is, the modeler would recognize that the entity *lecture* is in a relatively unevolved state of controlled evolution.

Third Normal Form

A relation is in third normal form if it is in second normal form and if no transitive dependency exists among its columns. A transitive dependency exists if there is a set of columns *Y* that is determined by one set of columns *X* and determines another

Fragment 25-6

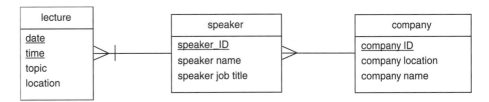

Fragment 25-7

column Z. That is, if the relation includes a set of columns X, a set of columns Y, and an individual column Z, then

$$X \rightarrow Y$$
$$Y \rightarrow Z$$

If you generate the default schema for Fragment 25-6, you will produce a relation that is in 2NF but not in 3NF. That is, a transitive dependency would exist among the columns of the Speaker relation. Specifically,

speaker_ID $\rightarrow$ company-ID

company_ID $\rightarrow$ company name

But Fragment 25-6 is a poor LDS; it reflects an early, relatively unevolved state of controlled evolution. The *company ID* attribute should be promoted, and the attributes *company location* and *company name* should be relocated to the entity resulting from the promotion.

Compared to Fragment 25-6, 25-7 is a better LDS. It would yield a default schema all of whose relations are in 3NF.

Fourth Normal Form

A relation is in fourth normal form if and only if it is in third normal form and there are no nontrivial multivalued dependencies.

This definition is accurate but not terribly helpful. To pursue this line of discourse, we'd have to define "multivalued dependency," and then we'd have to define

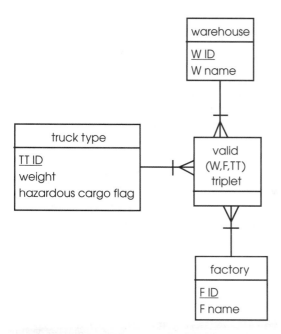

Fragment 25-8

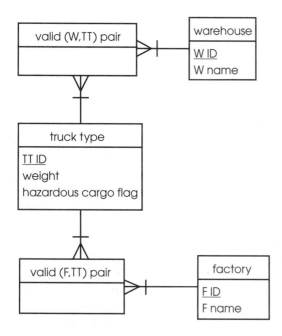

Fragment 25-9

what constitutes a trivial one. We leave this task to the authors of database textbooks. For our purpose, an example will suffice.

We are not being cavalier here. Remember, part of our message is that you do not need to think terribly hard about normal forms or normalization, provided that you work to generate good LDSs that are faithful to the users' information needs. By glossing over some of the more tedious aspects of normalization, we are reinforcing that message.

The example: Suppose your in-progress LDS looks like Fragment 25-8. Suppose further that the users indicate the following:

- Some warehouses cannot accommodate all trucks. (Some trucks are too big to maneuver into position at some warehouses.)
- Some factories cannot accommodate all trucks. (Some factories have old-fashioned loading docks that do not work with newer trucks.)
- Based on nothing more than these restrictions, each instance of *valid (W,F,TT) triplet* indicates that it is acceptable to deliver products from that factory to that warehouse in a truck of that type.

If you generate the default relational schema from Fragment 25-8, the resulting relation corresponding to the *valid (W,F,TT) triplet* entity will not be in fourth normal form. But as a master data modeler considering the users' assertions, you would never generate a schema from Fragment 25-8 because you would recognize that the fragment reflects an unevolved state of the LDS. Specifically, you would realize that you are not finished with The Flow—that you need to perform the Flow investigation "Seek further evolution for the chicken-feet-in shape."

In fact, according to the user assertions, you would replace Fragment 25-8 with Fragment 25-9. And based on the users' assertions, the default schema generated from Fragment 25-9 includes relations that are in fourth (or higher) normal form.

Fifth Normal Form

A relation is in fifth normal form if no remaining lossless, nontrivial projections are possible.

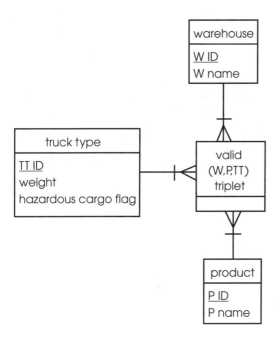

Fragment 25-10

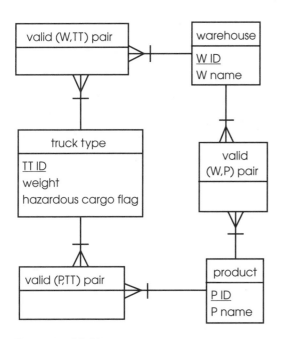

Fragment 25-11

Once again, understanding this definition would require further definitions: projection, nontrivial projection, and lossless projection. Other authors have covered that, and we're not going to repeat here what they've said elsewhere.

As is our custom, however, we will give you an example. Suppose your in-progress LDS looks like Fragment 25-10. Suppose further that the users indicate the following:

- Some warehouses cannot accommodate all trucks. (Some trucks are too big to maneuver into position at some warehouses.)
- Some warehouses cannot accommodate all products. (Some products require refrigerated warehouses.)
- Some trucks cannot accommodate all products. (Some products must be transported in trucks approved for carrying hazardous materials.)
- Based on nothing more than these restrictions, each instance of *valid (W,P,TT) triplet* indicates that it is acceptable to deliver that product to that warehouse in a truck of that type.
- If you generate the default relational schema from Fragment 25-10, the resulting relation corresponding to the *valid (W,P,TT) triplet* entity will not be in fifth normal form.

But as a master data modeler considering the users' assertions, you would never generate a schema from Fragment 25-10 because you would recognize that the fragment reflects an unevolved state of the LDS. Specifically, you would realize that you are not finished with The Flow—that you need to perform the Flow investigation "Seek further evolution for the chicken-feet-in shape."

In fact, according to the users' assertions, you would replace Fragment 25-10 with Fragment 25-11. And based on the users' assertions, the default schema generated from Fragment 25-11 includes relations that are in fifth normal form.

Summary

The relational model provides the theoretical basis for the commercial DBMS products, which in general do not strictly adhere to that model.

There is a mechanical procedure for generating a default relational schema based on any well-formed LDS. If the LDS faithfully represents your users' information needs, each relation of the resulting schema will be in high normal form. In more detail, here is the good news about normal forms:

1. If in your LDS each descriptor describes the correct entity and you use the simple mapping, then your relations will be at least 3NF. (Novice modelers quickly become skilled enough to help users place descriptors correctly.)
2. If you perform all the steps of controlled evolution and you avoid overidentification and you achieve the first trait in this list, then your relations will be in 5NF.

Exercises

1. Choose an RDBMS and draw an LDS that corresponds to its catalog. (You should expect to see a mix of singular and plural table names.)
2. Repeat question 1 for several different RDBMSs and compare their catalogs.
3. Take a real schema that you are familiar with, print it out, and then try to explain it to someone who knows nothing about it.
4. Repeat question 3, but before talking to others, reverse engineer the schema into an LDS. (Be alert for nonsimple mappings and the existence of tables instead of relations.)
5. Repeat question 3 for several different schemas. Think about improvements you might make in each schema.

26
Chapter

Cookbook:
Recipes for
Data Modelers

A shape is useful because it is content neutral, so you can use it on many different data models. To become a data modeler ready to help any users from any culture, you have mastered shapes (among other things).

Unlike a shape, a recipe is not content neutral. Rather, a recipe is a content-specific data-modeling fragment worth studying and reusing. Recipes deserve your attention because they occur frequently.

Recognizing a recipe differs from recognizing a shape. Remember, you recognize a shape through its structure (e.g., the arrangement of entities, chicken feet, and bars). You recognize a recipe by recognizing similarity in both structure and content. For example, if you are modeling airplane flights, you might say, *An airport is like a node in a directed graph*. We use "like" rather than "identical to" because a master data modeler, like a master chef, is not rigidly bound to a recipe but can readily handle variations on it.

In this chapter, we present recipes from discrete mathematics, a topic taught to computer science freshman and integral to computing. You may wonder why we include them. Well, they apply even to the first LDS you saw, Fragment 1-1: A creature achieves a set (not a bag or sequence) of skills; Figure 1-1, like Fragment 26-17, shows a matrix for data. We see students making rapid progress when they ask questions like *Do we remember a set or a sequence of achievements by a creature?*

This cookbook of recipe explanations appears without instances because by now you know how to visualize instances. So, as you study each recipe, you should create sample instances.

You should also ask yourself these questions:

- *Where have I seen situations like this recipe?*
- *What else could be remembered?*
- *What shapes apply?*
- *What steps of The Flow apply?*
- *How does this recipe compare to others?*

As you reflect upon your own modeling experiences, stuff this cookbook with notes and recipes of your own, and occasionally reorganize your recipes—doing so will help you see new connections among them.

Besides using these recipes for data modeling, we also use them to understand difficult scientific and mathematical writing. We reverse engineer the subscripted variables of a research paper into an LDS. Poorly written technical articles can become clear with the help of an LDS. Here is a simple exercise: Take the variables A_j, B_{ij}, C_{ijk}, and D_i, and draw an LDS.

> Increase this cookbook's value by writing down LDS situations that fit each recipe. Add your own recipes, too.

Set Recipes

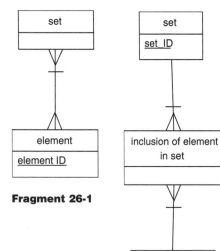

Fragment 26-1

Fragment 26-2

To accommodate any number of sets of elements, use Fragment 26-1. Note: Since a set is identified by its elements, the null set cannot be accommodated. Also, do not think in terms of changing a set because a set with different elements is a different set.

To accommodate any number of sets of elements, including the null set, use Fragment 26-2. Note: A set is not identified by its elements, as it was in Fragment 26-1.

To accommodate any number of bags of elements, including the null bag, use Fragment 26-3. Note: A bag, also called a multiset, can have an element in it more than once.

To accommodate any number of sequences of elements, use Fragment 26-4. Note: An element can appear at more than one position in a sequence.

To accommodate any number of unordered pairs of elements, use Fragment 26-5. Note: An unordered pair is a set with the degree of the link *elements of set* restricted to exactly two.

To accommodate any number of ordered pairs of elements, use Fragment 26-6. Note: An ordered pair is not a set.

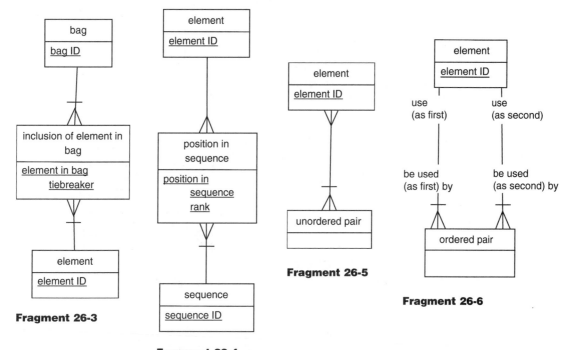

Fragment 26-3

Fragment 26-4

Fragment 26-5

Fragment 26-6

Graph Recipes

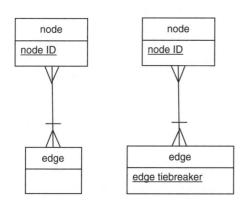

Fragment 26-7

Fragment 26-8

To accommodate an undirected graph of nodes and edges, use Fragment 26-7. Note: The graph must be unary; that is, it must have at most one edge between nodes. If the degree of the link *nodes of edge* is restricted to exactly two, then the graph is called a binary graph.

To accommodate an undirected multigraph of nodes and edges, use Fragment 26-8. Note: The graph can accommodate more than one edge between nodes.

To accommodate a directed graph of nodes and directed arcs, use Fragment 26-9. Note: The graph is binary (every directed arc has two, perhaps identical, nodes) and can accommodate more than one directed arc between nodes, but not in the same direction.

To accommodate a directed multigraph of nodes and directed arcs, use Fragment 26-10.

To accommodate a specialized directed multigraph of nodes and directed arcs where a node can be a source, limb,

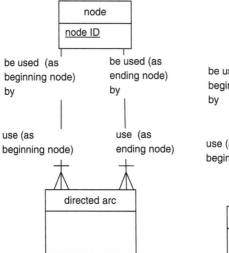

Fragment 26-9

Fragment 26-10

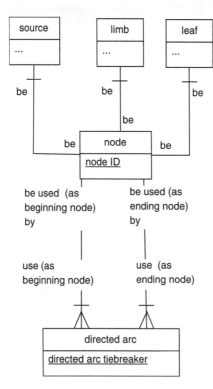

Fragment 26-11

or sink node, use Fragment 26-11. Note: Other descriptors (indicated by an ellipsis[1]) can be remembered about each kind of node.

To accommodate a directed graph augmented with remembered paths, use Fragment 26-12. Note: A path is a sequence of nodes, and a node can appear more than once in a path.

To accommodate a multigraph augmented with remembered paths, use Fragment 26-13. Note: A path is now a sequence of directed arcs, and a directed arc can appear more than once in a path.

To accommodate a directed graph with single-source broadcasting, use Fragment 26-14. Note: An arc can have possibly many beginning nodes and possibly many ending nodes.

---

[1] Do not misunderstand us. The ellipses stand for descriptors, including links, not just attributes.

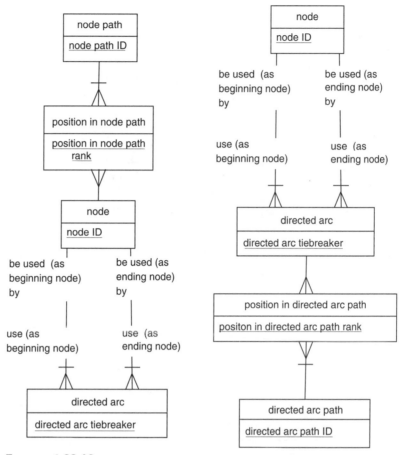

Fragment 26-12

Fragment 26-13

A multisource broadcasting arc is also possible, but we have never seen one. To make such an entity, add a chicken foot so that an arc can have many beginning nodes.

To accommodate any number of directed graphs, use Fragment 26-15, which modifies Fragment 26-9. Note: The other graph fragments can be similarly extended to support multiple graphs.

Matrix Recipes

To accommodate a plain matrix, use Fragment 26-16.

To accommodate a matrix with annotations for each row and each column, use Fragment 26-17. Note: If row and column are about the same variable, then use Fragment 26-6 or 26-10. (Graphs can be represented in matrix forms.)

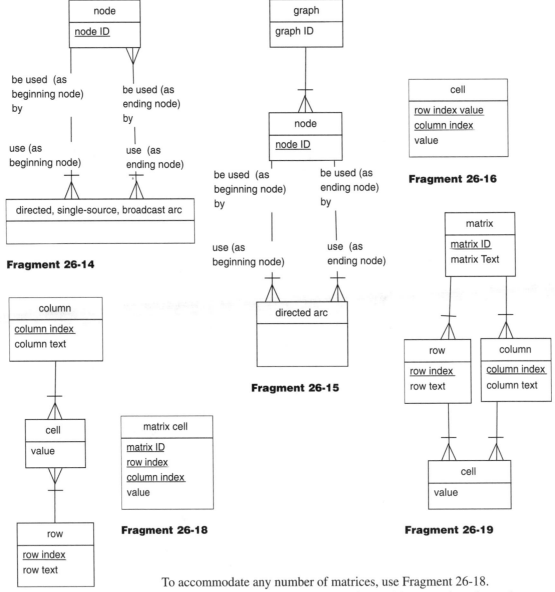

Fragment 26-14

Fragment 26-15

Fragment 26-16

Fragment 26-17

Fragment 26-18

Fragment 26-19

To accommodate any number of matrices, use Fragment 26-18.

To accommodate any number of matrices, with annotations for each row or column, use Fragment 26-19.

You should be able to modify these matrix recipes to accommodate matrices with just one and with two or more dimensions.

You will often see set and graph data represented in matrix form. To solidify your understanding, review the set and graph recipes and see how they connect to matrix recipes. Here is an important difference: *element ID* and *node ID* are nominal scale attributes, but *row index* and *column index* can be nominal, ordinal, or numeric scale.

Taxonomy and Near Taxonomy Recipes

Review the section "Changing the Level of Abstraction," in Chapter 20.

In this section we present several fragments that accommodate data that is a taxonomy or nearly so. The dictionary defines a taxonomy as a multilevel classification, especially of plants or animals, into phyla, species, and so on. A taxonomy is a special kind of graph—a tree.

Here are some collections of words that fit, or nearly fit, this definition:

(a) manufacturing: product, component, subcomponent, assembly, subassembly, and part;
(b) soils science: order, suborder, great group, subgroup, family, soils series, and subseries;
(c) geopolitical unit: state, county, district, township, and parcel;
(d) education: university, college, school, department, program, and course;
(e) company: area; region, division, department, and project;
(f) publishing: book, part, chapter, section, subsection, subsubsection, paragraph, sentence, clause, and word.

Notice in these examples that some units have a set of subunits, while others have a sequence of subunits.

Here are some sample factors that can complicate your taxonomies:

(a) in manufacturing: an assembly has no subassembly and a part appears in more than one subassembly;
(b) in soils science: a family has no subseries and a soil interpretation can describe several different taxonomic levels;
(c) in education: several different levels can offer courses, and a course can be cooffered by two different organizational units.

You need to think about four questions concerning a taxonomy:

(1) *Do levels have largely the same descriptors?* (Choose between a multiple-chicken-feet-across and a one-many reflexive relationship.)
(2) *At what levels does the taxonomy connect to the rest of the LDS?* (Perhaps complicate the LDS to connect entities correctly.)
(3) *Are there any degenerate instances?* (Perhaps complicate the LDS to identify entities correctly.)
(4) *Does the data truly fit a hierarchy, or is it a directed acyclic graph?* (Perhaps complicate the LDS to represent a many-many relationship correctly.)

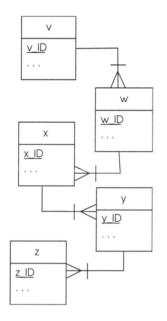

Fragment 26-20

To accommodate taxonomy data where there are different descriptors (indicated by an ellipsis) at different levels, use Fragment 26-20. To accommodate taxonomy where there are the same descriptors at different levels, use Fragment 26-21.

To accommodate taxonomy where there are the same descriptors at different levels, use Fragment 26-21.

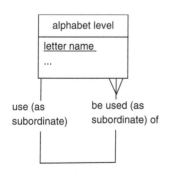

Fragment 26-21

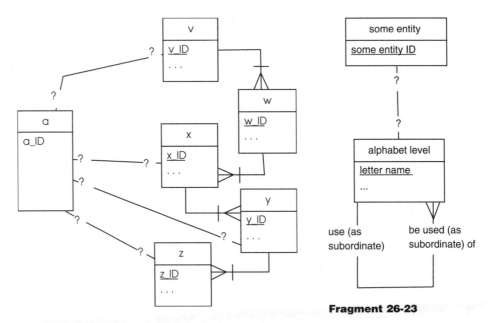

Fragment 26-22

Fragment 26-23

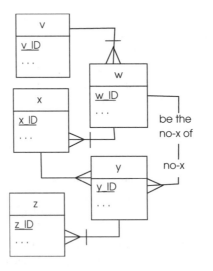

Fragment 26-24

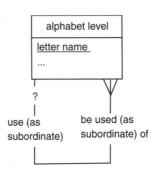

Fragment 26-25

To accommodate taxonomy data connecting the rest of the LDS at several levels, use Fragment 26-22, which is in progress. Note: Connections are not possible at all levels.

To accommodate connecting taxonomy data to the LDS where the taxonomy has largely the same descriptors at each level, use Fragment 26-23. Note: This fragment does not forbid connections at some levels, as the previous fragment did.

To accommodate near-taxonomy data, that is, with degenerate levels, use Fragment 26-24. Note: A *w* can have *x*'s or no *x*'s but still have *y*'s. Note also, *y* is now an independent entity.

The taxonomy recipes will evolve into something more complicated if any of the degree-one links become degree many. For example, you and users revisit Fragment 26-25, pursue The Flow step "Seek many-many relationship," and conclude yes.

Exercises

1. For each recipe, find a set of user words that fit it. Make up instances for the words.
2. Repeat exercise 1 several times until you have mastered each recipe.

Story Interlude

Scrape Off Barnacles

Liz was a student in a training class at company X. She had worked on one particular relational DBMS since she graduated from college and joined the company. During class she did not like when I used other than relation-like ways of depicting sample instances. I would put instances on the board and ask, *Is this OK?* Liz's reaction was no, not because of the content but because of the form. She saw the world in terms of those simple tables and thought that it was <u>the</u> correct view. She thought a data model was a means of showing a relational schema. It took most of a week for Liz to begin to scrape off those barnacles and allow herself to think of WHAT without HOW.

Moral: *Some experienced, successful technologists have trouble letting go of HOW.*

A Pause That Refreshes

At company X, urgency caused me to make a mistake. We had a looming deadline for a project and were pushing the pace by bringing in out-of-town users and having prolonged modeling meetings. I was running a meeting and things were going well for a while, but then I got confused. Since we needed to make progress and the users were leaving soon, we kept at it. However, I lost focus, and while evolution occurred, it was more haphazard than controlled. Finally, I came to my senses; I called a time-out and told the users to go eat, check e-mail, or whatever for two hours. I took the first hour off to refresh myself and let things simmer. During the second hour, I ruminated on the LDS by myself. By the time the users came back, I had found the source of my confusion. We revisited a suspect portion of the LDS, modified it, and went back to making real progress via controlled evolution.

My mistake was not calling a timeout when *I* needed one.

Moral: *Sometimes the best thing to do is to call a timeout.*

Explosive Mixtures

At company X, programmers wanted to attend a data-modeling meeting. While programmers are a vital and precious resource, Tom, the leader of the modeling group, said no, because each time the programmers came to a data-modeling meeting, they caused trouble. Tom said they would observe for a bit and then disrupt by saying something like *We can combine these four entities into a single, more general entity. That way, our programs will be able to make fewer declarations.*

Their behavior was only natural. They have a provincial view of processing (akin to users' provincial view of data). They are rewarded for getting things done, often within a crushingly short time frame. They exhibited classic hacker impatience.

Moral: *Keep programmers out of data-modeling meetings.*

Explosive Separations

At company X, after several projects that started with data modeling were remarkably successful, a project the modelers considered easy was a total failure. A later review found that the only notable difference from successful projects was that the failed project's programmers were off-site and did not have ready access to modelers. Those programmers found it easiest to make their own interpretations when they were uncertain about a portion of the LDS.

Moral: *Keep programmers nearby.*

My Life's Work

I was modeling brain data with Casey, a cognitive scientist with ties to neuroscience. In The Flow we were at the stage "Seek many-many relationship," and I asked the normal *Chicken foot here?* question. Casey paused for a bit, obviously deep in thought, before replying with *My life's work is demonstrating that you should put a chicken foot there.* The question I had asked was *Can a neuron have more than one plasticity mechanism?* Casey said, *Wow! I've always struggled to talk about my work. This LDS allows me to say succinctly what I'm about.*

Moral: *An LDS is a vehicle for communication.*

This story has another lesson for you. Casey, like a number of users, quickly grasped what data modeling is about. He was not dependent on me, so I did not insist on controlling our meetings; I lightly guided the process.

Moral: *Some users deserve nearly free rein.*

Smart Modelers

Content-neutral modelers ask shape-based questions that employ user words that are already on the model. Users often conclude that the modelers know a lot about the content.

Here are just two of numerous available examples: At agency X, the economists wanted to know how I had learned so much about the scientists' realm, and at company Y, a research chemist reacted to my shape-based question with *That's a really good question.* (It took a day for the chemists to come up with an answer.)

Moral: *Users think good modelers are amazingly knowledgeable about the users' realm.*

Fish Versus Fishing

My early industrial training classes were only partly successful. The students understood what I said but only partly inculcated data modeling into their work. I gave them fish, but they did not become master fishermen.

When a similar opportunity came up at company X, I proposed a several-pronged attack. I still taught classes as before. However, before the class, I reverse-engineered one of their applications from documentation, brought my model to class, and used it in class. In addition to hearing my words, they heard their own words. They quickly saw the usefulness of LDS as a vehicle for communicating about their data. After the class, first I modeled with the users as they observed; then a novice modeler would run a short meeting with me and others observing. During a postmortem after each session, we would go over good and bad things that had happened and address concerns that the novice had. They became a staff of full-time, self-sufficient modelers. As they got better, I faded out, except to train more novices and occasionally to troubleshoot. The troubleshooting often occurred at a "nerd club," a fairly regular after-work meeting where modelers discussed and debated hard shapes and situations without having to worry about users. (A few users did attend.) Finally, company X had a necessary ingredient: management support.

Moral: *Create a data-modeling culture.*

Summary

You can use these stories now.

- Study them.
- Learn the morals.
- Avoid the mistakes we and others made.
- Emulate our successful practices.
- Fit our stories to your modeling contexts.
- Craft your own stories and share them with others.

Bon voyage!

Exercise

Read Chapter 10 in G. Klein's *Sources of Power: How People Make Decisions,* MIT Press, Cambridge, MA, 1999. Then write down how you see things differently than you did before acquiring LDS skills.

Appendix

Exercises
for Mastery

When you have mastered data modeling, you will be able to lead a group of users comfortably through a successful modeling project. To attain that level of skill mastery, you must practice. The exercises at the end of each chapter focus, naturally, on practicing the chapter's material. Our intent in this appendix is to allow you to practice the whole skill as deeply as you can without real users.

Here are several points for you to consider:

* There are many paths to mastery. Take time to think about what you are doing and why. Do not hurry through the exercises to get "the" answer as fast as possible. You should think about what works best for you.
* Mastering a skill is not a linear process. You should expect to stumble, to make mistakes, and to learn from mistakes. Do not be surprised if, after struggling for a while, you suddenly acquire a sense of competency.[1] Keep snapshots of your work so that you can review it and assess your progress.
* This book is a reference. As you do this exercises, you should find yourself rereading and thinking more deeply about parts of the book.
* Data modeling is not a solitary process, and learning to model is not something you can do entirely by yourself. You can read this book and do some of its

---

[1] One final reminder: You will never master data modeling if you fail to keep your model well formed and fail to anchor your understanding with instances.

exercises by yourself, but you cannot claim you are a master modeler unless you have done it aloud and with others.

Our experience is that people acquire modeling skills best by working in teams, where everybody speaks and listens carefully. (In class, a team of three works best.) You should, if you can, work with other students or colleagues, observe modeling meetings, and get feedback from master modelers.

- You can model whether you know a lot or next to nothing about the to-be-modeled domain. Be brave: Since data modelers work in a content-neutral fashion, they can model anything.
- Up to a point, you (and your team) can practice data modeling without users.
  - You can serve as both user and modeler, or you can play the role of user for others. You have to supply the conflict coming from differing provincial points of view.
  - You can reverse engineer an existing system from an entire database, from a DBMS schema, from manuals, and from the forms and file formats of reports and transactions. This documentation serves as a surrogate for users.

As you do the following exercises, you should practice:

- saying LDS sentences, visualizing allowed instances, and visualizing disallowed instances. See Chapters 3 though 5.
- finding, naming, and using LDS shapes. See Chapters 7 through 12. (Make a copy of your LDS, and solidify your perception of shapes by circling each shape and writing down its name.)
- keeping the LDS syntactically valid, securing good names (for entities and attributes) and labels (for links). See Chapters 13 through 16.
- controlling evolution, choosing which questions to ask users, and gradually modifying an LDS. See Chapters 18 through 20.
- applying the six good habits. See Chapter 2.
- finding and using recipes. See Chapter 26.
- applying the morals of the data-modeling stories. See the Story Interludes.

In each exercise you are asked to create an LDS. Without being explicitly told, you should also do the following:

- Show instances that are accommodated and not accommodated. See Chapter 5.
- Document the LDS. See Chapter 17.
- Compare your answers with the answers produced by classmates or colleagues.

1. Movies

A. Suppose we were going to make a database out of the movie guide that appears in the local newspaper. It states <u>what</u> is playing, plus <u>where</u> and <u>when</u>.
  - Create an LDS for the data. Be sure to think at least about these words: movie, theater, location, rating, review, reviewer, show, producer, director, actor, popcorn size.
  - Write down the sentences for the LDS. (See Chapter 3.)

B. Evolve your answer to part A into another LDS, and state what decisions necessitated the changes. Feel free to add entities or descriptors. (Here are some ideas: triple features, customer ratings, handicap accessibility, seat reservations, discounts, and overbookings.)

C. Create an LDS for what movie historians want to remember. (To get ideas, visit one of the movie sites on the Web.)

2. Classroom Schedule

The university's classroom scheduling department has hired you to develop a model for their data. Your liaison has e-mailed you the following description of their operations.

> The Classroom Scheduling Department handles the allocation of rooms to classes every quarter. Each university building has been assigned a unique four-letter building code, apart from its name. I don't think we have any two buildings on campus with the same name. A building usually has several rooms available for use as classrooms, and we keep track of their capacities. The registrar's office supplies us with the expected enrollment for each class being offered, usually as a simple text file that looks like this:

CSci 5113 75

EE 5723   40

SEng 5115 35

> For class scheduling, we have defined nonoverlapping periods, starting at specific times. For example, period 1 each day starts at 8:30 A.M., period 2 starts at 9:45 A.M., and so on. For a class scheduled for period 4 on Mondays, Wednesdays, and Fridays, we have to find and allocate a room. We usually manage to assign just one room for all of the class periods, but sometimes we're forced to use more than one. Oh, another thing—between quarters, we send out an e-mail message asking the class instructors whether they have a preference for a particular building in which to have their classes. You know how these professors are; they often insist on classrooms in their own building! We try to keep them happy. . . . Anyway, if you have any questions, feel free to send me e-mail.

A. Prepare a response to this message:
   - Create an LDS to represent the information contained in it.
   - Document any assumptions you might have made.
   - Make a list of questions or clarifications you need from your liaison.

B. Consider the time unit of allocation in the scheduling process. In the description, it is a period. You're not told how long that is—does it matter? What if we wanted to allow variable amounts of time for a class? A class might meet for two periods on Mondays but only one period each on Wednesdays and Fridays. Can your LDS handle that?

C. Consider changing the decision that all classes are scheduled in terms of fixed-size periods. What units/chunks of allocation would be meaningful? How would your LDS be affected if the unit of time was 5 minutes instead of a period? What if it was a nanosecond?

D. Modify your LDS so that it supports many universities, each of which has its own schedule.

E. Consider the effect of exceptional instances on your LDS. For example, suppose that a few rooms are known by more than one place name (at the University of Minnesota, due to some old turf wars, a particular room is both ME 12 and EE 25).

3. Election

The city of Wentbridge elects a new city council (seven members) every two years. Here are the details.

Voting Details

- In each election, each citizen casts at most one ballot.
- Each ballot contains the names of the candidates. There are at least eight candidates.
- To cast a ballot, a citizen checks the name of each desirable candidate. (Note that a citizen can check any number of names. On a single ballot, a citizen effectively endorses each and every "acceptable" candidate.)
- Some citizens cast "protest ballots" in which they check no candidate names whatsoever.

Counting Details

Step 0: If fewer than half the citizens voted, the board of elections nullifies the results and schedules another election.

Step 1: If more than 10 percent of the ballots are protest ballots, the board of elections nullifies the results and schedules another election.

Step 2: The board of elections counts the ballots and ranks the candidates according to the number of checkmarks each candidate receives.

Step 3: The board of elections informs the first-place candidate of his or her margin of victory over the second-place candidate. (The margin of victory is the number of checkmarks separating the two candidates.)

Step 4: The first-place candidate grants each of his "extra" checkmarks to one of the other candidates. (For example, if G. Allen wins by 1000 votes, she can grant 900 of these "extra" checkmarks to G. Burns and 100 to S. Caesar.)

Step 5: The first-place candidate occupies one of the seats on the city council, leaving six vacant seats.

Step 6: The board of elections reranks the remaining candidates according to the total number of checkmarks they have received—either from the voters or from already victorious candidates.

Step 7: The top-ranked candidate wins a seat on the city council and grants his or her extra votes to remaining candidates.

Step 8: If there are remaining vacant seats on the city council, the board of elections returns to step 6 to determine the next winning candidate.

Step 9: The seventh and final candidate elected to the city council becomes the chairperson.

A. Create an LDS to express the results of one election, including the results of the vote-counting process.

B. Expand your LDS so that it can accommodate several elections.

4. Appointments

A. Construct a well-formed, high-quality LDS for your personal appointments calendar.

B. What is idiosyncratic about your appointments that would render the LDS a bad fit for other people?

5. Dictionary

A dictionary, e.g., *Webster's New World Dictionary,* is a useful database in paper form. Think of the entire book as the database.

A. Your task is to draw a well-formed, high-quality LDS for the database and to discuss the boundary decisions that you made. Here are some questions to consider: *Are page numbers important? How might the LDS evolve? What would you do if a thesaurus capability were added to the database?*

B. Visit one of the several dictionary Web pages, draw an LDS based on what you see, and compare it to your LDS from part A.

C. How, if at all, would the LDS change if the database were for crossword puzzles or Scrabble?

6. Web Usage

Your users are in the business of tracking Web usage, collecting statistics, and selling the data at an obscene profit. The following is all they're willing to let you know about their business.

A page on the World Wide Web has a title and some text and can be identified by its URL (uniform resource locator) string. For each page, we need to remember its size in kilobytes and the date it was last modified. A page may also contain hypertext links to other pages. For each such link, we must remember the linked text (the text you click on to fetch the linked page).

A page is made available on the Web by a server program. Of particular interest to us are the server software's name and version number. Servers can be contacted on the network by specifying their hostname and port number. No two servers can have the same hostname-port number pair. Whenever a Web browser downloads a page, the server increments a counter to keep track of the number of hits on the page. In addition, we are interested in tracking the effectiveness of hypertext links. So with each link, we need to maintain a count of the number of times the link was followed, that is, clicked on.

A. Given this brief description, develop an LDS. Make a list of questions you want to ask the users.

B. Just as you're finishing up the Web page model, another user walks in, peers over your shoulder at the LDS, and points out that the URL of a Web page isn't just a string. It is, she says, composed of a protocol name (like http, gopher, or mailto), a hostname, a port number, and a pathname. The hostname and port number identify the Web server of this page, as before. How would you modify your LDS to accommodate this added information?

7. Grades

A. Create an LDS suitable for capturing the grades associated with this course (if you are taking a course).

B. Evolve the LDS so that it can accommodate many different courses.

C. Evolve the LDS so that it accommodates just the final grades that the university remembers. What about changes in grades?

8. Bicycles

Johnny's A-Robic Borrowing Corp. rents bicycles. They have offices in cities in the United States. Rentals are intercity, intracity, or one-way. Johnny's research group does simulations to predict the inventory level (kinds and numbers of bikes available) at, and the flow (of bikes) between, offices. They also get reports of actual inventory and flow. Johnny wants a database so that he can get reports, for example, comparing expected versus actual rentals.

Your tasks are to draw an initial LDS based on this brief description and prepare a list of questions that you want to ask Johnny and his employees.

9. Sales

Think about a sales database and construct an LDS using the following words: customer, region, salesman, saleswoman, territory, order, line item, product, backorder, ship-to address, bill-to address, terms, quantity, unit price, ship date, order date, invoice #.

Explain any assumptions or additions you make.

10. Classified Ads

Joey's Junk Mail, Inc., makes and sells booklets of classified ads.

A. Your tasks are to design an LDS for a system that will help them develop and save booklets; prepare a list of questions that you want to ask Joey and his pals.

B. Add customer billing to the LDS.

11. Telephone Book

Think about telephone books.

A. Create an LDS for the residential telephone book. Ignore formatting.
B. Add formatting.
C. Create an LDS for the business phone book. Be sure to think about planned, available, and sold space; space sellers and their commissions; the day a customer proofreads artwork; other dates.

12. Course Schedule

A. If you are a student, create an LDS for this semester's class schedule at your university. If available, use the class schedule paper booklet. Treat the booklet as the database. Focus on what is offered, where, when, by whom, and with what prerequisites. (Hints: Do not expect prerequisite to be an attribute; look for exceptional instances.)

   Include a discussion on the quality of the LDS. How do you know that it covers all the data? What hard decisions did you make? Describe the ease or difficulty your team had in forming the LDS.
B. If they are included in your class schedule booklet, add other content: fees, campus maps, exam schedules, and so on.

13. Reverse Engineer a Database Schema or Application System

You can repeat this exercise as many times as you like.

   Find a nontrivial but modest-size relational database schema or application system at your workplace or elsewhere. For the schema:

- Reverse engineer the schema or system from documentation (DBMS catalog, manuals, file formats, forms, etc.), that is, deduce the LDS. Keep a log of what assumptions you make in the process, what problems you encountered, and so on.
- Prepare a list of questions you would like to ask users.
- Prepare and give a 10- to 15-minute presentation to other teams, assuming that they are data modelers, about your experience with this assignment.
- Listen to other teams present. Critique their model and their presentation of it.

The remaining exercises are challenging because you need skills in choosing an appropriate level of abstraction (see Chapter 20) and because the data is graph-like (see Chapter 26).

14. Airline Schedule

Warning: An airline schedule is about what is planned for a time period, generally a week. Each week the airline flies according to the schedule, with some deviations. A schedule does not represent individual flights.

A. Obtain an airline schedule for a small carrier, or visit the carrier's Web site. Create an LDS to support the data.
B. Obtain an airline schedule for a major carrier, or visit the carrier's Web site. Create an LDS to support the data.
C. Compare your answers to parts A and B. Explain their differences both in words and with noteworthy examples.
D. Add flight reservations. (This is really hard!)

15. Model

Suppose your data is a mathematical model that consists of

- a set of states
- a set of input symbols
- a transition function that maps state-symbol pairs to sets of states
- an initial state
- a set of final states

A. Create an LDS for the model.
B. Modify the LDS so that you can remember sessions, where for one session you trace the sequence of inputs and states.
C. Modify your LDS to allow the transition function to be probabilistic.
D. Modify your LDS to support many models.

16. Process

Suppose your data is a bunch of process models, each consisting of

- a set of tasks, each with a name, duration, and cost
- for each task, its immediate possible successors and the probability, p, of each successor being selected
- a set of initial tasks called starting points, each with a motto
- a set of final tasks, each with a goal name and a goal-reached logo

A. Create an LDS for the models.
B. Evolve your LDS to support versioning of models.
C. Evolve your LDS to support remembering traces of model execution.

17. Rules

A. Create a fine-grain LDS for the rules in a rule-based expert system. (For information on grain, see Chapter 26.)
B. Create a one-entity (a very coarse-grain) LDS for the rules in a rule-based expert system, and evolve it in small steps to your LDS for part A.

Index

Database Design for Mere Mortals
A Hands-On Guide to Relational Database Design
Michael J. Hernandez

Sound design can save you hours of development time before you write a single line of code. Based on the author's years of experience teaching this material, *Database Design for Mere Mortals* is a straightforward, platform-independent tutorial on the basic principles of relational database design. Database design expert Michael J. Hernandez introduces the core concepts of design theory and method without the technical jargon. *Database Design for Mere Mortals* will provide any developer with a commonsense design methodology for developing databases that work.

0-201-69471-9 • Paperback • 480 pages • ©1997

The Practical SQL Handbook, Third Edition
Using Structured Query Language
Judith S. Bowman, Sandra L. Emerson, and Marcy Darnovsky

The Practical SQL Handbook is the best-selling guide to learning SQL—the standard language for accessing information in relational databases. This book not only teaches SQL as it has been established by the ANSI standards committee but also as the language is used to solve real business problems. Step-by-step you'll learn the basic vocabulary and functions of the language and the processes and issues involved in developing robust applications. This book provides a thorough grounding in the basics of database design, security, and integrity. You will learn SQL pragmatically, by creating a sample database and then working through dozens of examples with it.

0-201-44787-8 • Paperback • 496 pages • ©1996

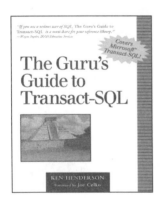

The Guru's Guide to Transact-SQL
Ken Henderson

Since its introduction more than a decade ago, the Microsoft SQL Server query language, Transact-SQL, has become increasingly popular and more powerful. The current version sports advanced features such as OLE Automation support, cross-platform querying facilities, and full-text search management. This book is the consummate guide to Microsoft Transact-SQL. From data type nuances to complex statistical computations to the bevy of undocumented features in the language, *The Guru's Guide to Transact-SQL* imparts the knowledge you need to become a virtuoso of the language as quickly as possible. This book contains the information, explanations, and advice needed to master Transact-SQL and develop the best possible Transact-SQL code. Some 600 code examples not only illustrate important concepts and best practices, but also provide working Transact-SQL code that can be incorporated into your own real-world DBMS applications.

0-201-61576-2 • Paperback • 592 pages • ©2000

Introduction to SQL, Third Edition
Mastering the Relational Database Language
Rick van der Lans

According to Ian Cargill of Soliton Software, Rick van der Lans has written "a first class book. A thorough and well-written introduction to a complex subject. I wish this book had been available when I was learning SQL." SQL was, is, and always will be the database language for relational database systems such as Oracle, DB2, Sybase, Informix, and Microsoft SQL Server. *Introduction to SQL* describes, in depth, the full capacity of SQL as it is implemented by the commercial databases, without neglecting the most recent changes to the standard, bringing the book up to date and fully compliant with SQL3. Unique in the extent of its coverage, this book takes you from the beginning to the end of SQL, the concepts to the practice, the apprentice to the master.

0-201-59618-0 • Paperback • 720 pages • ©2000

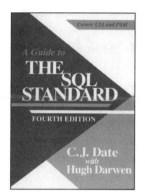

A Guide to the SQL Standard, Fourth Edition
C.J. Date with Hugh Darwen

The SQL language has established itself as the lingua franca for database management; it provides the basis for systems interoperability, application portability, client/server operation, distributed databases, and more. SQL is supported by just about every DBMS on the market today. SQL2—or, to give it its official name, the International Standard Database Language SQL (1992)—represents a major set of extensions to the earlier SQL standard. For a start, the new specification is well over 600 pages, compared with less than 100 for the original version. No database professional can afford to ignore it. This Fourth Edition of *A Guide to the SQL Standard* covers extensive integrity support, powerful new operators, and national and international character data support—all features of SQL2; comprehensive date and time support and a clear explanation of the complexities of Dynamic SQL—features of SQL. This book provides a tutorial treatment of SQL2.

0-201-96426-0 • Paperback • 544 pages • ©1997

Practical Issues in Database Management
A Reference for the Thinking Practitioner
Fabian Pascal

Three decades ago relational technology put the database field on a sound, scientific foundation for the first time. But the database industry—vendors, users, experts, and the trade press—has essentially flouted its principles, focusing instead on a "cookbook," product-specific approach, devoid of conceptual understanding. The consequences have been costly: DBMS products, databases, development tools, and applications don't always perform up to expectation or potential, and they can encourage the wrong questions and provide the wrong answers. *Practical Issues in Database Management* is an attempt to remedy this intractable and costly situation. Written for database designers, programmers, managers, and users, it addresses the core, commonly recurring issues and problems that practitioners—even the most experienced database professionals—seem to systematically misunderstand.

0-201-48555-9 • Paperback • 288 pages • ©2000

Register
Your Book

at www.aw.com/cseng/register

You may be eligible to receive:
- Advance notice of forthcoming editions of the book
- Related book recommendations
- Chapter excerpts and supplements of forthcoming titles
- Information about special contests and promotions throughout the year
- Notices and reminders about author appearances, tradeshows, and online chats with special guests

Contact us

If you are interested in writing a book or reviewing manuscripts prior to publication, please write to us at:

Editorial Department
Addison-Wesley Professional
75 Arlington Street, Suite 300
Boston, MA 02116 USA
Email: AWPro@aw.com

Addison-Wesley

Visit us on the Web: http://www.aw.com/cseng